Information Security and Cryptography
Texts and Monographs

For further volumes:
http://www.springer.com/series/4752

Alexander W. Dent · Yuliang Zheng
Editors

Practical Signcryption

Foreword by Moti Yung

Editors
Dr. Alexander W. Dent
Royal Holloway
University of London
Information Security Group
TW20 0EX Egham, Surrey
United Kingdom
a.dent@rhul.ac.uk

Prof. Yuliang Zheng
University of North Carolina, Charlotte
Dept. Software & Information Systems
University City Blvd. 9201
Charlotte, NC 28223
USA
yzheng@uncc.edu

Series Editors

Prof. Dr. David Basin
Prof. Dr. Ueli Maurer
ETH Zürich
Switzerland
basin@inf.ethz.ch
maurer@inf.ethz.ch

ISSN 1619-7100
ISBN 978-3-540-89409-4   e-ISBN 978-3-540-89411-7
DOI 10.1007/978-3-540-89411-7
Springer Heidelberg Dordrecht London New York

Library of Congress Control Number: 2010935931

ACM Computing Classification (1998): E.3, K.4.4

Cover design: KuenkelLopka GmbH, Heidelberg

Printed on acid-free paper

Springer is part of Springer Science+Business Media (www.springer.com)

Foreword

Scientific exploration follows many directions, and this is as true for a technological science like "cryptography" as it is for any physical science. One central scientific direction involves finding new notions, new primitives, and new methods; defining them; implementing them; and then showing and proving the characteristics of these findings. In modern cryptography, the definition of new basic primitives and their security properties has been one of the primary activities of the last few decades (since the field was conceived in the later part of the twentieth century).

Once a primitive is defined, a number of investigative directions take place: One direction is showing the basic tools (mathematical assumptions and basic cryptographic functions) that are necessary and sufficient for the primitive. A second direction involves finding more efficient implementations, where efficiency is measured in terms of the complexity of the primitive (such as the time it takes, the space it consumes, the messages used, the rounds of communication employed). A third direction is extending the properties of the basic primitive and modifying it to achieve other interesting important tasks, or making sure it operates in a different environment than it was originally intended for. Yet, a fourth direction is finding system's needs and applications that crucially exploit the primitive (either inherently, as a functional enhancement of an application or as a contributor to efficiency improvement); this direction eventually leads to actual working systems that can be exploited by actual computing systems. Note that other directions for investigation are known, such as reductions between primitives, generalization of primitives into a super-primitive. Once a primitive is born, its development often progresses in quite unexpected and mysterious ways.

Two of the cornerstones of modern cryptography are public-key encryption as implemented via public-key cryptosystems and digital signatures as implemented by signature schemes. Public-key cryptosystems are a concealment mechanism. Employing the cryptosystem enables a party (a sender) to encrypt a confidential message to a second party (a receiver) without the need to share an initial secret; the only thing needed is for the receiver to publicize the public portion of its key (the encryption key), while keeping secret the decryption key. Digital signatures, on the other hand, are an integrity mechanism. These enable a party to send a message with a signature tag that verifies the origin of the message (i.e., authenticates the sender) to any receiver; the only thing needed is for the sender to initially publicize its public verification key while keeping secret the corresponding signing key.

There are a very high number of variations of the concepts of public-key cryptosystems and digital signature schemes. Many properties have been added, and the definition and characteristic of these primitive, as well as efficient implementations of them and their variations, have been thoroughly investigated. These primitives have also been implemented as important underlying components in various security protocols used to secure computing and communication infrastructures (the Internet, the Web, the mobile networks, and so on).

The book "*Practical Signcryption*" by Alex Dent and Yuliang Zheng considers a very interesting primitive, originally the brainchild of Yuliang Zheng, called "Signcryption." The name of this primitive tells it all: It is a primitive that combines the functionality of digital signatures and that of public-key encryption. Often in science, when primitives are defined, there is an issue with their combination and interoperability. Note that in computer science in general, the notion of combination is very important, since complex structures need to be developed in pieces, and therefore modularity is a critical notion which enables the development of pieces which can be combined into more complete systems. Combination can be performed in many ways. For example, one can envision a simple concatenation of the primitives (i.e., performing the first and then the second); however, even such a simple combination presents a challenge in cryptographic research, since the combination may not preserve the security properties of each of the components.

Signcryption is a result of realizing that often one wants to send a message that is concealed (readable only by the intended receiver) and authenticated (verified as originating from the specified sender). This combination is natural in numerous applications. The original motivation for "signcryption" (which is a much shorter word than the expression "signature and encryption") was to gain efficiency, namely to allow both actions to be done more efficiently than just a serial composition of the two components (e.g., to get a shorter cryptogram representing both encryption and signature than is obtained merely by first encrypting the message into a ciphertext and then signing the ciphertext).

Once the above was shown possible, at that very moment, a new primitive was born and the book covers the many aspects of developments around this primitive of signcryption. These developments include achieving efficient constructions, achieving provably secure constructions under various models, getting efficient schemes in various algebraic domains, getting new techniques to design the primitives in various settings, and getting applications and actual implementations of it. The book covers all these areas by chapters that are written by the world-renowned cryptographers who have been in the frontier of research and who have actually been responsible for many of these numerous interesting developments. Note further that the authors of the various chapter demonstrate, by their wide geographical spread, the global nature of advanced cryptographic research nowadays.

The story of signcryption has taught us that "combining natural primitives" has strong research and development potential in many ways, and especially it has a good chance in reducing complexities when measured against a naive combination.

In fact, I learned this lesson myself and applied it a few years after signcryption had been conceived. Together with J. Katz, we studied the combination of private key encryption and message authentication codes (which is the "symmetric key cryptography" equivalent of what signcryption is in the "public-key cryptography" area). This primitive, now called "authenticated encryption," which has also been studied by a number of other groups has found numerous applications and is an outcome of the approach pioneered by the notion of signcryption.

The "Practical Signcryption" book can be a handbook on the state of the art of signcryption, specifically, and, at the same time, can serve as a way to historically view how this specific subject has evolved. On a more general level, the book can serve as an example how cryptographic primitives are conceived and how research in this general area evolves, going through various stages from the theoretical and mathematical development stage all the way to the practical stage (i.e., into systems and standardization). In other words, the book serves two purposes: (1) it is the definitive source on signcryption and (2) it is also a prototypical example to learn from how research on cryptographic primitives is performed by the cryptographic research community. Indeed, the book on combining cryptographic primitives, itself, combines these two purposes in a very elegant way! I think the book is, in fact, a fundamental and timely contribution to the cryptographic literature, and I congratulate Alex, Yuliang, and the various chapter authors for their unique achievement!

New York, NY   Moti Yung
April 2010

Preface

The concept for this book was initially created because we believe that signcryption is a fundamentally useful technology that is under-used in practical applications. It often seems bizarre to us that implementations will use complex modular exponentiation optimizations to achieve small efficiency improvements while ignoring the 50% efficiency saving that can be made by combining confidentiality and integrity protection operations into a single signcryption operation! We hope that the book will convince researchers, implementors, and standardization bodies to consider the use of efficient signcryption technologies in their work.

This book is the result of a long project and we would like to thank all of the authors for their efforts and their patience. We would also like to thank Springer-Verlag for their patience.

Yuliang Zheng would particularly like to thank Hideki Imai for his pioneering work in coded modulation which inspired him to develop signcryption. The endeavor to develop signcryption came to fruition while Yuliang was with the beautiful Mornington Peninsula campus of Monash University in Australia. He is indebted to ex-colleagues at Monash for their support during the initial stage of development of signcryption. In addition to authors of chapters of this book, Yuliang would also like to thank those researchers whose work on signcryption could not be included into this book. Their contributions to the design and analysis, as well as practical applications, of signcryption techniques are equally significant. Furthermore, Yuliang would like to extend his gratitude to colleagues at the University of North Carolina at Charlotte for numerous discussions on research over the past decade. Finally Yuliang would like to thank his wife Quinnie and two wonderful children for their continued love, support, and patience.

Alex Dent would particularly like to thank the Information Security Group in Royal Holloway, University of London, for their support during the writing/editing of this book. It should also be acknowledged that part of the work of editing this book was undertaken while Alex was visiting the Computer Science Department of New York University and the Graduate Center of the City University of New York. He would like to thank them for the opportunity to visit their universities. Lastly, he would like to thank his family for their continued support and Carrie for being such a wonderful person.

Some of the individual chapter authors would also like to acknowledge the help that they have received. These include

- John Malone-Lee (Chap. 6) would like to thank Wenbo Mao whose idea it was originally to use the RSA function for signcryption in this way.
- Yevgeniy Dodis (Chap. 8) would like to thank Jee Hea An and Tal Rabin for their collaboration on the subject of signcryption.
- Josef Pieprzyk (Chap. 9) was supported by Australian Research Council Discovery grants DP0663452 and DP0987734.
- Xavier Boyen (Chap. 10) would like to thank Paulo Barreto for useful feedback on an early draft of the chapter.
- Alex Dent (Chap. 11) would like to thank Colin Boyd for taking the time to read and comment on this chapter. These comments much improved the chapter.

London, UK   Alexander W. Dent
Charlotte, NC   Yuliang Zheng
May 2010

Contents

Contributors

Jee Hea An San Diego, CA, USA

Joonsang Baek Cryptography and Security Department, Institute for Infocomm Research (I2R), Singapore, Singapore, jsbaek@i2r.a-star.edu.sg

Paulo S. L. M. Barreto Architecture and Networking Lab (LARC), Department of Computer and Digital Systems Engineering (PCS), Escola Politécnica, University of São Paulo, São Paulo, Brazil, pbarreto@larc.usp.br

Tor E. Bjørstad Department of Informatics, The Selmer Center, University of Bergen, Bergen, Norway, tor.bjorstad@ii.uib.no

Xavier Boyen Chair of Cryptography and Information Security, Montefiore Institute, Université de Liège, Liège, Belgium, xb@boyen.org

Yang Cui National Institute of Advanced Industrial Science and Technology (AIST), Research Center for Information Security (RCIS), Tokyo, Japan, y-cui@aist.go.jp

Alexander W. Dent Information Security Group, University of London, Egham TW20 0EX, Surrey, UK, a.dent@rhul.ac.uk

Yevgeniy Dodis Cryptography Group, Department of Computer Science, New York University, New York, NY, USA, dodis@cs.nyu.edu

Goichiro Hanaoka National Institute of Advanced Industrial Science and Technology (AIST), Research Center for Information Security (RCIS), Tokyo, Japan

Benoît Libert Crypto Group, Microelectronics Laboratory, Université catholique de Louvain, Louvain, Belgium, benoit.libert@uclovain.be

John Malone-Lee Torus Insurance, London, UK

Noel McCullagh School of Computing, Dublin City University, Dublin, Ireland

Josef Pieprzyk Department of Computing, Center for Advanced Computing – Algorithms and Cryptography, Macquarie University, Sydney, Australia, josef@comp.mq.edu.au

David Pointcheval CNRS, ENS and INRIA, Paris, France,
david.pointcheval@ens.fr

Jean-Jacques Quisquater Crypto Group, Microelectronics Laboratory, Université
catholique de Louvain, Louvain, Belgium

Tal Rabin IBM T. J. Watson Research Center, Hawthorne, NY, USA,
talr@us.ibm.com

Ron Steinfeld Department of Computing, Center for Advanced Computing –
Algorithms and Cryptography, Macquarie University, Sydney, Australia,
josef@comp.mg.edu.au

Yuliang Zheng University of North Carolina, Charlotte, NC, USA,
yzheng@uncc.edu

Chapter 1
Introduction

Yuliang Zheng

1.1 Historical Development of Signcryption

1.1.1 Coded Modulation

In a typical communications system, data from an originator undergoes a sequence of transformations prior to being transported to its intended recipient. These transformations may include *source encoding* to compress the data or remove unwanted redundant information from the data, *authentication tagging* to ensure the detection of unauthorized modification, *encryption* to prevent the data from being accessible to unauthorized parties while en route, *error correction encoding* to allow the recipient to detect and correct transmission errors, and finally *modulation* of data signals for transmission over a communications channel between the originator and the recipient. Generally the communications channel is not only prone to transmission error but also considered to be insecure. Upon arriving at the recipient, the data is subject to matching decoding transformations in reserve order. Figure 1.1 depicts the various operations on data while traveling across a communications channel. Note that in the figure, authentication is applied before encryption is carried out. Alternatively, encryption can be applied first, followed by authentication.

Error-correcting codes and modulation techniques have been at the core of digital communications engineering and research from the mid-twentieth century. As a typical communications channel has only a limited bandwidth, one of the central questions is how to minimize the loss of effective data transmission rate incurred by error-correcting codes. Another important question is how to reap the full benefits of an increased data transmission rate offered by multi-level/phase modulation without suffering worsening interference among signals. While a great number of error-correcting codes and modulation techniques had been discovered accompanying the advent of digital communications after the Second World War, historically, error correction and modulation had always been carried out separately.

Y. Zheng (✉)
University of North Carolina, Charlotte, NC, USA
e-mail: yzheng@uncc.edu

A.W. Dent, Y. Zheng (eds.), *Practical Signcryption*, Information Security
and Cryptography, DOI 10.1007/978-3-540-89411-7_1,
© Springer-Verlag Berlin Heidelberg 2010

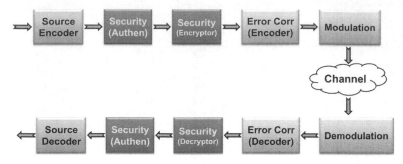

Fig. 1.1 A communications system

During the 1970s, researchers embarked on the pursuit of techniques for combining error correction and modulation with the aim of achieving performance gain without requiring the expansion of bandwidth or incurring a significant reduction of data transmission rate. The most successful of those efforts was represented by the work of Ungerboeck [190–193] and, independently, of Imai and Hirakawa [97] (see also [197]). Ungerboeck focused on blending together trellis or convolution codes and multi-level modulation without sacrificing bandwidth efficiency, whereas Imai and Hirakawa had the same goal but used a different approach, which was to combine block error-correcting codes and multi-level modulation.

Coded modulation addresses simultaneously two issues that appear mutually contradictory: (1) high transmission reliability and (2) high transmission efficiency. The hybrid technique, whether it is based on trellis codes or block error-correcting codes, makes reliable and bandwidth-efficient data transmission a reality (see Fig. 1.2).

1.1.2 Musings on Blending

The 1980s were an exciting period for those who worked in telecommunication. At the time, Professor Hideki Imai led a number of research projects at Yoko-

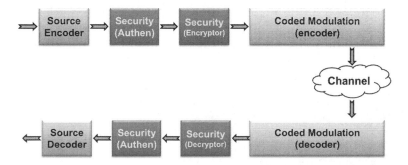

Fig. 1.2 Coded modulation for bandwidth-efficient communications

hama National University in Japan. These projects covered virtually all important technical aspects pertaining to data processing and communications. Specifically, the research projects addressed source coding, cryptography, error-correcting codes, modulation, and coded modulation.

I joined Professor Imai's group to pursue my graduate studies in the mid-1980s. Although my research area was cryptography, I was fortunate to be able to participate in weekly seminars with fellow students who worked on a range of different research projects. I still vividly remember that at one of the long seminars that extended well into the late evening, a fellow student started to explain the Imai-Hirakawa coded multi-level modulation technique [97] when I felt somewhat tired after a long day's studies and discussions. I was immediately intrigued by the idea of blending error-correcting codes and modulation together to obtain a better solution than applying them separately. Over the next few years I maintained strong interest in coded modulation. What I felt most fascinating was not only the beauty of ideas behind the technology but also the amazing velocity at which the technology was perfected, standardized, and applied in practice.

As a cryptographic researcher witnessing the rapid maturing and adoption of coded modulation in digital communications, I asked myself a quite natural question whether it was feasible to combine two cryptographic primitives into something that would be more efficient than employing the two primitives separately. The question accompanied me during the entire remaining period of my graduate studies. Years after I finished my PhD and moved "Down Under", I found it hard for me to stay completely away from musings on the same question.

Two of the most important functions of modern cryptography are the assurance of data confidentiality and that of data integrity. Confidentiality can be achieved using encryption algorithms or ciphers, whereas integrity can be provided by the use of authentication techniques.

Encryption algorithms fall into one of two broad groups: private key encryption and public key encryption. Likewise, authentication techniques can be categorized by private key authentication algorithms and public key digital signatures. When examining a cryptographic algorithm, one needs to take into account not only the strength or level of security the algorithm can offer but also the computational time it takes to perform the algorithm, together with the message expansion incurred by the algorithm. When two cryptographic algorithms offer a similar level of security, computational time and message expansion become a focal point of comparison. As a rule, smaller computational time and shorter message expansion are generally considered more desirable.

While both private key encryption and private key authentication admit very fast computation with minimal message expansion, public key encryption and digital signatures generally require heavy computation, such as exponentiations involving very large integers, together with message expansion proportional to security parameters (such as the size of a large composite integer or the size of a large finite field). Figure 1.3 illustrates the computational and message overhead incurred when digital signatures and public key encryption are applied in succession to a message.

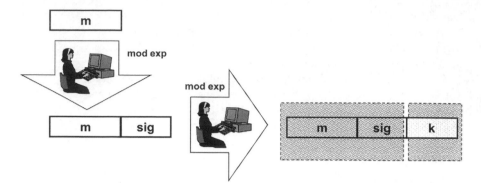

Fig. 1.3 Digital signature followed by public key encryption

I realized that there were at least two types of combinations that appeared to be meaningful in practice:

1. private key encryption combined with private key authentication and
2. public key encryption combined with digital signatures.

I also realized that the most important goal of a successful combination of two different cryptographic algorithms should be for the resultant solution not only to be faster to compute but also to admit shorter message expansion, when compared to applying the two original algorithms separately.

I set my sight on the second type of combinations, namely combinations of public key encryption and digital signatures, for a number of reasons:

1. Future widespread use of battery-powered small devices such as smart cards, smart phones, personal digital assistants (PDAs), electronic passports, electronic wallets, and other types of gadgets would require new public key cryptographic techniques that consume as little battery power as possible.
2. Applications in a resource-constrained environment such as contactless wireless identification tokens and unattended remote data collection systems would require the use of public key cryptographic algorithms that not only are fast to compute but also introduce minimum data expansion.
3. Finding combined public key cryptographic solutions appeared more challenging.
4. I felt that my experience in designing techniques for "immunizing" public key encryption against chosen ciphertext attacks [210, 211] would be useful in addressing the new challenge. The essence of these "immunization" techniques was to use authentication tags, especially those generated by a (keyed) one-way hash algorithm, to transform an unstructured plaintext into a highly structured one prior to the application of public key encryption. The transformation incapacitates a chosen ciphertext attacker who attempts to create a new ciphertext without already knowing the corresponding plaintext. Some of the ideas were

later elaborated as the "random oracle" model and plaintext awareness by other researchers and constituted an important foundation for public key encryption that admitted provable security.

1.1.3 Signcryption

After setting as my goal the combination of public key encryption and digital signatures, I narrowed down candidate algorithms to ElGamal public key encryption and signature, especially those that relied for their security on the hardness of discrete logarithm on a *subgroup* of a large finite field, due to their outstanding efficiency as well as the availability of their counterparts on elliptic curves.

1.1.3.1 ElGamal Public Key Encryption and Signature in a Subgroup

The specific version of ElGamal public key encryption and digital signatures I was interested in involved three parameters that were public to all:

1. p: a large prime.
2. q: a prime factor of $p - 1$.
3. g: an integer in the range of $[1, \ldots, p - 1]$ with order q modulo p.

Consider two users Alice and Bob. Alice has a private key x_a chosen uniformly at random from $[1, \ldots, q - 1]$. She also has $y_a = g^{x_a} \bmod p$ as her matching public key. Likewise, Bob's private key is an integer x_b chosen uniformly at random from $[1, \ldots, q - 1]$ and his public key is $y_b = g^{x_b} \bmod p$.

Now assume that Alice wishes to send a message m to Bob in a secure manner. Alice first looks up Bob's public key y_b in a public key directory. She then picks a random integer x from $[1, \ldots, q - 1]$ and calculates $t = y_b^x \bmod p$. This is followed by employing an appropriate one-way hash algorithm $hash$ to compute from t an encryption key $k = hash(t)$ for an appropriate private key cipher (E, D). Finally Alice sends to Bob the following pair of data items as a ciphertext of m:

$$\text{ElGamal Encryption: } (c_1, c_2) = (g^x \bmod p, \ E_k(m))$$

where E is the encryption algorithm of the private key cipher.

Upon receiving (c_1, c_2), Bob can recover k by computing $k = hash(c_1^{x_b} \bmod p)$. He can then use k and the decryption algorithm D of the same private key cipher to decrypt c_2 and obtain m.

Alice's signature on a message m is composed of two numbers r and s which are defined as

$$\text{ElGamal Signature: } (r, s) = (g^x \bmod p, \ (hash(m) - x_a \cdot r)/x \bmod (p - 1))$$

where x is a random number picked from $[1, \ldots, q - 1]$ and *hash* is an appropriate one-way hash algorithm. Bob and any other party can verify the authenticity of Alice's signature on the message m by using her publicly available key y_a.

There are numerous variants of and improvements to the original ElGamal signature. The most notable ones include the NIST Digital Signature Standard (DSS) or Digital Signature Algorithm (DSA) [149] and the Schnorr signature [173]. These two signature techniques are defined as

$$\text{DSS: } (r, s) = ((g^x \bmod p) \bmod q, \ (hash(m) + x_a \cdot r)/x \bmod q)$$
$$\text{Schnorr: } (r, s) = (hash(g^x \bmod p, m), \ (x - x_a \cdot r) \bmod q)$$

Two more interesting variants are obtained by further shortening variants of the DSS. These two shortened versions are called SDSS1 and SDSS2 and are defined as

$$\text{SDSS1: } (r, s) = (hash(g^x \bmod p, m), \ x/(r + x_a) \bmod q)$$
$$\text{SDSS2: } (r, s) = (hash(g^x \bmod p, m), \ x/(1 + x_a \cdot r) \bmod q)$$

1.1.3.2 Basic Signcryption Algorithms

Looking closely at the ElGamal encryption and signature algorithms, one notices that both contains the following item:

$$g^x \bmod p$$

This quantity can be viewed as playing the role of an "ephemeral key" in both algorithms. An interesting question is *whether it is possible to let the same "ephemeral key" serve as a conduit linking the encryption and signature algorithms together.*

Further, one notices that $g^x \bmod p$ does not explicitly appear in any of the four variants of the ElGamal signature described above. Nevertheless the quantity can be easily derived from these signatures by a signature verifier. All these four variants exhibit a significantly shorter signature size than the original ElGamal signature. This brings up yet another interesting question, that is *whether it is possible to combine ElGamal encryption and signature in such a way that the resultant algorithm does not contain $g^x \bmod p$.*

After a number of trials and errors, I was able to firm up my thinking in the southern winter of 1996. The outcome, which I called "signcryption," was a nice combination of ElGamal encryption and signature that answered both questions above in the affirmative. I will explain the combination that is based on SDSS1. In describing the signcryption technique, I use *Hash* to denote a one-way hash algorithm, *KH* to denote a keyed one-way hash algorithm, and (E, D) a private key cipher.

Basic Algorithm
Signcryption of m by Alice the Sender

1. Pick x uniformly at random from $[1, \ldots, q-1]$,
   and let $k = Hash(y_b^x \bmod p)$.
   Split k into k_1 and k_2 of appropriate length.
2. $c = E_{k_1}(m)$.
3. $r = KH_{k_2}(m)$.
4. $s = x/(r + x_a) \bmod q$.
5. Output (c, r, s) as the ciphertext to be sent to Bob.

Basic Algorithm
Unsigncryption of (c, r, s) by Bob the Recipient

1. Recover k from r, s, g, p, y_a and x_b
   by $k = Hash((y_a \cdot g^r)^{s \cdot x_b} \bmod p)$.
2. Split k into k_1 and k_2.
3. $m = D_{k_1}(c)$.
4. Output m as a valid message originated from Alice
   only if $KH_{k_2}(m) = r$. Output "Reject" otherwise.

The technique was first detailed in a patent application in Oct. 1996 [207], although the research paper was not published until almost a year later at Crypto'97 [203, 204].

1.1.4 Provably Secure Signcryption

Following the publication of the basic signcryption algorithm discussed above, finding formal proofs for both confidentiality and unforgeability of the algorithm emerged as the next challenge. I was fortunate to have Ron Steinfeld joining my lab at Monash University as a PhD student in the southern fall of 1999. Ron took my advice to look into formal proofs for the security of signcryption. We soon realized that identifying a right security model for signcryption was of most importance. In late 1999 we made the first step in that direction: we were able to find a security proof for the unforgeability of a factoring-based signcryption algorithm. The result was presented at ISW2000 [184], leaving proofs for the confidentiality of the signcryption algorithm as an open problem.

I welcomed Joonsang Baek to join my lab as a PhD student in early 2000. Shortly after his arrival, Joonsang started to work with Ron and myself on security proofs for signcryption. The joint research turned out to be extremely fruitful, resulting in the establishment of a strong security model for signcryption in the multi-user setting and formal security proofs for both unforgeability and confidentiality in that model [12, 13].

Independent of work at my lab, An, Dodis, and Rabin succeeded in obtaining proofs for the security of a broad class of joint public key encryption and digital signatures in the two-user setting [10]. These results and our results for the multi-user setting were mutually complementary, representing an important step toward designing signcryption that admits provable security.

The original signcryption algorithm required a few tweaks in order for its security to be proved with mathematical rigor [12, 13]. The tweaked algorithm employs two separate one-way hash algorithms G and H. The former was used to generate a key for a private key cipher whereas the latter to compute the value of r. In addition, both Alice's public key and Bob's public key participated in the hash computation of r, whereby the ciphertext was tightly bound to both Alice and Bob, thwarting possible abuse by dishonest Alice or Bob.

Provably Secure Algorithm
Signcryption of m by Alice the Sender

1. Pick x uniformly at random from $[1, \ldots, q - 1]$.
2. $k = y_b^x \bmod p$.
3. $\tau = G(k)$.
4. $c = E_\tau(m)$.
5. $r = H(m, y_a, y_b, k)$.
6. If $r + x_a = 0 \pmod{q}$ then go back to Step 1;
   otherwise let $s = x/(r + x_a) \bmod q$.
7. Output (c, r, s) as the ciphertext to be sent to Bob.

Provably Secure Algorithm
Unsigncryption of (c, r, s) by Bob the Recipient

1. $k = (y_a g^r)^{s \cdot x_b} \bmod p$.
2. $\tau = G(k)$.
3. $m = D_\tau(c)$.
4. If $H(m, y_a, y_b, k) = r$ then output m as a valid message originated from Alice; otherwise output "Reject".

1.2 Extensions, Standardization, and Future Research Directions

Signcryption has since been extended to elliptic curves [209], integer factorization [131, 184, 206], and pairings [122]. Furthermore researchers have designed

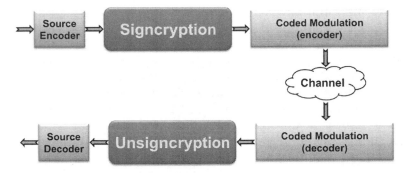

Fig. 1.4 Signcryption in a communications system

numerous signcryption techniques that have additional useful properties such as hybrid constructions for long messages [37, 73], direct verifiability by a third party [15], threshold [80], blindness [199], with an identity as public key [51], certificateless [16], proxy [85], and many others. This book serves as an introduction to all the practical forms of signcryption. For further references, the reader is directed to "Signcryption Central" (www.signcryption.org) which serves as an information portal for recent developments in the field.

In a different direction, Jutla studied the integration of private key encryption and private key message authentication, giving rise to *authenticated encryption* or *authencryption* [112].

More recently, the significance of signcryption in real-world applications has gained recognition by experts in data security. Since 2007, a technical committee within the International Organization for Standardization (ISO/IEC JTC 1/SC 27) has been developing an international standard for signcryption techniques [102]. Techniques to be included in the standard must meet ISO's stringent requirements, especially those pertinent to security, performance, and maturity.

In conclusion, I would like to bring the reader's attention to Fig. 1.4 which depicts a communications system where both coded modulation and signcryption are employed, achieving gains not only in communications efficiency and reliability but also in data security, all with minimal overhead. One cannot help but ask, Are additional types of blending still possible?

1.3 Notation and Security Notions

The development of signcryption schemes was preceded by, and makes use of, many other types of cryptographic scheme; it is not our intention to describe each of these earlier systems in detail, but a certain amount of introduction is necessary in order to explain the development of signcryption schemes effectively. In this section, we will give notation and security notions that will be used throughout the rest of the book.

1.3.1 Algorithms and Assignment

We follow the now common notation of using an arrow to denote assignment. If f is a function, then $y \leftarrow f(x)$ denotes the assignment to the variable y the value of the function f applied to the value x. Similarly, if $\mathcal{A}$ is a *deterministic* algorithm, then $y \leftarrow \mathcal{A}(x)$ denotes the assignment to the variable y the value obtained by running the algorithm $\mathcal{A}$ on the input x. If $\mathcal{A}$ has access to the oracle $\mathcal{O}$, then we write $y \leftarrow \mathcal{A}^{\mathcal{O}}(x)$.

For a probabilistic algorithm $\mathcal{A}$, we write $y \xleftarrow{R} \mathcal{A}(x)$ to denote the assignment to the variable y the value obtained by running the algorithm $\mathcal{A}$ on the input x using a fresh set of random coins. If we wish to specify that $\mathcal{A}$ is run using a specific set of coins R, then we write $y \leftarrow \mathcal{A}(x; R)$. Furthermore, if S a finite set, then we write $y \xleftarrow{R} S$ to denote the assignment to y of an element of S chosen uniformly at random. This allows us to use the symbol "$=$" to be used in algorithms to denote the comparison of two variables.

We will often wish to assess the probability that an event S occurs given that a series of related random variables have been defined according to a set of distributions $(X, Y, Z, \ldots)$. We write this as

$$\Pr[S : X, Y, Z, \ldots] \tag{1.1}$$

Hence,

$$\Pr[b = b' : b \xleftarrow{R} \{0, 1\}, \ b' \xleftarrow{R} \{0, 1\}] \tag{1.2}$$

denotes the probability that a bit b is equal to the bit b' when both b and b' are drawn uniformly at random from the set $\{0, 1\}$. Thus,

$$\Pr[b = b' : b \xleftarrow{R} \{0, 1\}, \ b' \xleftarrow{R} \{0, 1\}] = 1/2 \tag{1.3}$$

We will often want to show that an "efficient" algorithm only has a "small" probability of breaking a cryptographic scheme or solving a mathematical problem. All of our algorithms will be parameterized by some security parameter k. In our terms, an "efficient" algorithm is a *probabilistic, polynomial-time* (PPT) algorithm. A probabilistic algorithm $\mathcal{A}$ is polynomial time if there exists a polynomial p for which $\mathcal{A}(x)$ always terminates within $p(k)$ steps, regardless of the value of the random coins. In our terms, a probability is "small" if it is negligible in the security parameter. A function f is negligible in the security parameter if for all polynomials p there exists an integer $N(p)$ such that $f(k) \leq 1/|p(k)|$ for all $k \geq N(p)$. We will occasionally use the shorthand $negl(k)$ to denote a negligible function and use the notation $f(x) \leq g(x) + negl(k)$ to represent the fact that $|f(k) - g(k)|$ is a negligible function.

Lastly, if x and y are bitstrings, then $|x|$ is the length of x in bits and $x\|y$ is the concatenation of x and y. Furthermore, (x, y) is a binary representation of the ordered pair of x and y.

1.3.2 Signature Schemes

The first cryptographic primitive that we wish to consider is a digital signature scheme. A signature scheme is a public key primitive that provides origin authentication, data integrity, and non-repudiation for a piece of data. It is one of the two components that a signcryption scheme seeks to emulate.

1.3.2.1 Signature Schemes with Appendix

A signature scheme with appendix (or simply "a signature scheme") is characterized by three polynomial-time algorithms ($\mathtt{SigKeyGen}$, $\mathtt{Sign}$, $\mathtt{Verify}$):

- The key generation algorithm $\mathtt{SigKeyGen}$ is a probabilistic algorithm that takes as input the security parameter 1^k and outputs a key pair (sk^{sig}, pk^{sig}), written $(sk^{sig}, pk^{sig}) \xleftarrow{R} \mathtt{SigKeyGen}(1^k)$. The private signing key sk^{sig} is kept secret. The public verification key pk^{sig} is widely distributed.
- The signing algorithm $\mathtt{Sign}$ is a probabilistic algorithm that takes as input a message m and the private key sk^{sig}, and outputs a signature s, written $s \xleftarrow{R} \mathtt{Sign}(sk^{sig}, m)$.
- The verification algorithm $\mathtt{Verify}$ is a deterministic algorithm that takes as input a message m, a signature s, and a public verification key pk^{sig}. It outputs either a success symbol $\top$ to indicate the signature is correct or a failure symbol $\bot$ to denote that the signature is incorrect.

We require that for any key pair $(sk^{sig}, pk^{sig}) \xleftarrow{R} \mathtt{SigKeyGen}(1^k)$ and message m, we have that $\mathtt{Verify}(pk^{sig}, m, s) = \top$ whenever $s \xleftarrow{R} \mathtt{Sign}(sk^{sig}, m)$.

A signature scheme with appendix produces signature values that are designed to be appended to a message as the message is being sent from a sender to a receiver. The signature is not designed to convey any part of the message and hence the entire message has to be sent along with the signature. We stress that the signature scheme does not provide confidentiality protection: while the signature is not designed to convey any information about the message, there is no guarantee that an attacker cannot determine any information about the message from the signature.

1.3.2.2 Signature Schemes with Message Recovery

An alternative to a signature scheme with appendix is a signature scheme with message recovery. A signature scheme with message recovery allows the message to be recovered from the signature.[1] Sending a signature with message recovery is typically more bandwidth efficient than sending the concatenation of a message and a signature with appendix.

The syntax of a signature scheme with message recovery is very similar to a signature scheme with appendix. A signature scheme with message recovery is defined by a triple of polynomial-time algorithms (SigKeyGen, Sign, Verify):

- The key generation algorithm SigKeyGen is a probabilistic algorithm that takes as input the security parameter 1^k and outputs a key pair (sk^{sig}, pk^{sig}), written $(sk^{sig}, pk^{sig}) \xleftarrow{R} \text{SigKeyGen}(1^k)$. The private signing key sk^{sig} is kept secret. The public verification key pk^{sig} is widely distributed.
- The signing algorithm Sign is a probabilistic algorithm that takes as input a message m and the private key sk^{sig} and outputs a signature s, written $s \xleftarrow{R} \text{Sign}(sk^{sig}, m)$.
- The verification algorithm Verify is a deterministic algorithm that takes as input a signature s and a public verification key pk^{sig}. It outputs either a message m or a failure symbol $\perp$ to denote that the signature is incorrect, written $m \leftarrow \text{Verify}(pk^{sig}, s)$.

We require that for any key pair $(sk^{sig}, pk^{sig}) \xleftarrow{R} \text{SigKeyGen}(1^k)$ and message m, we have that $\text{Verify}(pk^{sig}, s) = m$ whenever $s \xleftarrow{R} \text{Sign}(sk^{sig}, m)$.

1.3.2.3 Security

The security requirements for a signature scheme were first described by Goldwasser et al. [91]. We present these security requirements using the syntax of a signature scheme with appendix; similar requirements exist for a signature scheme with message recovery. In both cases, we seek to bound the probability that an efficient attacker can create a false signature. This probability is assessed via the following game between a probabilistic, polynomial-time (PPT) attacker and a hypothetical challenger:

1. The challenger generates a key pair $(sk^{sig}, pk^{sig}) \xleftarrow{R} \text{SigKeyGen}(1^k)$.
2. The attacker runs $\mathcal{A}^{\mathcal{O}}(1^k, pk^{sig})$. The attacker has access to an oracle $\mathcal{O}$ (which will be described subsequently). The attacker terminates by outputting a message m^* and a signature s^*.

---

[1] Technically, a signature scheme with message recovery often only allows part of the message (sometimes called the *recoverable* part of the message) to be recovered from the signature. The remaining part of the message (sometimes called the *non-recoverable* part of the message) has to be sent along with signature. This is known as partial message recovery. However, any signature scheme with partial message recovery can be transformed into a scheme with full message recovery by concatenating the non-recoverable part of the message with the signature. Hence, in this book, we will only consider signature schemes with full message recovery.

The attacker has access to an oracle $\mathcal{O}$. The power of this oracle defines the *attack model* for the attack: it specifies the power that the attacker has in the attack.

- In a *chosen message attack* (CMA), the attacker has access to a signature oracle, which takes as input a message m and outputs a signature $s \overset{R}{\leftarrow} \text{Sign}(sk^{sig}, m)$. A chosen message attack seeks to emulate the normal mode of use of a signature scheme, in which an attacker can observe signatures produced by a legitimate party, perhaps in some adversarially chosen way.
- In a *no-message attack* (NMA), the oracle gives no response. This is equivalent to an attack model in which the attacker does not have access to the oracle.

The attacker attempts to forge a signature. There are two ways which we can assess whether the attacker succeeds in forging a signature.

- In the *existential unforgeability* (UF) game, the attacker is said to win if it outputs a pair (m^*, s^*) where $\text{Verify}(pk^{sig}, m^*, s^*) = \top$ and the attacker never queried the signature oracle with the message m^*.
- A slightly stronger notion of security is that of *strong existential unforgeability* (sUF). The attacker is said to win the strong unforgeability game if it outputs a pair (m^*, s^*) where $\text{Verify}(pk^{sig}, m^*, s^*) = \top$ and the attacker never queried the signature oracle with the message m^* and received the response s^*.

The difference between the two games is that in the unforgeability game the attacker is attempting to forge a signature on an unsigned message, whereas in the strong unforgeability game the attacker is attempting to either forge a signature on an unsigned message *or* forge a new signature on a previously signed message.

Definition 1.1 (Secure signature scheme) A signature scheme is said to be GOAL-ATK secure (where $\text{GOAL} \in \{\text{UF,sUF}\}$ and $\text{ATK} \in \{\text{NMA,CMA}\}$) if the probability that an attacker can win the GOAL game with oracle access as defined in the ATK model is negligible as a function of the security parameter for all probabilistic, polynomial-time attackers.

1.3.2.4 Weakened Security Notions for Finite Message Spaces

So far we have considered signature schemes that take arbitrary messages $m \in \{0, 1\}^*$ as input; however, we may consider weakened security notions for signature schemes that have a finite message space $\mathcal{M}$. For a finite message space, we may define a new attack model and success criteria.

In the case of the success criteria, we may ask the attacker to produce a forged signature for a randomly chosen message $m^* \overset{R}{\leftarrow} \mathcal{M}$. This leads to a new description for the attack game that a probabilistic, polynomial-time attacker $\mathcal{A}$ is playing:

1. The challenger generates a key pair $(sk^{sig}, pk^{sig}) \overset{R}{\leftarrow} \text{SigKeyGen}(1^k)$ and a message $m^* \overset{R}{\leftarrow} \mathcal{M}$.
2. The attacker runs $\mathcal{A}^{\mathcal{O}}(1^k, pk^{sig}, m^*)$. The attacker has access to an oracle $\mathcal{O}$. The attacker terminates by outputting a signature s^*.

Again, we may define two success criteria for this security game:

- In the *universally unforgeability* (uUF) game, the attacker is said to win if $\mathtt{Verify}(pk^{sig}, m^*, s^*) = \top$ and the attacker never queried the signature oracle with the message m^*.
- In the *strong universally unforgeability* (suUF) game, the attacker is said to win if $\mathtt{Verify}(pk^{sig}, m^*, s^*) = \top$ and the attacker never queried the signature oracle with the message m^* and received the response s^*.

Clearly, any scheme that is existentially unforgeable (respectively, strongly existentially unforgeable) is universally unforgeable (respectively, strong universally unforgeable).

In the case of the attack model, we can consider a situation where the attacker is given access to an oracle $\mathcal{O}$ that will return a randomly chosen message $m \xleftarrow{R} \mathcal{M}$ and a signature $s \xleftarrow{R} \mathtt{Sign}(sk^{sig}, m)$ on that message. We term this a *random message attack* (RMA). It is easy to see that this attack model lies between the notions of a no message attack (NMA) and a chosen message attack (CMA).

Definition 1.2 (Secure signature scheme) A signature scheme with a finite message space is said to be GOAL-ATK secure (where GOAL∈ {UF,sUF,uUF,suUF} and ATK∈{NMA,RMA,CMA}) if the probability that an attacker can win the GOAL game with oracle access as defined in the ATK model is negligible as a function of the security parameter for all probabilistic, polynomial-time attackers.

1.3.3 Public Key Encryption

The other cryptographic primitive that a signcryption scheme seeks to emulate is public key encryption. This primitive provides confidentiality protection for a message, although it does not guarantee data integrity or provide origin authentication.

1.3.3.1 Syntax

A public key encryption scheme consists of three polynomial-time algorithms (EncKeyGen, Encrypt, Decrypt):

- The key generation algorithm EncKeyGen is a probabilistic algorithm that takes as input a security parameter 1^k and outputs a key pair (sk^{enc}, pk^{enc}), written $(sk^{enc}, pk^{enc}) \xleftarrow{R} \mathtt{EncKeyGen}(1^k)$. The public encryption key pk^{enc} is widely distributed, while the private decryption key sk^{enc} should be kept secret. The public key defines a message space $\mathcal{M}$ and a ciphertext space $\mathcal{C}$.
- The encryption algorithm Encrypt is a probabilistic algorithm that takes a message $m \in \mathcal{M}$ and the public key pk^{enc} as input and outputs a ciphertext $C \in \mathcal{C}$, written $C \xleftarrow{R} \mathtt{Encrypt}(pk^{enc}, m)$.

- The decryption algorithm Decrypt is a deterministic algorithm that takes a ciphertext $C \in \mathcal{C}$ and the private key sk^{enc} as input and outputs either a message $m \in \mathcal{M}$ or the failure symbol $\perp$, written $m \leftarrow \text{Decrypt}(sk^{enc}, C)$.

For correctness, we require that for all key pairs $(pk^{enc}, sk^{enc}) \xleftarrow{R} \text{EncKeyGen}(1^k)$ and messages $m \in \mathcal{M}$, we have that $m \leftarrow \text{Decrypt}(sk^{enc}, C)$ whenever $C \xleftarrow{R} \text{Encrypt}(pk^{enc}, m)$.

In some cases, it may be advantageous for public/private key pairs to be based on some common parameters—e.g., a description of a group, a generator for that group, some randomly generated group elements. If this is required, then we assume the existence of a Setup algorithm which outputs these common parameters *param*. This algorithm must be run by some trusted entity (which is trusted to run the algorithm correctly, securely delete any internal data, and widely publish the results). The common parameters *param* are assumed to be an implicit input to the other algorithms in the scheme.

1.3.3.2 Security

A secure encryption scheme is one in which a ciphertext reveals no information about the underlying message. The generally accepted notion of security for an encryption scheme is given by the *indistinguishability* (IND) game. In this game, an attacker is considered to be a pair of probabilistic, polynomial-time algorithms $\mathcal{A} = (\mathcal{A}_1, \mathcal{A}_2)$. For a public key encryption scheme, the IND games run as follows:

1. The challenger generates a key pair $(sk^{enc}, pk^{enc}) \xleftarrow{R} \text{EncKeyGen}(1^k)$.
2. The attacker runs $\mathcal{A}_1^{\mathcal{O}}(1^k, pk^{enc})$ to produce a pair of equal length messages (m_0, m_1) and some state information α.
3. The challenger randomly chooses a bit $b \xleftarrow{R} \{0, 1\}$ and computes the challenge ciphertext $C^* \xleftarrow{R} \text{Encrypt}(pk^{enc}, m_b)$.
4. The attacker runs $\mathcal{A}_2^{\mathcal{O}}(C^*, \alpha)$ to produce a bit b'.

The attacker wins the game if $b = b'$. The attacker's advantage is defined to be

$$Adv_{\mathcal{A}}^{IND}(k) = |\Pr[b = b'] - 1/2| \tag{1.4}$$

Just as with signature schemes, the oracle defines the power that the attacker has in the attack model. There are two options:

- In a *chosen ciphertext attack* (CCA2), the attacker has access to a decryption oracle, which takes as input a ciphertext $C \in \mathcal{C}$ and outputs the message $m \leftarrow \text{Decrypt}(sk^{enc}, C)$. The only restriction is that $\mathcal{A}_2$ is not allowed to query the decryption oracle on the challenge ciphertext C^*.
- In a *chosen plaintext attack* (CPA), the oracle gives no response. Again, this is equivalent to an attack model in which the attacker does not have access to an oracle.

Definition 1.3 (Secure public key encryption scheme) A public key encryption scheme is said to be IND-ATK secure (where ATK∈{CPA,CCA2}) if the advantage that an attacker has in winning the IND game with oracle access as defined in the ATK model is negligible as a function of the security parameter for all probabilistic, polynomial-time attackers.

Lastly, we provide a useful lemma which can help bound the advantage of an attacker.

Lemma 1.1 *If $\mathcal{A}$ is an attacker with advantage $Adv_{\mathcal{A}}^{IND}$, then*

$$2 \cdot Adv_{\mathcal{A}}^{IND} = |\Pr[b' = 0 \mid b = 0] - \Pr[b' = 0 \mid b = 1]| \qquad (1.5)$$

1.3.3.3 Weakened Security Notions for Finite Message Spaces

Just as for signature schemes, if we know that the message space $\mathcal{M}$ of a public key encryption scheme is finite, then we may consider weaker security notions. In particular, we can consider a notion of one-way (OW) security. In this game, the attacker is considered to be a probabilistic, polynomial-time algorithm $\mathcal{A}$. The OW attack game is as follows:

1. The challenger generates a key pair $(sk^{enc}, pk^{enc}) \xleftarrow{R} \texttt{EncKeyGen}(1^k)$, a message $m^* \xleftarrow{R} \mathcal{M}$, and a ciphertext $C^* \xleftarrow{R} \texttt{Encrypt}(pk^{enc}, m^*)$.
2. The attacker runs $\mathcal{A}(1^k, pk^{enc}, C^*)$. $\mathcal{A}$ outputs a message m.

The attacker is said to win the OW-CPA game if $m = m^*$.

Definition 1.4 (One-way public key encryption scheme) A public key encryption scheme is said to be OW-CPA secure if the probability that an attacker has in winning the OW-CPA game is negligible as a function of the security parameter for all probabilistic, polynomial-time attackers.

One-way (OW) security is, conceptually, a weaker notion of security than indistinguishability (IND). Indeed, a scheme that is IND-CPA secure and has a message space $\mathcal{M} = \{0, 1\}^{\ell(k)}$, where $\ell(k)$ is a polynomial in the security parameter k, is necessarily OW-CPA secure.

1.3.4 Symmetric Encryption

While signcryption is a public key primitive, we will frequently make use of a symmetric encryption scheme as a subroutine in a larger primitive.

1.3.4.1 Syntax

A symmetric encryption scheme is a pair of deterministic algorithms (Enc, Dec):

- The encryption algorithm Enc takes as input a symmetric key K and a message $m \in \mathcal{M}$ and outputs a ciphertext $C \in \mathcal{C}$, written $C \leftarrow \text{Enc}_K(m)$.
- The decryption algorithm Dec takes as input a symmetric key K and a ciphertext $C \in \mathcal{C}$ and outputs either a message $m \in \mathcal{M}$ or the failure symbol $\perp$, written $m \leftarrow \text{Dec}_K(C)$.

For correctness, for any symmetric key K, we require that $m = \text{Dec}_K(\text{Enc}_K(m))$.

1.3.4.2 One-Time Security

The security requirements for symmetric encryption are similar to that of public key encryption. Again, it makes use of the *indistinguishability* (IND) security game and an attacker which is considered to be a pair of probabilistic, polynomial-time attackers $(\mathcal{A}_1, \mathcal{A}_2)$. The one-time notion of security works as follows:

1. The challenger generates a random key $K \xleftarrow{R} \{0, 1\}^k$.
2. The attacker runs $\mathcal{A}_1(1^k)$ to produce a pair of equal length messages (m_0, m_1) and some state information α.
3. The challenger randomly chooses a bit $b \xleftarrow{R} \{0, 1\}$ and computes the challenge ciphertext $C^* \leftarrow \text{Enc}_K(m_b)$.
4. The attacker runs $\mathcal{A}_2^{\mathcal{O}}(C^*, \alpha)$ to produce a bit b'.

Again, the attacker wins the game if $b = b'$ and the attacker's advantage is defined to be

$$Adv_{\mathcal{A}}^{OT}(k) = |Pr[b = b'] - 1/2| \tag{1.6}$$

Once again, the power of the attack model is defined by the oracle $\mathcal{O}$ and there are two possibilities for the oracle:

- In a *chosen ciphertext attack* (CCA), the attacker has a decryption oracle, which takes as input a ciphertext C and outputs a message $m \leftarrow \text{Dec}_K(C)$. The only restriction is that the attacker is not allowed to query the decryption oracle on the challenge ciphertext C^*.
- In a *chosen plaintext attack* (CPA), the decryption oracle gives no response. This is equivalent to an attack model in which the attacker does not have access to an oracle.

Note that, even in the CCA attack model, the attacker only has access to the oracle after the challenge ciphertext is issued.

Definition 1.5 (Secure Symmetric Encryption Scheme) A symmetric encryption scheme is said to be IND-ATK secure (where ATK$\in$\{CPA,CCA\}) if the advantage that an attacker has in winning the IND game with oracle access as defined in the ATK model is negligible as a function of the security parameter for all probabilistic, polynomial-time attackers.

1.3.5 Message Authentication Codes

A message authentication code (MAC) is a checksum value that can be computed on a message using a secret symmetric key to assure a recipient of the integrity and origin of the message. In many ways, it can be viewed as the symmetric version of a digital signature scheme, although it cannot provide a non-repudiation service without the involvement of a trusted third party.

A message authentication code (MAC) is defined by a deterministic MAC algorithm MAC. This algorithm takes as input a symmetric key K and a message $m \in \mathcal{M}$ and outputs a fixed length output tag.

The security requirement for a MAC scheme is similar to that of a digital signature scheme. An attacker is considered to be a probabilistic, polynomial-time algorithm $\mathcal{A}$ that runs in the following security model:

1. The challenger generates a random key $K \xleftarrow{R} \{0, 1\}^k$.
2. The attacker runs $\mathcal{A}(1^k)$ to produce a message m and a MAC tag tag. During its execution, the MAC algorithm is allowed to access a MAC oracle, which takes as input a message m and outputs $MAC_K(m)$.

The attacker wins the game if $MAC_K(m) = tag$ and m was never queried to the MAC oracle.

Definition 1.6 (Secure MAC Algorithm) A MAC algorithm is said to be secure if the advantage that an attacker has in winning the above game is negligible as a function of the security parameter for all probabilistic, polynomial-time attackers.

Part I
Security Models for Signcryption

Chapter 2
Security for Signcryption: The Two-User Model

Jee Hea An and Tal Rabin

2.1 Introduction

Signcryption is a cryptographic primitive designed to simultaneously provide confidentiality and integrity protection in a communication (see Chap. 1 for a more detailed description of the role of signcryption in a communication architecture). It is a public-key primitive and can be viewed as the public-key version of the symmetric-key primitive known as *authenticated encryption*; indeed, the two primitives share many similarities at a high level. Signcryption was originally proposed by Zheng [203, 204] with the intention that the primitive should satisfy "Cost(Signature & Encryption) ≪ Cost(Signature) + Cost(Encryption)." This inequality can interpreted in a number of ways:

- A signcryption scheme should be more computationally efficient than a naive combination of public-key encryption and digital signatures.
- A signcryption scheme should produce a signcryption "ciphertext" which is shorter than a naive combination of a public-key encryption ciphertext and a digital signature.
- A signcryption scheme should provide greater security guarantees and/or greater functionality than a naive combination of public-key encryption and digital signatures.

Of course, we would ideally aim to produce a scheme which gave all three advantages; however, in the absence of such a scheme, any one of these advantages may be useful depending on the nature of the application for which signcryption is being used. A discussion of the potential uses of signcryption in practical applications is given in Chap. 12.

This chapter provides a formal definition for the security of signcryption in the *two-user setting* and analysis of the security of signcryption schemes that are constructed by generically composing signature and encryption schemes in the public-

T. Rabin(✉)

IBM T.J. Watson Research Center, Hawthorne, NY, USA

e-mail: talr@us.ibm.com

A.W. Dent, Y. Zheng (eds.), *Practical Signcryption*, Information Security
and Cryptography, DOI 10.1007/978-3-540-89411-7_2,
© Springer-Verlag Berlin Heidelberg 2010

key setting. The first attempt to produce security models for signcryption was given by Steinfeld and Zheng [184]; however, this work only proposed a security model for the integrity protection property of a signcryption scheme. This chapter will be based on the more complete treatment given by the work of An et al. [10]. The problem of defining the security of signcryption in the public-key setting is more involved than the corresponding task in the symmetric setting [26, 117] due to the asymmetric nature of the former. The asymmetry of keys makes a difference in the notions of both authenticity and privacy on two major fronts which are addressed in this chapter.

The first difference for the public-key setting is that the security of the signcryption needs to be defined in the *multi-user* setting, where issues with users' identities need to be addressed. In contrast, authenticated encryption in the symmetric setting can be fully defined in a much simpler *two-user* setting. We argue that there is interest in the two-user setting in the public-key setting even though it does not provide all the security guarantees. There are quite a few subtle issues with defining the security of signcryption in the (simpler) two-user setting and thus starting in this setting highlights these delicate issues and is non-trivial.

The asymmetry of the public-key setting not only makes a difference in the multi-user and two-user settings but also makes a difference in the adversary's position depending on its knowledge of the keys. We give two definitions for security of signcryption depending on whether the adversary is an "outsider" (i.e., a third party who only knows the public information) or "insider" (i.e., a legal user of the network, either the sender or the receiver, or someone that knows the secret key of either the sender or the receiver). We call the former "outsider security" and the latter "insider security."

In this chapter, we will define security notions for both insider and outsider security in terms of both privacy (i.e., indistinguishability against chosen ciphertext attack, IND-CCA2) and authenticity (i.e., strong unforgeability against chosen message attack, sUF-CMA). We then analyze the security of the signcryption schemes that are constructed by generically composing signature and encryption schemes in the following three methods: Encrypt-and-Sign ($\mathcal{E}\&\mathcal{S}$), Encrypt-then-Sign ($\mathcal{E}t\mathcal{S}$), and Sign-then-Encrypt ($\mathcal{S}t\mathcal{E}$). As observed in [26, 117] in the symmetric setting, we show that the parallel $\mathcal{E}\&\mathcal{S}$ method does not provide even the weak IND-CPA security for privacy nor does it provide the strongest sUF-CMA security for authenticity (although it provides slightly weaker UF-CMA security) in either insider or outsider security models.

For the sequential $\mathcal{E}t\mathcal{S}$ and $\mathcal{S}t\mathcal{E}$ methods, we consider the following cases: security corresponding to the operation performed *last* (i.e., authenticity in the $\mathcal{E}t\mathcal{S}$ method and privacy in the $\mathcal{S}t\mathcal{E}$ method) and security corresponding to the operation performed *first* (i.e., privacy in the $\mathcal{E}t\mathcal{S}$ method and authenticity in the $\mathcal{S}t\mathcal{E}$ method). We show that the security of the last operation is *preserved* in both the insider and the outsider security models—that is, the $\mathcal{E}t\mathcal{S}$ method inherits the authenticity property of the base signature scheme and the $\mathcal{S}t\mathcal{E}$ method inherits the privacy property of the base encryption scheme. However, we show that the security of the first operation may or may not be preserved depending on the security models and the strengths of security considered. In the strong insider security model, the security of the first operation is *not* preserved against the strongest security notions of privacy and authenticity (i.e., IND-CCA2 and sUF-CMA security) although it is preserved against weaker security notions (e.g., IND-CPA, IND-gCCA2 [10], and UF-CMA security). In the weaker outsider security model, on the other hand, the security of the first operation can even be *amplified* as long as the security of the last operation is strong enough, exactly as in the symmetric setting [9, 26, 117].

2.2 Definition of Signcryption in the Two-User Setting

The definition of signcryption is a little bit more involved than the corresponding definition of authenticated encryption in the symmetric setting. Indeed, in the *symmetric* setting, we only have one specific pair of users who (1) share a single key; (2) trust each other; (3) "know who they are"; and (4) only care about being protected from "the rest of the world." In contrast, in the *public*-key setting, each user independently publishes its public keys, after which it can send/receive messages to/from any other user. In particular, (1) each user should have an explicit identity (associated with its public key); (2) each signcryption has to explicitly contain the (presumed) identities of the sender S and the receiver R; (3) each user should be protected from every other user. As we have said, complete security notions for signcryption schemes should be defined in the *multi-user* setting. However, the two-user setting provides important insights into the subtleties of signcryption and so we will provide the definitions for the two-user setting as a gentle introduction to the subject. We will provide full multi-user security models in Chap. 3.

2.2.1 Two Security Notions in the Two-User Setting

2.2.1.1 Syntax

A signcryption scheme Π consists of five algorithms, $\Pi = (\texttt{Setup}, \texttt{KeyGen}_S, \texttt{KeyGen}_R, \texttt{Signcrypt}, \texttt{Unsigncrypt})$:

- The (possibly randomized) setup algorithm $\texttt{Setup}$ takes as input a security parameter 1^k and outputs any common parameters *param* required by the signcryption schemes. This may include the security parameter 1^k, the description of a group $\mathbb{G}$ and a generator g for that group, choices for hash functions or symmetric encryption schemes, etc.

  It is important to note that this algorithm does not output a secret key. In fact, it may be important that the algorithm does not leak any information about the common parameters *except* those values which are explicitly stated as being part of the output. The security of the scheme may be jeopardized if extra information about the common parameters is leaked; for example, if the common parameters include two group elements g and h, then security may be jeopardized if the setup algorithm leaks the discrete logarithm of h with the respect to g. Hence, all users must trust that the setup algorithm is computed correctly and securely.

- The randomized sender key generation algorithm KeyGen_S takes as input the common parameters *param* and outputs a pair of keys (sk_S, pk_S), where sk_S is the sender's signing key, which is kept secret, and pk_S is the sender's verification key pair (pk_S, pk_R), which is made public; we write $(sk_S, pk_S) \xleftarrow{R} \mathrm{KeyGen}_S(param)$.

- The randomized receiver key generation algorithm KeyGen_R takes as input the common parameters *param* and outputs a pair of keys (sk_R, pk_R), where sk_R is the receiver's decryption key, which is kept secret, and pk_R is the receiver's encryption key, which is made public; we write $(sk_R, pk_R) \xleftarrow{R} \mathrm{KeyGen}_R(param)$. In a complete system, a user would have two key pairs: a pair (sk_S, pk_S) which is used when the user is sending a message and a pair (sk_R, pk_R) which is used when the user is receiving a message. It is possible for a user to have a single key pair (sk, pk) which is used for both sending and receiving messages—this issue is discussed in depth in Sect. 5.4—but the simpler two-key presentation suits our purposes for now. We note that we may always set $pk = (pk_S, pk_R)$ and $sk = (sk_S, sk_R)$ and so our presentation is an example of the more general case.

- The randomized *signcryption* (sign/encrypt) algorithm $\mathrm{Signcrypt}$ takes as input the common parameters *param*, the sender's secret key sk_S, the receiver's public key pk_R, and a message m from the associated message space $\mathcal{M}$. It internally flips some coins and outputs a signcryption ciphertext C; we will typically write $C \leftarrow \mathrm{Signcrypt}(sk_S, pk_R, m)$ or $C \leftarrow \mathrm{Signcrypt}(m)$ (omitting *param*, sk_S and pk_R for brevity).

- The deterministic *unsigncryption* (verify/decrypt) algorithm $\mathrm{Unsigncrypt}$ takes as input the common parameters *param*, the sender's public key pk_S, the receiver's secret key sk_R, and the signcryption ciphertext C. It outputs either $m \in \mathcal{M}$ or an error symbol $\perp$ which indicates that the message was not encrypted or signed properly. We write $m \leftarrow \mathrm{Unsigncrypt}(pk_S, sk_R, C)$ or $m \leftarrow \mathrm{Unsigncrypt}(C)$ (again, omitting the common parameters and keys).

We require that $\mathrm{Unsigncrypt}(\mathrm{Signcrypt}(m)) = m$ for any $m \in \mathcal{M}$.

2.2.1.2 Security of Signcryption

Fix the sender S and the receiver R. The security goal is to provide both authenticity and privacy of communicated data. In the symmetric setting, since the sender and the receiver share the same secret key, the only security model that makes sense is one in which the adversary is modeled as a third party or an *outsider* who does not know the shared secret key. However, in the public-key setting, the sender and the receiver do not share the same secret key but each has his/her own secret key. Due to this asymmetry of the secret keys, we need to protect the data not only from an outsider but also from an *insider* who is a legal user of the system (i.e., the sender or the receiver themselves or someone who knows either the sender's secret key or the receiver's secret key). Hence, we have an additional security notion in the public-key setting and we call it *insider security*. As opposed to the insider security, we call the security against an outsider *outsider security*, which is the security that is also considered in the symmetric setting.

Outsider Security

We define security against the strongest security notions of authenticity (the analogs of UF-CMA or sUF-CMA for digital signature schemes) and privacy (the analog of IND-CCA2 for public-key encryption schemes). Weaker notions could easily be defined as well. We assume that the adversary $\mathcal{A}$ has the public information (pk_S, pk_R). It also has oracle access to the functionalities of both the sender and the receiver. Specifically, it can mount a chosen message attack on the sender by asking the sender to produce a signcryption C of an arbitrary message m. In other words, $\mathcal{A}$ has access to the *signcryption oracle*. Similarly, it can mount a chosen ciphertext attack on the receiver by giving the receiver any candidate signcryption C and receiving back the message m (where m could be $\perp$), i.e., $\mathcal{A}$ has access to the *unsigncryption oracle*. Notice, $\mathcal{A}$ cannot by itself run either the signcryption or the unsigncryption oracles due to the lack of corresponding secret keys sk_S and sk_R.

To break the UF-CMA security of the signcryption scheme, $\mathcal{A}$ has to come up with a *valid* signcryption C (i.e., a ciphertext C for which the unsigncryption oracle does not return $\perp$) of a "new" message m, which it did not ask the sender to signcrypt earlier (note that $\mathcal{A}$ is not required to "know" m when producing C although $\mathcal{A}$ can always compute m by querying the unsigncryption oracle with C). The signcryption scheme is said to be *outsider secure* in the UF-CMA sense if any PPT $\mathcal{A}$ has a negligible chance of succeeding in the UF-CMA attack. To break the sUF-CMA security of the signcryption scheme, $\mathcal{A}$ has to come up with a valid signcryption C which was not returned by the sender earlier (note that C's unsigncryption output m does not have to be "new"). Formally, we consider a game played between a hypothetical challenger and a PPT attacker $\mathcal{A}$:

1. The challenger generates common parameters $param \xleftarrow{R} \mathsf{Setup}(1^k)$, a sender key pair $(sk_S, pk_S) \xleftarrow{R} \mathsf{KeyGen}_S(param)$, and a receiver key pair $(sk_R, pk_R) \xleftarrow{R} \mathsf{KeyGen}_R(param)$.
2. The attacker runs $\mathcal{A}$ on the input $(param, pk_S, pk_R)$. The attacker may query a signcryption oracle with a message $m \in \mathcal{M}$ to receive the signcryption ciphertext $C \xleftarrow{R} \mathsf{Signcrypt}(sk_S, pk_R, m)$. The attacker may also query an unsigncryption oracle with a ciphertext C to receive the message $m \leftarrow \mathsf{Unsigncrypt}(pk_S, sk_R, C)$. The attacker terminates with the output of a ciphertext C.

The attacker wins the UF-CMA game if (1) $m \leftarrow \mathsf{Unsigncrypt}(pk_S, sk_R, C)$ satisfies $m \neq \perp$ and (2) if m was never submitted to the signcryption oracle. The attacker wins the sUF-CMA game if (1) $m \leftarrow \mathsf{Unsigncrypt}(pk_S, sk_R, C)$ satisfies $m \neq \perp$ and (2) the signcryption oracle never returned C. The signcryption scheme is said to be *outsider secure* in the (s)UF-CMA sense if every PPT attacker $\mathcal{A}$ has a negligible chance of succeeding in the (s)UF-CMA attack.

To break the IND-CCA2 security of the signcryption scheme, $\mathcal{A}$ has to come up with two equal-length messages m_0 and m_1. One of these will be signcrypted at random, the corresponding signcryption challenge C^* will be given to $\mathcal{A}$ and $\mathcal{A}$ has to guess which message was signcrypted. Here, $\mathcal{A}$ is forbidden to query the unsigncryption oracle on the challenge C^*. Formally, we consider a game played between a challenger and a PPT attacker $\mathcal{A} = (\mathcal{A}_1, \mathcal{A}_2)$:

1. The challenger generates common parameters $param \overset{R}{\leftarrow} \mathtt{Setup}(1^k)$, a sender key pair $(sk_S, pk_S) \overset{R}{\leftarrow} \mathtt{KeyGen}_S(param)$, and a receiver key pair $(sk_R, pk_R) \overset{R}{\leftarrow} \mathtt{KeyGen}_R(param)$.
2. The attacker runs $\mathcal{A}_1$ on the input $(param, pk_S, pk_R)$. The attacker may query a signcryption oracle with a message $m \in \mathcal{M}$ to receive the signcryption ciphertext $C \overset{R}{\leftarrow} \mathtt{Signcrypt}(sk_S, pk_R, m)$. The attacker may also query an unsigncryption oracle with a ciphertext C to receive the message $m \leftarrow \mathtt{Unsigncrypt}(pk_S, sk_R, C)$. The attacker terminates with the output of two equal-length messages $m_0, m_1 \in \mathcal{M}$ and some state information α.
3. The challenger chooses $b \overset{R}{\leftarrow} \{0, 1\}$ and computes the challenge ciphertext $C^* \overset{R}{\leftarrow} \mathtt{Signcrypt}(sk_S, pk_R, m_b)$.
4. The attacker runs $\mathcal{A}_2$ on the input of the challenge ciphertext C^* and the state information α. The attacker may query the signcryption and unsigncryption oracles as before, with the exception that the attacker is forbidden from submitting the ciphertext C^* to the unsigncryption oracle. The attacker terminates with the output of a bit b'.

The attacker wins if $b = b'$ and the attacker's advantage is defined to be

$$\varepsilon = |Pr[b = b'] - 1/2|$$

The signcryption scheme is said to be *outsider secure* in the IND-CCA2 sense if every PPT attacker $\mathcal{A}$ has a negligible advantage in the IND-CCA2 attack.

Insider Security

Security notions for insider security are similar to those for outsider security, except that the attacker is given one of the private keys of the users. In the (s)UF-CMA game, the attacker is given the private key of the receiver, indicating that the attacker is the receiver and that the signcryption scheme prevents a receiver from forging a signcryption ciphertext that purports to be from the sender. This is a necessary condition if non-repudiation is to be achieved. In the IND-CCA2 game, the attacker is given the private key of the sender, indicating that the attacker is the sender and that the signcryption scheme prevents a sender from deciphering a signcryption ciphertext that has previously been produced. This means that the signcryption scheme protects the confidentiality of messages even if the sender's private key is subsequently leaked to an attacker.

The formal model for insider (s)UF-CMA security is as follows:

1. The challenger generates common parameters $param \xleftarrow{R} \texttt{Setup}(1^k)$, a sender key pair $(sk_S, pk_S) \xleftarrow{R} \texttt{KeyGen}_S(param)$, and a receiver key pair $(sk_R, pk_R) \xleftarrow{R} \texttt{KeyGen}_R(param)$.

2. The attacker runs $\mathcal{A}$ on the input $(param, pk_S, sk_R, pk_R)$. The attacker may query a signcryption oracle with a message $m \in \mathcal{M}$ to receive the signcryption cipher-text $C \xleftarrow{R} \texttt{Signcrypt}(sk_S, pk_R, m)$. (The attacker need not be given access to an unsigncryption oracle as it can compute the unsigncryption algorithm itself using sk_R.) The attacker terminates with the output of a ciphertext C.

The attacker wins the UF-CMA game if (1) $m \leftarrow \texttt{Unsigncrypt}(pk_S, sk_R, C)$ satisfies $m \neq \perp$ and (2) if m was never submitted to the signcryption oracle. The attacker wins the sUF-CMA game if (1) $m \leftarrow \texttt{Unsigncrypt}(pk_S, sk_R, C)$ satisfies $m \neq \perp$ and (2) the signcryption oracle never returned C. The signcryption scheme is said to be *insider secure* in the (s)UF-CMA sense if every PPT attacker $\mathcal{A}$ has a negligible chance of succeeding in the (s)UF-CMA attack.

The formal model for insider IND-CCA2 security is as follows:

1. The challenger generates common parameters $param \xleftarrow{R} \texttt{Setup}(1^k)$, a sender key pair $(sk_S, pk_S) \xleftarrow{R} \texttt{KeyGen}_S(param)$, and a receiver key pair $(sk_R, pk_R) \xleftarrow{R} \texttt{KeyGen}_R(param)$.

2. The attacker runs $\mathcal{A}_1$ on the input $(param, pk_S, sk_S, pk_R)$. The attacker may query an unsigncryption oracle with a ciphertext C to receive the message $m \leftarrow \texttt{Unsigncrypt}(pk_S, sk_R, C)$. (Again, the attacker does not need to be given access to a signcryption oracle as it can compute the signcryption functionality using sk_S.) The attacker terminates with the output of two equal-length messages $m_0, m_1 \in \mathcal{M}$ and some state information α.

3. The challenger chooses $b \xleftarrow{R} \{0, 1\}$ and computes the challenge ciphertext $C^* \xleftarrow{R} \texttt{Signcrypt}(sk_S, pk_R, m_b)$.

4. The attacker runs $\mathcal{A}_2$ on the input of the challenge ciphertext C^* and the state information α. The attacker may query the unsigncryption oracle as before, with the exception that the attacker is forbidden from submitting the ciphertext C^* to the unsigncryption oracle. The attacker terminates with the output of a bit b'.

The attacker wins if $b = b'$ and the attacker's advantage is defined to be

$$\varepsilon = |\Pr[b = b'] - 1/2|$$

The signcryption scheme is said to be *insider secure* in the IND-CCA2 sense if every PPT attacker $\mathcal{A}$ has a negligible advantage in the IND-CCA2 attack.

We also present an equivalent, but more elegant, definition of the insider security model. This more elegant treatment is rarely used in practice but does highlight the relationship between signcryption schemes and the related concepts of public-key encryption and digital signatures. We note that given any signcryption scheme $\Pi = (\texttt{Setup}, \texttt{KeyGen}_S, \texttt{KeyGen}_R, \texttt{Signcrypt}, \texttt{Unsigncrypt})$, we can define a corresponding *induced* signature scheme $\mathcal{S} = (\texttt{SigKeyGen}, \texttt{Sign}, \texttt{Verify})$ and encryption scheme $\mathcal{E} = (\texttt{EncKeyGen}, \texttt{Encrypt}, \texttt{Decrypt})$:

- *Signature scheme $\mathcal{S}$.* The key generation algorithm $\texttt{SigKeyGen}$ runs *param* $\overset{R}{\leftarrow} \texttt{Setup}(1^k)$, $(sk_S, pk_S) \overset{R}{\leftarrow} \texttt{KeyGen}_S(param)$, and $(sk_R, pk_R) \overset{R}{\leftarrow} \texttt{KeyGen}_R$ *(param)*. We set the signing key to $sk^{sig} = (param, sk_S, pk_S, pk_R)$ and the verification key to $pk^{sig} = (param, pk_S, sk_R, pk_R)$, namely, the public verification key (available to the adversary) *contains the secret key of the receiver R*. To sign a message m, $\texttt{Sign}(m)$ outputs $C = \texttt{Signcrypt}(m)$, while the verification algorithm $\texttt{Verify}(C)$ runs $m \leftarrow \texttt{Unsigncrypt}(C)$ and outputs $\top$ if and only if $m \neq \bot$. We note that the verification is indeed polynomial time since pk^{sig} includes sk_R.
- *Encryption scheme $\mathcal{E}$.* The key generation algorithm $\texttt{EncKeyGen}$ runs *param* $\overset{R}{\leftarrow} \texttt{Setup}(1^k)$, $(sk_S, pk_S) \overset{R}{\leftarrow} \texttt{KeyGen}_S(param)$, and $(sk_R, pk_R) \overset{R}{\leftarrow}$ $\texttt{KeyGen}_R(param)$. We set the encryption key to $pk^{enc} = (param, sk_S, pk_S, pk_R)$ and the decryption key to $sk^{enc} = (param, pk_S, sk_R, pk_R)$, namely the public encryption key (available to the adversary) *contains the secret key of the sender S*. To encrypt a message m, $\texttt{Encrypt}(m)$ outputs $C = \texttt{Signcrypt}(m)$, while the decryption algorithm $\texttt{Decrypt}(C)$ simply outputs $\texttt{Unsigncrypt}(C)$. We note that the encryption is indeed polynomial time since pk^{enc} includes sk_S.

The signcryption scheme is insider (s)UF-CMA secure if the induced signature scheme is (s)UF-CMA secure. The signcryption scheme is insider IND-CCA2 secure if the induced encryption scheme is IND-CCA2 secure.

2.2.2 Discussions on the Security Notions

2.2.2.1 Should we Require Non-Repudiation?

We note that the conventional notion of digital signatures supports *non-repudiation*. Namely, the receiver R of a correctly generated signature s of the message m can hold the sender S responsible for the contents of m. Indeed, presenting s to a third party is sufficient for R to prove that m was indeed signed by S as long as the signature scheme that is used to generate s is unforgeable and publicly verifiable. On the other hand, non-repudiation does not *automatically* follow from the definition of signcryption. Although signcryption allows the *receiver* to be convinced that m was sent by S, it does not necessarily enable a third party to verify this fact because the verification of the authenticity of the message m may involve the receiver's secret key, depending on how the signcryption scheme is built.

We believe that non-repudiation should not be part of the *definition* of signcryption security because the necessity of this property varies depending on the applications. Indeed, non-repudiation might be needed in some applications, while explicitly undesirable in others (e.g., this issue is the essence of undeniable [58] and chameleon [119] signature schemes). We will therefore not discuss this issue any further in this chapter. The issue of non-repudiation in signcryption schemes is discussed further in Sects. 4.6 and 6.5.

2.2.2.2 Insider vs. Outsider Security

We illustrate some of the differences between insider and outsider security. For example, insider security for authenticity implies non-repudiation "in principle." Namely, non-repudiation is certain at least when the receiver R is willing to reveal its secret key sk_R (since this induces a regular signature scheme) and may be possible by other means (e.g., with the use of an appropriate zero-knowledge proof). In contrast, outsider security leaves open the possibility that the receiver R can generate—using its secret key—valid signcryptions of messages that were not actually sent by the sender S. In such a case, non-repudiation cannot be achieved no matter what the receiver R does.

Despite the above issues, however, it might still seem that the distinction between insider and outsider security is a bit contrived, especially for privacy. Intuitively, outsider security protects the privacy of the receiver R from outside intruders who do not know the secret key of the sender S. On the other hand, insider security assumes that the sender S *is* the intruder attacking the privacy of the receiver R. But since the sender S is the *only* user that can send valid signcryptions from S to R, this seems to make little sense. Similarly for authenticity, if non-repudiation is *not* an issue, then insider security seems to make little sense as it assumes that the receiver R is the intruder attacking the authenticity of the sender S, and, simultaneously, the *only* user that needs to be convinced of the authenticity of the (received) data. In many settings *outsider security might be all one needs* for privacy and/or authenticity. Still, there are some cases where the extra strength of the insider security might be important. For example, assume an adversary A happens to steal the key of the sender S. Even though now A can send forged messages "from S to R," we still might not want A to understand previous (or even future) recorded signcryptions sent from the honest sender S to the receiver R. Similarly, if an adversary A happens to steal the key of the receiver R, we still might not want A to send forged messages "from S to R," although A can now understand signcryption messages sent from the honest sender S to the receiver R. Insider security will meet these security requirements, while the outsider security might not.

Finally, we note that *achieving* outsider security could be significantly easier than insider security. One such example will be seen in Theorems 2.3 and 2.4. Another example is given by An [7] and shows that authenticated encryption in the *symmetric setting* could be used to build outsider secure signcryption, but not insider secure signcryption. A final example is the outsider secure signcryption KEM produced by Dent [73] which is discussed in Sect. 7.3. In summary, one should carefully examine if one really needs the extra guarantees of insider security.

2.3 Generic Compositions of Signature and Encryption

In this section, we discuss three methods of constructing signcryption schemes that are based on generic composition of signature and encryption: Encrypt-and-Sign ($\mathcal{E}\&\mathcal{S}$), Sign-then-Encrypt ($\mathcal{St\mathcal{E}}$), and Encrypt-then-Sign ($\mathcal{Et\mathcal{S}}$).

2.3.1 Construction

Let $\mathcal{E} = (\texttt{EncKeyGen}, \texttt{Encrypt}, \texttt{Decrypt})$ be an encryption scheme and $\mathcal{S} = (\texttt{SigKeyGen}, \texttt{Sign}, \texttt{Verify})$ be a signature scheme. All three methods use the same common parameter algorithm and key generation algorithms—see Fig. 2.1. Essentially, the schemes require no common parameters, while the sender and receiver key generation algorithms are the key generation algorithms for the signature and encryption schemes, respectively. The three construction methods are the "Encrypt-and-Sign" ($\mathcal{E}\&\mathcal{S}$) method—see Fig. 2.2; the "Encrypt-then-Sign" ($\mathcal{Et\mathcal{S}}$) method—see Fig. 2.3; and the "Sign-then-Encrypt" ($\mathcal{St\mathcal{E}}$) method—see Fig. 2.4.

$\texttt{Setup}(1^k)$:
  $param \leftarrow 1^k$
  Return $param$

$\texttt{KeyGen}_S(param)$:
  $(sk^{sig}, pk^{sig}) \xleftarrow{R} \texttt{SigKeyGen}(1^k)$
  $(sk_S, pk_S) \leftarrow (sk^{sig}, pk^{sig})$
  Return (sk_S, pk_S)

$\texttt{KeyGen}_R(param)$:
  $(sk^{enc}, pk^{enc}) \xleftarrow{R} \texttt{EncKeyGen}(1^k)$
  $(sk_R, pk_R) \leftarrow (sk^{enc}, pk^{enc})$
  Return (sk_R, pk_R)

Fig. 2.1 The key generation algorithms for the generic compositions

$\texttt{Signcrypt}(sk_S, pk_R, m)$:
  Parse sk_S as sk^{sig}
  Parse pk_R as pk^{enc}
  $c \xleftarrow{R} \texttt{Encrypt}(pk^{enc}, m)$
  $\sigma \xleftarrow{R} \texttt{Sign}(sk^{sig}, m)$
  $C \leftarrow (c, \sigma)$
  Return C

$\texttt{Unsigncrypt}(pk_S, sk_R, C)$:
  Parse pk_S as pk^{sig}
  Parse sk_R as sk^{enc}
  Parse C as (c, σ)
  $m \leftarrow \texttt{Decrypt}(sk^{enc}, c)$
  If $\texttt{Verify}(pk^{sig}, m, \sigma) = \perp$ then return $\perp$
  Otherwise return m

Fig. 2.2 The Encrypt-and-Sign ($\mathcal{E}\&\mathcal{S}$) scheme

$\texttt{Signcrypt}(sk_S, pk_R, m)$:
  Parse sk_S as sk^{sig}
  Parse pk_R as pk^{enc}
  $c \xleftarrow{R} \texttt{Encrypt}(pk^{enc}, m)$
  $\sigma \xleftarrow{R} \texttt{Sign}(sk^{sig}, c)$
  $C \leftarrow (c, \sigma)$
  Return C

$\texttt{Unsigncrypt}(pk_S, sk_R, C)$:
  Parse pk_S as pk^{sig}
  Parse sk_R as sk^{enc}
  Parse C as (c, σ)
  If $\texttt{Verify}(pk^{sig}, m, \sigma) = \perp$ then return $\perp$
  $m \leftarrow \texttt{Decrypt}(sk^{enc}, c)$
  Return m

Fig. 2.3 The Encrypt-then-Sign ($\mathcal{Et\mathcal{S}}$) scheme

```
Signcrypt(sk_S,pk_R,m):              Unsigncrypt(pk_S,sk_R,C):
  Parse sk_S as sk^sig                 Parse pk_S as pk^sig
  Parse pk_R as pk^enc                 Parse sk_R as sk^enc
  σ ←^R Sign(sk^sig,m)                 m‖σ ← Decrypt(sk^enc,C)
  C ←^R Encrypt(pk^enc,m‖σ)            If Verify(pk^sig,m,σ) = ⊥ then return ⊥
  Return C                             Otherwise return m
```

Fig. 2.4 The Sign-then-Encrypt ($\mathcal{StE}$) scheme

2.3.2 Security of the Parallel Composition Method

Among the above three generic composition methods, the "Encrypt-and-Sign" ($\mathcal{E\&S}$) method allows computing encryption and signature in parallel, while in the other two methods, they are computed sequentially. However, in terms of security, it is easy to see that $\mathcal{E\&S}$ does *not* preserve privacy since the signature will reveal information about the message m (regardless of whether the adversary is an insider or an outsider). To be more formal, we give an attacker $\mathcal{A} = (\mathcal{A}_1, \mathcal{A}_2)$ against the IND-CCA2 property of the signcryption scheme. The attack works in two phases:

- The attacker $\mathcal{A}_1$ outputs two distinct equal-length messages from the message space (m_0, m_1).

The challenger randomly signcrypts one message to give a challenge ciphertext $(c^*, \sigma^*) \overset{R}{\leftarrow} \text{Signcrypt}(sk_S, pk_R, m_b)$. This challenge ciphertext is given to the attacker.

- The attacker $\mathcal{A}_2$ checks whether σ^* is a valid signature on m_0 or m_1 by computing $\text{Sign}(pk_S, m_0, \sigma^*)$ and $\text{Sign}(pk_S, m_1, \sigma^*)$. The attacker returns the appropriate bit b.

This may seem like a technicality, but the prospect of the digital signature leaking information about the message is very real. There is no requirement on the digital signature to preserve the confidentiality of the message. Indeed, digital signatures with message recovery, discussed in Sect. 1.3.2, guarantee that the signature will reveal the underlying message. These signature schemes still meet the strong notions of (s)UF-CMA security, but have absolutely no confidentiality properties.

Although $\mathcal{E\&S}$ does not preserve privacy, it is easy to see that it preserves the UF-CMA security. Intuitively, if an adversary against the UF-CMA security of the signcryption scheme built using $\mathcal{E\&S}$ succeeds, it means it succeeded in forging a signature for a "new" message, which is exactly what it means to break the UF-CMA security of the underlying signature scheme. However, for the sUF-CMA security (a stronger authenticity property), the $\mathcal{E\&S}$ method does not necessarily yield a secure signcryption scheme for a similar reason as in the privacy case (both the encryption part and the signature part need to be unforgeable). Notice that these results hold in both insider and outsider security models.

2.3.3 Security of the Sequential Composition Methods

In the strong insider security model, where the adversary knows all of the secret keys except for the one being attacked, signcryption security can only be based on the security of the underlying component whose secret key is unknown to the adversary. For example, in the case of confidentiality, the only key that the adversary does not know is the private key of the encryption scheme. In other words, the privacy of the signcryption scheme can only be based on the security of the public-key encryption scheme. Similarly, the integrity protection property of the signcryption scheme can only be based on the security of the digital signature scheme. Hence, preserving the security property of the underlying component is the best we can hope to achieve with insider security. However, we show that this may not always be achieved—that is, in the sequential composition methods (i.e., $\mathcal{E}t\mathcal{S}$ and $\mathcal{S}t\mathcal{E}$), depending on the order of composition and the strength of the security property considered, the security of the underlying component may or may not be preserved. We show this difference by dividing the security into two cases depending on whether we consider the signcryption security property corresponding to the operation performed *first* or *last*.

When we consider the security of signcryption corresponding to the security of the operation performed *last* (i.e., authenticity in the $\mathcal{E}t\mathcal{S}$ method and privacy in the $\mathcal{S}t\mathcal{E}$ method), the security of the base component is preserved. In other words, the security of the last operation is inherited by the signcryption scheme—that is, the $\mathcal{E}t\mathcal{S}$ method inherits the authenticity of the base signature scheme and the $\mathcal{S}t\mathcal{E}$ method inherits the privacy of the base encryption scheme. Notice that in this case the security of the signcryption scheme does *not* depend on the security of the other component (i.e., the operation performed first). This is true regardless of the security models (i.e., regardless of whether we consider the insider or outsider security model).

If we consider the signcryption security corresponding to the security of the operation performed *first* (i.e., privacy in the $\mathcal{E}t\mathcal{S}$ method and authenticity in the $\mathcal{S}t\mathcal{E}$ method), then results differ depending on the security models and the composition methods. In the insider security model, the security of the first operation is *not* preserved against the strongest security notions of privacy and authenticity (i.e., IND-CCA2 security and sUF-CMA security) although it is preserved against weaker security notions (e.g., IND-CPA, IND-gCCA2 [10], and UF-CMA security). This is because the adversary who knows the secret key of the other component (i.e., the signature scheme in the $\mathcal{E}t\mathcal{S}$ method and the encryption scheme in the $\mathcal{S}t\mathcal{E}$ method) can manipulate the given signcryption ciphertext by re-signing it and submitting the modified ciphertext as a unsigncryption oracle query (in the attack against the IND-CCA2 security of the $\mathcal{E}t\mathcal{S}$ method) or re-encrypting it and submit the modified ciphertext as a forgery (in the attack against the sUF-CMA security of the $\mathcal{S}t\mathcal{E}$ method). Intuitively, this tells us that achieving the strongest security corresponding to the security of the operation performed first is not possible when the adversary knows the secret key of the operation performed last.

However, in the outsider security model (where the adversary does not know any secret keys) the results are quite different. The security of the operation performed last can help enhance the security of the operation performed first—that is, a security property stronger than that of the first operation can be achieved as long as the security of the last operation is strong enough. Indeed, it turns out that, for the $\mathcal{E}t\mathcal{S}$ method, IND-CCA2 security can be achieved from the IND-CPA security of the base encryption scheme (which is the first operation) with the help of the sUF-CMA security of the base signature scheme (which is the last operation). For the $\mathcal{S}t\mathcal{E}$ method, sUF-CMA security can be achieved from the UF-NMA security of the base signature scheme (which is the first operation) with the help of the IND-CCA2 security of the base encryption scheme (which is the last operation).

We now summarize the results in the following theorems. Theorem 2.1 states that the signcryption security corresponding to the security of the last operation is preserved in both insider and outsider security models. In order to show that, we consider only the strongest security notions (i.e., insider IND-CCA2 security for privacy and insider sUF-CMA security for authenticity) as representative cases since the proofs for other weaker notions are very similar except a few minor definitional differences.

Theorem 2.1 *If $\mathcal{S}$ is sUF-CMA secure, then the signcryption scheme Π built using the $\mathcal{E}t\mathcal{S}$ method is sUF-CMA secure in the insider security model. If $\mathcal{E}$ is IND-CCA2 secure, then the signcryption scheme Π built using the $\mathcal{S}t\mathcal{E}$ method is IND-CCA2 secure in the insider security model.*

Proof (1) sUF-CMA security of $\mathcal{E}t\mathcal{S}$ in the insider security model

Let $\mathcal{A}'$ be a forger against the sUF-CMA security of Π built using the $\mathcal{E}t\mathcal{S}$ method in the insider security model. We can easily construct a forger $\mathcal{A}$ against the sUF-CMA security of the signature scheme $\mathcal{S}$ that has identical probability of forging signatures. Let (sk_S^{sig}, pk_S^{sig}) be the keys of $\mathcal{S}$. Given the signing oracle Sign and the public verification key pk_S^{sig}, $\mathcal{A}$ picks a pair of encryption keys $(sk_R^{enc}, pk_R^{enc}) \xleftarrow{R}$ EncKeyGen(1^k). $\mathcal{A}$ then hands $(pk_S^{sig}, sk_R^{enc}, pk_R^{enc})$ to $\mathcal{A}'$ as the public key of the induced signature scheme. $\mathcal{A}$ can easily simulate the signcryption query of $\mathcal{A}'$ for any message m' by first creating $e' \xleftarrow{R}$ Encrypt(pk_R^{enc}, m') and then asking the signing oracle for $\mathcal{S}$ to sign e'. Finally, when $\mathcal{A}'$ produces a forgery C for $\mathcal{E}t\mathcal{S}$, $\mathcal{A}$ outputs C as well. For sUF-CMA security, it is easy to see that if C is a valid and "new" signcryption (i.e., either the encryption part or the signature part is new), then C is a valid and "new" signature too (i.e., either the message part or the signature part is new).

(2) IND-CCA2 security of $\mathcal{S}t\mathcal{E}$ in the insider security model

Let $\mathcal{A}'$ be a distinguisher against the IND-CCA2 security of a scheme Π built using the $\mathcal{S}t\mathcal{E}$ method in the insider security model. We can easily construct a distinguisher $\mathcal{A}$ against the IND-CCA2 security of the encryption scheme $\mathcal{E}$ as follows. Let (sk_R^{enc}, pk_R^{enc}) be the key pair of $\mathcal{E}$. Given the public encryption key pk_R^{enc} and the decryption oracle Decrypt, $\mathcal{A}$ picks a pair of signing keys $(sk_S^{sig}, pk_S^{sig}) \xleftarrow{R}$ SigKeyGen(1^k). $\mathcal{A}$ then hands $(sk_S^{sig}, pk_S^{sig}, pk_R^{enc})$ to $\mathcal{A}'$, as the public key of the induced encryption scheme. To simulate the unsigncryption query C' made by $\mathcal{A}'$,

$\mathcal{A}$ first decrypts C' into $m'\|\sigma'$ using its own decryption oracle and then checks if σ' is a valid signature of m' and returns m' if s' is valid and $\perp$ if not. Next, when $\mathcal{A}'$ outputs a pair of messages m_0 and m_1, $\mathcal{A}$ outputs $m_0\|s_0$ and $m_1\|s_1$, where $s_i = \texttt{Sign}(sk_S^{sig}, m_i)$. $\mathcal{A}$ gives $\mathcal{A}'$ the same challenge $C = \texttt{Encrypt}(pk_R^{enc}, m_b\|s_b)$ it gets. Finally, $\mathcal{A}$ outputs the same guess b' that $\mathcal{A}'$ outputs. It is easy to see that $\mathcal{A}$ has the same probability of being correct as $\mathcal{A}'$ has. □

The following theorem states that when considering the signcryption security corresponding to the operation performed first, the strongest security properties (IND-CCA2 security for $\mathcal{E}t\mathcal{S}$ and sUF-CMA security for $\mathcal{S}t\mathcal{E}$) cannot be achieved in the insider security model.

Theorem 2.2 *Let $\mathcal{E}$ be any encryption scheme and $\mathcal{S}$ be a probabilistic signature scheme, then the signcryption scheme Π built using the $\mathcal{E}t\mathcal{S}$ method is not IND-CCA2 secure in the insider security model. Let $\mathcal{S}$ be any signature scheme and $\mathcal{E}$ be a probabilistic encryption scheme, then the signcryption scheme Π built using the $\mathcal{S}t\mathcal{E}$ method is not sUF-CMA secure in the insider security model.*

Proof (1) $\mathcal{E}t\mathcal{S}$ is *not* IND-CCA2 secure in insider security model

We show that the $\mathcal{E}t\mathcal{S}$ method cannot achieve IND-CCA2 security in the insider security model by constructing a distinguisher $\mathcal{A}$ against the IND-CCA2 security of Π built using the $\mathcal{E}t\mathcal{S}$ method. Let $\mathcal{S}$ and $\mathcal{E}$ be the base signature and encryption schemes whose key pairs are (sk_S^{sig}, pk_S^{sig}) and (sk_R^{enc}, pk_R^{enc}), respectively. Let $pk^{enc} = (sk_S^{sig}, pk_S^{sig}, pk_R^{enc})$ be the induced encryption key and let $sk^{enc} = (sk_R^{enc}, pk_S^{sig}, pk_R^{enc})$ be the induced decryption key. Given the induced decryption oracle $\texttt{Decrypt}$ and the induced encryption key pk^{enc}, $\mathcal{A}$ picks two messages (m_0, m_1), where $m_0 = 0$ and $m_1 = 1$, and then outputs them to get the challenge ciphertext $C = (c, \sigma)$. Next, $\mathcal{A}$ gets the message part c and re-signs c by computing a "new" signature $\sigma' \overset{R}{\leftarrow} \texttt{Sign}(sk_S^{sig}, c)$ of c, where $\sigma' \neq \sigma$, and then queries the induced decryption oracle with $C' = (c, \sigma')$. Notice that since we assumed $\mathcal{S}$ is probabilistic (not deterministic), with a non-negligible probability one can find a different signature for the same message in polynomial time. Since $C' \neq C$, and σ' is a valid signature of c, $\mathcal{A}$ can obtain the decryption of c. Once the decrypted message m is obtained, $\mathcal{A}$ compares it with its own message pair (m_0, m_1) and outputs the bit b where $m_b = m$.

(2) $\mathcal{S}t\mathcal{E}$ is *not* sUF-CMA secure in insider security model

We show that the $\mathcal{S}t\mathcal{E}$ method cannot achieve sUF-CMA security in the insider security model by constructing a forger $\mathcal{A}$ against the sUF-CMA security of a scheme Π built using the $\mathcal{S}t\mathcal{E}$ method. Let $\mathcal{S}$ and $\mathcal{E}$ be the base signature and encryption schemes whose key pairs are (sk_S^{sig}, pk_S^{sig}) and (sk_R^{enc}, pk_R^{enc}), respectively. Let $sk^{sig} = (sk_S^{sig}, pk_S^{sig}, pk_R^{enc})$ be the induced signature key and let $pk^{sig} = (sk_R^{enc}, pk_S^{sig}, pk_R^{enc})$ be the induced verification key. Given the induced signing oracle $\texttt{Sign}$ and the induced verification key pk^{sig}, the forger $\mathcal{A}$ picks a message m and queries $\texttt{Sign}$ with m to get the answer C. $\mathcal{A}$ then decrypts C using the decryption key sk_R^{enc} to get $m\|s = \texttt{Decrypt}(sk_R^{enc}, C)$, re-encrypt $m\|s$ to get

$C' = \text{Encrypt}(pk_R^{enc}, m\|s)$, where $C' \neq C$, and returns C' as a forgery. Notice that since $\mathcal{E}$ is a probabilistic encryption scheme (as opposed to deterministic), with a non-negligible probability, $\mathcal{A}$ can get C' in polynomial time such that $C' \neq C$ when re-encrypting $m\|s$. Since C' was never returned by the signing oracle Sign (i.e., $C' \neq C$) and s is a valid signature of m, C' is considered as a valid forgery against sUF-CMA of Π. □

Notice the negative results in Theorem 2.2 hold regardless of the strength of the security of the base encryption and signature schemes. Intuitively, this means that the security of the first operation is not protected by the last operation because both the security goals to achieve (i.e., IND-CCA2 and sUF-CMA) and the capabilities given to the adversary (i.e., having the secret key of one of the parties in the insider security model) are very strong. Notice that if we weaken the security goals (e.g., IND-gCCA2 security [10] and UF-CMA security), then the security may be preserved, as shown in [10]. Notice also that if we weaken the capabilities given to the adversary (e.g., if it is not given the secret keys as in the outsider security model), then the security may even be amplified, as shown in the next two theorems.

Unlike the insider security model, we show that in the weaker outsider security model, it is possible to amplify the security of encryption using signatures as well as the security of signatures using encryption, exactly like in the symmetric setting [9, 26, 117]. In particular, we can obtain a IND-CCA2 secure signcryption scheme via the $\mathcal{E}t\mathcal{S}$ method from a IND-CPA secure base encryption scheme with the aid of a "strong" base signature scheme. Similarly, we can obtain the sUF-CMA security via the $\mathcal{S}t\mathcal{E}$ method from a UF-NMA secure base signature scheme with the aid of a "strong" base encryption scheme. This shows that the outsider security model in the two-user setting is quite similar to the symmetric setting: namely, from the adversarial point of view the sender and the receiver "share" the secret key (sk_S, sk_R). We state this in the next two theorems. Specifically, the first theorem states that the $\mathcal{E}t\mathcal{S}$ method amplifies privacy and the second theorem states that the $\mathcal{S}t\mathcal{E}$ method amplifies authenticity.

Theorem 2.3 *If $\mathcal{E}$ is IND-CPA secure and $\mathcal{S}$ is sUF-CMA secure, then the signcryption scheme Π built using $\mathcal{E}t\mathcal{S}$ is IND-CCA2 secure in the outsider security model.*

Proof Let $\mathcal{A}'$ be the adversary breaking IND-CCA2 security of the Encrypt-then-Sign signcryption scheme $\mathcal{E}t\mathcal{S}$ in the outsider security model. Recall, $\mathcal{A}'$ only knows (pk_S^{sig}, pk_R^{enc}) and has access to the signcryption and the unsigncryption oracles Signcrypt and Unsigncrypt. By assumption, $|\Pr[b' = b] - 1/2|$ is negligible, where the probability is taken over all the randomness needed to perform the run of $\mathcal{A}'$ (as described in Sect. 2.2), b is the real index of the message being signcrypted, and b' is the guess of $\mathcal{A}'$.

We define the event FORGED to be the event where the adversary $\mathcal{A}'$ manages to generate a value $C' = (c', \sigma')$ on which it calls its unsigncryption oracle Unsigncrypt where C' satisfies the following properties:

1. C' passes the signature validation step, i.e., $\text{Verify}(pk_S^{sig}, c', \sigma') = \top$ and
2. C' was not given to $\mathcal{A}'$ by the signcryption oracle Signcrypt.

We split the executions of $\mathcal{A}'$ into two groups: (a) the runs in which $\mathcal{A}'$ has an event FORGED and (b) runs when no such event happens. The distinction between these two cases is that in (a) the adversary uses the unsigncryption oracle in a meaningful way. In case (b) the unsigncryption oracle can be completely simulated, i.e., either the unsigncryption oracle responds with failure or it is a query which has been asked to the signcryption oracle previously. Formally, we can show the following via an application of Bayes theorem:

$$
\begin{aligned}
&|\Pr[b' = b] - 1/2| \\
&\quad = |\Pr[\mathcal{A}'\ \text{WINS}] - 1/2| \\
&\quad = |\Pr[\mathcal{A}'\ \text{WINS} \mid \neg\text{FORGED}]\Pr[\neg\text{FORGED}] \\
&\qquad + \Pr[\mathcal{A}'\ \text{WINS} \mid \text{FORGED}]\Pr[\text{FORGED}] - 1/2| \\
&\quad = |\Pr[\mathcal{A}'\ \text{WINS} \mid \neg\text{FORGED}](1 - \Pr[\text{FORGED}]) \\
&\qquad + \Pr[\mathcal{A}'\ \text{WINS} \mid \text{FORGED}]\Pr[\text{FORGED}] - 1/2| \\
&\quad = |\Pr[\mathcal{A}'\ \text{WINS} \mid \neg\text{FORGED}] - 1/2 \\
&\qquad - (\Pr[\mathcal{A}'\ \text{WINS} \mid \neg\text{FORGED}] - \Pr[\mathcal{A}'\ \text{WINS} \mid \text{FORGED}])\Pr[\text{FORGED}]| \\
&\quad \leq |\Pr[\mathcal{A}'\ \text{WINS} \mid \neg\text{FORGED}] - 1/2| \\
&\qquad + |\Pr[\mathcal{A}'\ \text{WINS} \mid \neg\text{FORGED}] - \Pr[\mathcal{A}'\ \text{WINS} \mid \text{FORGED}]|\Pr[\text{FORGED}] \\
&\quad \leq |\Pr[\mathcal{A}'\ \text{WINS} \mid \neg\text{FORGED}] - 1/2| + \Pr[\text{FORGED}]
\end{aligned}
$$

Hence, it is sufficient to bound $|\Pr[\mathcal{A}'\ \text{WINS} \mid \neg\text{FORGED}] - 1/2|$ and $\Pr[\text{FORGED}]$ by negligible functions to show our results. We will show these results in two cases.

Case 1: $\Pr[\text{FORGED}]$ is negligible

We show that we can construct a forger $\mathcal{A}$ which breaks sUF-CMA security of signature scheme $\mathcal{S}$ with probability at least $\Pr[\text{FORGED}]$. The assumption that the signature scheme is sUF-CMA secure shows that $\Pr[\text{FORGED}]$ is negligible. Given the signing oracle Sign and the public verification key pk_S^{sig}, the forger $\mathcal{A}$ picks a pair of encryption keys $(sk_R^{enc}, pk_R^{enc}) \xleftarrow{R}$ EncKeyGen(1^k). $\mathcal{A}$ then picks a random bit b for the index of the message being signcrypted and hands (pk_S^{sig}, pk_R^{enc}) to $\mathcal{A}'$ as the public key of the signcryption scheme. For each signcryption query m of $\mathcal{A}'$, $\mathcal{A}$ simulates the signcryption oracle Signcrypt by first encrypting m using the generated encryption key pk_R^{enc} to get $c' \xleftarrow{R}$ Encrypt(pk_R^{enc}, m) and asking its own signing oracle Sign to sign c' to obtain σ'. For each unsigncryption query $C' = (c', \sigma')$, $\mathcal{A}$ simulates the unsigncryption oracle by first checking Verify(pk_S^{sig}, c', σ') $= \top$ and then decrypting c' using the decryption key sk_R^{enc}. If C' is a valid signcryption ciphertext, but C' was not returned by the signcryption oracle, then FORGED has occurred and $\mathcal{A}$ (correctly) outputs (c', σ') as an sUF-CMA forgery. If $\mathcal{A}'_1$ outputs (m_0, m_1) to be signcrypted in the first stage, then $\mathcal{A}$ computes the challenge ciphertext C^* of the message m_b using the signcryption method above. If $\mathcal{A}'$ terminates without the event FORGED occurring, then $\mathcal{A}$ terminates without output. Hence, $\mathcal{A}$ wins the sUF-CMA game if and only if FORGED occurs and so $\Pr[\text{FORGED}]$ is bounded by the success probability of $\mathcal{A}$ in winning the sUF-CMA security game against the signature scheme $\mathcal{S}$.

Case 2: $|\Pr[\mathcal{A}' \text{ WINS} \mid \neg\text{FORGED}] - 1/2|$ is negligible

First, we note that since FORGED does not occur, we have that any query $C' = (c', \sigma')$ to the unsigncryption oracle must have one of the following two forms: (a) $\text{Verify}_S(c') = \bot$ or (b) C' was already returned by Signcrypt on some query m'. For a type (a) query, the oracle's correct response is $\bot$. For a type (b) query, the oracle's correct response is m'. In both cases, $\mathcal{A}$ will "know" the correct response returned by the unsigncryption oracle. Overall, the unsigncryption oracle is useless: $\mathcal{A}'$ can compute all the answers by itself; hence, CPA security suffices for the encryption scheme.

Formally, we show that we can construct an adversary $\mathcal{A}$ which would break the IND-CPA security of $\mathcal{E}$. Given the public encryption key pk_R^{enc}, $\mathcal{A}$ picks a signature key pair (sk_S^{sig}, pk_S^{sig}) and gives (pk_S^{sig}, pk_R^{enc}) to $\mathcal{A}'$ as the public keys of the signcryption scheme. For each signcryption oracle query m, $\mathcal{A}$ simulates the signcryption oracle by first encrypting m using the given encryption key pk_R^{enc} to get $c' \xleftarrow{R} \text{Encrypt}(pk_R^{enc}, m)$ and then signing c' using the picked signing key sk_S^{sig} to get $\sigma' \xleftarrow{R} \text{Sign}(sk_S^{sig}, c')$. $\mathcal{A}$ keeps track of all the tuples (m, c', σ') that were simulated by the signcryption oracle in a table. For each unsigncryption query $C' = (c', \sigma')$, $\mathcal{A}$ returns $\bot$ to $\mathcal{A}'$ if C' is a type (a) query or it returns the corresponding m by using the table kept in the signcryption oracle simulation if C' is a type (b) query. If $\mathcal{A}'$ outputs (m_0, m_1), then $\mathcal{A}$ outputs (m_0, m_1) and gets the challenge ciphertext c. $\mathcal{A}$ then signs c to get $\sigma \xleftarrow{R} \text{Sign}(sk_S^{sig}, c)$ and gives $C = (c, \sigma)$ to $\mathcal{A}'$ as the challenge ciphertext. When $\mathcal{A}'$ outputs a guess bit b', $\mathcal{A}$ outputs the same bit. It is clear that if FORGED does not happen, $\mathcal{A}$ simulates the correct environment for $\mathcal{A}'$. Hence $\mathcal{A}$ succeeds in the IND-CPA game against the public-key encryption scheme with overall advantage equal to that of $\mathcal{A}'$ in the IND-CCA2 game against the signcryption scheme. □

Theorem 2.4 *If $\mathcal{E}$ is IND-CCA2 secure and $\mathcal{S}$ is UF-NMA secure, then the signcryption scheme Π built using the $\mathcal{S}t\mathcal{E}$ method is sUF-CMA secure in the outsider security model.*

Proof Let $\mathcal{A}'$ be an adversary attacking sUF-CMA security of the signcryption scheme built using the $\mathcal{S}t\mathcal{E}$ method in the outsider security model. Recall, $\mathcal{A}'$ only knows (pk_S^{sig}, pk_R^{enc}), but has access to signcryption and the unsigncryption oracles Signcrypt and Unsigncrypt. Let $m_1, \ldots, m_t$ be the queries $\mathcal{A}'$ asks the signcryption oracle and $C_1, \ldots, C_t$ be the corresponding answers. Without loss of generality, we assume that $\mathcal{A}'$ never asks its unsigncryption oracle any query C' which is the same as any one of C_i's returned by the signcryption oracle. Indeed, there is no need for $\mathcal{A}$ to ask such a query since it already knows the answer m_i.

Now, we use the standard hybrid argument. Let Env_0 denote the usual environment for $\mathcal{A}'$, which honestly answers all the signcryption and unsigncryption queries of $\mathcal{A}'$. Specifically, the signcryption query m_i is answered by computing $\sigma_i \xleftarrow{R} \text{Sign}(sk_S^{sig}, m_i)$ and returning $C_i \xleftarrow{R} \text{Encrypt}(pk_R^{enc}, m_i \| \sigma_i)$. Let $Succ_0(\mathcal{A}')$ be the success probability (i.e., that of breaking sUF-CMA security of the signcryption) of $\mathcal{A}'$ in Env_0. Next, we define the following "hybrid" environments Env_j, $1 \leq j \leq t$. Each Env_j is identical to Env_0 above, except for one aspect: for the first j queries m_i ($1 \leq i \leq j$) to the signcryption oracle, instead of returning $C_i \overset{R}{\leftarrow} \texttt{Encrypt}(pk_R^{enc}, m_i \| \sigma_i)$, Env_i returns a random encryption of 0: $C_i \overset{R}{\leftarrow} \texttt{Encrypt}(pk_R^{enc}, 0)$. We let $Succ_j(\mathcal{A}')$ be the success probability of $\mathcal{A}'$ in Env_j. Notice, Env_t answers all t queries "incorrectly" (i.e., all signcryption oracle queries are answered with random encryptions of 0).

We make two claims: (1) assuming IND-CCA2 security of $\mathcal{E}$, no PPT adversary $\mathcal{A}'$ can distinguish Env_{j-1} from Env_j with non-negligible probability, for any $1 \leq j \leq t$, i.e., $|Succ_{j-1}(\mathcal{A}') - Succ_j(\mathcal{A}')| \leq negl(k)$, and (2) assuming UF-NMA security of $\mathcal{S}$, $Succ_t(\mathcal{A}') \leq negl(k)$, for any PPT $\mathcal{A}'$. Combined, claims (1) and (2) imply our theorem, since t is polynomial and we have

$$
\begin{aligned}
Succ_0(\mathcal{A}') &\leq (Succ_0(\mathcal{A}') - Succ_1(\mathcal{A}')) + \cdots \\
&\quad \cdots + (Succ_{t-1}(\mathcal{A}') - Succ_t(\mathcal{A}')) + Succ_t(\mathcal{A}') \\
&\leq (t+1) \cdot negl(k) \\
&= negl(k)
\end{aligned}
$$

Proof of Claim (1)

If for some $\mathcal{A}'$, $|Succ_{j-1}(\mathcal{A}') - Succ_j(\mathcal{A}')| > \varepsilon$ for non-negligible ε, then we construct an adversary $\mathcal{A}$ that will break the IND-CCA2 security of $\mathcal{E}$ with probability ε as follows. Let (sk_R^{enc}, pk_R^{enc}) be the key pair for the encryption scheme $\mathcal{E}$. Given the public encryption key pk_R^{enc} and access to the decryption oracle $\texttt{Decrypt}$, $\mathcal{A}$ picks a pair of signing keys $(sk_S^{sig}, pk_S^{sig}) \overset{R}{\leftarrow} \texttt{SigKeyGen}(1^k)$ and gives (pk_S^{sig}, pk_R^{enc}) to $\mathcal{A}'$. $\mathcal{A}$ simulates all the unsigncryption queries C' of $\mathcal{A}'$ by using its own decryption oracle on C' to obtain (m, σ), then verifying the signature σ it gets back, before returning the message m to $\mathcal{A}'$. Simulation of the signcryption oracle is more intricate. $\mathcal{A}$ simulates the answers to the first $(j-1)$ signcryption oracle queries m_i "incorrectly," by returning $C_i \leftarrow \texttt{Encrypt}(pk_R^{enc}, 0)$ to $\mathcal{A}'$ (i.e., returning an encryption of 0). At the jth query m_j of $\mathcal{A}'$, $\mathcal{A}$ computes $\sigma_j \overset{R}{\leftarrow} \texttt{Sign}(sk_S^{sig}, m_j)$ and outputs $(0, m_j \| \sigma_j)$ to get the challenge ciphertext C_j (which is an encryption of either 0 or $m_j \| \sigma_j$). $\mathcal{A}$ then gives C_j to $\mathcal{A}'$ as a signcryption of m_j. From that point on, all the remaining signcryption queries m_i ($j < i \leq t$) are answered "correctly" (i.e., by computing $C_i \overset{R}{\leftarrow} \texttt{Encrypt}(pk_R^{enc}, m_i \| \sigma_i)$ where $\sigma_i \overset{R}{\leftarrow} \texttt{Sign}(sk_S^{sig}, m_i)$).

After $\mathcal{A}'$ returns a candidate forgery C, $\mathcal{A}$ checks if C is indeed a valid forgery by (1) checking that C is "new" (i.e., C was never returned to $\mathcal{A}'$ by $\mathcal{A}$ as an answer to a signcryption query in the signcryption oracle simulation) and (2) C is "valid" ($\mathcal{A}$ can check this by using its decryption oracle on C to get the presumed message/signature pair $m \| \sigma$ and verifying that σ is a valid signature of m). If so, $\mathcal{A}$ guesses that the challenge ciphertext C_j was the encryption of $m_j \| \sigma_j$ (i.e., $\mathcal{A}'$ was run in Env_{j-1}), else it guesses that the challenge ciphertext C_j was an encryption of 0. By a method similar to Lemma 1.1, we can show that $\mathcal{A}$'s advantage is $\varepsilon/2$, which is negligible as the encryption scheme is IND-CCA2 secure. However, to complete the proof of claim (1), we also need to check that $\mathcal{A}$ never asked its decryption oracle the challenge ciphertext C_j. We assumed that $\mathcal{A}'$ never asks its unsigncryption oracle any query C_i which was returned by the signcryption oracle. Since $\mathcal{A}$ only uses the decryption oracles to answer unsigncryption queries of $\mathcal{A}'$ and to decrypt C, this is indeed so.

Proof of Claim (2)

We note that in Env_t (where the signcryption answers are simulated by encrypting 0) the queries to the signcryption oracle are "useless": $\mathcal{A}'$ could have gotten the answers by itself by computing $\texttt{Encrypt}(pk_R^{enc}, 0)$. More formally, assuming $\mathcal{A}'$ forges a new signcryption with probability ε in Env_t, we can build a forger $\mathcal{A}$ for the signature scheme $\mathcal{S}$ that will contradict the UF-NMA security of $\mathcal{S}$. Let (sk_S^{sig}, pk_S^{sig}) be the keys of the signature scheme $\mathcal{S}$. Given the public verification key pk_S^{sig}, $\mathcal{A}$ picks a pair of encryption keys $(sk_R^{enc}, pk_R^{enc}) \xleftarrow{R} \texttt{EncKeyGen}(1^k)$ and gives (pk_S^{sig}, pk_R^{enc}) to $\mathcal{A}'$ as the public key of the signcryption scheme. From there on, $\mathcal{A}$ simulates the unsigncryption queries C' by computing $m' \| \sigma' = \texttt{Decrypt}(sk_R^{enc}, C')$ and returning m' if $\texttt{Verify}(pk_R^{sig}, m', \sigma') = \top$. It also simulates the signcryption queries by returning $\texttt{Encrypt}(pk_R^{enc}, 0)$. When $\mathcal{A}'$ returns a forged ciphertext C, $\mathcal{A}$ outputs the forged message/signature pair (m, σ) where $m \| \sigma = \texttt{Decrypt}(sk_R^{enc}, C)$. It is easy to see that $\mathcal{A}$ exactly recreates Env_t and forges a signature only if $\mathcal{A}'$ forges a signcryption. Hence $Succ_t$ is negligible. $\square$

2.4 Multi-user Setting

As we have mentioned, the two-user setting provides us with insight into some interesting aspects of signcryption, but one really needs multi-user security for most applications of signcryption. Formal definitions for the security of signcryption in a multi-user setting will be discussed in depth in Chap. 3. In this section, we will provide a brief introduction to multi-user security and the relationship between multi-user security and the generic signcryption constructions.

2.4.1 Syntax

So far we have concentrated on a network of two users: the sender S and the receiver R. Once we move to the full-fledged multi-user network, several new concerns arise. First, users must have identities. We denote by ID_U the identity of user U. We do not impose any constraints on the identities, other than they should be easily recognizable by everyone in the network and that users can easily obtain the public key pk_U from ID_U (e.g., ID_U could be pk_U or ID_U might enable another user to obtain pk_U from a public-key infrastructure). Next, we change the syntax of the signcryption algorithm $\texttt{Signcrypt}$ to both take and output the identity of the sender and the receiver. Specifically, (1) the signcryption algorithm for user S, on input

$(m, ID_{R'})$, uses $pk_{R'}$ to generate $(C, ID_S, ID_{R'})$ and (2) the unsigncryption algorithm for user R, on input $(C, ID_{S'}, ID_R)$, uses $pk_{S'}$ and outputs a message m' or the "failure" symbol $\perp$.

2.4.2 Security

To break the outsider security between a pair of designated users S and R, $\mathcal{A}$ is assumed to have all the secret keys besides sk_S and sk_R and has access to the signcryption oracle of S (which it can call with *any* $ID_{R'}$ and not just ID_R) and the unsigncryption oracle for R (which it can call with *any* $ID_{S'}$ and not just ID_S).

To break the sUF-CMA security of the signcryption scheme, the attacker $\mathcal{A}$ has to come up with a "valid" signcryption (C, ID_S, ID_R) of a message m where $\mathcal{A}$ did not receive (C, ID_S, ID_R) as the result of a signcryption oracle query. It is important to note that we do allow the attacker to attempt to generate a forgery by querying the signcryption oracle on $(m, ID_{R'})$ for $ID_R \neq ID_{R'}$ to receive $(C, ID_S, ID_{R'})$ and outputting (C, ID_S, ID_R). This is equivalent to saying that the attacker should not be able to "translate" a signcryption ciphertext intended for R' into a ciphertext intended for R.

Similarly, to break IND-CCA2 security of the signcryption scheme, the attacker $\mathcal{A}$ has to generate messages m_0 and m_1 for which it can distinguish the ciphertext $\mathtt{Signcrypt}(m_0, ID_S, ID_R)$ from the ciphertext $\mathtt{Signcrypt}(m_1, ID_S, ID_R)$. Of course, given a challenge (C, ID_S, ID_R), $\mathcal{A}$ is disallowed to query the unsigncryption oracle for R on the challenge (C, ID_S, ID_R), although queries of the form $(C, ID_{S'}, ID_R)$, where $ID_{S'} \neq ID_S$, are allowed.

We define insider security in an analogous manner. The only difference is that in addition to all the information given to the adversary in the outsider security model, the adversary is given the receiver's secret key, sk_R, when attacking authenticity (i.e., sk_S is the only secret that is not given to the adversary in this case) and the sender's secret key, sk_S, when attacking privacy (i.e., sk_R is the only secret that is not given to the adversary in this case).

2.4.3 Extending Signcryption

We can see that the signcryption algorithms that are built by generic composition of encryption and signature schemes (i.e., $\mathcal{E}t\mathcal{S}$ and $\mathcal{S}t\mathcal{E}$) are not secure in the multi-user setting. If the $\mathcal{E}t\mathcal{S}$ method is used in the multi-user setting, then the adversary $\mathcal{A}$ can easily break the CCA2 security, even in the outsider model. Indeed, given the challenge $C = (c, \sigma, ID_S, ID_R)$, where $c \xleftarrow{R} \mathtt{Encrypt}(pk_R, m_b)$ and $\sigma \xleftarrow{R} \mathtt{Sign}(sk_S, c)$, $\mathcal{A}$ can replace the sender's signature with its own by computing $C' = (c, \sigma', ID_{S'}, ID_R)$, where $\sigma' \xleftarrow{R} \mathtt{Sign}(sk_{S'}, c)$. If $\mathcal{A}$ queries the unsigncryption oracle on C' then the oracle will respond with m_b and $\mathcal{A}$ can trivially break the IND-CCA2 security of the scheme. A similar attack on authenticity holds for the $\mathcal{S}t\mathcal{E}$ scheme. In the $\mathcal{S}t\mathcal{E}$ scheme, the adversary $\mathcal{A}$ can easily break the sUF-CMA security in the outsider model. It can ask S to signcrypt a message m for R' and get $C = (\texttt{Encrypt}(pk_{R'}, m\|\sigma), ID_S, ID_{R'})$, where $\sigma \overset{R}{\leftarrow} \texttt{Sign}(pk_S, m)$. Then, it can recover $m\|\sigma$ using $sk_{R'}$ and forge the signcryption ciphertext $C' = (\texttt{Encrypt}(pk_R, m\|\sigma), ID_S, ID_R)$.

The generic composition methods suffer from the above types of attacks in the multi-user setting, because the signature and encryption used in the signcryption can easily be separated and are not "bound together" with the proper identities of the sender and receiver (unlike the two-user setting or the symmetric setting). The adversary can easily replace the signature or encryption with its own signature or encryption. We show how to fix this problem by "binding together" the signature and encryption used in the signcryption with the proper identities of the sender and receiver. The following rules can effectively bind the encryption and signature with proper identities of the sender and receiver and hence can be used to make the signcryption schemes built by generic composition secure in the multi-user setting (i.e. withstand above types of attacks).

1. Whenever *encrypting* something, include the identity of the *sender ID_S* together with the encrypted message.
2. Whenever *signing* something, include the identity of the *receiver ID_R* together with the signed message.
3. On the receiving side, whenever the identity of either the sender or the receiver does not match what is expected, output $\perp$.

Hence, we get the following new analogs for the $\mathcal{E}t\mathcal{S}$ and $\mathcal{S}t\mathcal{E}$ schemes:

- The $\mathcal{E}t\mathcal{S}$ signcryption scheme returns the signcryption ciphertext (c, σ, ID_S, ID_R) where $c \overset{R}{\leftarrow} \texttt{Encrypt}(pk_R, m\|ID_S)$ and $\sigma \overset{R}{\leftarrow} \texttt{Sign}(sk_S, c\|ID_R)$.
- The $\mathcal{S}t\mathcal{E}$ signcryption scheme returns the signcryption ciphertext (c, ID_S, ID_R) where $c \overset{R}{\leftarrow} \texttt{Encrypt}(pk_R, m\|\sigma\|ID_S)$ and $\sigma \overset{R}{\leftarrow} \texttt{Sign}(sk_S, m\|ID_R)$.

For both schemes, the unsigncryption algorithms work in the obvious manner. Intuitively, it is easy to see that the above rules "bind" the encryption and signature used in the signcryption with proper identities of the sender and receiver, because it includes the intended sender and receiver identities in the ciphertext.

However, it is important to ensure that the identities cannot be tampered within the ciphertext itself. If the encryption scheme used in the signcryption is malleable (i.e., underlying plaintext can be modified without being detected), the adversary may be able to modify the identities in the ciphertext which makes having the identities moot. For example, in the $\mathcal{E}t\mathcal{S}$ method, if the underlying encryption scheme is only IND-CPA secure, the adversary may be able to modify the ciphertext to replace the sender's identity with its own and strip off the sender's signature and replace it with its own signature and identity. Hence, it is important to assume that the underlying encryption scheme is non-malleable (or CCA2 secure) for the signcryption scheme built by the $\mathcal{E}t\mathcal{S}$ method to be secure even in the outsider model. This is different from the result in the two-user setting, where the encryption scheme can be just IND-CPA secure for the signcryption built from the $\mathcal{E}t\mathcal{S}$ method to be (IND-CCA2 and sUF-CMA) secure in the outsider model. This tells us that the security proven in the two-user setting does *not* automatically translate into security in the multi-user setting even if we follow above rules to "bind" the signature and encryption with identities. In general, when analyzing the security of the signcryption scheme built from the generic composition methods following the above rules in the multi-user setting, the assumptions for the underlying encryption and signature schemes should be "strong enough" (i.e., IND-CCA2 or sUF-CMA secure) so that the identities bound to the signature and encryption cannot be altered.

Chapter 3
Security for Signcryption: The Multi-User Model

Joonsang Baek and Ron Steinfeld

3.1 Introduction

This chapter presents security models for confidentiality and unforgeability of signcryption schemes in the multi-user setting. A family of security models for signcryption in both two-user and multi-user settings was presented by An et al. [10] in their work on signcryption schemes built from black-box signature and encryption schemes—see Chap. 2. (The first well-defined security model for unforgeability of signcryption schemes in the two-user setting was given earlier by Steinfeld and Zheng [184].) These models are referred to as the "ADR model" in this chapter. Multi-user models for confidentiality and unforgeability also appeared independently in the work of Baek et al. [12, 13] on the security of Zheng's original signcryption scheme. These multi-user models are referred to as the "BSZ model" throughout the rest of this chapter. The BSZ models are equivalent to certain multi-user ADR models. For consistency with Chap. 2, we use in this chapter the terminology introduced by ADR to classify multi-user attack models as insider or outsider models.

A central difference between the multi-user BSZ model and the two-user ADR models is the extra power of the adversary. In the BSZ model, the attacker may choose receiver (resp. sender) public keys when accessing the attacked users' signcryption (resp. unsigncryption) oracles. In signcryption schemes built from separate signature and encryption primitives, this extra power can be easily dealt with by a "semi-generic" conversion which converts any scheme secure in the two-user model to one secure in the multi-user model, as described in Sect. 2.4. But for signcryption schemes that share some functionality between the signature and the encryption components, such as is the case for Zheng's signcryption scheme, described in Sect. 3.3 and in further detail in Sect. 4.3, the extra power of the adversary in the multi-user model may be much more significant, and a careful case-by-case analysis is required to establish security of such schemes in the multi-user model.

J. Baek (✉)
Cryptography and Security Department, Institute for Info Comm Research (I2R), Singapore, Singapore
e-mail: jsbaek@i2r.a-star.edu.sg

A.W. Dent, Y. Zheng (eds.), *Practical Signcryption*, Information Security and Cryptography, DOI 10.1007/978-3-540-89411-7_3,

This chapter is organized as follows. Section 3.2 contains definitions for and discussions about the BSZ model for both confidentiality and unforgeability of signcryption in the multi-user setting. We also discuss the extra power available to the adversary in the multi-user BSZ model vs. the two-user ADR model. Finally, in Sect. 3.3, we review Zheng's signcryption scheme and its security as an application of the multi-user BSZ model. This analysis is done to demonstrate the difference between the ADR security model and the BSZ security model. Further analysis of this signcryption scheme and its variants is given in Sect. 4.3.

3.2 The BSZ Model

In this section, we review the definitions of confidentiality and unforgeability of signcryption in the BSZ model in great detail. Throughout this chapter, we will use the same notational syntax for generic signcryption schemes as is defined in Sect. 2.2.1.

3.2.1 Confidentiality of Signcryption in the Multi-User BSZ Model

As in the two-user setting covered in Chap. 2, the multi-user setting also has two types of models depending on the identity of the attacker: an *insider* model and an *outsider* model. We discuss the two models in turn.

Outsider Security

The outsider model assumes an attack by an entity who does not know either of the attacked users' secret keys (i.e., the attacker does not know the sender or receiver's secret keys). In the BSZ model, this confidentiality notion of signcryption is specially termed "indistinguishability of signcryptext against chosen ciphertext attack with access to 'flexible' signcryption/unsigncryption oracles (FSO/FUO-IND-CCA2)." The indistinguishability of signcryptext (abbreviated by "IND") here means that there is no polynomial-time adversary that can learn any information about the plaintext from the signcryptext except for its length. In contrast to the standard chosen ciphertext attack for encryption schemes [148, 164], in the chosen ciphertext attack for signcryption, it is assumed that an adversary has access to two oracles that perform signcryption and unsigncryption. Importantly, in the signcryption case, these oracles are *flexible* in the sense that the adversary can freely choose the public keys with which those oracles perform signcryption and unsigncryption. (Note that this feature is unique in the BSZ model.) In the following, we review the formal definition of the multi-user outsider confidentiality in the FSO/FUO-IND-CCA2 sense.

Definition 3.1 Let $\mathcal{A} = (\mathcal{A}_1, \mathcal{A}_2)$ be a two-stage adversary trying to break the confidentiality of messages between the (fixed) sender S and the (fixed) receiver R. Consider the following attack game:

1. The Setup algorithm is run and the resulting common parameters, denoted by *param*, is sent to any interested parties including S, R, and $\mathcal{A}_1$.
2. The KeyGen$_S$ and KeyGen$_R$ algorithms are run to generate S and R's public/private key pairs, denoted by (sk_S, pk_S) and (sk_R, pk_R), respectively. The public keys (pk_S, pk_R) are given to $\mathcal{A}_1$.
3. $\mathcal{A}_1$ submits a series of signcryption and unsigncryption queries. Each signcryption query consists of a pair (pk, m) where pk is a receiver's public key generated by $\mathcal{A}_1$ at will and m is a message. On receiving this, the signcryption oracle computes a signcryptext $C \overset{R}{\leftarrow}$ Signcrypt$(param, sk_S, pk, m)$ and returns it to $\mathcal{A}_1$. Each unsigncryption query consists of a pair (pk', C) where pk' denotes a sender's public key generated by $\mathcal{A}_1$ at will and C is a signcryptext. On receiving this, the unsigncryption oracle performs unsigncryption by computing Unsigncrypt$(param, pk', sk_R, C)$ and returns the result to $\mathcal{A}_1$.
4. $\mathcal{A}_1$ outputs a pair of equal-length plaintexts (m_0, m_1) and a state string α. On receiving this, the signcryption oracle picks $b \overset{R}{\leftarrow} \{0, 1\}$ at random, computes a target signcryptext $C^* \overset{R}{\leftarrow}$ Signcrypt$(param, sk_S, pk_R, m_b)$, and runs $\mathcal{A}_2$ on input (C^*, α).
5. $\mathcal{A}_2$ submits a number of signcryption/unsigncryption queries as $\mathcal{A}_1$ did in Step 3. A restriction here is that $\mathcal{A}_2$ is not allowed to query (pk_S, C^*) to the unsigncryption oracle. (Note, however, that $\mathcal{A}_2$ can query the unsigncryption oracle on (pk', C^*) for any $pk' \neq pk_S$ and on (pk_S, C) for any $C \neq C^*$.)
6. $\mathcal{A}_2$ outputs its guess $b' \in \{0, 1\}$ for the value of b chosen in Step 4.

$\mathcal{A}$ is said to win the game if $b' = b$. $\mathcal{A}$'s advantage is defined to be

$$\varepsilon = |Pr[b = b'] - 1/2|$$

We say that the signcryption scheme achieves *multi-user outsider confidentiality in the FSO/FUO-IND-CCA2 sense* if any polynomial-time adversary $\mathcal{A}$ wins the above game with negligible advantage.

We emphasize again that in the above definition, the signcryption and unsigncryption oracles are not constrained to be executed only under pk_R and pk_S, respectively—the receiver R and the sender S's public keys can be replaced by the public keys generated by the adversary. Accordingly, access to these oracles gives the adversary the full chosen-plaintext/ciphertext power with the ability to choose the sender and receiver's public keys, as well as the message and signcryptext.

Insider Security

Unlike the outsider setting where the attacker only knows the public keys of the attacked pair of users S and R, the insider model deals with the setting where an attacker, knowing the secret key of the sender S, tries to decrypt signcryptexts sent by that sender. Indeed, in order to give the attacker as much power as possible, we allow the attacker to choose the sender's key pair. The formal definition of this model is identical to the one given above for the outsider model, except for the following changes:

- In Step 2, the key generation algorithm is run just once, to generate the attacked receiver's key pair (sk_R, pk_R), and pk_R is given to $\mathcal{A}_1$.
- In Steps 3 and 5, $\mathcal{A}$ has access to R's unsigncryption oracle, but no signcryption oracle (as either S's keys are undefined or S's private key is known to the adversary).
- In Step 4, $\mathcal{A}_1$ outputs an attacked sender's key pair (sk_S, pk_S), in addition to (m_0, m_1, α). The key sk_S is used to produce the challenge signcryptext C^* as in the outsider model.

We call the corresponding security notion *multi-user insider confidentiality in the FSO/FUO-IND-CCA2 sense*.

Discussion

As also acknowledged in [10], the insider confidentiality model is under normal circumstances not of significant importance because it effectively assumes that the sender S is trying to decrypt (unsigncrypt) a signcryptext which was sent by herself. Thus, this model appears only useful in providing "forward secrecy," i.e., providing security under the special circumstances in which an adversary who breaks into S's system obtains her secret key in order to unsigncrypt a message previously signcrypted by S to R. As pointed out by Zheng in the full version of the original signcryption paper [204], this insecurity can be considered a positive feature, called "past message recovery", since it allows S to store signcryptexts and unsigncrypt them in the future when desired. In view of this discussion, we believe that for most applications it suffices for a signcryption scheme to achieve confidentiality in the "multi-user outsider" model. We should point out that a practical advantage of the outsider model is that it tends to be easier to achieve, and many natural and efficient schemes are secure in the outsider model but not secure in the insider model. (In particular, Zheng's original scheme [204] falls in this category.)

In Step 4, we have required that the attacker outputs both the public and the private key for the sender. It is possible to propose a stronger security model, similar to the secret key ignorant unforgeability notion described in Sect. 3.2.2, in which the attacker only outputs a sender public key pk_S in Step 4. The signcryption oracle then computes the associated private key sk_S and the signcryption of the message m_b as before. This means that the process of computing the challenge ciphertext is not necessarily polynomial time; however, this is not a problem, as there is no intrinsic requirement that a security model must be expressed as a polynomial-time process. (We only require that the signcryption scheme and the adversary are polynomial time.) The signcryption literature is currently confused as to which of these models best represents multi-user insider confidentiality, with some papers preferring the weaker notion of insider security and some papers preferring the stronger notion.

3.2.2 Unforgeability of Signcryption in the Multi-User BSZ Model

We now review the definition of unforgeability for signcryption in the multi-user model, again addressing the two settings of outsider and insider adversary in turn. We also discuss some further stronger unforgeability model variants ("strong" and "secret key ignorant" unforgeability).

Outsider Security

In this model, the adversary's goal is to forge a valid signcryptext from a given sender S to a given receiver R, where the adversary represents some third party. The adversary is given S and R's (random) public keys and has access to S's flexible signcryption oracle and R's flexible unsigncryption oracle, which will perform signcryption/unsigncryption for any message/ciphertexts and receiver/sender public keys chosen by the adversary at will. A more precise formal definition is presented in the following definition.

Definition 3.2 Let $\mathcal{A}$ be an adversary trying to forge a valid signcryptext from the sender S to the receiver R. Consider the following attack game:

1. The Setup algorithm is run and the resulting common parameters, denoted by *param*, is sent to any interested parties including S, R, and $\mathcal{A}$.
2. The KeyGen$_S$ and KeyGen$_R$ algorithms are run to generate S and R's public/private key pairs, denoted by (sk_S, pk_S) and (sk_R, pk_R), respectively. The public keys (pk_S, pk_R) are given to $\mathcal{A}$.
3. $\mathcal{A}$ submits a series of signcryption and unsigncryption queries. Each signcryption query consists of a pair (pk, m) where pk is a receiver's public key generated by $\mathcal{A}$ at will and m is a message. On receiving this, the signcryption oracle computes a signcryptext $C \xleftarrow{R} \text{Signcrypt}(param, sk_S, pk, m)$ and returns it to $\mathcal{A}$. Each unsigncryption query consists of a pair (pk', C) where pk' is a sender's public key generated by $\mathcal{A}$ at will and C is a signcryptext. On receiving this, the unsigncryption oracle computes the message $m \xleftarrow{R} \text{Unsigncrypt}(param, pk', sk_R, C)$ and returns it to $\mathcal{A}$.
4. $\mathcal{A}$ outputs a signcryptext C^*.

We say that $\mathcal{A}$ wins the game if the following requirements are satisfied: (1) C^* is a valid signcryptext from S to the receiver R (this means that the unsigncryption oracle which performs unsigncryption under the public key pk_S and the private key sk_R does not reject C^*) and (2) $\mathcal{A}$ did not query (pk_R, m^*) to the signcryption oracle, where m^* is the plaintext of the signcryptext C^* (i.e., the message m^* was never signcrypted to the receiver public key pk_R).

We say that the signcryption scheme achieves *multi-user outsider unforgeability in the FSO/FUO-UF-CMA sense* if any polynomial-time adversary $\mathcal{A}$ wins the above game with negligible probability.

Note that the above definition rules out both (i) a "conventional forgery," where the message m^* is "new", and (ii) a "receiver transfer forgery," where the forgery message m^* was previously queried to S's signcryption oracle but was never sign-crypted under the receiver key pk_R. We remark that the "receiver transfer forgery" was called a "double spending attack" in [204], due to its implication in e-commerce payment applications.

We should also emphasize that the above outsider model does not prevent forgery of valid signcryptexts by the receiver and hence the receiver cannot (unlike the situation with standard digital signatures) use a valid signcryptext to convince a third party that the message was sent by the sender. Consequently, the model does not allow for non-repudiation. Thus we view this model as useful only for assuring the receiver himself of the authenticity of the message.

Insider Security

The insider unforgeability model considers the setting in which the adversary is the receiver R. Accordingly, in this model, the adversary chooses the keys of R. The formal definition is identical to the outsider notion except for the following modifications:

- In Step 2, only the sender key generation algorithm is run, in order to generate the attacked sender's public/private key pair (sk_S, pk_S).
- In Step 3, $\mathcal{A}$ has access to S's signcryption oracle, but no unsigncryption oracle (note that R's keys are not yet defined).
- In Step 4, $\mathcal{A}$ outputs a receiver's public/private key pair (sk_R, pk_R) and a sign-cryptext C^*. The conditions of winning the game are as in the outsider model.

We call the corresponding security notion *multi-user insider unforgeability in the FSO/FUO-UF-CMA sense*.

Since this model rules out forgeries even by the receiver, a valid signcryptext may be used to convince a third party that the sender sent the message, thus also giving an opportunity for non-repudiation. However, there is no intrinsic algorithm which produces the evidence that demonstrates that a signcryptext is a signcryption of a particular message and from a particular sender, without revealing the receiver's private key. The concept of non-repudiation is discussed in more detail in Sects. 2.2.2, 4.6, and 5.6.

Strong Unforgeability

As in the two-user setting, the above models may be considered a "weak" form of unforgeability since they do not prevent the creation of new valid signcryptexts corresponding to an existing signcrypted message. In some applications, such as authenticated key exchange protocols, one may demand that such forgeries also be ruled out. The corresponding unforgeability notions are called *Strong Unforgeability* (sUF) and can be defined in either the outsider or the insider model. The change required to the above weak unforgeability formal definitions is to modify the second attacker winning condition as follows: (2) $\mathcal{A}$ did not receive C^* as a response to a query (pk_R, m^*) to the signcryption oracle, where pk_R is R's public key.

Note that $\mathcal{A}$ would still win the strong unforgeability game if he received C^* as response to a signcryption query (pk, m) with $pk \neq pk_R$ (a "receiver transfer" forgery). A scheme that is secure in the strong unforgeability model is said to be *multi-user insider unforgeable in the FSO/FUO-sUF-CMA sense*.

Secret Key Ignorant Unforgeability

Again, we note that in the insider security model the adversary is asked to output a valid receiver's key pair (sk_R, pk_R). We can weaken this security model to simply requiring the attacker to output a receiver public key pk_R. The winning conditions remain the same; however, it may require the computation of the receiver private key sk_R in order to verify that C^* is a valid signcryptext from S to R. The original security model ensures security in situations where an attacker must register their public keys with some trusted authority (such as a PKI) in such a way that proves the user knows the private key corresponding to the public key that it is registering. This ensures that if the adversary outputs a valid public key pk_R then it must also prove that it knows the corresponding private key sk_R. However, security in the secret key ignorant (SKI) model ensures security in situations where users are not required to prove knowledge of a private key sk_R when registering the public key pk_R. This security model may be harder to achieve in practice, but the security guarantees may be invaluable in some situations.

Furthermore, in some signcryption schemes, particularly Zheng's scheme [204] described in Sects. 3.3 and 4.3, convincing a third party of the validity of a signcryptext (i.e., achieving non-repudiation) without compromising the receiver's secret key requires a carefully designed signcryptext validity verification protocol to be run between the receiver and the third party. (For example, such a protocol may be a zero-knowledge proof of membership for the appropriate "language"—see the protocols in [204] for further details.) However, the above insider unforgeability definition is not sufficiently strong to support such a verification protocol, since it does not rule out forgeries of valid signcryptexts for which the attacker does not know the corresponding receiver's secret key. (The adversary may instead just know some information related to the secret key which still suffices for passing the signcryptext validity verification protocol with the third party.)

To address both these issues, one may strengthen the above insider unforgeability definition to also rule out "secret key ignorant" (SKI) forgeries in which the adversary does not know the receiver's secret key. The formal definition involves the following change to the insider FSO/FUO-UF-CMA model:

- In Step 4, $\mathcal{A}$ outputs a receiver's public key pk_R and a signcryptext C^*. The conditions of winning the game are as in the outsider model, where the private key sk_R corresponding to pk_R is computed by the challenger in verifying the forgery. (Note that the challenger does not run in polynomial time in this definition.)

We call the corresponding security notion *multi-user insider unforgeability in the FSO/FUO-UF-CMA-SKI sense*. Note that this is the full BSZ multi-user insider unforgeability model defined in [13].

3.2.3 Further Discussions on the Multi-User BSZ Model

3.2.3.1 The Extra Power of Multi-User Model vs. Two-User Model

The extra power given to the adversary in the multi-user model is the ability to access *flexible* signcryption and unsigncryption oracles which allow the adversary to specify the receiver's and sender's public keys (respectively) in addition to the message and signcryptext (respectively). In a practical application, such an attack might be conducted by the adversary by requesting a new public key certificate from the Certificate Authority (CA) each time he wants to query the sender's signcryption oracle with a new public key of his choice. A signcryption scheme meeting the multi-user model must be secure even if the adversary can get public key certificates issued for as many public keys as it wishes. In some applications it may be possible to place significant constraints on the public keys in such a way that additional checks by the CA ensure that users "know" the private key associated with their public key. However, we believe that for the sake of wide applicability one should be conservative and avoid such assumptions if possible.

We emphasize that the security of signcryption in the two-user model *does not* imply security in the multi-user model. Furthermore, there is no known *efficient* (in particular, not using encryption/signature primitives) generic conversion of a "two-user secure" signcryption scheme into a "multi-user secure" one. (The "semi-generic" efficient conversion given by ADR in Sect. 2.4 only works for the schemes which are built from separate signature and encryption primitives.) More precisely, we prove the following theorem.

Theorem 3.1 *There exists a signcryption scheme unforgeable in the two-user model but forgeable in the multi-user model.*

Proof Let Π = (Setup, KeyGen$_S$, KeyGen$_R$, Signcrypt, Unsigncrypt) be a signcryption scheme *unforgeable* in the two-user model. Let (sk_S, pk_S) be a single sender S's private/public key pair. Similarly let (sk_R, pk_R) be a single receiver R's private/public key pair. Suppose that $sk_S = b_1 b_2 \cdots b_n$ where $b_i \in \{0, 1\}$ for $i = 1, \ldots, n$. (Namely, b_i represents each bit of the private key sk_S.)

We now construct a signcryption scheme Π' = (Setup', KeyGen$'_S$, KeyGen$'_R$, Signcrypt', Unsigncrypt') as follows:

- Setup', KeyGen$'_S$, KeyGen$'_R$ are identical to Setup, KeyGen$_S$, KeyGen$_R$.
- Signcrypt'$(param, sk_S, pk_R, m) = b_i \| $Signcrypt$(param, sk_S, pk_R, m)$, where $i \leftarrow f(pk_R)$ is determined as a function of pk_R. We choose this function f to be efficiently computable and onto $\{1, \ldots, n\}$, so for each $i \in \{1, \ldots, n\}$ there exists a receiver public key pk_i (which is easily computable) such that $f(pk_i) = i$.
- Unsigncrypt' ignores the first bit of signcryptexts, processing the remaining portion identically to the Unsigncrypt algorithm of Π.

In the two-user model, a forging adversary for Π' can only query the sender's signcryption oracle with one receiver public key, which is fixed for the whole attack, and hence in this model, the forger can only get a single bit of the secret key. Consequently the new scheme is still unforgeable. In the multi-user model, however, the adversary can quickly get all the bits of the sender's secret key by querying the signcryption oracle with just n different receiver public keys, so the scheme is easily forgeable in the multi-user setting. Note that the scheme remains forgeable in the multi-user setting, for the same reason, even after applying the "semi-generic" conversion of [10] described in Sect. 2.4. □

3.2.3.2 One Key Pair Generation vs. Two Key Pair Generation

Before moving to the next section, we make the following comments on the key generation algorithm in the multi-user BSZ model. In our definition of the multi-user security model presented in this chapter, we assume the traditional PKI setting in which each user *generates two independent key pairs*, one for sending (authentication) and the other for receiving (confidentiality). In most signcryption schemes, the sender and receiver's key generation algorithms are identical, and a user may wish to use a single key pair for both sending and receiving. However, such a *one key generation* setting opens up additional capabilities for attacks and requires some modifications to the security models. Namely, the models should be modified to allow the adversary to access two additional oracles: the sender's unsigncryption oracle and the receiver's signcryption oracle (except in the case of the insider security models where only a single oracle needs to be added). Due to this difference in attack models, it is important to state whether the one key generation setting is assumed or not when analyzing the security of a signcryption scheme. More details are given in Sect. 5.4.

3.3 Example: The Security of Zheng's Signcryption Scheme in the BSZ Model

As an example of how the BSZ model can be applied, we discuss the security of Zheng's original signcryption scheme [203]. However, we postpone giving a formal description of Zheng's scheme and stating its security formally until Chap. 4. The purpose of this section is to explain how the different types of security in the BSZ model have meaning in analyzing security of a given signcryption scheme. We give a description of the scheme in Fig. 3.1.

In terms of confidentiality, Zheng's original signcryption scheme is proven to be multi-user outsider secure in the FSO/FUO-IND-CCA2 sense, in the random oracle model [29], relative to the "Gap Diffie–Hellman (GDH) [152]" problem. (Readers are referred to Sect. 4.2 for precise definition of the GDH problem.) The reason why Zheng's original signcryption scheme does not provide insider confidentiality is as follows. An adversary that knows the sender's private key x_S and the signcryptext (c, r, s) can easily compute $x = s(r + x_S)$ and so compute the symmetric key $\tau = G(y_R^x)$ and the corresponding message $m = \text{Dec}_\tau(c)$.

In terms of unforgeability, Zheng's signcryption scheme achieves unforgeability in the multi-user insider secret-key-ignorant FSO-UF-CMA-SKI sense, in the random oracle model, assuming that the Gap Discrete Log (GDL) problem is hard.

Setup(1^k)

   Pick a random large prime p with
      a k-bit prime q dividing $p-1$.
   Pick $g \in \mathbb{Z}_p^*$ of order q.
   Choose an one-time symmetric-key
      encryption scheme $SE = (\text{Enc}, \text{Dec})$
      with key space $\mathcal{K}$ and ciphertext space $\mathcal{C}$
   Pick cryptographic hash functions:
      $G : \{0,1\}^* \rightarrow \mathcal{K}$
      $H : \{0,1\}^* \rightarrow \mathbb{Z}_q$
   $param \leftarrow (p,q,g,SE,G,H)$
   Return $param$

KeyGen$_S$($param$)

   $x_S \xleftarrow{R} \mathbb{Z}_q; y_S \leftarrow g^{x_S}$
   $sk_S \leftarrow (x_S, y_S); pk_S \leftarrow y_S$
   Return (sk_S, pk_S)

KeyGen$_R$($param$)

   $x_R \xleftarrow{R} \mathbb{Z}_q; y_R \leftarrow g^{x_R}$
   $sk_R \leftarrow (x_R, y_R); pk_R \leftarrow y_R$
   Return (sk_R, pk_R)

Signcrypt($param, sk_S, pk_R, m$)

   Parse sk_S as (x_S, y_S); Parse pk_R as y_R
   If $y_R \notin \langle g \rangle \setminus \{1\}$ then return $\perp$
   $x \xleftarrow{R} \mathbb{Z}_q; K \leftarrow y_R^x; \tau \leftarrow G(K)$
   $bind \leftarrow pk_S \| pk_R; r \leftarrow H(m \| bind \| K)$
   $c \leftarrow \text{Enc}_\tau(m)$
   If $r + x_S = 0$ then return $\perp$
   $s \leftarrow x/(r + x_S)$
   $C \leftarrow (c, r, s)$
   Return C

Unsigncrypt($param, pk_S, sk_R, C$)

   Parse sk_R as (x_R, y_R); Parse pk_S as y_S
   If $y_S \notin \langle g \rangle \setminus \{1\}$ then return $\perp$
   Parse C as (c, r, s)
   If $r \notin \mathbb{Z}_q$ or $s \notin \mathbb{Z}_q$ or $c \notin \mathcal{C}$
      Return $\perp$
   $\omega \leftarrow (y_S g^r)^s; K \leftarrow \omega^{x_R}; bind \leftarrow pk_S \| pk_R$
   $\tau \leftarrow G(K); m \leftarrow \text{Dec}_\tau(c)$
   If $H(m \| bind \| K) = r$ then return m
   Else return $\perp$

Fig. 3.1 Zheng's signcryption scheme

Informally, the GDL problem is, given g^a for random $a \in \mathbb{Z}_q^*$, to compute a with the help of a Decisional Diffie–Hellman (DDH) oracle which, on input (g, g^a, g^b, z), outputs 1 if $z = g^{ab}$ and 0 otherwise. (Readers are referred to Sect. 4.2 for precise definition of the GDL problem.) Note that the GDL problem is possibly a harder problem than the GDH problem.

To understand why the hardness of GDL problem is *necessary* for the unforgeability of Zheng's scheme in the multi-user model, but not necessary in the two-user model, one can show that, using an efficient algorithm to solve the GDL problem as a subroutine, an adversary that breaks unforgeability of Zheng's scheme in the multi-user setting can be constructed as follows. The adversary is given the sender's public key $y_S = g^{x_S}$ and runs the GDL algorithm to recover the sender's secret key x_S. When the GDL algorithm wishes to check whether a tuple of the form $(g, y_S = g^{x_S}, u, z)$ is a valid Diffie–Hellman tuple (i.e., whether $z = u^{x_S}$ or not), where u and z are chosen by the GDL algorithm, the unforgeability adversary queries the sender's signcryption oracle on an arbitrary message m with receiver's public key set to be u. When the signcryption oracle returns signcryptext (c, r, s), the adversary checks whether $H(m \| y_S \| u \| (z \cdot u^r)^s)$ is equal to r. If $z = u^{x_S}$, we have that $(z \cdot u^r)^s = u^{(x_S + r)s}$ is equal to the key K used by the signcryption oracle, and the adversary's test will pass, while if $z \neq u^{x_S}$, the adversary's test will fail with overwhelming probability. Hence, a multi-user unforgeability adversary can use a GDL algorithm to break the system by testing validity of Diffie–Hellman tuples via queries to the attacked sender's signcryption algorithm. Note the attack cannot be mounted in the two-user model, where the receiver's public key in signcryption queries cannot be controlled by the adversary. This is another example which shows that evaluating the two-user security of a signcryption scheme is not sufficient for establishing its multi-user security.

In view of its strong multi-user confidentiality and unforgeability properties, Zheng's scheme would be suitable for use in a wide range of application environments, even in settings where user public keys are registered without proving knowledge of the corresponding secret keys. But due to the scheme's lack of insider confidentiality, it may not be suitable for applications in which the sender's key is likely to be compromised (for example, a highly mobile sending device which may be easily lost). In such environments, the loss of the sender's key would potentially compromise all past messages sent by the sender, whereas for an insider-secure scheme, a quick revocation of the sender's key can prevent security breaches from occurring.

Part II
Signcryption Schemes

Chapter 4
Signcryption Schemes Based on the Diffie–Hellman Problem

Paulo S.L.M. Barreto, Benoît Libert, Noel McCullagh, and
Jean-Jacques Quisquater

4.1 Introduction

In this chapter we examine various signcryption schemes based on the Diffie–Hellman problem. Importantly, this set of schemes includes the original signcryption scheme by Zheng [203] and also several constructions with enhanced properties, for example, the scheme by Bao and Deng [15].

Zheng's discovery was extremely practical and insightful, it removed the construction of cryptographic schemes from the purely mathematical and instead focused on how cryptographic primitives were used in practice.

From a practical point of view, often when information is considered sensitive enough to be encrypted it must also be signed. Intuitively, if we think of information as important enough to warrant encrypting, then it is also be useful to know the authority behind the message. For example, a company internal memo, say with projected sales figures, would need to be signed by an appropriate authority to carry any weight, while it would also need to be encrypted so only the specified company employees could access it.

Zheng's original construction was very efficient. It was built on a modification of the ElGamal signature and carefully exploits randomness reuse to authenticate and encrypt the message more efficiently than simply encrypting the message using ElGamal encryption.

We see that while the original scheme had message origin authentication from the receivers viewpoint, it had no clear and efficient non-repudiation property—see Sect. 3.3. We will go on to see the problems in trying to incorporate efficient non-repudiation. Obviously no scheme where a signature on the message is transmitted in the clear can enjoy the indistinguishability of ciphertexts property. Gamage et al. [86] unknowingly avoided the latter problem by carefully appending a signature on the ciphertext. Therefore any third party would be able to determine the origin of the

B. Libert (✉)
Crypto Group, Microelectronics Laboratory, Université Catholique
de Louvain, Louvain, Belgium
e-mail: benoit.libert@uclouvain.be

A.W. Dent, Y. Zheng (eds.), *Practical Signcryption*, Information Security
and Cryptography, DOI 10.1007/978-3-540-89411-7_4,
© Springer-Verlag Berlin Heidelberg 2010

ciphertext, if not the actual content of the message. As we will see, this unfortunately does not completely solve non-repudiation concerns.

In 2002, Shin et al. [178] proposed a Diffie–Hellman style construction that enjoys a secure and efficient non-repudiation procedure allowing receivers to convince a third party of the origin of a message. In 2005, Malone-Lee [130] suggested a similar technique and proposed a scheme extending Schnorr's signature scheme [173] that was additionally supported by a proof of unforgeability.

4.2 Diffie–Hellman Problems

Definition 4.1 Let k be a security parameter and p be a k-bit prime number. Let us consider a cyclic group $\mathbb{G}$ of order p with a random generator g.

- The *Discrete Logarithm* problem (DL) is to compute a given $(g, g^a) \in \mathbb{G}^2$ for randomly chosen $a \xleftarrow{R} \mathbb{Z}_p^*$. An algorithm $\mathcal{B}$ has advantage ε if the probability that $\mathcal{B}$ outputs the correct solution is at least ε.
- The *Computational Diffie–Hellman* problem (CDH) is to compute $g^{ab} \in \mathbb{G}$ given $(g, g^a, g^b) \in \mathbb{G}^3$ for randomly chosen $a, b \xleftarrow{R} \mathbb{Z}_p^*$. An algorithm $\mathcal{B}$ has advantage ε if the probability that $\mathcal{B}$ outputs the correct solution is at least ε.
- The *Decisional Diffie–Hellman* problem (DDH) is to distinguish the distribution of "Diffie–Hellman tuples" $D_{DH} := \{(g, g^a, g^b, g^{ab}) \mid a, b \xleftarrow{R} \mathbb{Z}_p^*\}$ from that of "random tuples" $D_{\mathrm{rand}} := \{(g, g^a, g^b, g^c) \mid a, b, c \xleftarrow{R} \mathbb{Z}_p^*\}$. We say that an algorithm $\mathcal{B}$ solving the DDH problem has advantage ε if

$$\left| \Pr[\mathcal{B}(g, g^a, g^b, g^{ab}) = 1 \mid a, b \xleftarrow{R} \mathbb{Z}_p^*] - \Pr[\mathcal{B}(g, g^a, g^b, g^c) = 1 \mid a, b, c \xleftarrow{R} \mathbb{Z}_p^*] \right|$$

is at least ε. Solving a DDH instance amounts to decide whether $c = ab \bmod p$ given a tuple $(g, g^a, g^b, g^c) \in \mathbb{G}^3$.
- The *Gap Diffie–Hellman* problem (GDH) is the problem of solving the CDH problem on (g, g^a, g^b) with the help of a DDH oracle which, on input of a tuple $(g^x, g^y, g^z) \in \mathbb{G}^3$, will return 1 if $z = xy \bmod p$ and 0 otherwise. An algorithm $\mathcal{B}$ has advantage ε if the probability that $\mathcal{B}$ outputs a correct solution to the CDH problem is at least ε.
- The *Gap Discrete Logarithm* problem (GDL) is the problem of solving a DL problem on (g, g^a) with the help of a DDH oracle (described above). An algorithm $\mathcal{B}$ has advantage ε if the probability that $\mathcal{B}$ outputs a correct solution to the DL problem is at least ε.

The Gap Diffie–Hellman assumption was introduced by Okamoto and Pointcheval [152] with the motivation of providing security proofs for signature schemes with special properties. It is stronger than its variant termed "Strong Diffie–

Hellman assumption" previously considered in [2].[1] The latter posits the infeasibility of solving a CDH instance (g, g^a, g^b) with the help of a *restricted* DDH oracle which, on input of a pair $(X, Y) \in \mathbb{G}^2$, will return 1 if $Y = X^a$ and 0 otherwise.

4.3 Zheng's Construction and Its Variants

This section presents the first realization of the signcryption primitive, as proposed by Zheng [203] in 1997. It was built on a modification of the ElGamal signature scheme [81] dubbed SDSS (as a shorthand for Shortened Digital Signature Scheme). In this scheme, the signer holds a public/private key pair (pk, sk) where $pk = g^{sk} \in \mathbb{G}$ and $sk \xleftarrow{R} \mathbb{Z}_p^*$. A signature on a message m is a pair

$$(r, s) = \left(h(m \| g^x), \frac{x}{r + sk} \bmod p \right)$$

where $h : \{0, 1\}^* \to \mathbb{Z}_p^*$ is a hash function and x is a random element from $\mathbb{Z}_p^*$. A signature (r, s) can be verified by checking whether $r = h\big(m \| (pk \cdot g^r)^s\big)$.

Zheng's signcryption algorithm relies on a careful reuse of the random value x to implement a non-interactive Diffie–Hellman key agreement using the recipient's public key. We first describe the variant for which a security proof was provided in [12, 13] before showing several modifications considered in the late 1990s.

4.3.1 Zheng's Original Scheme

The specification of Zheng's signcryption scheme is given in Fig. 4.1. The specification involves a symmetric encryption scheme, as described in Sect. 1.3.4. The key property of the scheme is that a signature (r, s) allows re-computing the group element

$$g^x = (pk_S \, g^r)^s \bmod p$$

---

[1] The latter assumption should not be confused with another assumption introduced by Boneh and Boyen [42] and named "q-Strong Diffie–Hellman." The assumption of [42] is very different and states the intractability of computing a pair $(c, g^{1/(c+a)}) \in \mathbb{Z}_p \times \mathbb{G}$ given $(g, g^a, g^{(a^2)}, \ldots, g^{(a^q)})$ for randomly chosen $a \xleftarrow{R} \mathbb{Z}_p^*$. This problem is described in more detail in Chap. 5.

Setup(1^k)

    Pick a random large prime p with
        a k-bit prime q dividing $p-1$.

    Pick $g \in \mathbb{Z}_p^*$ of order q.

    Choose an one-time symmetric-key
        encryption scheme $SE = (\text{Enc}, \text{Dec})$
        with key space $\mathcal{K}$ and ciphertext space $\mathcal{C}$

    Pick cryptographic hash functions:

        $G : \{0,1\}^* \to \mathcal{K}$

        $H : \{0,1\}^* \to \mathbb{Z}_q$

    $param \leftarrow (p,q,g,SE,G,H)$

    Return $param$

KeyGen$_S$($param$)

    $x_S \xleftarrow{R} \mathbb{Z}_q; y_S \leftarrow g^{x_S}$

    $sk_S \leftarrow (x_S, y_S); pk_S \leftarrow y_S$

    Return (sk_S, pk_S)

KeyGen$_R$($param$)

    $x_R \xleftarrow{R} \mathbb{Z}_q; y_R \leftarrow g^{x_R}$

    $sk_R \leftarrow (x_R, y_R); pk_R \leftarrow y_R$

    Return (sk_R, pk_R)

Signcrypt($param, sk_S, pk_R, m$)

    Parse sk_S as (x_S, y_S); Parse pk_R as y_R

    If $y_R \notin \langle g \rangle \setminus \{1\}$ then return $\bot$

    $x \xleftarrow{R} \mathbb{Z}_q; K \leftarrow y_R^x; \tau \leftarrow G(K)$

    $bind \leftarrow pk_S \| pk_R; r \leftarrow H(m \| bind \| K)$

    $c \leftarrow \text{Enc}_\tau(m)$

    If $r + x_S = 0$ then return $\bot$

    $s \leftarrow x/(r + x_S)$

    $C \leftarrow (c, r, s)$

    Return C

Unsigncrypt($param, pk_S, sk_R, C$)

    Parse sk_R as (x_R, y_R); Parse pk_S as y_S

    If $y_S \notin \langle g \rangle \setminus \{1\}$ then return $\bot$

    Parse C as (c, r, s)

    If $r \notin \mathbb{Z}_q$ or $s \notin \mathbb{Z}_q$ or $c \notin \mathcal{C}$

        Return $\bot$

    $\omega \leftarrow (y_S g^r)^s; K \leftarrow \omega^{x_R}; bind \leftarrow pk_S \| pk_R$

    $\tau \leftarrow G(K); m \leftarrow \text{Dec}_\tau(c)$

    If $H(m \| bind \| K) = r$ then return m

    Else return $\bot$

Fig. 4.1 Zheng's original scheme

generated by the signer. The quantity simultaneously acts as a component of the signature scheme and an ephemeral Diffie–Hellman key in a non-interactive key agreement, as in the ElGamal [81] or ECIES [2] public key encryption schemes.

    The scheme is remarkable in terms of efficiency since the sender jointly authenticates and encrypts the message thanks to a single modular exponentiation; hence, the scheme is almost as efficient as the ECIES public key encryption scheme on which it is based [2].

    An inherent limitation of this scheme is that receivers have no secure and efficient way to convince a third party that the sender is the actual originator of the message m. A suggestion given in [203, 204] was to let the receiving party forward $\kappa \leftarrow \omega^{sk_R} \bmod p$ and $\langle c, r, s \rangle$ to the third party. The receiver then had to provide a zero-knowledge proof that the logarithm of pk_R for the base g equals the discrete logarithm of κ with respect to the base $\omega = (pk_S g^r)^s \bmod p$. Unfortunately, as shown in [159], disclosing $\kappa = \omega^{sk_R} \bmod p$ and the pair (r, s) gives away $g^{sk_S sk_R}$ which harms the confidentiality of any subsequent communication between both parties.

    Somewhat surprisingly, a formal security proof for Zheng's scheme remained lacking until 2002 [12, 13]. The following security results are proven in [12, 13] in the model of Baek, Steinfeld, and Zheng described in Chap. 3. Theorem 4.1 states that this scheme protects the confidentiality of messages in the multi-user outsider FSO/FUO-IND-CCA2 security model, while Theorem 4.2 establishes the unforgeability property in the multi-user insider secret-key-ignorant FSO-UF-CMA-SKI security model. Both proofs resort to the random oracle methodology [29].

Theorem 4.1 *If the GDH problem is hard and the symmetric encryption scheme is IND-CPA secure, then Zheng's scheme is multi-user outsider FSO/FUO-IND-CCA2 secure in the random oracle model. Concretely, if there exists*

- *an attacker $\mathcal{A} = (\mathcal{A}_1, \mathcal{A}_2)$ against the multi-user outsider FSO/FUO-IND-CCA2 security that runs in time t, makes at most q_{sc} queries to the signcryption oracle, makes at most q_{usc} queries to the unsigncryption oracle, makes at most q_G queries to the G-oracle, makes at most q_H queries to the H-oracle, and has advantage $Adv_{\mathcal{A}}^{IND}(k)$,*

then there exists

- *an algorithm $\mathcal{B}$ that runs in time $O(t^2)$, makes at most $(q_G + q_H)(q_{sc} + q_{usc})$ queries to the DDH oracle and has advantage $Adv_{\mathcal{B}}^{GDH}(k)$ in solving the Gap Diffie–Hellman problem, and*
- *an attacker $\mathcal{B}' = (\mathcal{B}'_1, \mathcal{B}'_2)$ against the IND-CPA property of the symmetric encryption scheme that runs in time $O(t^2)$ and has advantage $Adv_{\mathcal{B}'}^{SYM}(k)$*

such that

$$Adv_{\mathcal{A}}^{IND}(k) \leq 2Adv_{\mathcal{B}}^{GDH}(k) + Adv_{\mathcal{B}'}^{SYM}(k)$$
$$+ \frac{q_{sc}(q_G + q_H + q_{sc} + q_{usc} + 2)}{2^{k-1}} + \frac{(q_H + 2q_{usc})}{2^{k-1}}$$

Theorem 4.2 *If the Gap Discrete Logarithm problem is hard, then Zheng's scheme is multi-user insider secret-key-ignorant FSO-UF-CMA-SKI secure in the random oracle model. More precisely, if there exists*

- *an attacker $\mathcal{A}$ that runs in time t, makes at most q_{sc} queries to the signcryption oracle, makes at most q_G queries to the G-oracle, makes at most q_H queries to the H-oracle and breaks the security of the scheme with probability $Adv_{\mathcal{A}}^{UF}(k)$*

then there exists

- *an algorithm $\mathcal{B}$ that breaks the Gap Discrete Logarithm problem that runs in time $O(t^2)$, makes at most $2q_{sc}(q_G + q_H) + 2q_H$ queries to the DDH oracle, and has advantage $Adv_{\mathcal{B}}^{GDL}(k)$*

such that

$$Adv_{\mathcal{B}}^{UF}(k) \leq 2\big(q_H \, Adv_{\mathcal{A}}^{GDL}(k)\big)^{1/2} + \frac{q_{sc}(q_{sc} + q_G + q_H) + q_H + 1}{2^k - 1}$$

We mention that Zheng's construction was revisited in several recent works [37, 72] which analyze it in a hybrid setting. We refer the reader to Chap. 7 for a detailed study of this canonical scheme in such a model.

4.3.2 The Bao–Deng Modification

In 1998, Bao and Deng [15] proposed a modification of Zheng's construction that aims to allow receivers to efficiently convince a third party of the origin of a received message and thus provide the non-repudiation property of digital signatures. This scheme is described in Fig. 4.2.

This method allows a receiver to convince a court of the sender's authorship for m by simply revealing m and (r, s) which is nothing but a signature on m.

Unfortunately, this non-repudiation procedure seriously harms the confidentiality of the scheme which obviously becomes insecure under any definition of privacy based on the idea of indistinguishable encryptions [90]. Indeed, the ciphertext contains a signature (r, s) on the plaintext and thus leaks information on the latter. An adversary can easily decide which one of m_0 and m_1 is the message enciphered by a given ciphertext (c, r, s) by simply checking the signature (r, s) for m_0 and m_1. This security concern was reported for the first time by Shin et al. [178] who described another scheme built on the DSA signature with the motivation to overcome this limitation. Other constructions (such as [196, 201]) turn out to suffer from a similar weakness.

Setup(1^k)
  Pick a random large prime p with
    a k-bit prime q dividing $p - 1$.
  Pick $g \in \mathbb{Z}_p^*$ of order q.
  Choose an one-time symmetric-key
    encryption scheme $SE = (\text{Enc}, \text{Dec})$
    with key space $\mathcal{K}$ and ciphertext space $\mathcal{C}$
  Pick cryptographic hash functions:
    $G : \{0,1\}^* \rightarrow \mathcal{K}$
    $H : \{0,1\}^* \rightarrow \mathbb{Z}_q$
  $param \leftarrow (p, q, g, SE, G, H)$
  Return $param$

KeyGen$_S$($param$)
  $x_S \xleftarrow{R} \mathbb{Z}_q; y_S \leftarrow g^{x_S}$
  $sk_S \leftarrow (x_S, y_S); pk_S \leftarrow y_S$
  Return (sk_S, pk_S)

KeyGen$_R$($param$)
  $x_R \xleftarrow{R} \mathbb{Z}_q; y_R \leftarrow g^{x_R}$
  $sk_R \leftarrow (x_R, y_R); pk_R \leftarrow y_R$
  Return (sk_R, pk_R)

Signcrypt($param, sk_S, pk_R, m$)
  Parse sk_S as (x_S, y_S); Parse pk_R as y_R
  If $y_R \notin \langle g \rangle \setminus \{1\}$ then return $\bot$
  $x \xleftarrow{R} \mathbb{Z}_q; K \leftarrow y_R^x; \omega \leftarrow g^x$
  $\tau \leftarrow G(K); c \leftarrow \text{Enc}_\tau(m)$
  $bind \leftarrow pk_S \| pk_R; r \leftarrow H(m \| bind \| \omega)$
  If $r + x_S = 0$ then return $\bot$
  $s \leftarrow x / (r + x_S)$
  $C \leftarrow (c, r, s)$
  Return C

Unsigncrypt($param, pk_S, sk_R, C$)
  Parse sk_R as (x_R, y_R); Parse pk_S as y_S
  If $y_S \notin \langle g \rangle \setminus \{1\}$ then return $\bot$
  Parse C as (c, r, s)
  If $r \notin \mathbb{Z}_q$ or $s \notin \mathbb{Z}_q$ or $c \notin \mathcal{C}$
    Return $\bot$
  $\omega \leftarrow (y_S g^r)^s; K \leftarrow \omega^{x_R}; bind \leftarrow pk_S \| pk_R$
  $\tau \leftarrow G(K); m \leftarrow \text{Dec}_\tau(c)$
  If $H(m \| bind \| \omega) = r$ then return m
  Else return $\bot$

Fig. 4.2 The Bao–Deng scheme

4.3.3 A Modification with Public Verifiability

In 1999, Gamage et al. [86] suggested a modification of the Bao–Deng scheme which allows anyone (e.g., firewalls) to publicly verify the origin of a ciphertext without learning anything about the plaintext. The scheme is given in Fig. 4.3.

Setup(1^k)
  Pick a random large prime p with
    a k-bit prime q dividing $p-1$.
  Pick $g \in \mathbb{Z}_p^*$ of order q.
  Choose an one-time symmetric-key
    encryption scheme $SE = (\text{Enc}, \text{Dec})$
    with key space $\mathcal{K}$ and ciphertext space $\mathcal{C}$
  Pick cryptographic hash functions:
    $G : \{0,1\}^* \to \mathcal{K}$
    $H : \{0,1\}^* \to \mathbb{Z}_q$
  $param \leftarrow (p, q, g, SE, G, H)$
  Return $param$

KeyGen$_S$($param$)
  $x_S \xleftarrow{R} \mathbb{Z}_q; y_S \leftarrow g^{x_S}$
  $sk_S \leftarrow (x_S, y_S); pk_S \leftarrow y_S$
  Return (sk_S, pk_S)

KeyGen$_R$($param$)
  $x_R \xleftarrow{R} \mathbb{Z}_q; y_R \leftarrow g^{x_R}$
  $sk_R \leftarrow (x_R, y_R); pk_R \leftarrow y_R$
  Return (sk_R, pk_R)

Signcrypt($param, sk_S, pk_R, m$)
  Parse sk_S as (x_S, y_S); Parse pk_R as y_R
  If $y_R \notin \langle g \rangle \setminus \{1\}$ then return $\perp$
  $x \xleftarrow{R} \mathbb{Z}_q; K \leftarrow y_R^x; \omega \leftarrow g^x$
  $\tau \leftarrow G(K); c \leftarrow \text{Enc}_\tau(m)$
  $bind \leftarrow pk_S \| pk_R; r \leftarrow H(c \| bind \| \omega)$
  If $r + x_S = 0$ then return $\perp$
  $s \leftarrow x/(r + x_S)$
  $C \leftarrow (c, r, s)$
  Return C

Unsigncrypt($param, pk_S, sk_R, C$)
  Parse sk_R as (x_R, y_R); Parse pk_S as y_S
  If $y_S \notin \langle g \rangle \setminus \{1\}$ then return $\perp$
  Parse C as (c, r, s)
  If $r \notin \mathbb{Z}_q$ or $s \notin \mathbb{Z}_q$ or $c \notin \mathcal{C}$
    Return $\perp$
  $\omega \leftarrow (y_S g^r)^s; K \leftarrow \omega^{x_R}; bind \leftarrow pk_S \| pk_R$
  $\tau \leftarrow G(K); m \leftarrow \text{Dec}_\tau(c)$
  If $H(c \| bind \| \omega) = r$ then return m
  Else return $\perp$

Fig. 4.3 The Gamage et al. scheme

In this scheme, a ciphertext (c, r, s) can be thought of as containing a signature (r, s) on the encrypted message c. This is accomplished in such a way that a firewall can verify that (r, s) is a valid signature on c. It is worth stressing that this approach departs from a naive Encrypt-then-Sign composition (see Chap. 2) in that c is enciphered using a symmetric key derived from a Diffie–Hellman "session key" generated by the randomness x that is involved in the signing procedure.

This modification avoids the security concern encountered in the Bao–Deng construction, but it unfortunately does not provide an efficient method allowing receivers to prove the origin of the plaintext m to third parties.

The security of the above scheme was never explicitly analyzed in the multi-user setting and its original description [86] did not specify to hash $bind$ along with c and ω in the calculation or r.[2] To make it easier to observe the differences among schemes, we nevertheless retain the binding information among the inputs of the hash function.

4.4 An Encrypt-then-Sign Composition

In [108], Jeong et al. proposed a construction combining a non-interactive Diffie–Hellman key agreement with any strongly unforgeable signature scheme and any

---

[2] Neither did the original specification—given in [203]—of Zheng's proposal. It was in [12] that the binding information was taken as argument by H for the first time (in order to prove security in the multi-user setting).

$\texttt{Setup}(1^k)$
   Pick a cyclic group $\mathbb{G}$ whose order is a
      k-bit prime p and a generator $g \in \mathbb{G}$
   Choose an IND-CPA secure symmetric-key
      encryption scheme $SE = (\texttt{Enc}, \texttt{Dec})$
      with key space $\mathcal{K}$ and ciphertext space $\mathcal{C}$
   Pick a cryptographic hash function:
      $H : \{0,1\}^* \to \mathcal{K}$
   Pick a strongly unforgeable signature scheme
      $\Sigma = (\texttt{SigKeyGen}, \texttt{Sign}, \texttt{Verify})$
   $param \leftarrow (\mathbb{G}, g, p, SE, \Sigma, H)$
   Return $param$

$\texttt{KeyGen}_S(param)$:
   $(sk_S, pk_S) \xleftarrow{R} \texttt{SigKeyGen}(1^k)$.
   Return (sk_S, pk_S)

$\texttt{KeyGen}_R(param)$
   $x_R \xleftarrow{R} \mathbb{Z}_q; y_R \leftarrow g^{x_R}$
   $sk_R \leftarrow (x_R, y_R); pk_R \leftarrow y_R$
   Return (sk_R, pk_R)

$\texttt{Signcrypt}(param, sk_S, pk_R, m)$
   $x \xleftarrow{R} \mathbb{Z}_p^*; \omega \leftarrow g^x$
   $\tau \leftarrow H(pk_S \| pk_R^x); c \leftarrow \texttt{Enc}_\tau(m)$
   $\sigma \xleftarrow{R} \texttt{Sign}(sk_S, \omega \| c)$
   $C \leftarrow (\omega, c, \sigma)$
   Return C

$\texttt{Unsigncrypt}(param, pk_S, sk_R, C)$
   Parse C as (ω, c, σ)
   If $\omega \notin \mathbb{G} \setminus \{1\}$ or $c \notin \mathcal{C}$
      Return $\perp$
   If $\texttt{Verify}(pk_S, \omega \| c, \sigma) = \perp$
      Return $\perp$
   $K \leftarrow \omega^{sk_R}; \tau \leftarrow H(pk_S \| K)$
   $m \leftarrow \texttt{Dec}_\tau(c)$
   Return m

Fig. 4.4 The Jeong et al. scheme

semantically secure secret key cryptosystem, which they termed the DHEtS scheme. The security of signature schemes is discussed in Sect. 1.3.2. The scheme is described in Fig. 4.4.

At a high level, it bears resemblance with a previous proposal [7] which was itself inspired from the ECIES public key encryption scheme [2].

Proofs of security were given in [108]. The confidentiality security is proven in the multi-user outsider confidentiality FSO/FUO-IND-CCA2 security model. The unforgeability is proven in the multi-user insider strong unforgeability FSO-sUF-CMA security model. Similar to proofs given in [2], they do not involve random oracles [29] but the proof of confidentiality requires a complex assumption (that eventually looks as strong as the random oracle model). This "Oracle Diffie–Hellman assumption" [2] posits the hardness of distinguishing the hash value $H(g^u \| g^{ab})$ from a random string of the same length given $(u, g, g^a, g^b) \xleftarrow{R} \mathbb{Z}_p^* \times \mathbb{G}^3$ even with the help of an oracle which returns $H(X_1 \| X_2^b)$ on input of arbitrary pairs $(X_1, X_2) \in \mathbb{G}_2$ with $X_2 \neq g^a$.

It is also worth mentioning that this scheme is as essentially slow as using the Encrypt-then-Sign techniques—when the encryption layer is implemented with the ECIES cryptosystem [2]—described in Chap. 2.

4.5 A Scheme with Unforgeability Based on Factoring

In 2000, Steinfeld and Zheng [184] described a scheme which is provably unforgeable assuming the hardness of factoring. This construction extends a signature

$\text{Setup}(1^k, 1^\lambda)$

    Choose random k-bit primes p, q such that
        $p - 1, q - 1$ have no prime factors smaller
        than $2^{\ell(k)}$ and such that the multiplicity of
        2 in $ord_{\mathbb{Z}_p^*}(g)$ is different than in $ord_{\mathbb{Z}_q^*}(g)$

    $N \leftarrow pq$

    Choose a large bound $S \ll \sqrt{N}$

    Choose $g \in \mathbb{Z}_N^*$ of large order $ord_{\mathbb{Z}_N^*}(g) < S/2$

    Choose an IND-CPA secure symmetric-key
        encryption scheme $SE = (\text{Enc}, \text{Dec})$
        with key space $\mathcal{K}$ and ciphertext space $\mathcal{C}$

    Pick cryptographic hash functions:

        $H : \{0,1\}^* \rightarrow \{0,1\}^{\ell(k)}$

        $G : \mathbb{Z}_N \rightarrow \mathcal{K} \times \{0,1\}^{\ell'(k)}$

    $param \leftarrow (N, g, S, G, H, SE, \ell'(k))$

    Return $param$

$\text{KeyGen}_S(param)$

    $sk_S \overset{R}{\leftarrow} \{0, \dots, S-1\}$

    $pk_S \leftarrow g^{-sk_S} \bmod N$

    Return (sk_S, pk_S)

$\text{KeyGen}_R(param)$

    $sk_R \overset{R}{\leftarrow} \{0, \dots, S-1\}$

    $pk_R \leftarrow g^{-sk_R} \bmod N$

    Return (sk_R, pk_R)

$\text{Signcrypt}(param, sk_S, pk_R, m)$

    $r \overset{R}{\leftarrow} \{0, \dots, S-1\}$

    $K \leftarrow pk_R^r \bmod N;\ (\tau_1, \tau_2) \leftarrow G(K)$

    $c \leftarrow \text{Enc}_{\tau_1}(m)$

    $bind \leftarrow pk_S \| pk_R;\ e \leftarrow H(m \| bind \| \tau_2)$

    $y \leftarrow r + e \cdot sk_S$ (computed in $\mathbb{Z}$)

    $C \leftarrow (c, e, y)$

    Return C

$\text{Unsigncrypt}(param, pk_S, sk_R, C)$:

    Parse C as (c, e, y)

    If $e \notin \{0,1\}^{\ell(k)}$ or $c \notin \mathcal{C}$

        Return $\perp$

    $K \leftarrow (g^y \cdot pk_S^e)^{-sk_R} \bmod N$

    $(\tau_1, \tau_2) \leftarrow G(K);\ bind \leftarrow pk_S \| pk_R$

    $m \leftarrow \text{Dec}_{\tau_1}(c)$

    If $r \neq H(m \| bind \| \tau_2)$

        Return $\perp$

    Return m

Fig. 4.5 The Steinfeld–Zheng scheme

scheme due to Pointcheval [162] (which is itself a modification of the GPS signature scheme [89]) and can be seen as performing a Diffie–Hellman operation in a group of hidden order. The scheme is described in Fig. 4.5. In this description, the notation $ord_{\mathbb{G}}(g)$ stands for the order of an element g in a group $\mathbb{G}$.

The Steinfeld–Zheng method requires a trusted party to generate system-wide parameters that include an RSA modulus $N = pq$ of particular shape: as in [162], the security proof requires that all odd prime factors of $\varphi(N)$ be larger than a certain bound 2^ℓ. Neither the sender nor the receiver is allowed to know the prime factors of N. They must have confidence in the authority, which is assumed not to maliciously generate N or use its knowledge of the prime factors to mount an attack. However, this authority is not needed beyond the setup phase and can be shut down after having carried out its task.

As in [89, 162], the element y is calculated in $\mathbb{Z}$, without a modular reduction.

This scheme is not endowed with a practical non-repudiation procedure. Steinfeld and Zheng proved (in the random oracle model) its unforgeability in the two-user setting under a factoring assumption which slightly differs from the standard one: the RSA modulus N has indeed a specific shape and an element g of large (though much smaller than $\sqrt{N}$) order is also public. Finding a proof of confidentiality in a suitable model was left as an open problem [184].

4.6 Schemes with Non-repudiation

In 2002, Shin et al. [178] were the first to notice the security weakness in the Bao–Deng [15] and Yum and Lee [201] schemes. To solve these problems, they put forth the first example of a Diffie–Hellman style construction that enjoys a secure and efficient non-repudiation procedure allowing receivers to convince third parties of the sender's authorship of a plaintext.

With the same motivations, Malone-Lee [130] independently suggested a similar technique and came up with a scheme extending Schnorr's signature scheme[173]. This section gives a description of those schemes.

4.6.1 A DSA-Based Construction

This system, called SC-DSA+ by Shin et al. [178] and described in Fig. 4.6, is an extension of a modified version of the DSA signature [149].

Receivers can extract a non-repudiation material from the ciphertext and hand it to third parties as evidence of the plaintext's origin. To this end, they only have to forward m, $bind$, τ_2 together with the pair (e_1, e_2) to the judge who can simply verify a (modified) DSA signature: the message is accepted if $H(m\|bind\|\tau_2) = se_1 \bmod q$ where $s = ((g^{e_1}pk_S^{e_2} \bmod p) \bmod q)/e_2 \bmod q$. From a security point of view, including τ_2 among the arguments of H is crucial since the scheme would be subject to the same weakness as the Bao–Deng construction otherwise.

Setup(1^k)
  Pick a random large prime p with
    a k-bit prime q dividing $p-1$.
  Pick $g \in \mathbb{Z}_p^*$ of order q.
  Choose an one-time symmetric-key
    encryption scheme $SE = (\mathrm{Enc}, \mathrm{Dec})$
    with key space $\mathcal{K}$ and ciphertext space $\mathcal{C}$
  Pick cryptographic hash functions:
    $G : \{0,1\}^* \to \mathcal{K} \times \{0,1\}^{\ell'(k)}$
    $H : \{0,1\}^* \to \mathbb{Z}_q$
  $param \leftarrow (p,q,g,SE,G,H,\ell'(k))$
  Return $param$

KeyGen$_S(param)$
  $x_S \xleftarrow{R} \mathbb{Z}_q$; $y_S \leftarrow g^{x_S}$
  $sk_S \leftarrow (x_S, y_S)$; $pk_S \leftarrow y_S$
  Return (sk_S, pk_S)

KeyGen$_R(param)$
  $x_R \xleftarrow{R} \mathbb{Z}_q$; $y_R \leftarrow g^{x_R}$
  $sk_R \leftarrow (x_R, y_R)$; $pk_R \leftarrow y_R$
  Return (sk_R, pk_R)

Signcrypt$(param, sk_S, pk_R, m)$
  Parse sk_S as (x_S, y_S); Parse pk_R as y_R
  If $y_R \notin \langle g \rangle \setminus \{1\}$ then return $\bot$
  $x \xleftarrow{R} \mathbb{Z}_q^*$; $\omega \leftarrow g^x$; $K \leftarrow y_R^x$
  $(\tau_1, \tau_2) \leftarrow G(K)$; $c \leftarrow \mathrm{Enc}_{\tau_1}(m)$
  $r \leftarrow \omega \bmod q$; $bind \leftarrow pk_S\|pk_R$
  $h \leftarrow H(m\|bind\|\tau_2)$; $s \leftarrow (h + x_S \cdot r)/x \bmod q$
  $e_1 \leftarrow h/s \bmod q$; $e_2 \leftarrow r/s \bmod q$
  $C \leftarrow (c, e_1, e_2)$
  Return C

Unsigncrypt$(param, pk_S, sk_R, C)$
  Parse pk_S as y_S; Parse sk_R as (x_R, y_R)
  Parse C as (c, e_1, e_2)
  If $c \notin \mathcal{C}$ or $e_1, e_2 \notin \mathbb{Z}_q^*$
    Return $\bot$
  $\omega \leftarrow g^{e_1}y_S^{e_2} \bmod p$; $K \leftarrow \omega^{x_R} \bmod p$
  $(\tau_1, \tau_2) \leftarrow G(K)$; $m \leftarrow \mathrm{Dec}_{\tau_1}(c)$
  $bind \leftarrow pk_S\|pk_R$; $r \leftarrow \omega \bmod q$
  $s \leftarrow r/e_2 \bmod q$; $h \leftarrow H(m\|bind\|\tau_2)$
  If $h \neq s \cdot e_1$ then return $\bot$
  Return m

Fig. 4.6 The Shin et al. scheme

Shin et al. [178] proved the confidentiality of SC-DSA+ in a variant of the model of Baek et al. [12, 13] in which the attacker has access to a fixed signcryption oracle, rather than a flexible signcryption oracle—see Chap. 3, under the Gap Diffie–Hellman assumption. Their security model does not take into account information that may be leaked if the attacker requests non-repudiation information for some ciphertexts. They did not provide a formal proof of unforgeability and settled for arguing that if the DSA signature is existentially unforgeable, so is SC-DSA+.

4.6.2 A Scheme Built on Schnorr's Signature Scheme

In 2005, Malone-Lee [130] described another system which is somewhat similar to SC-DSA+. It was built on Schnorr's signature scheme [173] and dubbed SCNINR as a shorthand for "Signcryption with Non-Interactive Non-Repudiation." This scheme is described in Fig. 4.7.

For non-repudiation purposes, the recipient has to forward m, $bind$, τ_2, and (r, s) to a third parties who can simply verify a Schnorr signature.

Malone-Lee [130] proved the security of the SCNINR scheme in a multi-user model drawing inspiration from the one considered by Bellare et al. [22] for public key encryption. Malone-Lee's security model lies somewhere between the two-user model (see Chap. 2) and the multi-user model (see Chap. 3). The model allows for the existence of multiple users; however, none of these users are considered to be

Setup(1^k)
  Pick a random large prime p with
    a k-bit prime q dividing $p-1$.
  Pick $g \in \mathbb{Z}_p^*$ of order q.
  Choose an one-time symmetric-key
    encryption scheme $SE = (\text{Enc}, \text{Dec})$
    with key space $\mathcal{K}$ and ciphertext space $\mathcal{C}$
  Pick cryptographic hash functions:
    $G : \{0,1\}^* \to \mathcal{K} \times \{0,1\}^{\ell'(k)}$
    $H : \{0,1\}^* \to \mathbb{Z}_q$
  $param \leftarrow (p, q, g, SE, G, H, \ell'(k))$
  Return $param$

KeyGen$_S$($param$)
  $x_S \xleftarrow{R} \mathbb{Z}_q; y_S \leftarrow g^{x_S}$
  $sk_S \leftarrow (x_S, y_S); pk_S \leftarrow y_S$
  Return (sk_S, pk_S)

KeyGen$_R$($param$)
  $x_R \xleftarrow{R} \mathbb{Z}_q; y_R \leftarrow g^{x_R}$
  $sk_R \leftarrow (x_R, y_R); pk_R \leftarrow y_R$
  Return (sk_R, pk_R)

Signcrypt($param, sk_S, pk_R, m$)
  Parse sk_S as (x_S, y_S); Parse pk_R as y_R
  If $y_R \notin \langle g \rangle \setminus \{1\}$ then return $\perp$
  $x \xleftarrow{R} \mathbb{Z}_q^*; \omega \leftarrow g^x; K \leftarrow y_R^x$
  $(\tau_1, \tau_2) \leftarrow G(K); c \leftarrow \text{Enc}_{\tau_1}(m)$
  $bind \leftarrow pk_S \| pk_R; r \leftarrow H(m \| bind \| \omega \| \tau_2)$
  $s \leftarrow x - r \cdot x_S \bmod q$
  $C \leftarrow (c, r, s)$
  Return C

Unsigncrypt($param, pk_S, sk_R, C$)
  Parse pk_S as y_S; Parse sk_R as (x_R, y_R)
  Parse C as (c, r, s)
  If $c \notin \mathcal{C}$ or $r, s \notin \mathbb{Z}_q$
    Return $\perp$
  $\omega \leftarrow pk_S^r g^s \bmod p; K \leftarrow \omega^{x_R} \bmod p$
  $(\tau_1, \tau_2) \leftarrow G(K); m \leftarrow \text{Dec}_{\tau_1}(c)$
  $bind \leftarrow pk_S \| pk_R$.
  If $H(m \| bind \| \omega \| \tau_2) \neq r$
    Return $\perp$
  Return m

Fig. 4.7 Malone-Lee's SCNINR scheme

under the control of the attacker and therefore the model may be considered to be closer to a two-user outsider model. The model also allows the attacker access to oracles which simulate the non-repudiation process, thus proving the security of the scheme even in situations in which the attacker can observe non-repudiation interactions.

In this multi-user scenario, and using the random oracle model, the confidentiality of SCNINR is proved under the CDH assumption while the unforgeability relies on the Discrete Logarithm assumption. While the confidentiality property rests on the CDH assumption, it is worth pointing out that the proof of this fact only holds for a very specific choice of groups [111] where the DDH problem is easy (and where CDH and GDH problems are thus equivalent) and that might be inherently more subject to attacks than general groups. However, as mentioned in [130], the confidentiality can be proven under the stronger GDH assumption when the scheme is implemented with general groups.

4.7 The CM Scheme

In 2006 [37], Bjørstad and Dent showed a general framework for constructing (hybrid) signcryption schemes[3] from certain key encapsulation mechanisms

$\text{Setup}(1^k)$
  Pick a group $\mathbb{G}$ whose order is a
    k-bit prime p and with a generator $g \in \mathbb{G}$
  Choose an one-time symmetric-key
    encryption scheme $SE = (\text{Enc}, \text{Dec})$
    with key space $\mathcal{K}$ and ciphertext space $\mathcal{C}$
  Pick cryptographic hash functions:
    $G : \mathbb{G} \to \mathcal{K}$
    $H : \mathbb{G} \to \mathbb{G}$
    $H' : \{0,1\}^* \to \mathbb{Z}_p$
  $param \leftarrow (\mathbb{G}, g, p, SE, G, H, H')$
  Return $param$

$\text{KeyGen}_S(param)$
  $x_S \overset{R}{\leftarrow} \mathbb{Z}_q; y_S \leftarrow g^{x_S}$
  $sk_S \leftarrow (x_S, y_S); pk_S \leftarrow y_S$
  Return (sk_S, pk_S)

$\text{KeyGen}_R(param)$
  $x_R \overset{R}{\leftarrow} \mathbb{Z}_q; y_R \leftarrow g^{x_R}$
  $sk_R \leftarrow (x_R, y_R); pk_R \leftarrow y_R$
  Return (sk_R, pk_R)

$\text{Signcrypt}(param, sk_S, pk_R, m)$
  Parse sk_S as (x_S, y_S); Parse pk_R as y_R
  If $y_R \notin \langle g \rangle \setminus \{1\}$ then return $\bot$
  $x \overset{R}{\leftarrow} \mathbb{Z}_q; K \leftarrow y_R^x$
  $\tau \leftarrow G(K); c \leftarrow \text{Enc}_\tau(m)$
  $h \leftarrow H(K); v \leftarrow h^x; z \leftarrow h^{x_S}$
  $r \leftarrow H'(c\|pk_S\|pk_R\|g\|z\|h\|K\|v)$
  $s \leftarrow x + r \cdot x_S \bmod p$
  $C \leftarrow (c, z, r, s)$
  Return C

$\text{Unsigncrypt}(param, pk_S, sk_R, C)$
  Parse sk_R as (x_R, y_R); Parse pk_S as y_S
  If $y_S \notin \langle g \rangle \setminus \{1\}$ then return $\bot$
  Parse C as (c, z, r, s)
  If $c \notin \mathcal{C}$ or $z \notin \mathbb{G}$ or $r, s \notin \mathbb{Z}_p$
    Return $\bot$
  $K \leftarrow (g^s \cdot y_S^{-r})^{x_R}$
  $h \leftarrow H(K); v \leftarrow h^s \cdot z^{-r}$
  If $r \neq H'(c\|pk_S\|pk_R\|g\|z\|h\|K\|v)$
    Return $\bot$
  $\tau \leftarrow G(K); m \leftarrow \text{Dec}_\tau(c)$
  Return m

Fig. 4.8 The CM scheme

---

[3] More hybrid constructions are described in Chap. 7.

(KEMs) termed tag-KEMs [4, 5]. They notably described yet another Diffie–Hellman-like construction based on Chevallier-Mames' signature scheme [62].

This particular system, depicted in Fig. 4.8, is slightly less efficient than schemes that have been covered so far in this chapter. In comparison with the scheme of Fig. 4.1, for instance, it incurs longer ciphertexts and two extra exponentiations at the sender's end. However, the CM scheme inherits the advantage of the underlying signature scheme, which is a tight security reduction (in the random oracle model) to a well-studied intractability assumption (in this case, the hardness of the CDH problem). This feature turns out to be rare in the realm of Diffie–Hellman style constructions. Indeed, the unforgeability of previously known schemes was only demonstrated under relatively loose reductions to less classical assumptions (such as the Gap Discrete Logarithm or the Gap Diffie–Hellman assumption).

On the other hand, the security of the CM signcryption scheme was only analyzed in the two-user setting with respect to both confidentiality and unforgeability. It is an interesting open problem to see whether its security can be established in the same adversarial model as that of Zheng's system.

Chapter 5
Signcryption Schemes Based on Bilinear Maps

Paulo S.L.M. Barreto, Benoît Libert, Noel McCullagh, and Jean-Jacques Quisquater

5.1 Introduction

As has been established in the previous chapters, signcryption is a cryptographic primitive which combines the message integrity, message origin authentication, and (if possible) signature non-repudiation properties of a traditional digital signature with the privacy-preserving property of a public key encryption scheme.

The last chapter discussed the construction of signcryption schemes based on the Diffie–Hellman problem. In this chapter we look at signcryption schemes resulting from bilinear maps, also commonly called "pairings." Since computing a bilinear map can be significantly slower than computing an exponentiation in a group of the same order, the development of signcryption schemes based on bilinear maps only makes sense if these schemes can provide an advantage over the simpler and potentially more efficient Diffie–Hellman-based schemes. This can be in the form of an improved security analysis or some extra property of the scheme. In this section, we discuss some of these advantages such as ciphertext anonymity and detachable signatures, and give examples of schemes that enjoy these properties.

Pairings were first brought to the attention of the cryptographic community when Menezes, Okamoto, and Vanstone described an attack using the Weil pairing to efficiently convert the Elliptic Curve Discrete Logarithm Problem (EC-DLP) to the Discrete Logarithm Problem in a finite field, which can be solved in sub-exponential time [138]. This is referred to as the MOV attack in the literature.

In 2000, Joux used bilinear maps in the construction of the first pairing-based cryptographic protocol [109]. This was a tripartite Diffie–Hellman key agreement protocol, and as such was subject to the man-in-the-middle attack. Importantly, it was the first non-destructive use of pairings in the literature.

A third paper, by Boneh and Franklin [45, 46], really got cryptographers excited by the new possibilities afforded by bilinear maps. It closed a long-standing open problem in cryptography. The problem of constructing an efficient, secure

B. Libert (✉)
Crypto Group, Microelectronics Laboratory, Université catholique
de Louvain, Louvain, Belgium
e-mail: benoit.libert@uclouvain.be

A.W. Dent, Y. Zheng (eds.), *Practical Signcryption*, Information Security
and Cryptography, DOI 10.1007/978-3-540-89411-7_5,
© Springer-Verlag Berlin Heidelberg 2010

identity-based encryption (IBE) scheme was proposed by Shamir in 1984 [177]. In his paper Shamir proposed the first identity-based signature scheme, but left the construction of an identity-based encryption scheme as an open problem. Seventeen years later, in 2001, an efficient solution was proposed by Boneh and Franklin. This solution made use of bilinear maps.

Since the original paper by Boneh and Franklin there have been many identity-based and, indeed, non-identity-based protocols based on pairings. In addition to IBE [45, 46], we also have many flavors of identity-based signatures [18, 57], key agreement schemes [59, 137], and, as we shall see in Chap. 10, identity-based signcryption schemes.

5.2 Bilinear Map Groups

Definition 5.1 Let k be a security parameter and p be a k-bit prime number. Let us consider groups $(\mathbb{G}_1, \mathbb{G}_2, \mathbb{G}_T)$ of order p and let g_1, g_2 be generators of $\mathbb{G}_1$ and $\mathbb{G}_2$, respectively. We say that $(\mathbb{G}_1, \mathbb{G}_2, \mathbb{G}_T)$ are *bilinear map groups* if there exists a bilinear map $e : \mathbb{G}_1 \times \mathbb{G}_2 \to \mathbb{G}_T$ with the following properties:

1. Bilinearity: $\forall (u, v) \in \mathbb{G}_1 \times \mathbb{G}_2 \; \forall a, b \in \mathbb{Z}$, we have $e(u^a, v^b) = e(u, v)^{ab}$.
2. Non-degeneracy: $\forall u \in \mathbb{G}_1, e(u, v) = 1 \; \forall v \in \mathbb{G}_2$ if and only if $u = 1_{\mathbb{G}_1}$.
3. Computability: $\forall (u, v) \in \mathbb{G}_1 \times \mathbb{G}_2, \; e(u, v)$ is efficiently computable.

In addition to the above general properties, the constructions described in this chapter additionally need an efficient, publicly computable (but not necessarily invertible) isomorphism $\psi : \mathbb{G}_2 \to \mathbb{G}_1$ such that $\psi(g_2) = g_1$. Many other pairing-based protocols (such as short signatures [47, 48]) require the availability of such an isomorphism, either in the implementation of schemes themselves or in their security proofs.

Such bilinear map groups are known to be instantiable with ordinary elliptic curves such as MNT curves [144] and the kind of curves studied by Barreto and Naehrig [20]. In practice, $\mathbb{G}_1$ is a p-order cyclic subgroup of such a curve $E(\mathbb{F}_r)$ while $\mathbb{G}_2$ is a subgroup of $E(\mathbb{F}_{r^\alpha})$, where α is the "embedding degree of the group" (i.e., the smallest integer α for which the order p of the group divides $r^\alpha - 1$). The group $\mathbb{G}_T$ is the set of p-th roots of unity in the finite field $\mathbb{F}_{r^\alpha}$. In this case, the trace map can be used as an efficient isomorphism ψ as long as $\mathbb{G}_2$ is properly chosen [183] within $E(\mathbb{F}_{r^\alpha})$.

The property of *computability* is ensured by Miller's famous algorithm [140, 141]—the detail of which is beyond the scope of this chapter. In p-order cyclic subgroups of curves of embedding degree α, the complexity of Miller's algorithm is dominated by $O(\log p)$ operations in the extension field $\mathbb{F}_{r^\alpha}$ containing the group $\mathbb{G}_T$. Computing a pairing is generally significantly more expensive than computing an elliptic curve scalar multiplication. Using a naïve implementation of Miller's algorithm, a pairing computation is more than α^2 times slower than a scalar multiplication on $E(\mathbb{F}_r)$. On the other hand, a recent paper by Scott [174] estimates that most optimized algorithms for an embedding degree $\alpha = 2$ end up with a running time which is from two to four times as long as an RSA decryption. Regardless, pairing-based cryptographic protocols usually strive to minimize the number of pairing calculations they involve.

Some specific cryptographic protocols require the use of symmetric pairings, where $\mathbb{G}_1 = \mathbb{G}_2$ and ψ is the identity mapping. Such symmetric pairings have the additional commutativity property: for any pair $u, v \in \mathbb{G}_1^2$, $e(u, v) = e(v, u)$. Admissible mappings of this kind can be derived from the Weil and Tate pairings using special endomorphisms called "distortion maps" [194] that are known to only exist on a particular kind of curve termed "supersingular" in the literature.[1] Supersingular curves may be more susceptible to attacks than ordinary curves. Indeed, several optimization tricks for them [17] require the use of fields of small characteristic. The problem is that the MOV and Frey–Rück reductions [82, 138] reduce the discrete logarithm problem over the elliptic curve to the discrete logarithm problem in a finite field, and the discrete logarithm problem in a finite field is much easier to solve in fields of small characteristic [65] than in fields of large characteristic and similar overall size. Since this threat is well known, it is usually thwarted by increasing field sizes to maintain a sufficient level of security. Therefore, protocols where bandwidth requirements have to be minimized (e.g., [47, 48]) usually avoid supersingular curves whenever possible.

5.3 Assumptions

The security of the first scheme described in this chapter relies on a natural variant of the Diffie–Hellman problem introduced in [47, 48].

Definition 5.2 The *co-Diffie–Hellman (co-CDH)* problem in bilinear map groups $(\mathbb{G}_1, \mathbb{G}_2)$ is to compute $g_1^{ab} \in \mathbb{G}_1$ given $(g_1, g_2, g_1^a, g_2^b) \in (\mathbb{G}_1 \times \mathbb{G}_2)^2$ for random values $a, b \xleftarrow{R} \mathbb{Z}_p^*$. The advantage of a co-CDH solver is defined as the probability of finding g_1^{ab} taken over the random choice of a, b and the solver's coin tosses. In the following, we call $\mathrm{Adv}^{co-CDH}(t, k)$ the maximal probability, taken over the random choice of $a, b \in \mathbb{Z}_p^*$ and the adversary's coin tosses, of solving a random co-CDH instance within time t when the security parameter is $k = \lfloor \log p \rfloor$.

The security properties of the second scheme described in the chapter rest on the intractability of the following problems introduced in [41, 42] which extend ideas from [143, 170].

Definition 5.3 Consider a set of bilinear map groups $(\mathbb{G}_1, \mathbb{G}_2, \mathbb{G}_T)$.

---

[1] In fact, a curve $E(\mathbb{F}_r)$ is said to be supersingular if its number of points $\#E(\mathbb{F}_r)$ is such that $t = r + 1 - \#E(\mathbb{F}_r)$ is a multiple of the characteristic of $\mathbb{F}_r$.

- The *q-Diffie–Hellman Inversion problem* (*q*-DHI) consists of computing the value $g_1^{1/x} \in \mathbb{G}_1$ given a tuple $(g_1, g_2, g_2^x, g_2^{(x^2)}, \ldots, g_2^{(x^q)}) \in \mathbb{G}_1 \times \mathbb{G}_2^{q+1}$ for a randomly drawn $x \xleftarrow{R} \mathbb{Z}_p^*$.
- The *q-Strong Diffie–Hellman problem* (*q*-SDH) consists of computing a pair $(c, g_1^{1/(x+c)}) \in \mathbb{Z}_p \times \mathbb{G}_1$, given elements $(g_1, g_2, g_2^x, g_2^{(x^2)}, \ldots, g_2^{(x^q)}) \in \mathbb{G}_1 \times \mathbb{G}_2^{q+1}$ for a random $x \xleftarrow{R} \mathbb{Z}_p^*$.

Again, the advantage of solvers is defined as their probability, taken over the random choice of x and their own coin tosses, of finding the appropriate group element. In the following, we denote by $\mathrm{Adv}^{q\text{-DHI}}(t, k)$ (resp. $\mathrm{Adv}^{q\text{-SDH}}(t, k)$) the maximal probability of solving a random q-DHI (resp. q-SDH) instance within time t when the security parameter is $k = \lfloor \log p \rfloor$.

It should be emphasized that the strength of these assumptions grows with the parameter q (which will be the number of random oracle queries allowed for adversaries in games modeling their security). Since this parameter must be reasonably large—the upper bound $q \approx 2^{60}$ is frequently used in the literature—for proofs to be meaningful, those assumptions are notably less trustworthy than the standard computational Diffie–Hellman assumption.

However, despite recent concerns [61] regarding the hardness of the above problems, it still seems reasonable to use this scheme with an appropriate adjustment of key size. For instance, $|p| \approx 256$ seems to suffice if we settle for a security level equivalent to AES implemented with 128-bit keys.

5.4 Signcryption for Anonymous Communications

The schemes that we present in this chapter are anonymous and have "detachable signatures." The term "detachable signature" means that the output of the unsigncryption algorithm is a plaintext and some authentication material that can be forwarded to third parties who can check its validity using publicly available information. This is clearly equivalent to the notion of non-interactive non-repudiation proposed by Malone-Lee and discussed in Sect. 4.6.2.

Similar to certain identity-based signcryption schemes [51, 60], the constructions described in this chapter are meant to provide anonymous ciphertexts which do not reveal information on the identity of their author or recipient, much in the fashion of *key-private* public key cryptosystems [21].

We therefore begin by presenting a new syntax for a signcryption scheme and new security definitions. In particular, we will assume that there exists a single key derivation algorithm, which produces keys that can be used for both signcryption and unsigncryption (see Sect. 3.2.3). We present models for confidentiality, unforgeability, and anonymity.

For our purposes, a signcryption scheme consists of tuple of algorithms (Setup, KeyGen, Signcrypt, Unsigncrypt, Verify). The syntax of the first three algorithms (Setup, KeyGen, Signcrypt) remain the same as before, except that the key generation algorithm KeyGen produces keys that can be used for both sign-cryption and unsigncryption. The unsigncryption algorithm takes as input a cipher-text C, a sender public key pk_S, and a receiver private key sk_R; it outputs either a message m and a detachable signature σ or an error symbol $\perp$. The verify algorithm is used to verify detached signatures. It takes as input a message m, a signature σ, and a receiver public key pk_R, and outputs either a valid symbol $\top$ or an invalid symbol $\perp$.

5.4.1 Message Privacy

The next definition captures message privacy: it is the equivalent of the multi-user insider confidentiality security model (FSO/FUO-IND-CCA2) presented in Sect. 3.2.1, except that we consider a single key generation algorithm.

Definition 5.4 We say that a signcryption scheme ensures *message privacy against chosen-ciphertext attacks* (we call this security notion insider FSO/FUO-IND-CCA2) if no PPT adversary has a non-negligible advantage in this game:

1. The challenger generates a private/public key pair (sk_U, pk_U). The private key sk_U is kept secret, while the public key pk_U is given to the adversary $\mathcal{A}$.
2. $\mathcal{A}$ first performs series of queries of the following kinds:

   - Signcryption queries: the adversary $\mathcal{A}$ produces a message $m \in \mathcal{M}$ and an arbitrary public key pk_R (which may differ from pk_U) and acquires the result $\mathtt{Signcrypt}(param, sk_U, pk_R, m)$.
   - Unsigncryption queries: $\mathcal{A}$ produces a ciphertext C, a sender's public key pk_S, and acquires the result of $\mathtt{Unsigncrypt}(param, pk_S, sk_U, C)$, which consists of a signed plaintext (m, σ) if the obtained signed plaintext is valid for the sender's public key pk_S and the $\perp$ symbol otherwise.

   These queries can be asked adaptively: each query may depend on the answers to previous ones. After a number of queries, $\mathcal{A}$ produces equal-length messages m_0, m_1 and an arbitrary private key sk_S.
3. The challenge flips a coin $b \xleftarrow{R} \{0, 1\}$ and computes the challenge signcryption $C \xleftarrow{R} \mathtt{Signcrypt}(param, sk_S, pk_U, m_b)$ of m_b with the sender's private key sk_S and the public key pk_U. The ciphertext C is given to $\mathcal{A}$.
4. $\mathcal{A}$ performs new queries as in step 2 but he/she may not ask for the unsigncryp-tion of the challenge ciphertext C with respect to the public key pk_S (i.e., the public key that corresponds to sk_S). At the end of the game, he/she outputs a bit b' and wins if $b' = b$.

$\mathcal{A}$'s advantage is defined to be $Adv_{\mathcal{A}}^{IND}(k) := |\Pr[b' = b] - 1/2|$.

5.4.2 Ciphertext Unforgeability and Signature Unforgeability

We define notions for message integrity (unforgeability). The main notion of unforgeability is the same as in Chap. 3 with the exception that it is suitable for signcryption schemes with a single key generation algorithm.

Definition 5.5 We say that a signcryption scheme is *strongly existentially ciphertext unforgeable* against insider chosen message attacks (FSO/FUO-sUF-CMA) if no PPT adversary $\mathcal{F}$ has a non-negligible advantage in the following game:

1. The challenger generates a key pair (sk_U, pk_U) and pk_U is given to the forger $\mathcal{F}$.
2. The forger $\mathcal{F}$ queries the signcryption and unsigncryption oracles in an adaptive fashion as in Definition 5.4.
3. $\mathcal{F}$ eventually outputs a ciphertext C and a key pair (sk_R, pk_R). The forger wins if the result $\texttt{Unsigncrypt}(param, pk_U, sk_R, C)$ is a pair (m, σ) such that (m, σ) is a valid signature with respect to the public key pk_U and C was not the output of a signcryption query $\texttt{Signcrypt}(param, sk_U, pk_R, m)$ during the game.

As in Sect. 3.2.2, the forger is allowed to have obtained the forged ciphertext as the result of a signcryption query for a different receiver's public key to which the one that the claimed forgery pertains.

Since we are concerned with specific constructions which allow receivers to extract authentication material (such as an ordinary digital signature) from a ciphertext and to forward it to a third party, non-repudiation with respect to this embedded authentication material may be sufficient in many contexts. This requirement is captured by the notion of *signature unforgeability* which was introduced for the first time by Boyen [51] and is recalled below.

Definition 5.6 A scheme is *existentially signature unforgeable* against chosen message attacks (or has the FSO/FUO-ESUF-CMA security) if no PPT adversary $\mathcal{F}$ has a non-negligible advantage against a challenger in this game:

1. The challenger generates a key pair (sk_U, pk_U) and pk_U is given to the forger $\mathcal{F}$.
2. $\mathcal{F}$ adaptively performs a series of queries to the signcryption and unsigncryption oracles as in Definition 5.4.
3. $\mathcal{F}$ outputs a ciphertext C and a key pair (sk_R, pk_R) and wins if the result of $\texttt{Unsigncrypt}(param, pk_U, sk_R, C)$ is a pair (m, σ) such that the pair (m, σ) is valid with respect to the public key pk_U and no signcryption query involving the message m and some receiver's public key pk'_R resulted in a ciphertext C' for which the output of $\texttt{Unsigncrypt}(param, pk_U, sk'_R, C')$ is (m, σ).

Of course, considering non-repudiation with respect to underlying signatures (instead of ciphertexts) only makes sense for schemes where the receiver extracts a signature from the ciphertext.

A potential incentive to settle for signature unforgeability is that it may reduce the amount of data that receivers have to forward to third parties coping with non-repudiation disputes. For instance, the scheme described in Sect. 5.6 allows receivers to extract short signatures from ciphertexts.

In settings where signature unforgeability suffices, a complementary notion was also introduced in [51]. It was called *ciphertext authentication* and assures that a receiver is always convinced that a ciphertext was jointly signed and encrypted by the same person and was not subject to a kind of man-in-the-middle attack. The resulting model shares many similarities with the multi-user outsider unforgeability model described in Sect. 3.2.2, with the exception that it only applies to signcryption schemes with one key generation algorithm.

Definition 5.7 A signcryption scheme has the *ciphertext authentication* property (FSO/FUO-AUTH-CMA) if no PPT adversary $\mathcal{F}$ has a non-negligible advantage in the next game:

1. The challenger generates two key pairs (sk_S, pk_S) and (sk_R, pk_R); pk_S and pk_R are given to the forger.
2. The forger $\mathcal{F}$ performs queries to the signcryption oracles Signcrypt($param$, $sk_U, \cdot, \cdot$) and the unsigncryption Unsigncrypt($param$, $\cdot, pk_U, \cdot$), for both $U = S$ and $U = R$, as in previous definitions.
3. $\mathcal{F}$ produces a ciphertext C and wins if the result of Unsigncrypt($param$, pk_S, sk_R, C) is a pair (m, σ) such that (m, σ) is a valid signature for the public key pk_S and no signcryption query involving the message m and the receiver's public key pk_R produced in the ciphertext C.

We emphasize that the latter definition is only useful in complement to the signature unforgeability property. These properties should not be considered if one is merely concerned with the ciphertext unforgeability in the sense of Definition 5.5.

5.4.3 Anonymity

In [51], Boyen suggested other security properties for signcryption schemes. One of them was called *ciphertext anonymity* and can be thought of as extending the notion of *key privacy* as considered by Bellare et al. [21] for public key encryption schemes. Intuitively, a public key encryption scheme is anonymous if ciphertexts convey no information about the public key that was used to create them.

In the signcryption setting, the ciphertext anonymity property is satisfied if ciphertexts reveal no information about who created them nor about whom they are intended to. This intuition is captured by the definition below which transposes the one given in [51] to a traditional public key setting.

Definition 5.8 A signcryption scheme is said to be *ciphertext anonymous* (FSO/FUO-ANON-CCA) if no PPT distinguisher $\mathcal{D}$ has a non-negligible advantage in the following game:

1. The challenger generates two distinct key pairs (sk_{R_0}, pk_{R_0}) and (sk_{R_1}, pk_{R_1}). The distinguisher $\mathcal{D}$ is provided with pk_{R_0} and pk_{R_1}.
2. $\mathcal{D}$ adaptively performs queries to the signcryption and unsigncryption oracles for the key pairs (sk_{R_0}, pk_{R_0}) and (sk_{R_1}, pk_{R_1}) as in previous definitions. $\mathcal{D}$ eventually outputs two private keys sk_{S_0} and sk_{S_1} and a plaintext m.

3. The challenger then flips coins $b, b' \xleftarrow{R} \{0, 1\}$ and computes a challenge cipher-text $C \xleftarrow{R} \mathrm{Signcrypt}(param, sk_{S_b}, pk_{R_{b'}}, m)$.
4. $\mathcal{D}$ adaptively issues new queries as in step 2 with the restriction that $\mathcal{D}$ may not ask for the unsigncryption of pairs (C, pk_{S_j}), where $j \in \{0, 1\}$ and C is the challenge ciphertext, under either of the private keys sk_{R_0} or sk_{R_1}. Eventually, $\mathcal{D}$ outputs bits d, d' and wins if $(d, d') = (b, b')$.

The adversary's advantage is defined as $Adv_{\mathcal{D}}^{ANON}(k) := |\mathrm{Pr}[(d, d') = (b, b')] - \frac{1}{4}|$.

Again, this notion captures the security against insider attacks as the distinguisher is allowed to choose a pair of private keys among which the one used to create the challenge ciphertext is picked by the challenger.

5.5 A Tightly Secure Scheme

This section describes a signcryption scheme whose security is tightly related to the hardness of a natural variant of the Diffie–Hellman problem in bilinear map groups. It was originally proposed, in a slightly modified form, by Libert and Quisquater [123]. This method relies on the digital signature algorithm of Boneh et al. [47, 48]. In this scheme, private keys consist of an integer $x \in \mathbb{Z}_p^*$ and public keys consist of a group element $Y = g_2^x \in \mathbb{G}_2$. A signature on a message m has the shape $\sigma = H(m)^x \in \mathbb{G}_1$ (where the hash function H maps arbitrary mes-sages onto the cyclic group $\mathbb{G}_1$). This signature can be verified by checking that $e(\sigma, g_2) = e(H(m), Y)$. In order to enhance the concrete security of the reduc-tion in the proof of ciphertext unforgeability, a random quantity U that is used for encryption purposes also acts as a random salt to provide a tighter security reduction in the random oracle model [29].

The scheme may be viewed as a composition of a digital signature scheme which is existentially unforgeable against chosen message attacks (UF-CMA) [91] with a public key encryption scheme that is only secure against chosen plaintext attacks. In [10], it was already observed in the outsider security model that a sequential com-position in the "sign-then-encrypt" order can amplify rather than simply preserve the security properties of the underlying building blocks—see Theorem 2.3. This construction gives another example showing that a CCA-secure signcryption system (in the sense of Definition 5.4) may be obtained from weaker building blocks. Here, in some sense, the redundancies needed to achieve CCA security are embedded in the signature.

5.5.1 The Scheme

For the security of the scheme depicted in Fig. 5.1, it is crucial that the underlying symmetric encryption scheme be deterministic and one-to-one: for a given plaintext and symmetric key, there should be a single possible ciphertext. If it were possible

Setup(1^k)
  Pick a set of bilinear map groups
    $(\mathbb{G}_1, \mathbb{G}_2, \mathbb{G}_T)$ whose order is a prime
    p such that $2^{k-1} < p < 2^k$ and
    generators $(g_1, g_2) \in \mathbb{G}_1 \times \mathbb{G}_2$
    such that $g_1 = \psi(g_2)$
  Let ℓ_1 be the bitlength of elements of $\mathbb{G}_1$
  Choose an one-time symmetric-key
    encryption scheme $SE = (\text{Enc}, \text{Dec})$
    with key space $\mathcal{K}$ and ciphertext space $\mathcal{C}$
  Pick cryptographic hash functions:
    $H_1 : \{0,1\}^* \to \mathbb{G}_1^*$
    $H_2 : \mathbb{G}_1^2 \to \{0,1\}^{\ell_1}$
    $H_3 : \mathbb{G}_1^3 \to \mathcal{K}$
  $param \leftarrow (\mathbb{G}_1, \mathbb{G}_2, \mathbb{G}_T, p,$
                    $g_1, g_2, SE, H_1, H_2, H_3, \ell_1)$
  Return $param$

KeyGen($param$)
  $x_U \xleftarrow{R} \mathbb{Z}_p^*; y_U \leftarrow g_2^{x_U}$
  $sk_U \leftarrow x_U; pk_U \leftarrow y_U$
  Return (sk_U, pk_U)

Signcrypt(m, sk_S, pk_R)
  Parse sk_S as (x_S, y_S); Parse pk_R as y_R
  If $y_S, y_R \notin \mathbb{G}_2 \setminus \{1\}$ then return $\perp$
  $r \xleftarrow{R} \mathbb{Z}_p^*; u \leftarrow g_1^r$
  $v \leftarrow H_1(m\|u\|pk_S\|pk_R)^{x_S}$
  $w \leftarrow v \oplus H_2(u\|\psi(y_R)^r)$
  $\tau \leftarrow H_3(u\|v\|\psi(y_R)^r)$
  $z \leftarrow \text{Enc}_\tau(m)$
  $C \leftarrow (u, w, z)$
  Return C

Unsigncrypt(C, pk_S, sk_R):
  Parse pk_S as y_S; Parse sk_R as (x_R, y_R)
  If $y_S, y_R \notin \mathbb{G}_2 \setminus \{1\}$ then return $\perp$
  Parse C as (u, w, z)
  If $u \notin \mathbb{G}_1$ or $w \notin \{0,1\}^{\ell_1}$ or $z \notin \mathcal{C}$
    Return $\perp$
  $v \leftarrow w \oplus H_2(u\|u^{x_R})$
  If $v \notin \mathbb{G}_1$ then return $\perp$
  $\tau \leftarrow H_3(u\|v\|u^{x_R})$
  $m \leftarrow \text{Dec}_\tau(z)$
  If $e(v, g_2) \neq e(H_1(m\|u\|pk_S\|pk_R), y_S)$
    Return $\perp$
  Return (m, pk_R, v, u)

Fig. 5.1 The co-CDH-based scheme

to compute another encryption of the same plaintext m given $c = \text{Enc}(m)$, it would be possible to generate another ciphertext (u, w, z') given (u, w, z) and thus defeat the chosen ciphertext security of the whole scheme.

The receiver has to forward m, v, pk_R, and u to a third party to convince her that the message actually comes from the sender. Together with u and pk_R, the value v acts as a "detachable signature" that the receiver can extract from the ciphertext and transmit it to third parties. This signature is verified by checking that $e(v, g_2) = e(H_1(m\|u\|pk_S\|pk_R), y_S)$.

We note that the recipient's public key must be hashed together with the pair (m, u) in order to achieve the *strong* unforgeability according to Definition 5.5.

5.5.2 Efficiency

Three exponentiations in $\mathbb{G}_1$ are required in the signcryption algorithm, while one multiplication and two pairings must be performed at unsigncryption. The scheme is at least as efficient and more compact than most sequential compositions of the BLS signature [47, 48] with any CCA-secure Diffie–Hellman-based encryption scheme [11, 14, 68, 83, 84, 161, 181]. For example, a sequential combination of the BLS signature scheme [47, 48] with an ElGamal [81] encryption padded with the Fujisaki–Okamoto conversion [83] would involve an additional exponentiation at decryption because of the "re-encryption phase" which checks the validity of the ciphertext. With $\ell_1 \approx k \geq 171$, this construction saves about 171 bits of overhead (i.e., the difference between ciphertext and plaintext sizes) with respect to a composition of the BLS signature scheme with Fujisaki–Okamoto/ElGamal.

The scheme looks like a sequential composition of the BLS signature scheme [47, 48] with the hybrid KEM/DEM ElGamal encryption scheme proven secure by Cramer and Shoup [68]. Actually, the hybrid ElGamal scheme *must* be implemented with an IND-CCA2 symmetric encryption while the above system only needs a symmetric scheme that meets the very weak requirement of being semantically secure against passive attacks (that is an attack where the adversary has no encryption or decryption oracle in an indistinguishability scenario). Here, for fixed-length messages, the symmetric encryption could simply be a "one-time pad" of the message with a hash value of $u \| v \| \psi(Y_R)^r$.

5.5.3 Security

The original version [123] of this system (where τ was obtained by hashing v alone) was found [186, 198] not to meet its intended security properties. Although a chosen ciphertext attack was also given [187] against the modification suggested in [198], its variant detailed in Fig. 5.1 is immune to these attacks (and the countermeasures do not incur any significant additional cost).

The scheme is proven secure in the random oracle model (with a tight reduction) assuming the hardness of the co-CDH problem. The proof of the next theorem features a tight reduction to the co-CDH problem using the property (pointed out for the first time in [111] for a specific kind of pairing-friendly groups) that its decisional counterpart is easy: it can be easily tested whether a given tuple $(g_1, g_2, g_1^a, g_2^b) \in (\mathbb{G}_1 \times \mathbb{G}_2)^2$ satisfies $a = b$ by checking if $e(g_1, g_2^b) = e(g_1^a, g_2)$.

Theorem 5.1 *The scheme is FSO/FUO-IND-CCA2 secure in the random oracle model assuming that the co-CDH problem is hard and that the symmetric encryption scheme is IND-CPA secure. For any adversary $\mathcal{A}$ running in time t_A and making at most q_{sc} signcryption queries, q_{usc} unsigncryption queries, and q_{H_i} queries to random oracles H_i ($i = 1, 2, 3$), we have*

$$\mathrm{Adv}_{\mathcal{A}}(t_A, k) \leq \frac{q_{usc}}{2^{k-2}} + \mathrm{Adv}_{\mathcal{B}}^{co\text{-}CDH}(t', k) + \mathrm{Adv}_{\mathcal{B}}^{ind\text{-}cpa\text{-}sym}(t', |\mathcal{K}|)$$

where

- *$\mathrm{Adv}_{\mathcal{B}}^{co\text{-}CDH}(t', k)$ stands for the maximal probability of solving the co-CDH problem in time $t' \leq t_A + O(q_{usc} + q_{H_2} + q_{H_3})t_p + O(q_{H_1})t_{exp}$ when the security parameter is k and t_p, t_{exp} stand for the time complexity of a pairing evaluation and an exponentiation, respectively.*

-   $\text{Adv}_{\mathcal{B}}^{ind\text{-}cpa\text{-}sym}(t', |\mathcal{K}|)$ is the maximal advantage[2] of any adversary mounting a chosen plaintext attack on (Enc, Dec) within time t' when the key size is $|\mathcal{K}|$.

Proof The proof consists of a sequence of games where the first game is the real attack game, and in the last game the adversary is essentially a passive attacker against the symmetric encryption scheme (Enc, Dec). In the sequence, the event that the adversary $\mathcal{A}$ wins in Game i is denoted S_i.

Game 1 is the real attack game detailed in Definition 5.4. The adversary is given public parameters comprising $g_2 \in \mathbb{G}_2$ and $g_1 = \psi(g_2)$ and the receiver's public key is defined as $pk_u = g_2^b \in \mathbb{G}_2$ for some random $b \xleftarrow{R} \mathbb{Z}_p^*$ chosen by the simulator $\mathcal{B}$. The latter uses $sk_U = b$ to answer all signcryption/unsigncryption queries. Random oracle queries are dealt with in the standard way, by returning random values in the appropriate range. To maintain consistency and return identical outputs if the same random oracle query is made more than once, $\mathcal{B}$ keeps track of all these queries and their outputs in lists L_1, L_2, and L_3. In the challenge phase, $\mathcal{A}$ outputs a pair of messages m_0, m_1 and a sender's private key $sk_S^* = x_S^*$. The simulator $\mathcal{B}$ flips a fair coin $d \xleftarrow{R} \{0, 1\}$. It also chooses a random exponent $a \xleftarrow{R} \mathbb{Z}_p^*$ and successively computes ciphertext elements $u^* = g_1^a$, $v^* = H_1(m_d \| u^* \| g_2^{x_S^*} \| pk_u)^{x_S^*}$, $w^* = v^* \oplus H_2(u^* \| \psi(pk_u)^a)$, $\tau^* = H_3(u^* \| v^* \| \psi(pk_u)^a)$, and $z^* = \text{Enc}_{\tau^*}(m_d)$. The challenge ciphertext (u^*, w^*, z^*) is given to $\mathcal{A}$ who eventually outputs a bit d' and wins if $d' = d$. The adversary $\mathcal{A}$'s advantage is thus $|\Pr[S_1] - 1/2|$.

Game 2: In this game, the first ciphertext component $u^* = g_1^a$ is calculated at the beginning of the game. This change is purely conceptual and $\Pr[S_2] = \Pr[S_1]$.

Game 3 is the same as Game 2 but the simulator $\mathcal{B}$ aborts if the adversary ever queries the unsigncryption of a ciphertext (u, w, z) such that $u = u^* = g_1^a$ *before* the challenge phase. We call F_3 the latter event. Game 3 and Game 2 are clearly identical until it occurs and we have $|\Pr[S_3] - \Pr[S_2]| \le \Pr[F_3]$. Since u^* is independent of $\mathcal{A}$'s view until the challenge phase, we have $\Pr[F_3] \le q_{usc}/p \le q_{usc}/2^{k-1}$ so that $|\Pr[S_3] - \Pr[S_2]| \le q_{usc}/2^{k-1}$.

Game 4: We modify the treatment of random oracle queries as well as that of signcryption/unsigncryption queries. A difference with earlier games is that H_2 and H_3 queries are now handled using four lists L_2, L_2' and L_3, L_3'.

-   H_1 queries: If a hash query $H_1(m_i \| u_i \| pk_{S,i} \| pk_{R,i})$ is made, $\mathcal{B}$ first checks if the value of H_1 was previously defined for that input. If it was, the previously defined hash value $h_{1,i}$ is returned. Otherwise, $\mathcal{B}$ picks a random $t_i \xleftarrow{R} \mathbb{Z}_p^*$, returns $h_{1,i} \leftarrow g_1^{t_i} \in \mathbb{G}_1$, and inserts the tuple $(m_i, u_i, pk_{S,i}, pk_{R,i}, t_i)$ into L_1.
-   H_2 queries: If a hash query $H_2(u_i \| R_i)$ is made, for inputs $(u_i, R_i) \in \mathbb{G}_1^2$, $\mathcal{B}$ first scans list L_2 to see if there exists a record $(u_i, R_i, h_{2,i}, \beta)$ for some

---

[2] This advantage is usually defined as $|\Pr[d = d'] - 1/2|$ when the adversary chooses a pair equal-length plaintexts m_0, m_1, obtains $c = \text{Enc}_\tau(m_d)$ for a random key $\tau \xleftarrow{R} \mathcal{K}$ and a randomly drawn bit $d \xleftarrow{R} \{0, 1\}$, and outputs $d' \in \{0, 1\}$.

bit β. If so, the previously defined value $h_{2,i}$ is returned. Otherwise, $\mathcal{B}$ checks if (g_2, u_i, pk_u, R_i) is a valid co-Diffie–Hellman tuple (in our notation, we write $R_i = \text{co-DH}_{g_2}(u_i, pk_u)$) by checking whether $e(R_i, g_2) = e(u_i, pk_u)$.

- If yes, then $\mathcal{B}$ checks if L'_2 contains an entry of the shape $(u_i, ?, h_{2,i})$ for some string $h_{2,i} \in \{0, 1\}^{\ell_1}$. If yes, $h_{2,i}$ is returned and a record $(u_i, R_i, h_{2,i}, 1)$ is stored in L_2. If no entry $(u_i, ?, h_{2,i})$ exists in L'_2, $\mathcal{B}$ returns a random string $h_{2,i} \xleftarrow{R} \{0, 1\}^{\ell_1}$ and inserts $(u_i, R_i, h_{2,i}, 1)$ in L_2.
- If (g_2, u_i, pk_u, R_i) is not a co-DH tuple, $\mathcal{B}$ picks $h_{2,i} \xleftarrow{R} \{0, 1\}^{\ell_1}$ at random and stores the tuple $(u_i, R_i, h_{2,i}, 0)$ in L_2.

- H_3 queries: If a hash query $H_3(u_i \| v_i \| R_i)$ is made, then $\mathcal{B}$ proceeds as for answering H_2 queries, using lists L_3 and L'_3 to maintain the consistency and checking if (g_2, u_i, pk_u, R_i) is a co-Diffie–Hellman tuple, namely, L_3 contains entries of the form $(u_i, v_i, R_i, h_{3,i}, \beta)$, with $\beta \in \{0, 1\}$. If $\beta = 1$, then $H_3(u_i \| v_i \| R_i) = h_{3,i}$ and it holds that $R_i = \text{co-DH}_{g_2}(u_i, pk_u)$. If $\beta = 0$, then $H_3(u_i \| v_i \| R_i) = h_{3,i}$ and $R_i \neq \text{co-DH}_{g_2}(u_i, pk_u)$. The auxiliary list L'_3 contains entries $(u_i, v_i, ?, h_{3,i})$ such that a subsequent query $H_3(u_i \| v_i \| R_i)$ for which $R_i = \text{co-DH}_{g_2}(u_i, pk_u)$ should receive the answer $h_{3,i} \in \mathcal{K}$.
- Signcryption queries: If a signcryption query on a plaintext m and a recipient's public key pk_R is made, then $\mathcal{B}$ picks a random $r \xleftarrow{R} \mathbb{Z}_p^*$, computes $u = g_1^r \in \mathbb{G}_1$, and checks if L_1 contains a tuple (m, u, pk_u, pk_R, t) indicating that $h_1(m \| u \| pk_u \| pk_R)$ was previously set to be g_1^t. If no such tuple is found, $\mathcal{B}$ picks $t \xleftarrow{R} \mathbb{Z}_p^*$ and stores the entry (m, u, pk_u, pk_R, t) in L_1. It then computes $v = \psi(pk_u)^t = (g_1^b)^t \in \mathbb{G}_1$. The rest follows as in the signcryption process: $\mathcal{B}$ computes $\psi(pk_R)^r$ (for the pk_R specified by the adversary), simulates H_2 and H_3 to obtain $h_2 = H_2(u \| \psi(pk_R)^r)$ and $\tau = H_3(u \| v \| \psi(pk_R)^r)$, and then computes $w = v \oplus h_2$ and $z = \text{Enc}_\tau(m)$. The ciphertext (u, w, z) is returned to $\mathcal{A}$.
- Unsigncryption queries: For an unsigncryption query on a ciphertext $C = (u, w, z)$ and a sender's public key $pk_S \in \mathbb{G}_2$, $\mathcal{B}$ checks if list L_2 contains the sole possible tuple $(u, R, h_2, 1)$ for some $R \in \mathbb{G}_1$ and $h_2 \in \{0, 1\}^{\ell_1}$ (meaning that $R = \text{co-DH}_{g_2}(u, pk_u)$ and that $H_2(u \| R)$ was set to $h_2 \in \{0, 1\}^{\ell_1}$):

  - If such an entry exists, $\mathcal{B}$ obtains $v = w \oplus h_2$ and rejects C if $v \notin \mathbb{G}_1$. Otherwise, $\mathcal{B}$ obtains the secret key $\tau = H_3(u \| v \| R) \in \mathcal{K}$ (by simulating H_3) and sets $m = \text{Dec}_\tau(z)$. Then, $\mathcal{B}$ computes $H = H_1(m \| u \| pk_S \| pk_u) \in \mathbb{G}_1$ (by simulating H_1) and checks whether $e(v, g_2) = e(H, pk_S)$. If so, the information (m, pk_u, v, u) is returned. Otherwise, C is rejected.
  - If such an entry does not exist, then $\mathcal{B}$ checks if L'_2 contains an entry $(u, ?, h_2)$. If such an entry does not exist either, then $\mathcal{B}$ chooses $h_2 \xleftarrow{R} \{0, 1\}^{\ell_1}$ and stores $(u, ?, h_2)$ in L'_2, so as to preserve consistency and answer h_2 to a subsequent H_2 query on the input $u \| \text{co-DH}_{g_2}(u, pk_u)$. In either case, $\mathcal{B}$ obtains the h_2 value. It sets $v = w \oplus h_2 \in \{0, 1\}^{\ell_1}$ and rejects C if $v \notin \mathbb{G}_1$. Then, $\mathcal{B}$ scans lists L_3 and L'_3, in search for an entries of the shape $(u, v, R, \tau, 1)$

and $(u, v, ?, \tau)$, respectively. If no such entries exist, $\mathcal{B}$ picks $\tau \overset{R}{\leftarrow} \mathcal{K}$ at random and inserts a record $(u, v, ?, \tau)$ in L_3' to make sure that a future hash query $H_3(u\|v\|\text{co-DH}_{g_2}(u, pk_u))$ will get the answer τ. Finally, $\mathcal{B}$ computes $m = \text{Dec}_\tau(z)$. The ciphertext C is declared invalid if $e(v, g_2) \neq e(H, pk_S)$ where $H = H_1(m\|u\|pk_S\|pk_u)$. If the ciphertext is deemed valid, $\mathcal{A}$ is returned the information (m, pk_u, v, u).

It can be checked that the above simulation of the various oracles is consistent and $\mathcal{A}$'s view is not altered by these changes. It comes that $\Pr[S_4] = \Pr[S_3]$. We also note that the private key $sk_U = b$ is not explicitly used to answer signcryption or unsigncryption queries.

Game 5 modifies the way to answer unsigncryption queries and add a special rule that applies to *post-challenge* unsigncryption queries, namely, if $\mathcal{A}$ queries the unsigncryption of a ciphertext (u, w, z) such that $(u, w) = (u^*, w^*)$ after the challenge phase, $\mathcal{B}$ returns $\bot$. Two situations must be distinguished to see that this change does not significantly alter $\mathcal{A}$'s view.

- If the query pertains to the same sender's public key as in the challenge phase (i.e., $pk_S = pk_S^*$), we necessarily have $z \neq z^*$ (as the query is illegal otherwise). For such a ciphertext, the underlying $v = w^* \oplus H_2(u^*\|u^{*b})$ must be the same as the value v^* calculated in the challenge phase. Also, the same symmetric key $\tau^* = H_3(u^*\|v^*\|u^{*b})$ must be used to decipher z when the unsigncryption operation is carried out normally. Since $z \neq z^*$ and given that the encryption/decryption algorithms (Enc, Dec) are bijections, the plaintext $m = \text{Dec}_{\tau^*}(z)$ must be different from the plaintext m_d that was encrypted in the challenge phase. Hence, unless we have a collision $H_1(m\|u^*\|pk_S^*\|pk_u) = H_1(m_d\|u^*\|pk_S^*\|pk_u)$ (which occurs with probability smaller than $1/|p| < 1/2^{k-1}$ when H_1 is modeled as a random oracle), v^* cannot be a valid signature for the message $m\|u^*\|pk_S^*\|pk_u$ and the unsigncryption algorithm would certainly reject it.
- If the query is made for a different sender $pk_S \neq pk_S^*$ (and we may thus have $z = z^*$ or not), the unsigncryption algorithm would still reveal the same v^* as in the challenge phase and the same symmetric key $\tau^* = H_3(u^*\|v^*\|u^{*b})$ would be used to decipher z. If we denote by $m = \text{Dec}_{\tau^*}(z)$ the symmetric decryption of z under the key τ^*, the ciphertext (u^*, w^*, z) would only be accepted in earlier games in the event that $H_1(m_d\|u^*\|pk_S^*\|pk_u)^{sk_S^*} = H_1(m\|u^*\|pk_S\|pk_u)^{\log_g(pk_S)}$ (i.e., if the outputs of the random oracle H_1 are correlated in a very specific way for two different inputs). Since we are working in the random oracle model, this situation only occurs with probability $1/p < 1/2^{k-1}$.

Throughout all queries, the overall probability that the new rule causes $\mathcal{B}$ to reject a ciphertext that would have been deemed valid in earlier games is at most $q_{usc}/2^{k-1}$. We thus have $|\Pr[S_5] - \Pr[S_4]| \leq q_{usc}/2^{k-1}$.

Game 6 makes some last changes to the simulation. First, we modify the generation of the challenge ciphertext (u^*, w^*, z^*). The first element u^* is still set as $u_1^* = g_1^a$ ($\mathcal{B}$ does not explicitly know a—only g_1^a) but $w^* \xleftarrow{R} \{0, 1\}^{\ell_1}$ is now chosen at random and z^* is generated as an encryption $z^* = \mathrm{Enc}_{\tau^*}(m_d)$ under a perfectly random key $\tau^* \xleftarrow{R} \mathcal{K}$. The other change is that we define an event E and let the simulator halt if it ever occurs. Event E is the occurrence of one of the following situations.

E.1 $\mathcal{A}$ queries oracle H_2 on the input $(u^* \| R)$ such that $R = \mathrm{co\text{-}DH}_{g_2}(u^*, pk_u)$.
E.2 $\mathcal{A}$ queries oracle H_3 on an input $(u^* \| . \| R)$ such that $R = \mathrm{co\text{-}DH}_{g_2}(u^*, pk_u)$.

We see that $\mathcal{B}$ is able to detect occurrences of E.1 and E.2, which both reveal the value $R = \mathrm{co\text{-}DH}_{g_2}(g_1^a, g_2^b) = g_1^{ab}$. Since $\mathcal{B}$ never knows exponents a or b, it would solve an instance of the co-CDH problem if E.1 $\vee$ E.2 happens. We thus have $\Pr[E.1 \vee E.2] \leq \mathrm{Adv}_{\mathcal{B}}^{co\text{-}CDH}(t', k)$, where $t' \leq t_A + O(q_{usc} + q_{H_2} + q_{H_3})t_p + O(q_{H_1})t_{exp}$ is an upper bound on $\mathcal{B}$'s computation time that takes into account the unsigncryption queries as well as H_2 and H_3 queries, each requiring two pairing evaluations.

If event E does not occur, the symmetric key τ^* is completely independent of $\mathcal{A}$'s view. Guessing $d \in \{0, 1\}$ then amounts to carry out a chosen plaintext attack on the symmetric encryption scheme (Enc, Dec). Indeed, the only way for $\mathcal{A}$ to observe symmetric decryptions under τ^* would be to query the unsigncryption of ciphertexts of the shape (u^*, w^*, z). Such ciphertexts are precisely rejected by the oracle due to the rules introduced in Game 3 and Game 5. It comes that $|\Pr[S_6] - 1/2| = \mathrm{Adv}_{\mathcal{B}}^{ind\text{-}cpa\text{-}sym}(t')$. $\square$

We observe that the reduction is very tight. Up to negligible terms and assuming that $\mathrm{Adv}_{\mathcal{B}}^{ind\text{-}cpa\text{-}sym}(t')$ is negligible, algorithm $\mathcal{B}$ has the essentially same probability to solve the co-CDH problem as the adversary's advantage in breaking the scheme. The cost of the reduction is also bounded by an expression which is linear in the number of adversarial queries. That is the reason why u is included among the arguments of H_2. The scheme remains secure if v is concealed by a hash value of $\psi(pk_R)^r$ alone but the reduction entails a number of pairing evaluations that are quadratic in the number of adversarial queries.

Having a tight reduction to a computational problem is a notable feature of the scheme. It contrasts with other Diffie–Hellman-based constructions which are also CCA secure under tight reductions but rely on gap assumptions involving oracles that do not exist. This can be lifted by implementing those schemes over pairing-friendly groups (where some gap problems become equivalent to computational problems) but most of them keep relatively loose reductions with respect to unforgeability (the only notable exception being Bjørstad and Dent's CM scheme [37] discussed in Sect. 4.7). In the present system, the reductions are also efficient in the proof of ciphertext unforgeability.

Theorem 5.2 *Assume that an adversary* $\mathcal{F}$ *has advantage* $\mathrm{Adv}_{\mathcal{F}}(t, k)$ *over the FSO/FUO-sUF-CMA security of the scheme when running in time* t, *making* q_{sc}

signcryption queries, q_{usc} unsigncryption queries, and q_{H_i} queries on random oracles H_i (for $i = 1, 2, 3$). Then, there is an algorithm $\mathcal{B}$ which solves the co-CDH problem in $(\mathbb{G}_1, \mathbb{G}_2)$ with probability

$$\mathrm{Adv}_{\mathcal{B}}^{co\text{-}CDH}(t', k) \geq \mathrm{Adv}_{\mathcal{F}}(t, k) - \frac{q_{sc}(q_{H_1} + q_{sc} + q_{usc}) + 1}{2^{k-1}}$$

and within running time $t' \leq t + O(q_{H_2} + q_{H_3} + q_{usc})t_p + O(q_{sc})t_{exp}$, where t_p and t_{exp} stand for the time required for a pairing evaluation and an exponentiation in $\mathbb{G}_1$.

Proof The simulator $\mathcal{B}$ receives a random co-Diffie–Hellman instance (g_1^a, g_2^b). It uses $\mathcal{F}$ as a subroutine to solve that instance and plays the role of $\mathcal{F}$'s challenger. The forger $\mathcal{F}$ is initialized with the input $pk_u = g_2^b$ and performs adaptive queries that are handled by $\mathcal{B}$ as explained below (using lists as in the proof of Theorem 5.1):

- H_1 queries: If a hash query on a tuple $m \| u \| pk_S \| pk_R$ is made, then $\mathcal{B}$ checks to see if the latter was previously queried. If so, then $\mathcal{B}$ returns the same value. For a query on a new tuple $m \| u \| pk_S \| pk_R$, $\mathcal{B}$ picks $t \xleftarrow{R} \mathbb{Z}_q^*$ and defines $H_1(m \| u \| pk_S \| pk_R) = (g_1^a)^t \in \mathbb{G}_1$. The list L_1 is updated accordingly.
- H_2 queries and H_3 queries are dealt with as in Game 4, the proof of Theorem 5.1.
- Signcryption queries: If a signcryption query on a message m and a receiver's public key pk_R is made, $\mathcal{B}$ picks $r \xleftarrow{R} \mathbb{Z}_p^*$ and computes $u = g_1^r \in \mathbb{G}_1$. If H_1 is already defined on $m \| u \| pk_u \| pk_R$, $\mathcal{B}$ declares "failure" and halts. Otherwise, $\mathcal{B}$ picks $t \xleftarrow{R} \mathbb{Z}_p^*$, sets $H_1(m \| u \| pk_u \| pk_R) = g_1^t \in \mathbb{G}_1$, and updates L_1 accordingly. It then computes $v = \psi(pk_u)^t \in \mathbb{G}_1$, $h_2 = H_2(u \| \psi(pk_R)^r) \in \{0, 1\}^{\ell_1}$, $w = v \oplus h_2$, $\tau = H_3(u \| v \| \psi(pk_R)^r) \in \mathcal{K}$, and $z = \mathrm{Enc}_\tau(m) \in \mathcal{C}$. The ciphertext (u, w, z) is then returned to $\mathcal{F}$.
- Unsigncryption queries are handled exactly as in the proof of Theorem 5.1.

At the end of the game, $\mathcal{F}$ produces a ciphertext (u^*, w^*, z^*) and a recipient's public/private key pair (sk_R^*, pk_R^*). At that moment, $\mathcal{B}$ can unsigncrypt the ciphertext using sk_R^* and, if the ciphertext is a valid forgery for the sender's public key pk_u, $\mathcal{B}$ can extract the message m^* and the signature v^*. If the hash value $H_1(m^* \| u^* \| pk_u \| pk_R^*)$ was not explicitly defined by a query to the H_1 oracle during the simulation, then $\mathcal{B}$ reports "failure" and stops. Otherwise, $\mathcal{B}$ can extract v^* and the hash value $H_1(m^* \| u^* \| pk_u \| pk_R^*)$ must have been defined to be $(g_1^a)^{t^*}$, for some known $t^* \in \mathbb{Z}_p^*$. This implies that v^* must be equal to $(g_1^{ab})^{t^*}$, which yields the co-Diffie–Hellman value.

It is easy to see that the probability for $\mathcal{B}$ to fail in answering a signcryption query is not greater than $q_{sc}(q_{H_1} + q_{sc} + q_{usc})/p \leq q_{sc}(q_{H_1} + q_{sc} + q_{usc})/2^{k-1}$ (since at each signcryption query, there is at most $q_{H_1} + q_{sc} + q_{usc}$ elements in L_1). The probability that $\mathcal{F}$ succeeds without explicitly making the $H_1(m^* \| u^* \| pk_u \| pk_R^*)$ query can be bounded by considering the following three possibilities:

- If the value of $H_1(m^* \| u^* \| pk_u \| pk_R^*)$ is undefined by the simulation, then the probability that $\mathcal{F}$ wins is bounded by $1/2^{k-1}$ (since $\mathcal{F}$ must output a valid ciphertext).
- If the value of $H_1(m^* \| u^* \| pk_u \| pk_R^*)$ was defined by the signcryption oracle for some query on a message m and receiver public key pk_R, then we must have $m = m^*, pk_R = pk_R^*$, and that the associated value $u = u^*$. Since both ciphertexts must be valid, we have that $v = v^*$, and so $w = w^*$ and $\tau = \tau^*$. This means that $z = z^*$ by the deterministic nature of the symmetric encryption scheme. Hence, we conclude that $\mathcal{F}$ outputs the result of a signcryption query, which is a contradiction to the fact that $\mathcal{F}$ wins the game.
- If the value of $H_1(m^* \| u^* \| pk_u \| pk_R^*)$ was defined by the unsigncryption oracle, then $\mathcal{B}$ is still able to solve the co-CDH problem as the simulation of the unsigncryption oracle calls the simulated H_1 oracle for all its computations.

Hence, we can conclude that the probability that the algorithm fails is bounded by $q_{sc}(q_{H_1} + q_{sc} + q_{usc})/2^{k-1} + 1/2^{k-1}$ and the result follows. $\qquad \square$

A similar theorem to Theorem 5.1 links the anonymity property of the scheme to the co-CDH assumption.

5.6 A Scheme with Short Detachable Signatures

Figure 5.2 describes a signcryption scheme by Libert and Quisquater [124] with a shorter detachable signature. The construction relies on a signature scheme independently proposed by Zhang et al. [202] and Boneh-Boyen [42]. In the latter work, this scheme was shown to efficiently produce 160-bit signatures without requiring the use of a special hash function mapping messages to be signed onto an elliptic curve subgroup, unlike the original BLS short signature proposed in [47, 48]. In [42], it was also shown that this scheme has a more efficient security reduction in the random oracle model under the q-strong Diffie–Hellman assumption than the reduction given by Zhang et al. [202] under the q-Diffie–Hellman inversion assumption.

The protocol makes use of a (masked) signature as an ElGamal-like ephemeral key as well as a checksum showing that a message was properly encrypted. The sender first computes an exponent $r \leftarrow \gamma/(h_1(b_m \| m \| pk_S) + sk_S) \in \mathbb{Z}_p^*$ where γ is randomly chosen from $\mathbb{Z}_p^*$, $m \in \{0, 1\}^*$ is the message to sign and encrypt, and b_m is a message-dependent bit computed as a function of m and the private key sk_S according to Katz and Wang's proof technique [113]—this helps to achieve tight security reductions without introducing random "salts" in signatures. This exponent r is then used to compute an ephemeral Diffie–Hellman key g_1^r as in the ElGamal cryptosystem [81] and to scramble the secret γ using a hash value of $\psi(pk_R)^r$, while a digest of γ, $\psi(pk_R)^r$, and other elements is used to conceal the message m using a deterministic and one-to-one symmetric encryption scheme.

$\text{Setup}(1^k)$

   Pick a set of bilinear map groups
      $(\mathbb{G}_1, \mathbb{G}_2, \mathbb{G}_T)$ whose order is a prime
      p such that $2^{k-1} < p < 2^k$ and
      generators $(g_1, g_2) \in \mathbb{G}_1 \times \mathbb{G}_2$
      such that $g_1 = \psi(g_2)$ with $g_2 \xleftarrow{R} \mathbb{G}_2$

   Choose a one-time deterministic
      symmetric-key encryption scheme
      $SE = (\text{Enc}, \text{Dec})$ with key space $\mathcal{K}$
      and ciphertext space $\mathcal{C}$

   Pick cryptographic hash functions:
      $H' : \{0,1\}^* \to \{0,1\}$
      $H_1 : \{0,1\}^* \to \mathbb{Z}_p$
      $H_2 : \mathbb{G}_1^3 \to \{0,1\}^{k+1}$
      $H_3 : \{0,1\}^k \to \mathcal{K}$
      $param \leftarrow (\mathbb{G}_1, \mathbb{G}_2, \mathbb{G}_T, p,$
                  $g_1, g_2, SE, H', H_1, H_2, H_3)$

   Return $param$

$\text{KeyGen}(param)$

   $x_U \xleftarrow{R} \mathbb{Z}_p^*; \; y_U \leftarrow g_2^{x_U}$
   $sk \leftarrow x_U; \; pk \leftarrow y_U$
   Return (sk, pk)

$\text{Signcrypt}(param, sk_S, pk_R, m)$

   Parse sk_S as (x_S, y_S); Parse pk_R as y_R
   If $y_S, y_R \notin \mathbb{G}_2 \setminus \{1\}$ then return $\bot$
   $\gamma \xleftarrow{R} \mathbb{Z}_p^*$
   $b_m \leftarrow H'(sk_S, m)$
   $r \leftarrow \dfrac{\gamma}{H_1(b_m \| m \| pk_S) + x_S} \bmod p$
   $c_1 \leftarrow g_1^r$
   $c_2 \leftarrow (\gamma \| b_m) \oplus H_2(c_1 \| y_R \| \psi(y_R)^r)$
   $\tau \leftarrow H_3(\gamma \| b_m \| y_R \| \psi(y_R)^r)$
   $c_3 \leftarrow \text{Enc}_\tau(m)$
   $C \leftarrow (c_1, c_2, c_3)$
   Return C

$\text{Unsigncrypt}(param, pk_S, sk_R, C)$

   Parse pk_S as y_S; Parse sk_S as (x_S, y_S)
   Parse C as (c_1, c_2, c_3)
   If $c_1 \notin \mathbb{G}_1$, $c_2 \notin \{0,1\}^{k+1}$ or $c_3 \notin \mathcal{C}$
      Return $\bot$
   $(\gamma \| b_m) \leftarrow c_2 \oplus H_2(c_1 \| y_R \| c_1^{x_R})$
   If $\gamma \notin \mathbb{Z}_p^*$ then return $\bot$
   $\tau \leftarrow H_3(\gamma \| b_m \| y_R \| c_1^{x_R})$;
   $m \leftarrow \text{Dec}_\tau(c_3)$
   $\sigma \leftarrow c_1^{\gamma^{-1}}$
   If $e(\sigma, y_S \cdot g_2^{H_1(b_m \| m \| pk_S)}) \neq e(g_1, g_2)$
      Return $\bot$
   Return (m, b_m, σ)

Fig. 5.2 The SDH-based scheme

The use of a masked signature as a "one-time" Diffie–Hellman key allows the sparing of one exponentiation (actually an elliptic curve scalar multiplication) with respect to a sequential signature/encryption composition.

When computing the second component of the ciphertext, the receiver's public key and the first component (which is an embedded signature as well as a Diffie–Hellman ephemeral key) are hashed together with the "one-time" Diffie–Hellman key $\psi(pk_R)^r$ in order to simplify the security proof.

In order to convince a third party that a recovered message m originates from the sender S, the receiver reveals the detached signature σ, the message m, and the associated bit b_m to the third party who can run the regular signature verification algorithm (i.e., check that $e(g_1, g_2) = e(\sigma, y_S \cdot g_2^{H_1(b_m \| m \| pk_S)})$). The scheme thus provides detachable signatures that cannot be linked to their original ciphertext: the signature is masked by a randomly chosen factor γ and anyone observing a valid message–signature pair can use his/her private key to build a signcryption of that message–signature pair under his/her public key. The scheme thus provides *ciphertext unlinkability* in the sense of [51].

5.6.1 Efficiency

Besides a modular inversion, the sender only computes two exponentiations in $\mathbb{G}_1$. The receiver's workload is dominated by one pairing computation (as $e(g_1, g_2)$ can be included among the common public parameters param), two exponentiations in $\mathbb{G}_1$, and one exponentiation in $\mathbb{G}_2$.

The scheme is described in terms of asymmetric pairings and requires the existence of a publicly computable isomorphism $\psi : \mathbb{G}_2 \to \mathbb{G}_1$. It does not require the hashing of arbitrary strings onto cyclic elliptic curve subgroups. Hence, the kind of groups suggested in Sect. 4 of [183] may be employed here as they provide an asymmetric pairing configuration $e : \mathbb{G}_1 \times \mathbb{G}_2 \to \mathbb{G}_T$ with an efficiently computable isomorphism $\psi : \mathbb{G}_2 \to \mathbb{G}_1$. It has been reported that hashing onto $\mathbb{G}_2$ may be somewhat slow in such configurations. Such parameters allow the performance of the last step of the Unsigncrypt algorithm at a reasonable speed using the specific techniques for ordinary curves given by Barreto et al. [19].

Note that the two exponentiations that are the bulk of the sender's workload can be computed off-line (i.e., before knowing the message to be sent). Indeed, in an off-line phase, the sender can pick a random $r \xleftarrow{R} \mathbb{Z}_p^*$, compute $c_1 \leftarrow g_1^r$ and $\omega \leftarrow \psi(pk_R)^r$, store them in memory, and, then, once the message m is known, compute $\gamma \leftarrow r(H_1(b_m \| m \| pk_S) + sk_S) \bmod p$, $c_2 \leftarrow (\gamma \| b_m) \oplus H_2(c_1 \| pk_R \| \omega)$ and $c_3 \leftarrow \mathrm{Enc}_{H_3(\gamma \| b_m \| y_R \| \omega)}(m)$. In this case, care must be taken not to re-use the same r to sign and encrypt distinct messages because this would expose the private key.

From a bandwidth point of view, the scheme allows receivers to extract short signatures from a ciphertext when they wish to convince a judge of the sender's authorship of the message (e.g., signatures of length 256 bits, using the pairing-friendly groups suggested by Barreto and Naehrig [20]).

5.6.2 Anonymous Communications

Like the co-CDH-based scheme of Fig. 5.1, this scheme is meant to provide anonymous communications, where ciphertexts do not reveal the identity of the sender and the receiver. In such a situation, it may be the case that the receiver himself/herself does not know who the sender is upon receiving a ciphertext. We nevertheless remark that the sender's public key is only needed in the final step of the unsigncryption algorithm. A simple solution to the above problem is to have the sender append a short string ID_S that identifies him/her (or even his public key) to the message that is being signcrypted. The receiver then has to perform an online lookup in a public repository to fetch the appropriate public key pk_S.

The syntax of the unsigncryption algorithm is then slightly modified as this algorithm does not take the sender's public key pk_S as input any longer. A similar modification can be made to the scheme of Fig. 5.1.

5.6.3 Security

The original version of the scheme [124] was shown by Tan [188] to be vulnerable to a chosen ciphertext attack taking advantage of a key substitution attack on the underlying signature scheme [42, 202]. However, protecting the scheme against the attack of Tan [188] is rather straightforward using a standard countermeasure to immunize signature schemes from key substitution attacks: it suffices to hash the signer's public key along with the message to be signed. The resulting scheme is even more efficient than the improvement of Ma [128] (subsequently also broken by Tan [189]) as it allows for shorter detachable signatures.

The message confidentiality and existential signature unforgeability, respectively, rely (in the random oracle model) on the intractability of the q-Diffie–Hellman Inversion and q-strong Diffie–Hellman assumptions.

For convenience, the message confidentiality is proved under an equivalent formulation of the q-DHI assumption, which we call the $(q + 1)$-exponent problem in $(\mathbb{G}_1, \mathbb{G}_2)$. This consists of computing $g_1^{(x^{q+1})} \in \mathbb{G}_1$ given $(g_1, g_2, g_2^x, \ldots, g_2^{(x^q)})$. A proof of the following result can be found in [41] but we give it for completeness.

Lemma 5.1 *The q-Diffie–Hellman Inversion problem can be formulated as the problem of computing $g_1^{(x^{q+1})}$ on input of $(g_1, g_2, g_2^x, g_2^{(x^2)}, \ldots, g_2^{(x^q)}) \in \mathbb{G}^{q+1}$.*

Proof Given a sequence of elements $(g_1, g_2, g_2^x, \ldots, g_2^{(x^q)})$, where x is uniformly chosen in $\mathbb{Z}_p^*$, for which $g_1^{(x^{q+1})}$ should be found, one can easily construct a q-DHI instance $(y_1, y_2, y_2^A, y_2^{(A^2)}, \ldots, y_2^{(A^q)})$ by setting

$$y_1 = \psi(y_2) \qquad y_2 = g_2^{(x^q)} \qquad y_2^A = g_2^{(x^{q-1})} \qquad \cdots \qquad y_2^{(A^q)} = g_2$$

This implicitly defines the value $A = 1/x$. Any algorithm that computes the q-DHI solution $y_1^{1/A}$ thus reveals the value $g_1^{(x^{q+1})}$. □

Theorem 5.3 *The scheme is FSO/FUO-IND-CCA2 secure in the random oracle model assuming that the q-DHI problem is intractable and that the symmetric encryption scheme is IND-CPA secure. For any adversary $\mathcal{A}$ running in time t_A and making at most q_{sc} signcryption queries, q_{usc} unsigncryption queries, q_{H_i} queries to random oracles H_i ($i = 1, 2, 3$), and $q_{H'}$ queries to H', we have*

$$\mathrm{Adv}_{\mathcal{A}}(t_A, k) \leq \frac{q_{usc}}{2^{k-2}} + \frac{(q_{sc} + q_{usc})(q_{sc} + q_{usc} + q_{H_3}) + q}{2^{k-1}}$$
$$+ \mathrm{Adv}_{\mathcal{B}}^{q\text{-}DHI}(t', k) + \mathrm{Adv}_{\mathcal{B}}^{ind\text{-}cpa\text{-}sym}(t', |\mathcal{K}|)$$

where $\mathrm{Adv}_{\mathcal{B}}^{ind\text{-}cpa\text{-}sym}(t', |\mathcal{K}|)$ is defined as in Theorem 5.1 while $\mathrm{Adv}_{\mathcal{B}}^{q\text{-}DHI}(t', k)$ stands for the maximal probability of solving the q-DHI problem within running *time* $t' \leq t_A + O(q_{H_2} + q_{H_3} q_{usc}) t_p + O(q^2 + q_{H'} + q_{sc} + q_{usc}) t_{exp}$ *when the security parameter is* k *and* t_p *and* t_{exp} *denote the time complexity of a pairing evaluation and that of an exponentiation in* $\mathbb{G}_2$, *respectively.*

Proof The proof proceeds with a sequence of games. The first game is the real attack game, while in the final game the adversary has no better advantage than a passive adversary against the symmetric encryption scheme (Enc, Dec). Throughout the sequence, we call S_i the event that the adversary $\mathcal{A}$ wins (by correctly guessing the bit $d \in \{0, 1\}$ chosen by the challenger $\mathcal{B}$ in the challenge phase) in Game i.

Game 1 is the real attack game. The adversary $\mathcal{A}$ is provided with a random generator $h \xleftarrow{R} \mathbb{G}_2$, its image $g = \psi(h) \in \mathbb{G}_1$, as well as a receiver's public key $pk_U = X = h^x$. Throughout the game, the simulator $\mathcal{B}$ uses the private key $sk_U = x$ to answer signcryption and unsigncryption queries. Random oracle queries are answered by outputting random values in the appropriate range. This is done consistently in that, if an oracle is queried twice on the same input, the same output is returned by $\mathcal{B}$. To keep track of those queries, lists L', L_1, L_2, and L_3 are used to bookkeep all inputs and the matching outputs for oracles H', H_1, H_2, H_3. In the middle point of the game, $\mathcal{A}$ outputs a pair of messages (m_0, m_1) and a sender's private key $sk_S^* = x_S^*$. To generate the challenge ciphertext (c_1^*, c_2^*, c_3^*), the simulator $\mathcal{B}$ flips a fair binary coin $d \xleftarrow{R} \{0, 1\}$, randomly chooses $\gamma^* \xleftarrow{R} \mathbb{Z}_p^*$, and generates (c_1^*, c_2^*, c_3^*) as $c_1^* = g^{r^*}$, $c_2^* = (\gamma^* \| b_m^*) \oplus H_2(c_1^* \| X \| \psi(X)^{r^*})$, and $c_3^* = \text{Enc}_{\tau^*}(m_d)$ where $r^* = \gamma^* / (x_S^* + H_1(b_m^* \| m_d \| pk_S^*))$, $\tau^* = H_3(\gamma^* \| b_m^* \| X \| \psi(X)^{r^*}) \in \mathcal{K}$, and the bit $b_m^* \in \{0, 1\}$ is determined as $b_m^* = H'(x_S^*, m_d)$. In this game, the adversary has advantage $|\Pr[S_1] - 1/2|$.

Game 2 modifies the generation of the public generator $h \in \mathbb{G}_2$ and the public key X, namely, $\mathcal{B}$ defines values $(g_1, g_2, g_2^x, g_2^{(x^2)}, \ldots, g_2^{(x^q)}) \in \mathbb{G}_1 \times \mathbb{G}_2^{q+1}$ for a randomly chosen $x \xleftarrow{R} \mathbb{Z}_p^*$. To generate $h \in \mathbb{G}_2$, $g = \psi(h) \in \mathbb{G}_1$ and a public key $X = h^x \in \mathbb{G}_2$, $\mathcal{B}$ picks $w_1, \ldots, w_{q-1} \xleftarrow{R} \mathbb{Z}_p$, expands the polynomial $f(z) = \prod_{i=1}^{q-1} (z + w_i) = \sum_{i=0}^{q-1} c_i z^i$, and uses it to obtain a random generator $h \in \mathbb{G}_2$ and a public key X. These can be obtained by first computing

$$ h' = \prod_{i=0}^{q-1} (g_2^{(x^i)})^{c_i} = g_2^{f(x)} \quad \text{and} \quad X' = \prod_{i=1}^{q} (g_2^{(x^i)})^{c_{i-1}} = g_2^{xf(x)} = h'^x $$

We call F_2 the event that h' is the identity element of $\mathbb{G}$ (i.e., because $f(x) = 0$ when one of the w_i happens to be the exponent x). Since there are $q - 1$ values w_i and x is chosen at random, we have that the probability that $f(x) = 0$ is bounded by $(q - 1)/p$. It is easy to see that Game 1 and Game 2 are identical unless event F_2 occurs. Hence, $|\Pr[S_1] - \Pr[S_2]| \leq \Pr[F_2] \leq (q - 1)/p \leq (q - 1)/2^{k-1}$.

Game 3 changes the game so that part of the challenge ciphertext (c_1^*, c_2^*, c_2^*) is computed at the beginning of the game, namely, $\mathcal{B}$ chooses $a \xleftarrow{R} \mathbb{Z}_p$ at random and sets the first ciphertext component as $c_1^* = g^{(x+a)} = \psi(X) \cdot g^a \in \mathbb{G}_1$, which implicitly defines the encryption exponent as $r^* = a + x$. When $\mathcal{A}$ chooses messages m_0, m_1 and a sender's private key sk_S^* in the challenge phase, $\mathcal{B}$ computes $\gamma^* = r^*(sk_S^* + H_1(b_m^* \| m_d \| pk_S^*))$ after having determined the message-dependent bit $b_m^* = H'(sk_S^*, m_d)$ and computes parts c_2^* and c_3^* of the ciphertext as specified by the description of the scheme. This change is only conceptual and we have $\Pr[S_2] = \Pr[S_3]$.

Game 4 is the same as game 3 but $\mathcal{B}$ aborts if a pre-challenge unsigncryption query involves a ciphertext (c_1, c_2, c_3) such that $c_1 = c_1^*$. Unless this event, that we call F_4, occurs, Game 3 and Game 4 proceed identically and we have $\Pr[S_3 \wedge \neg F_4] = \Pr[S_4 \wedge \neg F_4]$ and $|\Pr[S_4] - \Pr[S_3]| \leq \Pr[F_4]$. Since c_1^* is independent of $\mathcal{A}$'s view until the challenge phase, we must have $\Pr[F_4] \leq q_{usc}/p \leq q_{usc}/2^{k-1}$.

Game 5 modifies the treatment of random oracle queries and the way to handle signcryption and unsigncryption queries. We note that, for the values $w_i \in \mathbb{Z}_p$ that are roots of the polynomial $f(z)$, $\mathcal{B}$ can compute $q_{sc} = q - 1$ pairs $(w_i, g^{\frac{1}{w_i+x}})$ using only $(g_1, g_2, \ldots, g_2^{x^q})$ (and without using the underlying x). Using the technique of [42], it obtains these pairs $(w_i, g^{\frac{1}{w_i+x}})$ by expanding $f_i(z) = f(z)/(z + w_i) = \prod_{i=0}^{q-2} d_i z^i$ and computing

$$\tilde{g}_i = \prod_{j=0}^{q-2} \psi(g_2^{(x^j)})^{\theta d_j} = g_1^{\theta f_i(x)} = g_1^{\theta \frac{f(x)}{x+w_i}} = g^{\frac{1}{x+w_i}}$$

for $i = 1, \ldots, q - 1$. Queries to random oracles H', H_1 and signcryption queries are now processed as follows:

- H' queries: When a query $H'(\alpha, m_i)$ is made, $\mathcal{B}$ checks if a tuple (α, m_i, b_{m_i}) appears in L'. If so, it returns the previously defined $b_{m_i} \in \{0, 1\}$. If no such tuple is found,

  - if $\alpha = x$ (which $\mathcal{B}$ can test by checking if $g_2^x = g_2^\alpha$ if it does not explicitly know x, as will be the case in later games), $\mathcal{B}$ looks up entries of the form $(?, m_i, b_{m_i})$ in L', returns the matching b_{m_i} if such an entry is found, and replaces the entry by (α, m_i, b_{m_i}). If no entry $(?, m_i, b_{m_i})$ is found, $\mathcal{B}$ responds with a random $b_{m_i} \xleftarrow{R} \{0, 1\}$ and stores (x, m_i, b_{m_i}) in L'.
  - if $\alpha \neq x$, $\mathcal{B}$ returns a random $b \xleftarrow{R} \{0, 1\}$ and stores (α, m_i, b) in L'.

- H_1 queries: These queries are indexed by a counter t that is initially set to 1. When a triple $\delta \| m \| X$ (involving the challenge public key X) is submitted in a H_1 query for a new message m, $\mathcal{B}$ looks up L' for a record $(?, m, b_m)$ (where ? is a placeholder for a currently unknown value). If no such record is found, $\mathcal{B}$ picks a random bit $b_m \xleftarrow{R} \{0, 1\}$ and stores $(?, m, b_m)$ in L' so that b_m will be associated with the message m from this point forward. The treatment of the hash query $H_1(\delta \| m \| X)$ then depends on $\delta \in \{0, 1\}$, namely, if $\delta = b_m$, $\mathcal{B}$ returns w_t, stores (δ, m, X, w_t) in L_1, and increments the counter t (in such a way that $\mathcal{B}$

is able to create a valid signature on m). Otherwise (i.e., if $\delta \neq b_m$), $\mathcal{B}$ returns a random $c \xleftarrow{R} \mathbb{Z}_p^*$ and stores (δ, m, X, c) in L_1. Should H_1 be queried again on the same $\delta \| m \| X$ later on, $\mathcal{B}$ will look up L_1 and output the value that was defined at the first occurrence of the query.

- H_2 queries are now processed using two lists L_2 and L_2'. On input $Y_{1,i} \| Y_{2,i} \| Y_{3,i}$: $\mathcal{B}$ first checks if H_2 was previously queried on the same input and, if so, returns the previously defined value. Otherwise, $\mathcal{B}$ checks if the tuple $(h, Y_{1,i}, Y_{2,i}, Y_{3,i})$ is a valid co-Diffie–Hellman tuple (in our notation, we write $Y_{3,i} = \text{co-DH}_h(Y_{1,i}, Y_{2,i})$) by verifying if

$$e(Y_{1,i}, Y_{2,i}) = e(Y_{3,i}, h).$$

If it is, $\mathcal{B}$ checks if L_2' contains a record $(Y_{1,i}, Y_{2,i}, ?, \zeta_i)$, for some $\zeta_i \in \{0, 1\}^{k+1}$ and where ? is a placeholder for a currently undetermined value. In this case, ζ_i is returned and an entry $(Y_{1,i}, Y_{2,i}, Y_{3,i}, \zeta_i, 1)$ is added in L_2. If no entry of the shape $(Y_{1,i}, Y_{2,i}, ?, \zeta_i)$ is in L_2', $\mathcal{B}$ returns a string $\zeta_i \xleftarrow{R} \{0, 1\}^{k+1}$ and inserts $(Y_{1,i}, Y_{2,i}, Y_{3,i}, \zeta_i, 1)$ in L_2. If $(h, Y_{1,i}, Y_{2,i}, Y_{3,i})$ is not a co-Diffie–Hellman tuple, $\mathcal{B}$ returns a random $\zeta_i \xleftarrow{R} \{0, 1\}^{k+1}$ and the entry $(Y_{1,i}, Y_{2,i}, Y_{3,i}, \zeta_i, 0)$ is added in L_2.

- H_3 queries: When a query $H_3(\gamma \| b_m \| pk_R \| Y)$ is made, $\mathcal{B}$ looks up the history L_3 of H_3 queries. If it already contains a record $(*, pk_R, \gamma, b_m, Y, \tau)$ for any value of $*$, then $\mathcal{B}$ returns $\tau \in \mathcal{K}$. Otherwise, $\mathcal{B}$ checks all entries of the form $(c_1, pk_R, \gamma, b_m, ?, \tau)$, for some $c_1 \in \mathbb{G}_1$, and tests whether one of them satisfies $Y = \text{co-DH}_h(c_1, pk_R)$. If so, it returns the matching $\tau \in \mathcal{K}$ and replaces the record by $(c_1, pk_R, \gamma, b_m, Y, \tau)$ in L_3. Otherwise, $\mathcal{B}$ returns a random $\tau \xleftarrow{R} \mathcal{K}$ and stores $(?, pk_R, \gamma, b_m, Y, \tau)$ in L_3.

- Signcryption queries on a plaintext m, for an arbitrary receiver's key pk_R: We assume that m was previously submitted in an H_1 query and that the message-dependent bit b_m was previously defined. Since $H_1(b_m \| m \| X)$ was (or will be) defined to be w_j for some $j \in \{1, \ldots, t\}$, $\mathcal{B}$ knows that $\tilde{g}_j = g^{1/(w_j + x)}$ appears as a valid signature on m from $\mathcal{A}$'s view. So, it computes $c_1 = \tilde{g}_j^\gamma \in \mathbb{G}_1$ for some $\gamma \xleftarrow{R} \mathbb{Z}_p^*$. It then checks if L_2 contains an entry $(c_1, pk_R, Y_3, \zeta, 1)$ (indicating that $Y_3 = \text{co-DH}_h(c_1, pk_R)$) or if L_2' contains a record of the form $(c_1, pk_R, ?, \zeta)$. If so, $\mathcal{B}$ sets $c_2 = (\gamma \| b_m) \oplus \zeta \in \{0, 1\}^{k+1}$. Otherwise, it sets $c_2 \xleftarrow{R} \{0, 1\}^{k+1}$ and inserts $(c_1, pk_R, ?, (\gamma \| b_m) \oplus c_2)$ in L_2'. If L_3 happens to already contain an entry $(*, pk_R, \gamma, b_m, ., \tau)$ comprising this particular γ, $\mathcal{B}$ fails (we call F_5 this event). Otherwise, it picks a random symmetric key $\tau \xleftarrow{R} \mathcal{K}$, sets $c_3 = \text{Enc}_\tau(m)$, and stores a record $(c_1, pk_R, \gamma, b_m, ?, \tau)$ in L_3 (in such a way that a subsequent $H_3(\gamma \| b_m \| pk_R \| \text{co-DH}_h(c_1, pk_R))$ obtains the answer τ). The resulting triple (c_1, c_2, c_3) is then returned to $\mathcal{A}$.

- Unsigncryption queries: When $\mathcal{A}$ submits a ciphertext $C = (c_1, c_2, c_3)$ together with a sender's public key pk_S, $\mathcal{B}$ checks whether list L_2 contains the unique entry $(c_1, X, Y, \zeta, 1)$ for some elements $Y \in \mathbb{G}_1$ and $\zeta \in \{0, 1\}^{k+1}$ (indicating that $Y = \text{co-DH}_h(c_1, X))$ or whether L'_2 contains the entry $(c_1, X, ?, \zeta)$ for some $\zeta \in \{0, 1\}^{k+1}$:

- If it does, $\mathcal{B}$ obtains $(\gamma \| b_m) = c_2 \oplus \zeta \in \{0, 1\}^{k+1}$, $\tau = H_3(\gamma \| b_m \| X \| Y)$ (by simulating H_3) and finally $m = \text{Dec}_\tau(c_3)$. Finally, $\mathcal{B}$ extracts $\sigma = c_1^{1/\gamma}$ and returns the plaintext m and the signature σ if the verification equation $e(\sigma, pk_S \cdot h^{H_1(b_m \| m \| pk_S)}) = e(g, h)$ is satisfied.
- If it does not, $\mathcal{B}$ randomly picks $\zeta \xleftarrow{R} \{0, 1\}^{k+1}$, $\tau \xleftarrow{R} \mathcal{K}$, and inserts $(c_1, X, ?, \zeta)$ into the list L'_2 (so that a subsequent H_2 query on $(c_1, X, \text{co-DH}_h(c_1, X))$ will be assigned the output ζ). It computes $(\gamma \| b_m) = c_2 \oplus \zeta \in \{0, 1\}^{k+1}$ and aborts in the unlikely event, which we call F'_5, that the obtained γ already appears somewhere in L_3 (since γ is almost uniform in $\mathbb{Z}_p$, event F'_5 only happens with negligible probability). Otherwise, it stores $(c_1, X, \gamma, b_m, ?, \tau)$ in L_3 (in such a way that a subsequent query $H_3(\gamma \| b_m \| X \| \text{co-DH}_h(c_1, X))$ will receive the answer τ). The latter is used to compute $m \leftarrow \text{Dec}_\tau(c_3)$. The signature $\sigma = c_1^{1/\gamma}$ is checked as above. If the verification succeeds, $\mathcal{B}$ returns (m, σ). Otherwise, it outputs $\perp$.

Unless event F_5 or F'_5 occurs at some query, $\mathcal{A}$'s view is not affected by the above modifications. We thus have $|\Pr[S_5] - \Pr[S_4]| \leq \Pr[F_5 \vee F'_5]$. It is easy to see that $\Pr[F_5 \vee F'_5] \leq (q_{sc} + q_{usc})(q_{sc} + q_{usc} + q_{H_3})/2^{k-1}$ since list L_3 never contains more than $q_{sc} + q_{usc} + q_{H_3}$ entries.

Game 6 changes the simulation of the unsigncryption oracle again and adds the following rule. *After* the challenge phase, if $\mathcal{A}$ queries the unsigncryption of a ciphertext (c_1, c_2, c_3) such that $(c_1, c_2) = (c_1^*, c_2^*)$, $\mathcal{B}$ returns $\perp$. We consider two cases:

- If the query is made for the same sender $pk_S = pk_S^*$, we must have $c_3 \neq c_3^*$. It is easy to see that for such a ciphertext the underlying values (γ, b_m) must be the same as the pair (γ^*, b_m^*) of the challenge ciphertext. Moreover, the same symmetric key $\tau^* = H_3(\gamma^* \| b_m^* \| X \| \psi(X)^{r^*})$ must be used to decipher c_3 when executing the unsigncryption operation. Since $c_3 \neq c_3^*$ and given that the symmetric encryption algorithm (Enc, Dec) is a bijection, the underlying plaintext $m = \text{Dec}_{\tau^*}(c_3)$ must be different from m_d. Therefore, unless we have a collision $H_1(b_m^* \| m \| pk_S^*) = H_1(b_m^* \| m_d \| pk_S^*)$ (which occurs with probability at most $1/|p| < 1/2^{k-1}$ when H_1 is viewed as a random oracle), the underlying c_1^{*1/γ^*} cannot be a valid signature for m.
- If the query is made for a different sender's public key $pk_S \neq pk_S^*$ (in which case, we may have $c_3 = c_3^*$ or $c_3 \neq c_3^*$), the unsigncryption operation would still reveal the same values $(\gamma, b_m) = (\gamma^*, b_m^*)$ as in the challenge phase and the same symmetric key $\tau^* = H_3(\gamma^* \| b_m^* \| X \| c_1^{*x})$ must be used to decipher c_3. However, if we denote by $m = \text{Dec}_{\tau^*}(c_3)$ the symmetric decryption of c_3 under that symmetric key τ^*, the ciphertext (c_1^*, c_2^*, c_3) would only be accepted in

previous games if $\log_g(pk_S) + H_1(b_m^* \| m \| pk_S) = x_S^* + H_1(b_m^* \| m_d \| pk_S^*)$. In the random oracle model, this only occurs with probability at most $1/p < 1/2^{k-1}$.

Throughout all queries, the probability that the new rule causes the rejection of a ciphertext that would not have been rejected in earlier games is at most $q_{usc}/2^{k-1}$. We thus have $|\Pr[S_6] - \Pr[S_5]| \le q_{usc}/2^{k-1}$.

Game 7 brings two changes to the simulation and first modifies the generation of the challenge ciphertext $C^* = (c_1^*, c_2^*, c_3^*)$ again. When $\mathcal{A}$ outputs messages m_0, m_1 together with a sender's private key $sk_S^* \in \mathbb{Z}_p^*$ in the challenge phase, $\mathcal{B}$ still computes c_1^* by choosing $a \xleftarrow{R} \mathbb{Z}_p^*$ and setting $c_1^* = g^{(x+a)} = \psi(X) \cdot g^a \in \mathbb{G}_1$. However, sk_S^* is no longer used to compute c_2^* and neither are the private key $sk_U = x$ and the encryption exponent $r^* = x + a$. Elements (c_2^*, c_3^*) are generated by drawing $c_2^* \xleftarrow{R} \{0, 1\}^{k+1}$ at random and computing $c_3^* = \text{Enc}_{\tau^*}(m_d)$, for a random bit $d \xleftarrow{R} \{0, 1\}$, using a random key $\tau^* \xleftarrow{R} \mathcal{K}$. The other change is that the simulator $\mathcal{B}$ immediately halts in the event, which we call E, that either of the following situations occurs:

E.1　$\mathcal{A}$ queries oracle H' on a pair $(x, *)$, where $x = sk_U = \log_g(X)$ is the private key. This can be tested by checking whether $X = h^\alpha$ at each query $H'(\alpha, *)$.

E.2　$\mathcal{A}$ queries oracle H_2 on an input $(c_1^* \| X \| Y)$ such that $Y = \text{co-DH}_h(c_1^*, X)$.

E.3　$\mathcal{A}$ queries oracle H_3 on an input $(\gamma \| b_m \| X \| Y)$ such that $Y = \text{co-DH}_h(c_1^*, X)$.

We observe that $\mathcal{B}$ can detect E.1, E.2, and E.3 without knowing the private key $sk_U = x$. Event E.1 directly allows solving a given instance of the q-DHI problem and so do events E.2 and E.3 as we will see.

Let us assume for now that event E does not occur. Since the proof takes place in the random oracle model, without knowing the value $H_2(c_1^* \| X \| \text{co-DH}_h(c_1^*, X))$, $\mathcal{A}$ has no information on $c_2^* \oplus H_2(c_1^* \| X \| \text{co-DH}_h(c_1^*, X))$ and cannot realize that the challenge ciphertext was not properly generated. Game 7 is then identical to Game 6, which allows writing $\Pr[S_7 \wedge \neg E] = \Pr[S_6 \wedge \neg E]$ and $|\Pr[S_7] - \Pr[S_6]| \le \Pr[E]$. Moreover, as long as event E.3 does not happen, the key τ^* that is used to compute c_3^* is perfectly independent of $\mathcal{A}$'s view and guessing the bit $d \in \{0, 1\}$ boils down to mounting a chosen plaintext attack on the symmetric cipher (Enc, Dec). Indeed, before Game 6, the only situation where $\mathcal{A}$ could possibly manage to see the result of a symmetric decryption under the key τ^* would be by creating a valid ciphertext of the form (c_1^*, c_2^*, c_3) and such ciphertexts are always rejected by the unsigncryption oracle from Game 6 onwards. We thus have $|\Pr[S_7] - 1/2| = \text{Adv}_{\mathcal{B}}^{ind\text{-}cpa\text{-}sym}(t')$, where t' is a bound on $\mathcal{B}$'s running time (which will be determined below).

We still have to explain how $\mathcal{B}$ can solve a q-DHI instance if event E.2 or event E.3 (as defined above) occurs. When, via H_2 or H_3 queries, $\mathcal{B}$ obtains the co-Diffie–Hellman value $Y = \text{co-DH}_h(c_1^*, X) = g^{x(x+a)} = g_1^{\theta x f(x)(x+a)}$, it expands $f'(z) = f'(z)(z + a) = \sum_{j=0}^{q} f_j z^j \in \mathbb{Z}_p[z]$ and, since $Y = \prod_{j=0}^{q} \psi(g_2^{(x^{j+1})})^{\theta f_j}$, $\mathcal{B}$ can compute

$$g_1^{(x^{q+1})} = \left[Y^{1/\theta} \cdot \prod_{j=0}^{q-1} \psi(g_2^{(x^{j+1})})^{-f_j} \right]^{\frac{1}{f_q}} \in \mathbb{G}_1$$

and solve the $(q+1)$-exponent instance.

From a computational point of view, $\mathcal{B}$'s running time is dominated by $q+2$ multi-exponentiations with q elements that reach an overall cost of $O(q^2)$ exponentiations. Computing $f(z)$ also involves a cost in $O(q^2)$ while computing each $f_i(z)$ implies $O(q)$ operations like the computation of the product $f'(z)(z+a)$. When handling H_2 and H_3 queries, $\mathcal{B}$ also has to compute $O(q_{H_2} + q_{H_3}q_{usc})$ pairings. Finally, answering H' queries, signcryption queries, and unsigncryption queries also implies exponentiations.

The probability that event E occurs can thus be bounded by

$$\Pr[E] \le \mathrm{Adv}_{\mathcal{B}}^{q\text{-}DHI}(t')$$

where $t' \le t_{\mathcal{A}} + O(q_{H_2} + q_{H_3}q_{usc})t_p + O(q^2 + q_{H'} + q_{sc} + q_{usc})t_{exp}$. □

The scheme does not necessarily provide ciphertext unforgeability; however, it can be shown to give signature unforgeability (see Sect. 5.4.2). This means that, while it might be possible for an attacker to produce a new valid ciphertext from a particular sender, it is not possible for an attacker to produce a ciphertext that gives rise to a new message/signature pair. In other words, the resulting signature must have been originally produced by the legitimate sender.

Theorem 5.4 *If an ESUF-CMA adversary $\mathcal{F}$ has non-negligible advantage in the game of Definition 5.6, we can break the q-Strong Diffie–Hellman assumption in the random oracle model. More precisely, for any forger $\mathcal{F}$ running in time t, making q_{H_i} queries to oracles H_i ($i = 1, 2, 3$), q_{usc} unsigncryption queries, and q_{sc} signcryption queries, there exists an algorithm $\mathcal{B}$ solving the q-SDH problem for $q = q_{H_1}$ such that*

$$\mathrm{Adv}_{\mathcal{F}}(t_{\mathcal{F}}, k) \le \left(1 + 2 \cdot \left(1 - \frac{q-1}{2^{k-1}} \right)^{-1} \right) \cdot \mathrm{Adv}_{\mathcal{B}}^{q\text{-}SDH}(t', k)$$
$$+ \frac{(q_{sc} + q_{usc})(q_{sc} + q_{usc} + q_{H_3}) + 2q - 1}{2^{k-1}}$$

where $t' \le t_{\mathcal{F}} + O(q_{H_2} + q_{H_3}q_{usc})t_p + O(q^2 + q_{H'} + q_{sc} + q_{usc})t_{exp}$ and t_p and t_{exp} stand for the same quantities as in Theorem 5.3.

Proof The proof consists of a sequence of five games. The first one is the real attack game described by Definition 5.6. In the last game, the simulator will be able to extract a solution to a q-SDH instance from its interaction with the adversary. In each game of the sequence, we call W_i the event that the adversary wins.

Game 1 is the real attack game. The adversary $\mathcal{F}$ is given a random generator $h \xleftarrow{R} \mathbb{G}_2$, $g = \psi(h) \in \mathbb{G}_1$ and a sender's public key $pk_U = X = h^x$. Throughout the game, the simulator $\mathcal{B}$ uses the private key $sk_U = x$ to answer signcryption and unsigncryption queries. Random oracle queries are handled in the standard way, by returning random values in the appropriate set and producing the same output if the same input is queried several times. The forger $\mathcal{F}$ eventually outputs a ciphertext $C^* = (c_1^*, c_2^*, c_3^*)$ and a key pair (sk_R^*, pk_R^*). He/she wins if the unsigncryption of C^* under sk_R^* and pk_u is a valid triple (m^*, b^*, σ^*) with respect to pk_u and if this triple was not trivially obtained by querying the signcryption oracle (as described in Step 3 of Definition 5.6). The advantage of $\mathcal{F}$ is defined as $Adv_{\mathcal{F}} = \Pr[W_1]$.

Game 2 modifies the generation of the generator h and the sender's public key X which are now calculated in the same way as in Game 2 in the previous proof. The generators $h \in \mathbb{G}_2$, $g = \psi(h) \in \mathbb{G}_1$, that are given to the forger $\mathcal{F}$ as a part of the output of the common key generation algorithm, and the public key $X = h^x$ are generated as in Game 2 in the proof of Theorem 5.3, namely, $\mathcal{B}$ chooses a random polynomial $f(z) = \prod_{i=1}^{q-1}(z+w_i)$, with $w_1, \ldots, w_{q-1} \xleftarrow{R} \mathbb{Z}_p$. Given values $(g_1, g_2, g_2^x, \ldots, g_2^{(x^q)})$, it computes $h' = g_2^{f(x)}$, $X' = h'^x$ and finally $h = h'^{\theta}$, $X = X'^{\theta}$ where $\theta \xleftarrow{R} \mathbb{Z}_p$. If $f(x)$ happens to be zero, $\mathcal{B}$ can directly solve the problem as in the proof of Theorem 5.3. At the beginning of the game, $\mathcal{B}$ hands the public key $pk_u = X = h^x$ to $\mathcal{F}$. It is easy to see that Game 1 and Game 2 are identical unless the polynomial $f(z)$ accidentally cancels in x. This event, which we call F_2, occurs with probability bounded by $(q-1)/p$. Hence, we have that $|\Pr[W_1] - \Pr[W_2]| \leq \Pr[F_2] \leq (q-1)/2^{k-1}$.

Game 3 modifies the treatment of all queries and handles them exactly in the same way as in game 5 in the proof of Theorem 5.3. In this game, the private key $sk_u = x$ is not explicitly used to answer queries. In particular, signcryption queries can be dealt with without it since, after having calculated h and the public key, $\mathcal{B}$ knows $q-1$ pairs of the form $(w_i, g^{\frac{1}{w_i+x}})$. We denote by F_3 and F_3' the events that $\mathcal{B}$ fails when answering a signcryption and an unsigncryption query, respectively (i.e., the same events as F_5 and F_5' in the proof of Theorem 5.3). Unless either F_3 or F_3' occurs at some query, $\mathcal{A}$'s view will not be affected by these changes and we have $|\Pr[W_3] - \Pr[W_2]| \leq \Pr[F_3 \vee F_3']$. As in the proof of Theorem 5.3, we have $\Pr[F_3 \vee F_3'] \leq (q_{sc} + q_{usc})(q_{sc} + q_{usc} + q_{H_3})/p$ since list L_3 always contains at most $q_{sc} + q_{usc} + q_{H_3}$ records.

Game 4 introduces a failure event F_4 which is the same as event E.1 in the proof of Theorem 5.3 (namely $\mathcal{A}$ queries oracle H' on a pair $(x, *)$). Clearly, if event F_4 occurs, $\mathcal{B}$ can detect it and directly solve the q-SDH instance. We thus find that $\Pr[F_4] \leq Adv^{q\text{-}SDH}(\mathcal{B})$ and $|\Pr[W_4] - \Pr[W_3]| \leq Adv^{q\text{-}SDH}(\mathcal{B})$.

Game 5 raises a new failure event F_5 and makes $\mathcal{B}$ abort when it occurs. When the adversary $\mathcal{F}$ halts and outputs a ciphertext $C^* = (c_1^*, c_2^*, c_3^*)$ and an arbitrary recipient's key pair $(sk_R^*, pk_R^* = h^{sk_R^*})$, $\mathcal{B}$ looks up the values $H_2(c_1^* \| pk_R^* \| c_1^{*sk_R^*})$ and $\tau^* = H_3(\gamma^* \| b_{m^*} \| pk_R^* \| c_1^{*sk_R^*})$, where $(\gamma^* \| b_{m^*}) = c_2^* \oplus H_2(c_1^* \| pk_R^* \| c_1^{*sk_R^*})$, in the history of random oracle queries (and simulates random oracles for itself if necessary). We define F_5 to be the event that the hash value $H_1(b_{m^*} \| m^* \| X)$ was never defined by the simulation. Since H_1 is modeled as a random oracle, the probability that $\mathcal{A}$ wins without having forced the simulation to define $H_1(b_{m^*}\|m^*\|X)$ is at most $1/p < 1/2^{k-1}$. We thus have $|\Pr[W_5] - \Pr[W_4]| \leq \Pr[F_5] \leq 1/2^{k-1}$.

We will now give an upper bound for $\Pr[W_5]$. When $\mathcal{F}$ outputs a fake signature embedded in a ciphertext $C^* = (c_1^*, c_2^*, c_3^*)$ and the key pair $(sk_R^*, pk_R^* = h^{sk_R^*})$, $\mathcal{B}$ can recover the fake triple $\left(m^*, b_{m^*}, \sigma^* = g^{1/(H_1(b_{m^*}\|m^*\|X)+x)}\right)$ that must be contained in C^* by successively computing $(\gamma^*\|b_{m^*}) = c_2 \oplus H_2(c_1^*\|pk_R^*\|c_1^{*sk_R^*})$, $\tau^* = H_3(\gamma^*\|b_{m^*}\|pk_R^*\|c_1^{*sk_R^*})$, $m^* = \mathrm{Dec}_{\tau^*}(c_3^*)$, and $\sigma^* = c_1^{*1/\gamma^*}$.

Let us first assume that m^* was never the input of a signcryption query. Then, with probability $1/2$, b_{m^*} differs from the message-dependent bit $b_{m^*}^*$ (that indicates how m^* should be signed with the private key corresponding to $pk_u = X$ in the underlying signature scheme) since the latter is independent of $\mathcal{F}$'s view. Recall that we have $\sigma^* = g^{1/(x+h_1^*)} = g_1^{\theta f(x)/(x+h_1^*)}$, where $h_1^* = H_1(b_{m^*}\|m^*\|X)$. As long as $b_{m^*} \neq b_{m^*}^*$, we have $h_1^* \notin \{w_1, \ldots, w_{q-1}\}$ with probability at least $1 - (q-1)/p$ (since H_1 is a random oracle) and $(x + h_1^*)$ does not divide $f(x)$. In this case, a q-SDH pair (h_1^*, g^*) can then be extracted by expanding $f(z)/(z + h_1^*)$ into

$$\frac{\gamma_{-1}}{z + h_1^*} + \sum_{i=0}^{q-2} \gamma_i z^i$$

and computing $g^* = \left[\sigma^{*1/\theta} \cdot \prod_{i=0}^{q-2} \psi(g_2^{(x^i)})^{-\gamma_i}\right]^{\frac{1}{\gamma_{-1}}}$.

In the event that m^* was the input of some signcryption query, the latter was answered by generating the underlying signature as $\sigma = g^{1/(x+H_1(b_{m^*}^*\|m^*\|X))}$ using the message-dependent bit $b_{m^*}^*$. It comes that the bit b_{m^*} must necessarily be different from $b_{m^*}^*$ as, according to Definition 5.6, the triple (m^*, b_{m^*}, σ^*) would not be a forgery otherwise. Since $b_{m^*} \neq b_{m^*}^*$, $\mathcal{B}$ can extract an SDH pair as in the first case. In either situation, we find that $\Pr[W_5] \leq 2 \cdot \mathrm{Adv}^{q\text{-}SDH}(\mathcal{B}) + (q-1)/2^{k-1}$. $\square$

In comparison with other schemes, the disadvantage of this one is a security reduction relying on somewhat strong assumptions as the value q must be fairly large.

Chapter 6
Signcryption Schemes Based on the RSA Problem

Alexander W. Dent and John Malone-Lee

6.1 Introduction

The first practical public-key encryption scheme and digital signature scheme were proposed in 1978 by Rivest et al. [165]. While the original public-key encryption scheme would not be considered secure by modern standards, the RSA transform has been the basis of dozens of public-key encryption schemes and digital signature schemes. These schemes have proven very successful and have been very widely deployed in industry. However, despite being widely used in the design of public-key encryption and digital signature schemes, the RSA transform has not been widely used in the construction of signcryption schemes.

The basic RSA transform makes use of two large prime numbers (p, q) and an integer e which is coprime to $p - 1$ and $q - 1$. The RSA public key contains an RSA modulus $N = pq$ and the encryption exponent e. The RSA private key consists of the RSA modulus N and the decryption exponent $d = e^{-1} \bmod (p - 1)(q - 1)$. Note that the decryption exponent can easily be computed if one knows the prime factorization of N. The public key defines a permutation on the set $\mathbb{Z}_N$ as $x \mapsto x^e \bmod N$. This permutation is undone via the inverse transformation $x \mapsto x^d \bmod N$.

The security of the RSA transform comes from the problem of computing e-th roots modulo N. Indeed, it has been shown that the problem of computing an RSA decryption exponent d from the RSA public key (N, e) is as difficult as factoring N, as knowledge of (N, e, d) is sufficient to factor N in polynomial time [135]. This fact explains the difficulty in using the RSA transform in signcryption schemes. For a signcryption scheme to be insider secure, it must be possible to reveal the private key of one of the parties without compromising security, which implies that the ability to factor that party's modulus must not impact the security of the scheme. Hence, any signcryption scheme that is purely based on the RSA transform requires two transforms: one using the sender's RSA parameters, upon which the security

A.W. Dent (✉)

Information Security Group, University of London, Egham TW20 0EX, Surrey, UK

e-mail: a.dent@rhul.ac.uk

A.W. Dent, Y. Zheng (eds.), *Practical Signcryption*, Information Security
and Cryptography, DOI 10.1007/978-3-540-89411-7_6,
© Springer-Verlag Berlin Heidelberg 2010

of the data origin authentication service depends, and one using the receiver's RSA parameters, upon which the security of the data confidentiality service depends. This implies that any RSA-based signcryption scheme must intrinsically involve at least two "expensive" operations. Furthermore, each of these operations must use a different modulus and so acts as a permutation of different sets. This incompatibility between the domains of the two RSA transforms further complicates the construction of an efficient signcryption scheme.

The aim of an RSA-based signcryption scheme is therefore to achieve good security guarantees, while minimizing the ciphertext expansion and using only two RSA transformations. In this chapter we will review the early attempts to construct signcryption schemes based on the use of RSA moduli before focusing our efforts on the signcryption schemes that can be derived from the use of the RSA transform and certain padding schemes. Schemes of this type were proposed by Malone-Lee and Mao [131] and by Dodis et al. [77, 78]. All of these padding schemes are based on Feistel networks, which are used to add redundancy and randomness to messages before applying the RSA transforms. The resulting padding schemes can also be thought of in terms of commitment schemes and therefore have some similarities to the signcryption schemes based on concealment discussed in Chap. 8.

6.2 The RSA Transform

The RSA transform was introduced by Rivest, Shamir, and Adleman in 1978 [165]. The formal statement of the problem is a little more complex than the colloquial description given in the previous section. The exact definition of the problem depends upon the distribution from which the two prime numbers p and q are drawn. For our purposes, this is defined by a probabilistic, polynomial-time RSA parameter generation algorithm RSAGen, which takes as input a security parameter 1^k and outputs two primes (p, q) with the property that $N = pq$ is a k-bit integer. The exact description of the distribution is important as certain distributions lead to easily solvable versions of the RSA problem. We define the Euler function ϕ as $\phi(N) = (p - 1)(q - 1)$. The formal description of the RSA problem is as follows:

Definition 6.1 Let k be a security parameter and RSAGen be an RSA parameter generation algorithm:

- Suppose that $(p, q) \xleftarrow{R} \text{RSAGen}(1^k)$ and $N \leftarrow pq$. The *factoring problem* is to compute (p, q) when given N.
- Suppose that $(p, q) \xleftarrow{R} \text{RSAGen}(1^k)$, $N \leftarrow pq$, $e \xleftarrow{R} \mathbb{Z}^*_{\phi(N)}$, and $y \xleftarrow{R} \mathbb{Z}_N$. The *RSA problem* is to compute x such that $x^e = y \bmod N$ when given (N, e, y).
- Suppose that $(p, q) \xleftarrow{R} \text{RSAGen}(1^k)$, $N \leftarrow pq$, and $y \xleftarrow{R} \mathbb{Z}_N$. The *e-th root problem* is to compute x such that $x^e = y \bmod N$ when given (N, y).
- Suppose that $(p, q) \xleftarrow{R} \text{RSAGen}(1^k)$, $N \leftarrow pq$, $e \xleftarrow{R} \mathbb{Z}^*_{\phi(N)}$, and $y \xleftarrow{R} \mathbb{Z}_N$. The $\ell'(k)$-*partial RSA problem* is to compute $x \in \{0, 1\}^{\ell'(k)}$ such that $(x \| x')^e = y \bmod N$ for some $x' \in \{0, 1\}^{k-\ell'(k)}$ when given (N, e, y).

The only difference between the RSA problem and the e-th root problem is that the encryption exponent e is fixed in the e-th root problem, while it is randomly chosen in the RSA problem. The choice of a specific value for e can lead to efficiency gains in the signcryption and unsigncryption algorithms, but the security of the scheme would then rely on the difficulty of the e-th root problem, which may be easier to solve than the RSA problem.

There is a direct relationship between the partial RSA problem and the RSA problem, as demonstrated by Coron et al. [67].

Lemma 6.1 *If $\mathcal{A}$ is an algorithm that solves the partial RSA problem with probability ε in time t, where $2^{k-1} < N < 2^k$, $\ell'(k) > 64$, and $k/\ell'(k)^2 < 2^{-6}$, then there exists an algorithm $\mathcal{B}$ that solves the RSA problem with success probability ε' in time t', where*

$$n = \left\lceil \frac{5k}{4\ell'(k)} \right\rceil$$
$$\varepsilon' \geq \varepsilon(\varepsilon^n - 2^{-k/8})$$
$$t' \leq nt + \mathrm{poly}(k)$$

With current research, the fastest method to solve either the RSA problem or the e-th root problem (for odd values of $e > 1$) is to factor the modulus N. However, no proof exists to show that this must always be the case, and it is possible that the RSA or e-th root problems are significantly easier than the corresponding factoring problem. As has already been mentioned, the exact method for generating the primes p and q is important, as some distributions for p and q lead to an easily solvable factoring problem. Luckily, it has been argued that, for sufficiently large k, it suffices to select p and q at random from all $k/2$-bit primes [166]. Several estimates have been given as to the security given by moduli of different lengths, with one of the most trusted recent estimations given by Lenstra [120]:

RSA modulus bit length	Conservative equivalent symmetric key length	Optimistic equivalent symmetric key length
1, 024	72	72
1, 280	78	80
1, 536	82	85
2, 048	88	95
3, 072	99	112
4, 096	108	125
8, 192	135	163

6.3 Dedicated RSA-Based Signcryption Schemes

Most RSA-based signcryption schemes are perhaps most correctly viewed as applications of generic constructions which make use of a padding scheme and a pair of trapdoor permutations. We will discuss these constructions in Sect. 6.4. However, there are two constructions which rely on the RSA-style techniques without relying directly on the RSA transform: the Steinfeld–Zheng construction [184] discussed in Sect. 4.5 and Zheng's extension of this scheme [206]. These schemes make use of techniques similar to Zheng's original Diffie–Hellman-based signcryption scheme (discussed in Sect. 4.3) but using a version of the Schnorr signature scheme in a (hidden) prime-order subgroup of $\mathbb{Z}_N^*$.

6.4 Signcryption from Padding Schemes

In this section we will develop the theory behind the construction of signcryption schemes from padding schemes [77, 78]. This will culminate in the "Two Birds One Stone" signcryption scheme proposed by Malone-Lee and Mao [131]. This scheme is described in Sect. 6.5. In all cases, the schemes only provide signcryption for fixed-length messages. However, this can be extended to cover the signcryption of messages of any length up to a given bound using a suitable padding scheme.

6.4.1 Trapdoor Permutations

A trapdoor permutation is defined by a probabilistic, polynomial-time generation algorithm Gen which takes as input a security parameter 1^k and outputs a pair of PPT functions $(f, f^{-1}) \overset{R}{\leftarrow} \mathtt{Gen}(1^k)$. Both of these functions are permutations over some set of bitstrings $\{0, 1\}^{\ell(k)}$ and each function is the inverse of the other.

Definition 6.2 (Trapdoor one-way function) The trapdoor permutation defined by Gen is one-way if every PPT attacker $\mathcal{A}$ has negligible probability in the following experiment:

$$\Pr[x = f^{-1}(y) : x \overset{R}{\leftarrow} \mathcal{A}(f, y), \ y \overset{R}{\leftarrow} \{0, 1\}^{\ell(k)}, \ (f, f^{-1}) \overset{R}{\leftarrow} \mathtt{Gen}(1^k)]$$

The RSA transform is believed to be a trapdoor one-way permutation, except that it is defined over the set $\mathbb{Z}_N$, rather than over a set of bitstrings $\{0, 1\}^{\ell(k)}$, which complicates the application of these techniques in practice. This problem will be discussed further as we introduce the different constructions.

6.4.2 Extractable Commitments

An *extractable commitment scheme* has all the properties of a standard commitment scheme. In addition it has the property that there is an *extraction algorithm* that, for any commitment, can extract a unique decommitment with high probability. This extraction algorithm has to "observe" the construction of the commitment. The extractable commitment schemes that are used in these constructions are all built from cryptographic hash functions and the formal security analysis of the resulting schemes is all done in the random oracle model [29]. We will not go into details of the security proofs here, suffice to say that the extraction algorithm only needs to observe the random oracle queries made during the construction of the commitment. The interested reader will find the details in [78].

Formally, an extractable commitment scheme consists of three PPT algorithms: Commit, Open, and Extract. Given a message m, Commit(m) outputs a pair (c, d). Here c represents a *commitment* to the message m and d the corresponding *decommitment*. The output of Open(c, d) is m if (c, d) is a valid commitment/decommitment pair for message m; otherwise the output is $\perp$. There is the usual correctness requirement that Open(Commit(m)) $= m$ for all messages m in the appropriate message space.

Informally, we require that the commitment hides all information about the underlying message and that there exists an extraction algorithm that can recover the correct decommitment corresponding to a commitment if it can observe the random oracle queries made while creating the commitment. More formally, we require the following:

- *Hiding*: For all PPT attackers $\mathcal{A} = (\mathcal{A}_1, \mathcal{A}_2)$, the following advantage $\varepsilon_{\text{hide}}$ is negligible:

$$\left| \Pr\left[b = b' : \begin{array}{l} (m, \omega) \xleftarrow{R} \mathcal{A}_1(1^k), (c_0, d) \xleftarrow{R} \texttt{Commit}(m), \\ c_1 \xleftarrow{R} \{0, 1\}^{|c_0|}, b \xleftarrow{R} \{0, 1\}, b' \xleftarrow{R} \mathcal{A}_2(c_b, \omega) \end{array} \right] - \frac{1}{2} \right|$$

- *Extractability*: If $\mathcal{A}$ is an algorithm, then let $T(\mathcal{A})$ denote the transcripts of all random oracle queries and responses made by $\mathcal{A}$ during its execution. Then we require that the following advantage ε_{ext} is negligible:

$$\Pr[\texttt{Extract}(c, T(\mathcal{A})) \neq d \wedge \texttt{Open}(c, d) \neq \perp : (c, d) \xleftarrow{R} \mathcal{A}(1^k)]$$

The extractability property implies the binding property that we would expect from a commitment scheme. Consider an algorithm $\mathcal{A}$ that outputs (c, d, d') where $d \neq d'$ but for which Open(c, d) $\neq \perp$ and Open(c, d') $\neq \perp$. Then we can conclude that Extract($c, T(\mathcal{A})$) $= d$ as (c, d) is a valid commitment. However, by the same argument, we can also conclude that Extract($c, T(\mathcal{A})$) $= d'$, which is a contradiction. Hence, we are forced to conclude that it is infeasible to construct an algorithm $\mathcal{A}$ which outputs (c, d, d').

We construct an extractable commitment scheme using a hash function $H \colon \{0, 1\}^{|d|} \to \{0, 1\}^{|c|}$. In the security proofs of Dodis et al. [77, 78], this hash function is modeled as a random oracle [29]. Suppose that we wish to commit to a message m. We first split m into two bitstrings m_1 and m_2 such that $m = m_1 \| m_2$. Next a random bitstring $r \in \{0, 1\}^{(|d| - |m_2|)}$ is chosen. The commitment and corresponding decommitment are computed as follows:

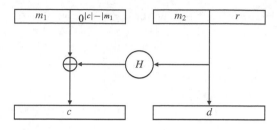

Fig. 6.1 An extractable commitment scheme

$$c \leftarrow (m_1 \| 0^{(|c|-|m_1|)}) \oplus H(m_2 \| r)$$
$$d \leftarrow m_2 \| r$$

Here $0^{(|c|-|m_1|)}$ denotes a string of $|c| - |m_1|$ zeros. Clearly this scheme is parameterized by $|m_1|$, $|m_2|$, $|c|$, and $|d|$. We give a graphical illustration in Fig. 6.1. The Open process involves computing $m_2 \| r \leftarrow d$ and $m_1 \| t \leftarrow c \oplus H(d)$. The message $m = m_1 \| m_2$ is returned only if $t = 0^{(|c|-|m_1|)}$; otherwise an error message $\perp$ is returned.

This scheme is a generalization that, given appropriate choices of parameters, and when used with particular Feistel padding schemes, reduces to existing padding schemes [30, 31]. If $|m_1| = 0$ and the P-Pad scheme, described in Sect. 6.4.3, is used, then this gives the PSS-R padding scheme [31]. Similarly, if $|m_2| = 0$ and the P-Pad scheme is used, then we obtain the OAEP padding scheme [30]. Both PSS and OAEP were designed by Bellare and Rogaway.

6.4.3 Padding-Based Signcryption Schemes

We are now in a position to describe the padding-based signcryption schemes. In all cases, the sender's public key will be a trapdoor one-way permutation $pk_S = f_S$ and the sender's private key will be the corresponding inverse permutation $sk_S = f_S^{-1}$. Similarly, the receiver's public key will also be defined by a trapdoor one-way permutation $pk_R = f_R$ and $sk_R = f_R^{-1}$. In all cases, the signcryption scheme will begin by applying an extractable commitment scheme to the message, resulting in the commitment pair (c, d). Then a padding scheme will be applied to create "shares" (w, s). Finally, the sender's and receiver's permutations will be applied to the shares in order to produce a ciphertext.

All of the padding schemes are based on *Feistel networks*. A Feistel network takes as input a pair (L, R) and makes use of a *round function* F. The output of one round of a Feistel network is (L', R') where

$$L' = R \quad \text{and} \quad R' = F(R) \oplus L$$

It is easy to see that such a procedure is invertible, even if F itself is not, as

$$R = L' \quad \text{and} \quad L = F(R) \oplus R'$$

All the padding schemes here will make use of one or more rounds of a Feistel network. The round functions are constructed using cryptographic hash functions

$$G : \{0, 1\}^* \to \{0, 1\}^{|d|} \quad \text{and} \quad H : \{0, 1\}^* \to \{0, 1\}^{|c|}$$

where $|c|$ and $|d|$ denote the lengths of c and d in the commitment scheme (respectively). We denote the padding operation Pad and the corresponding de-padding operation Depad. We also make use of an extractable commitment scheme with a commitment algorithm Commit and an opening algorithm Open. For security, we require that $|c|$, $|d|$, $|r|$, and $|c| - |m_1|$ are sufficiently large.

We define three padding schemes and the corresponding signcryption schemes: *parallel padding*, *sequential padding*, and *extended sequential padding*. We note that one important feature of these schemes is that they do not assume that users have separate keys for sending and receiving ciphertexts: a single transform f_U is sufficient for a user U to act as both sender and receiver. In order to incorporate this into the security model, we use the one-key model discussed in Sect. 3.2.3 and outlined in Sect. 5.4.

6.4.3.1 Signcryption Based on the Parallel Padding Scheme

The parallel padding scheme (P-Pad) is described in Fig. 6.2. The resulting signcryption scheme is given in Fig. 6.3 and is shown graphically in Fig. 6.4.

We quote the security results for completion. We give some intuition as to why these theorems hold in Sect. 6.4.4 and prove the security of a related scheme using similar techniques in Sect. 6.5.2.

$$
\begin{array}{ll}
\text{P-Pad}(m, pk_S, pk_R): & \text{P-Depad}(w, s, pk_S, pk_R): \\
\quad bind \leftarrow pk_S \| pk_R & \quad bind \leftarrow pk_S \| pk_R \\
\quad (c, d) \xleftarrow{R} \text{Commit}(m) & \quad d \leftarrow G(bind, w) \oplus s \\
\quad w \leftarrow c & \quad c \leftarrow w \\
\quad s \leftarrow G(bind, c) \oplus d & \quad m \leftarrow \text{Open}(c, d) \\
\quad \text{Return } (w, s) & \quad \text{Return } m
\end{array}
$$

Fig. 6.2 The parallel padding (P-Pad) scheme

$$
\begin{array}{ll}
\text{Signcrypt}(f_S^{-1}, f_R, m): & \text{Unsigncrypt}(f_S, f_R^{-1}, C): \\
\quad (w, s) \xleftarrow{R} \text{P-Pad}(m, f_S, f_R) & \quad \text{Parse } C \text{ as } (\chi, \psi) \\
\quad \chi \leftarrow f_R(w) & \quad w \leftarrow f_R^{-1}(\chi) \\
\quad \psi \leftarrow f_S^{-1}(s) & \quad s \leftarrow f_S(\psi) \\
\quad C \leftarrow (\chi, \psi) & \quad m \leftarrow \text{P-Depad}(w, s, f_S, f_R) \\
\quad \text{Return } C & \quad \text{Return } m
\end{array}
$$

Fig. 6.3 The parallel padding signcryption scheme

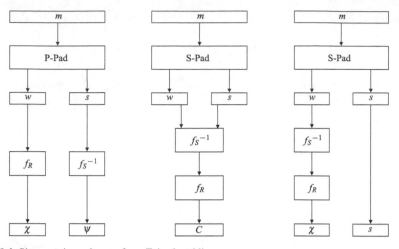

Fig. 6.4 Signcryption schemes from Feistel padding

Theorem 6.1 *For any algorithm, let q_S denote the number of signcryption queries made by the algorithm, q_U denote the number of unsigncryption queries made by the algorithm, and q_G denote the number of queries to the random oracle modeling the hash function G made by the algorithm. Let ε_{tdp} be the advantage of some attacker against the trapdoor one-way permutation, let ε_{hide} be the advantage of some attacker against the hiding property of the commitment scheme, and let ε_{ext} be the advantage of some attacker against the extractability property of the commitment scheme.*

If there exists a PPT attacker that has advantage ε_{cca} against the multi-user insider FSO/FUO-IND-CCA2 security property of the parallel padding signcryption scheme, then

$$\varepsilon_{cca} \leq \varepsilon_{tdp} + (q_S + 2)\big((q_S + q_G)2^{-|c|} + \varepsilon_{hide}\big) + q_U(\varepsilon_{ext} + 2^{-|d|}) + 2\varepsilon_{ext}$$

If there exists a PPT attacker that has advantage ε_{cma} against the multi-user insider FSO/FUO-sUF-CMA security property of the parallel padding signcryption scheme, then

$$\varepsilon_{cma} \leq q_G \varepsilon_{tdp} + q_S\big((q_S + q_G)2^{-|c|} + \varepsilon_{hide}\big) + (q_U + 2)\big(\varepsilon_{ext} + 2^{-|d|}\big) + 6\varepsilon_{ext}$$

Note that it is fairly simple to apply the two RSA transforms in the parallel padding scheme: one simply ensures that the two shares (w, s) are less than the corresponding moduli (N_R, N_S). This can be done either by setting $|w| = |N_R| - 1$ and $|s| = |N_S| - 1$ or by repeatedly running the commitment algorithm until the signcryption gives rise to values (w, s) which are in the correct range.

$$
\begin{array}{ll}
\text{S-Pad}(m, pk_S, pk_R): & \text{S-Depad}(w, s, pk_S, pk_R): \\
\quad bind \leftarrow pk_S \| pk_R & \quad bind \leftarrow pk_S \| pk_R \\
\quad (c, d) \xleftarrow{R} \text{Commit}(m) & \quad c \leftarrow H(w) \oplus s \\
\quad w \leftarrow G(bind, c) \oplus d & \quad d \leftarrow G(bind, c) \oplus w \\
\quad s \leftarrow H(w) \oplus c & \quad m \leftarrow \text{Open}(c, d) \\
\quad \text{Return } (w, s) & \quad \text{Return } m
\end{array}
$$

Fig. 6.5 The sequential padding (S-Pad) scheme

$$
\begin{array}{ll}
\text{Signcrypt}(f_S^{-1}, f_R, m): & \text{Unsigncrypt}(f_S, f_R^{-1}, C): \\
\quad (w, s) \xleftarrow{R} \text{S-Pad}(m, f_S, f_R) & \quad (w, s) \leftarrow f_S(f_R^{-1}(C)) \\
\quad C \leftarrow f_R(f_S^{-1}(w, s)) & \quad m \leftarrow \text{S-Depad}(w, s, f_S, f_R) \\
\quad \text{Return } C & \quad \text{Return } m
\end{array}
$$

Fig. 6.6 The sequential padding signcryption scheme

6.4.3.2 Signcryption Based on the Sequential Padding Scheme

The sequential padding (S-Pad) scheme is slightly more complicated than the parallel padding scheme: one extra round of Feistel network is required. The padding scheme is given in Fig. 6.5 and the signcryption scheme is given in Fig. 6.6. Again, the scheme is shown graphically in Fig. 6.4. The padding scheme is a two-round Feistel network using G as the round function in the first round and H as the round function in the second round.

Again, we state the security result for completion.

Theorem 6.2 *For any algorithm, let q_S denote the number of signcryption queries made by the algorithm, q_U denote the number of unsigncryption queries made by the algorithm, q_G denote the number of queries to the random oracle modeling the hash function G made by the algorithm, and q_H denote the number of queries to the random oracle modeling the hash function H made by the algorithm. Let ε_{tdp} be the advantage of some attacker against the trapdoor one-way permutation, ε_{hide} be the advantage of some attacker against the hiding property of the commitment scheme, and ε_{ext} be the advantage of some attacker against the extractability property of the commitment scheme.*

If there exists a PPT attacker that has advantage ε_{cca} against the multi-user insider FSO/FUO-IND-CCA2 security property of the sequential padding signcryption scheme, then

$$
\varepsilon_{cca} \le \varepsilon_{tdp} + (q_S + q_G + q_H)^2 2^{-|d|}
$$
$$
+ (q_S + q_U)\big((2q_G + q_S)2^{-|c|} + \varepsilon_{hide} + \varepsilon_{ext}\big) + 3q_G \varepsilon_{hide}
$$

If there exists a PPT attacker that has advantage ε_{cma} against the multi-user insider FSO/FUO-sUF-CMA security property of the sequential padding signcryption scheme, then

$$
\varepsilon_{cma} \le q_G \varepsilon_{tdp} + (q_S + q_G + q_H)^2 2^{-|d|}
$$
$$
+ (q_S + q_U)\big((q_G + q_S)2^{-|c|} + \varepsilon_{hide} + 4\varepsilon_{ext}\big)
$$

Note that the sequential signcryption scheme (and the extended sequential sign-cryption scheme) is not secure in the secret key ignorant model as the attacker can always set $f_S = f_R$ and remove the trapdoor permutations from the description of the signcryption scheme.

It is much harder to alter the sequential padding scheme so that it uses the RSA transform in place of arbitrary one-way permutations. This is due to the fact that the sender's RSA transform defines a permutation over $\mathbb{Z}_{N_S}$ and the receiver's RSA transform defines a permutation over $\mathbb{Z}_{N_R}$, and so the result of the first transform may not constitute a valid input to the second transform. The problem will be discussed in more depth when we discuss the RSA-TBOS scheme in Sect. 6.5.1.

6.4.3.3 Signcryption Based on the Extended Sequential Padding Scheme

The extended sequential padding scheme is identical to the sequential padding scheme. The difference is in how it is applied to construct a signcryption scheme. The net effect is, at the cost of a slightly longer ciphertext, one obtains a tighter proof of security when using extended sequential padding. The resulting X-Pad signcryption scheme is given in Fig. 6.7 and shown graphically in Fig. 6.4.

Theorem 6.3 *For any algorithm, let q_S denote the number of signcryption queries made by the algorithm, q_U denote the number of unsigncryption queries made by the algorithm, q_G denote the number of queries to the random oracle modeling the hash function G made by the algorithm, and q_H denote the number of queries to the random oracle modeling the hash function H made by the algorithm. Let ε_{tdp} be the advantage of some attacker against the trapdoor one-way permutation, ε_{hide} be the advantage of some attacker against the hiding property of the commitment scheme, and ε_{ext} be the advantage of some attacker against the extractability property of the commitment scheme.*

If there exists a PPT attacker that has advantage ε_{cca} against the multi-user insider FSO/FUO-IND-CCA2 security property of the extended sequential padding signcryption scheme, then

$$\varepsilon_{cca} \leq \varepsilon_{tdp} + \left(q_S + q_G + q_H\right)^2 2^{-|d|}$$
$$+ (q_S + q_U)\left((2q_G + q_S)2^{-|c|} + \varepsilon_{hide} + \varepsilon_{ext}\right) + 3q_G\varepsilon_{hide}$$

If there exists a PPT attacker that has advantage ε_{cma} against the multi-user insider FSO/FUO-sUF-CMA security property of the extended sequential padding signcryption scheme, then

$$
\begin{array}{ll}
\text{Signcrypt}(f_S^{-1}, f_R, m): & \text{Unsigncrypt}(f_S, f_R^{-1}, C): \\
(w, s) \xleftarrow{R} \text{S-Pad}(m, f_S, f_R) & \text{Parse } C \text{ as } (\chi, s) \\
\chi \leftarrow f_R(f_S^{-1}(w)) & w \leftarrow f_S(f_R^{-1}(C)) \\
C \leftarrow (\chi, s) & m \leftarrow \text{S-Depad}(w, s, f_S, f_R) \\
\text{Return } C & \text{Return } m
\end{array}
$$

Fig. 6.7 The extended sequential padding signcryption scheme

$$\varepsilon_{cma} \leq q_G \varepsilon_{tdp} + (q_S + q_G + q_H)^2 2^{-|d|}$$
$$+ (q_S + q_U)((q_G + q_S)2^{-|c|} + \varepsilon_{hide} + 4\varepsilon_{ext})$$

The security reductions lose the same amount of tightness in both the sequential and extended sequential padding-based schemes. However, the extended sequential padding-based scheme is perhaps to be regarded as more secure as the derived algorithm which breaks the trapdoor one-way permutation is more efficient. The details can be found in Dodis et al. [77]. Again, the problem of using RSA transform with this construction is discussed in Sect. 6.5.1.

6.4.4 Proof Intuition

Here we provide some intuition about how the notion of extractable commitments, as introduced in Sect. 6.4.2, can be used when arguing formally about the security of the resulting signcryption schemes. Our treatment is only intuitive. Formal results may be found in [77, 78].

We take the P-Pad signcryption scheme as an illustrative example. The semantic security proof for the P-Pad scheme by Dodis et al. [77, 78] holds under the assumption that the trapdoor permutation f_R is one-way. As part of the proof, we must show that the attacker is not able to break the security of the scheme by querying the unsigncryption oracle or the signcryption oracle. This is achieved by showing that we can use the properties of the random oracle model and the extractable commitment scheme to build a simulation of the signcryption and unsigncryption oracle without needing to invert the function f_R.

Consider a ciphertext (χ, ψ) submitted to the unsigncryption oracle. We may easily recover s as $f_S(\psi)$. In the random oracle model, we may record the inputs $bind\|c$ to the random oracle G and the respective outputs. Furthermore, due to the extractability property of the commitment scheme, for each input c we may determine if c is a valid commitment to some value and, if so, the corresponding decommitment d. Hence, we may search for a pair (c, d) such that $G(bind\|c) \oplus d = s$ and $f_R(c) = \chi$. If such a pair exists, then we can return the message $\mathtt{Open}(c, d)$. Otherwise we return the error symbol $\perp$.

Similarly, if we consider a signcryption query made on the message m, then we can use the random oracle to create a valid ciphertext. We first compute $(c, d) \xleftarrow{R} \mathtt{Commit}(m)$ and choose a random value for s. The ciphertext is computed as $\chi \leftarrow f_R(c)$ and $\psi \leftarrow f_S(s)$, and the random oracle is "fixed" so that $G(bind\|c) = s \oplus d$. It can be shown that, with high probability, this "fixing" of the random oracle is unnoticed by the adversary and so the adversary is given a valid signcryption of the message m.

However, it can be shown that the attacker must query the G-oracle on the commitment c^* used to create the challenge ciphertext in order to break the security of the scheme. (If the attacker does not query the G-oracle on c^*, then the attacker cannot learn any information about the corresponding decommitment d^* and so cannot learn any information about the message due to the hiding property of the commitment scheme.) If the attacker does query the G-oracle on c^* then the attacker has managed to invert f_R on the challenge ciphertext χ^*, which breaks the security of the trapdoor one-way permutation.

The unforgeability of the scheme follows for similar reasons. We can simulate signcryption and unsigncryption oracles as in the proof of confidentiality. However, in order to forge a signcryption on any message, it can be shown that this means the attacker must forge a signcryption on a *new* value of s, i.e., a value of s which the signcryption oracle has *not* used to produce a signcryption. Now, since $s = G(bind\|c) \oplus d$ and G is a random oracle, this is equivalent to inverting f_S on a random input, which breaks the security of the trapdoor one-way permutation.

6.5 Signcryption Based on RSA-TBOS

Independent of, and slightly prior to, the abstract treatment provided by Dodis et al. [77, 78], a similar padding-based scheme was proposed by Malone-Lee and Mao under the title of "Two Birds One Stone (TBOS)" signcryption [131]. We present a slightly modified treatment of that algorithm which can be proven secure in the multi-user model.

6.5.1 The TBOS Construction

The abstract TBOS scheme is given in Fig. 6.8. The scheme uses a version of the extractable commitment scheme described in Sect. 6.4.2, the parallel padding scheme described in Sect. 6.4.3.1, and trapdoor permutations in a manner similar to that of the sequential signcryption scheme described in Sect. 6.4.3.2. The overall result is that this construction is very similar to the sequential signcryption scheme, but uses a Feistel network with one fewer round. However, this efficiency gain comes at the cost of weakened security guarantees.

The original construction was designed and proven secure in a two-user model. However, we have reformulated the scheme in terms of a one-key multi-user model. A security proof for this construction is given in Sect. 6.5.2.

We now adapt this scheme to use the RSA permutation in place of an arbitrary trapdoor permutation. The RSA permutation is defined over the $\mathbb{Z}_N$ and, as dis-

$$
\begin{array}{ll}
\text{Signcrypt}(f_S^{-1}, f_R, m): & \text{Unsigncrypt}(f_S, f_R^{-1}, C): \\
\quad bind \leftarrow pk_S \| pk_R & \quad bind \leftarrow pk_S \| pk_R \\
\quad r \xleftarrow{R} \{0,1\}^{|d|-|m|} & \quad (w\|s) \leftarrow f_S(f_R^{-1}(C)) \\
\quad c \leftarrow H(bind, m\|r) & \quad m\|r \leftarrow G(bind, w) \oplus s \\
\quad d \leftarrow m\|r & \quad \text{If } H(bind, m\|r) = w \text{ return } m \\
\quad w \leftarrow c & \quad \text{Else return } \bot \\
\quad s \leftarrow G(bind, c) \oplus d & \\
\quad C \leftarrow f_R(f_S^{-1}(w\|s)) & \\
\quad \text{Return } C &
\end{array}
$$

Fig. 6.8 The TBOS signcryption scheme with an arbitrary permutation

cussed in the introduction, we require different values of N to be defined for the sender permutation and the receiver permutation. While we could have defined the abstract constructions in terms of permutations over arbitrary sets, which would allow the use of a single RSA transform, there is a problem in that the two permutations used in the signcryption constructions will necessarily act over different sets. In particular, if the sender public and private keys consist of the integers (N_S, e_S) and (N_S, d_S), and the receiver public/private key consists of the integers (N_R, e_R) and (N_R, d_R), then it is unclear how to perform signcryption if $f_S^{-1}(w, s) = (w\|s)^{d_S} \bmod N_S$ is an integer greater than N_R. Similarly, it is unclear how to perform unsigncryption if $f_R^{-1}(w, s) = (w\|s)^{d_R} \bmod N_R$ is an integer greater than N_S. We term this the domain problem of RSA signcryption.

The RSA-TBOS construction is given in Fig. 6.9. Note that this scheme does not make use of a Setup algorithm. By Theorems 6.4 and 6.5 and Lemma 6.1, the security of this scheme is related to the difficulty in solving the RSA problem. Further details can be found in [131].

The RSA-TBOS signcryption scheme deals with the domain problem in two ways. First, the signcryption algorithm fails if a random value r is chosen such that the result value of $w\|s$ is greater than N_S. If such a situation occurs, then the message can still be the subject of signcryption, but a different value of r should be chosen. It is unlikely that more than two values of r will need to be chosen. Second, if the intermediate ciphertext C' is greater than N_R then the signcryption algorithm computes a smaller, related value by forcing the most significant bit to

KeyGen$_S(1^k)$:
  $(p, q) \xleftarrow{R} \text{RSAGen}(1^k)$
  $N_S \leftarrow pq$
  $e_S \xleftarrow{R} \mathbb{Z}^*_{\phi(N)}$
  $d_S \leftarrow e_S^{-1} \bmod (p-1)(q-1)$
  $pk_S \leftarrow (N_S, e_S); sk_S \leftarrow (N_S, d_S)$
  Return (pk_S, sk_S)

KeyGen$_R(1^k)$:
  $(p, q) \xleftarrow{R} \text{RSAGen}(1^k)$
  $N_R \leftarrow pq$
  $e_R \xleftarrow{R} \mathbb{Z}^*_{\phi(N)}$
  $d_R \leftarrow e_R^{-1} \bmod (p-1)(q-1)$
  $pk_R \leftarrow (N_R, e_R); sk_R \leftarrow (N_R, d_R)$
  Return (pk_R, sk_R)

Signcrypt(sk_S, pk_R, m):
  Parse sk_S as (N_S, d_S)
  Parse pk_R as (N_R, e_R)
  $bind \leftarrow pk_S \| pk_R$
  $r \xleftarrow{R} \{0, 1\}^{|r|}$
  $w \leftarrow H(bind, m\|r)$
  $s \leftarrow (m\|r) \oplus G(bind, w)$
  If $w\|s > N_S$ then return $\perp$
  $C' \leftarrow (w\|s)^{d_S} \bmod N_S$
  If $C' > N_R$ then $C' \leftarrow C' - 2^{k-1}$
  $C \leftarrow C'^{e_R} \bmod N_R$
  Return C

Unsigncrypt(pk_S, sk_R, C):
  Parse pk_S as (N_S, e_S)
  Parse sk_R as (N_R, d_R)
  $bind \leftarrow pk_S \| pk_R$
  $C' \leftarrow C^{d_R} \bmod N_R$
  If $C' > N_S$ then return $\perp$
  $(w\|s) \leftarrow C'^{e_S} \bmod N_S$
  $m\|r \leftarrow s \oplus G(bind, w)$
  If $H(bind, m\|r) = w$ then return m
  $C' \leftarrow C' + 2^{k-1}$
  If $C' > N_S$ then return $\perp$
  $(w\|s) \leftarrow C'^{e_S} \bmod N_S$
  $m\|r \leftarrow s \oplus G(bind, w)$
  If $H(bind, m\|r) = w$ then return m
  Else return $\perp$

Fig. 6.9 The RSA-TBOS signcryption scheme

be zero. The result is guaranteed to be an integer in the correct domain. It may
be thought that this would lead to security or useability weaknesses, as there now
exist two potential messages which lead to the same ciphertext: the intermediate
ciphertext C' may occur as a result of a message m and a random value r which
gives rise to a pair (w, s) satisfying $(w\|s)^{es} \bmod N_S = C'$ or as the result of a
message m' and a random value r' which gives rise to a pair (w', s') satisfying
$(w'\|s')^{es} \bmod N_S = C' + 2^{k-1} > N_R$. However, since $(m, r) \neq (m', r')$ and H is
a random oracle, the probability that $H(bind, m\|r) = w$ and $H(bind, m'\|r') = w'$
is very small. Hence, with very high probability, only one solution will be a valid
ciphertext. This allows us to adapt the security proofs for the abstract construction
to the RSA-TBOS construction.

An unfortunate consequence of the solution to the domain problem in the RSA-
TBOS signcryption scheme is that the unsigncryption oracle may have to perform an
extra exponentiation in the unsigncryption process in order to recover the message
(or determine that the ciphertext is invalid). Malone-Lee and Mao [131] give two
methods of avoiding this problem:

- The first method is for the signcryption algorithm to fail if it produces a value
  $C' > N_R$. As with the case where the algorithm fails if $(w\|s) > N_S$, the sign-
  cryption algorithm could still act on the message, but a new value of r should be
  chosen.
- The second method is to append a bit b to the ciphertext which is set to 1 whenever the intermediate value C' is greater than N_R. In this case, the unsigncryption
  algorithm would always compute $C' \leftarrow C' + 2^{b(k-1)}$ as part of its unsigncryption
  process.

Although separate formal security arguments have not been presented for these
schemes, they would appear to be as secure as the original construction, as the
methods used in the proof for the simulation of the signcryption and unsigncryption
oracles can provide information as to the size of the intermediate value C'.

Lastly, we note that the scheme can easily be altered to provide non-repudiation.
To attest to a message m, the receiver only has to provide the intermediate value C'
computed during the unsigncryption process. It is simple to verify that this is the
correct intermediate value for the ciphertext, by checking that $C = f_R(C')$, and to
compute the corresponding message as in the normal unsigncryption process.

6.5.2 Security Proof for the TBOS Signcryption Scheme

Since we have reformulated the TBOS scheme in the multi-user model, we are
forced to re-prove the security of the scheme. The security of the abstract TBOS
scheme depends upon a non-standard assumption related to the hardness of inverting
a trapdoor one-way permutation.

Definition 6.3 (Partial bi-directional one-way permutations) Let k be a security
parameter and Gen define a family of trapdoor permutations over $\{0, 1\}^{\ell(k)}$ and

let $\ell'(k) \leq \ell(k)$ for all k. The family is partial bi-directional one-way if any PPT attacker $\mathcal{A}$ has negligible probability in the following experiment:

$$\Pr\left[f_2(f_1^{-1}(C)) = w\|s \ : \ \begin{array}{c} w \overset{R}{\leftarrow} \mathcal{A}(f_1, f_2, C), \ C \leftarrow \{0,1\}^{\ell(k)}, \\ (f_2, f_2^{-1}) \overset{R}{\leftarrow} \mathsf{Gen}(1^k), \ (f_1, f_1^{-1}) \overset{R}{\leftarrow} \mathsf{Gen}(1^k) \end{array} \right]$$

for some s, where $w \in \{0,1\}^{\ell'(k)}$.

The definition can be thought of as capturing the difficulty of finding even part of the inverse of the function $f_1 \circ f_2^{-1}$. This function is a permutation which is one-way in both directions; however, knowledge of one trapdoor allows the computation of the function in one direction. This strongly resembles the ordering of the use of permutations in the sequential padding signcryption schemes. Obviously, the problem of recovering the entire input $f_2(f_1^{-1}(C))$ given (f_1, f_2, C) is equivalent to the problem of recovering $f_1^{-1}(C)$ given (f_1, C). However, the problem of recovering part of the input of $f_2(f_1^{-1}(C))$ given (f_1, f_2, C) does not appear to be equivalent to the problem of recovering part of the input of $f_1^{-1}(C)$ from (f_1, C) except perhaps in special cases.

Theorem 6.4 *Let $\mathcal{A}$ be a PPT attacker against the multi-user one-key outsider FSO/FUO-IND-CCA2 security of the signcryption scheme with advantage ε_{cca} and suppose that $\mathcal{A}$ makes at most q_S queries to the signcryption oracle, q_U queries to the unsigncryption oracle, q_G queries to the random oracle modeling the hash function G, and q_H queries to the random oracle modeling the hash function H. Then there exists a PPT attacker $\mathcal{B}$ against the partial bi-direction one-way permutation with advantage ε_{tdp} such that*

$$\varepsilon_{cca} \leq (q_G + q_H + q_S)\varepsilon_{tdp} + (q_H + q_S)(q_G + q_H + q_S)2^{-|c|}$$
$$+(q_H + q_S)^2 2^{-|r|} + q_S 2^{-|r|} + q_U(2^{-|c|} + 2^{-(|c|+|d|)})$$

Proof Suppose that $\mathcal{A} = (\mathcal{A}_1, \mathcal{A}_2)$ is an attacker against the multi-user one-key outsider FSO/FUO-IND-CCA2 security of the signcryption scheme. Suppose that the attacker $\mathcal{A}$ is run using the challenge sender public key f_S^* and the challenge receiver public key f_R^*. We begin by explaining how we will simulate the oracles to which the attacker has access:

- *G-oracle*: If the G-oracle is queried with an input $(bind, w)$ then the oracle searches for an entry $(bind, w, t)$ on GLIST. If such an entry exists, then the oracle returns t. Otherwise, the oracle generates $t \overset{R}{\leftarrow} \{0,1\}^{|d|}$, stores $(bind, w, t)$ on GLIST, and returns t.
- *H-oracle*: If the H-oracle is queried with an input $(bind, m\|r)$ then the oracle searches for an entry $(bind, m\|r, w, C)$ on HLIST. If such an entry exists, then the oracle returns w. If $bind$ cannot be split into $f_S\|f_R$, then the oracle is simulated trivially in the same manner as the G-oracle. Otherwise, the oracle chooses $x \overset{R}{\leftarrow} \{0,1\}^{|c|+|d|}$, computes $y \leftarrow f_S(x)$ and $C \leftarrow f_R(x)$, and splits y as $y_1\|y_2$ where

$y_1 \in \{0, 1\}^{|c|}$ and $y_2 \in \{0, 1\}^{|d|}$. If the G-oracle is defined on $(bind, y_1)$ then the algorithm fails. If not, the algorithm stores $(bind, m\|r, y_1, C)$ on HLIST and $(bind, y_1, y_2 \oplus m\|r)$ on GLIST and returns y_1.

- *Signcryption*: If the signcryption oracle is queried on the sender public key $f_U \in \{f_S^*, f_R^*\}$, the receiver public key f_R, and the message m, then the oracle computes $bind \leftarrow f_U\|f_R$, chooses $r \xleftarrow{R} \{0, 1\}^{|r|}$ and $x \xleftarrow{R} \{0, 1\}^{|c|+|d|}$, computes $y \leftarrow f_U(x)$ and $C \leftarrow f_R(x)$, and splits y as $y_1\|y_2$ where $y_1 \in \{0, 1\}^{|c|}$ and $y_2 \in \{0, 1\}^{|d|}$. If the H-oracle is defined on $(bind, m\|r)$ or the G-oracle is defined on $(bind, y_1)$ then the algorithm fails. Otherwise, the oracle adds $(bind, m\|r, y_1, C)$ to HLIST, $(bind, y_1, y_2 \oplus m\|r)$ to GLIST, and returns C.
- *Unsigncryption*: If the unsigncryption oracle is queried on the sender public key f_S, the receiver public key $f_U \in \{f_S^*, f_R^*\}$, and the ciphertext C, then the oracle computes $bind \leftarrow f_S\|f_U$ and searches the HLIST for an entry $(bind, m\|r, x, C)$. If such an entry exists, then the oracle returns m. Otherwise, it returns $\perp$.

These simulations are perfect as long as one of the following four exceptions do not occur:

- The H-oracle is forced to define a G-oracle entry on some value $(bind, y_1)$ which is already defined. For each H-oracle query, y_1 is a randomly chosen value of $\{0, 1\}^{|c|}$. Since $|\text{GLIST}| \leq q_G + q_H + q_S$, we have that the probability that y_1 has been part of a previous query is bounded by $(q_G + q_H + q_S)2^{-|c|}$. Thus, when we consider all H-oracle queries, the probability that the simulation fails is bounded by $q_H(q_G + q_H + q_S)2^{-|c|}$.
- The signcryption oracle is forced to define a H-oracle query on some value $(bind, m\|r)$ which is already defined. However, since r is chosen at random and $|\text{HLIST}| \leq q_H + q_S$, we have that this occurs with probability at most $q_S(q_H + q_S)2^{-|r|}$.
- The signcryption oracle is forced to define a G-oracle query on some value $(bind, y_1)$ which is already defined. Again, since y_1 is chosen at random and $|\text{GLIST}| \leq q_G + q_H + q_S$, we have that this occurs with probability at most $q_S(q_G + q_H + q_S)2^{-|c|}$.
- The unsigncryption oracle returns $\perp$ for some valid ciphertext. This can only occur if the H-oracle has not been queried on the underlying values $(bind, m\|r)$ for which $H(bind, m\|r) = w$. Since H is a random oracle, the probability that $H(bind, m\|r)$ would be defined to be w is $2^{-|c|}$. Hence, the probability that the simulation fails is bounded by $q_U 2^{-|c|}$.

We define an algorithm which uses these simulated oracles to break the partial one-way property of the challenge user's public key. The algorithm $\mathcal{B}$ runs as follows:

1. $\mathcal{B}$ receives the public keys (f_1, f_2) and the challenge value C^*. $\mathcal{B}$ sets $f_S^* = f_2$ and $f_R^* = f_1$.
2. $\mathcal{B}$ runs $\mathcal{A}_1$ on (f_S^*, f_R^*). If $\mathcal{A}$ queries an oracle, then these are answered using the simulated oracles above, with the exception that $\mathcal{B}$ halts if $\mathcal{A}$ queries the

unsigncryption oracle with C^* and the sender public key f_S^*. $\mathcal{A}_1$ terminates with the output of two equal-length messages (m_0, m_1) and some state information ω.

3. $\mathcal{B}$ runs $\mathcal{A}_2$ on the input (C^*, ω). If $\mathcal{A}_2$ makes an oracle query, then these are answered using the simulated oracles above. $\mathcal{A}_2$ terminates with the output of a bit b'.

4. $\mathcal{B}$ selects a random input on GLIST and outputs this as the solution to the problem instance.

We now consider $\mathcal{B}$'s success probability. Let asterisks denote variables that would be associated with the computation of the challenge ciphertext C^*. Hence, we have that C^* is an encryption of $m^* \in \{m_0, m_1\}$ using randomness r^* and involve the computation of the intermediate variables $bind^*$, c^*, d^*, w^*, and s^*. $\mathcal{B}$'s simulation of $\mathcal{A}$'s environment is perfect unless one of the following events occurs:

- $\mathcal{A}_1$ queries the unsigncryption oracle on (f_S^*, C^*). Since C^* is chosen at random, we have that this occurs with probability bounded by $q_U 2^{-k}$.

- $\mathcal{A}_2$ makes an unsigncryption oracle query which returns $\bot$ as the correct entry $(bind^*, m^* \| r^*, y_1, C)$ is not included on HLIST. However, in this case we must have that $C = C^*$ and so the query is illegal. Therefore, the probability that this event occurs is 0.

- $\mathcal{A}$ makes a G-oracle, H-oracle, or signcryption oracle query which defines the G-oracle's action on $(bind^*, w^*)$. In this case, the simulation fails; however, it allows the possibility that $\mathcal{B}$ can recover the solution to the challenge. We let this event be denoted E and note that $\Pr[E] \geq (q_G + q_H + q_S)\varepsilon_{tdp}$. All of the further analysis is predicated on the event E not occurring.

- $\mathcal{A}$ makes an H-oracle on $(bind^*, m^* \| r^*)$. However, if E does not occur, then r^* is information theoretically hidden from the attacker $\mathcal{A}$. Thus, this H-oracle query can occur only with probability bounded by $q_H(q_H + q_S)2^{-|r|}$. We let this event be denoted by E'.

- $\mathcal{A}$ makes a signcryption oracle query which defines the action of the H-oracle on $(bind^*, m^* \| r^*)$. Since r is chosen at random during the simulation of the signcryption oracle, this occurs with probability bounded by $q_S 2^{-|r|}$.

Lastly, we note that if E and E' do not occur, then the attacker $\mathcal{A}$ can have no advantage in breaking the FSO/FUO-IND-CCA2 security of the signcryption scheme. Hence,

$$\varepsilon_{cca} \leq (q_G + q_H + q_S)\varepsilon_{tdp} + (q_H + q_S)(q_G + q_H + q_S)2^{-|c|}$$
$$+ (q_H + q_S)^2 2^{-|r|} + q_S 2^{-|r|} + q_U(2^{-|c|} + 2^{-(|c|+|d|)})$$

This concludes the proof. □

Theorem 6.5 *Let $\mathcal{A}$ be a PPT attacker against the multi-user insider FSO/FUO-sUF-CMA security of the signcryption scheme with advantage ε_{cma} and suppose that $\mathcal{A}$ makes at most q_S queries to the signcryption oracle, q_U queries to the unsigncryption oracle, q_G queries to the random oracle modeling the hash function*

G, and q_H queries to the random oracle modeling the hash function H. Then there exists a PPT attacker $\mathcal{B}$ against the one-way permutation with advantage ε_{tdp} such that

$$\varepsilon_{cma} \leq q_H \varepsilon_{tdp} + (q_H + q_S + 1)(q_G + q_H + q_S)2^{-|c|}$$
$$+ q_S(q_H + q_S)2^{-|r|} + (q_U + 1)2^{-|c|}$$

Proof Suppose that $\mathcal{A}$ is an attacker against the multi-user one-key insider FSO/FUO-sUF-CMA security of the signcryption scheme. Suppose that $\mathcal{A}$ is run on the challenge sender public key f_S^*. We simulate the oracles as in the previous theorem (with the exception that there is no pre-specified challenge receiver key f_R^* and a slight modification to the H-oracle which is described below). We describe an algorithm $\mathcal{B}$ which breaks the one-way security of f_S^*:

1. $\mathcal{B}$ receives the challenge function f_S^* and the challenge value y^*. $\mathcal{B}$ splits y^* as $w^* \| s^*$ where $w^* \in \{0, 1\}^{|c|}$.
2. $\mathcal{B}$ randomly chooses an index $i^* \xleftarrow{R} \{1, 2, \ldots, q_H\}$. This index defines $\mathcal{B}$'s "guess" as to the H-oracle query corresponding to the forgery that $\mathcal{A}$ eventually outputs.
3. $\mathcal{B}$ runs $\mathcal{A}$ on f_S^*. If $\mathcal{A}$ queries an oracle, then $\mathcal{B}$ answers using the simulators described in the previous theorem, with the exception of the i^*-th new query to the H-oracle:

   - If the i^*-th new query to the H oracle is on input $(bind^*, m^* \| r^*)$ where $bind^* = f_S^* \| f_S^*$, then $\mathcal{B}$ stores $(bind^*, m^* \| r^*, w^*, w^* \| s^*)$ on HLIST and $(bind^*, w^*, s^* \oplus m^* \| r^*)$ on GLIST and returns w^*.
   - If the i^*-th new query to the H oracle is on input $(bind^*, m^* \| r^*)$ where $bind^* \neq f_S^* \| f_S^*$, then $\mathcal{B}$ stores $(bind^*, m^* \| r^*, w^*, ?)$ on HLIST and $(bind^*, w^*, s^* \oplus m^* \| r^*)$ on GLIST and returns w^*.

   In either case, if the G-oracle is already defined on the input $(bind^*, w^*)$ then $\mathcal{B}$ terminates. $\mathcal{A}$ terminates with the output of a receiver key pair (f_R^*, f_R^{*-1}) and a ciphertext C.
4. $\mathcal{B}$ outputs $f_R^{*-1}(C)$.

For notational convenience, we let C^* denote the encryption of m^* using the randomness r^* using the public keys defined in $bind^*$. In other words, C^* is the ciphertext associated with the i^*-th query to the H-oracle. If $\mathcal{B}$'s simulation was perfect, then the entry $(bind^*, m^* \| r^*, w^*, C^*)$ would be added to HLIST instead of $(bind^*, m^* \| r^*, w^*, ?)$. $\mathcal{B}$ correctly simulates the oracles to which $\mathcal{A}$ has access unless (a) any of the four conditions identified in the previous theorem holds, (b) the G-oracle is already defined on $(bind^*, w^*)$, or (c) $\mathcal{A}$ submits the ciphertext C^* and the sender public key f_S to the unsigncryption oracle where $bind^* = f_S \| f_S^*$. We have already shown that condition (a) occurs with probability at most

$$(q_H + q_S)(q_G + q_H + q_S)2^{-|c|} + q_S(q_H + q_S)2^{-|r|} + q_U 2^{-|c|}$$

and, since w^* is chosen at random, condition (b) occurs with probability at most $(q_G + q_H + q_S)2^{-|c|}$.

In order that $\mathcal{B}$ should correctly invert the challenge, it must correctly inject the challenge into the correct H-oracle query. If $\mathcal{A}$ outputs a ciphertext for which the H-oracle is not defined on the underlying values $(bind, m\|r)$, then the probability that it is a correct forgery is bounded by $2^{-|c|}$. If $\mathcal{A}$ did make such a query, then this will be the i^*-th query to the H-oracle with probability $1/q_H$. If this event occurs, then $\mathcal{B}$ outputs the correct solution to the challenge problem.

We now claim that our simulation of the unsigncryption oracle is sufficient such that condition (c) does not occur. If $\mathcal{B}$ is going to successfully invert the challenge, then we will require that $bind^* = f_S^*\|f_R^*$. Recall that f_S^* is defined by the challenge instance, while f_R^* is defined by the attacker. Therefore, if $\mathcal{B}$ correctly guesses the value of i^* and condition (c) occurs, then $bind^* = f_S^*\|f_S^*$. However, in this case, we do add the correct value to HLIST and simulate unsigncryption correctly. We therefore conclude that

$$\varepsilon_{cma} \leq q_H\varepsilon_{tdp} + (q_H + q_S + 1)(q_G + q_H + q_S)2^{-|c|}$$
$$+ q_S(q_H + q_S)2^{-|r|} + (q_U + 1)2^{-|c|}$$

This concludes the proof. $\square$

Part III
Construction Techniques

Chapter 7
Hybrid Signcryption

Tor E. Bjørstad

7.1 Background

A major limitation of many common asymmetric cryptographic primitives is that
their computational efficiency is much worse than for corresponding symmetric-
key algorithms. Hybrid cryptography is the branch of asymmetric cryptography that
aims to overcome this weakness, by using symmetric primitives as components to
improve the overall performance and flexibility of a larger asymmetric scheme.

The canonical example of the hybrid approach is hybrid encryption. In these
schemes, a symmetric encryption algorithm, such as a block cipher in a secure mode
of operation, is used to overcome the relative slowness and restricted message space
of traditional public-key encryption schemes. Informally, this is done by using the
public-key scheme to transmit a one-time symmetric key in a secure manner and
using that key to encrypt subsequent communication with the symmetric cipher.
This yields an overall scheme which is fast, efficient, and practical, even when
encrypting long messages.

Although the basic concept of hybrid encryption has been common knowledge
in the cryptographic community for many years, a formal construction paradigm
was first suggested in the late 1990s by Cramer and Shoup [68]. Their KEM +
DEM model splits a hybrid encryption scheme into two parts: an asymmetric *key
encapsulation mechanism* (KEM) and a symmetric *data encapsulation mechanism*
(DEM). The main benefit of this model is that the security of the KEM and DEM can
be analyzed separately, under the knowledge that *generic* composition of a secure
KEM and a secure DEM is essentially as secure as the component parts. Although
not all hybrid encryption schemes fit into this framework, it has proven itself as a
useful model for analysis in both theory and practice.

The original signcryption scheme proposed by Zheng [203] (as discussed in
Sects. 3.3 and 4.3) is a natural example of the benefits of the hybrid approach in signcryption. Using a public-key signature scheme as his starting point, Zheng showed
how to reap the benefits of both signatures and encryption at a low additional cost,

T. E. Bjørstad (✉)
Department of Informatics, The Selmer Center, University of Bergen, Bergen, Norway
e-mail: tor.bjorstad@ii.uib.no

A.W. Dent, Y. Zheng (eds.), *Practical Signcryption*, Information Security
and Cryptography, DOI 10.1007/978-3-540-89411-7_7,
© Springer-Verlag Berlin Heidelberg 2010

by using a symmetric key encryption scheme as a black-box component. A similar approach is used in many of the most efficient signcryption schemes in the literature (see Chaps. 4, 5, and 6). Hence it is of interest to study how hybrid techniques can be used to build signcryption schemes in a more general setting, to gain a better understanding of how these efficient schemes work.

It turns out that the formal analysis of hybrid signcryption schemes is more complicated than that of hybrid encryption. This stems from the increased complexity of obtaining message authenticity and integrity in addition to confidentiality. As discussed at depth in Chaps. 2 and 3, it is necessary to consider not only straightforward attacks against the authenticity and confidentiality of messages, but also more complex issues such as the distinction between outsider and insider attacks. As we shall see in Sects. 7.3 and 7.4 entirely different construction paradigms are needed to obtain appropriate models for outsider-secure and insider-secure hybrid signcryption.

A formal composition model for hybrid signcryption was first proposed by Dent in 2004, yielding an efficient model for signcryption KEMs in the outsider-secure setting [71, 73]. Dent's construction of outsider-secure signcryption KEMs is directly analogous to the corresponding construction of regular encryption KEMs. However, it is fundamentally impossible to produce an insider-secure signcryption KEM in this model. A model for insider-secure signcryption KEMs was also proposed by Dent in [71, 72]. This model covers Zheng's original scheme. However, this construction is quite complex and has a poor security reduction. This meant that the concrete security of Zheng's scheme appears significantly worse when analyzed in Dent's model, than in the non-hybrid setting of original security proof [12, 13, 36].

An improved model for insider-secure hybrid signcryption was given by Bjørstad and Dent [37], based on encryption tag-KEMs [5, 4] rather than regular encryption KEMs. As it turns out, this model provides a simpler description of signcryption schemes than its predecessor, and the generic security reduction for the signcryption tag-KEM + DEM construction is better. Zheng's signcryption scheme remains the canonical example of an (insider-secure) hybrid signcryption scheme, as it may be expressed in the signcryption tag-KEM + DEM setting with only a minor modification. In this model, the concrete security analysis of Zheng's scheme yields a similar result to that of the original proof of security [12, 13, 37].

The formal security analysis of hybrid signcryption has historically been performed in the simpler two-user (ADR) model presented in Chap. 2, rather than in a full multi-user (BSZ) setting presented in Chap. 3. Meanwhile, the multi-user security model is more suitable in the analysis of insider-secure signcryption schemes, where it is a reasonable assumption that an adversary may corrupt or otherwise obtain the private keys of legitimate users. A proof of security of signcryption tag-KEMs in the multi-user model may also have further applications, for example, in analysis of efficient key establishment protocols (discussed in Chap. 11). Initial study of the multi-user security of signcryption tag-KEMs was first performed by Yoshida and Fujiwara [200], although this text somewhat extends their results.

This chapter will commence by introducing the basic construction of hybrid encryption schemes in the KEM + DEM setting in Sect. 7.2. Following this, the adaptation of hybrid encryption KEMs to outsider-secure signcryption KEMs will be described in Sect. 7.3. Finally, the use of tag-KEMs to describe insider-secure hybrid signcryption will be examined in detail in Sect. 7.4.

7.1.1 A Brief Word on Notation

This chapter contains many situations in which one algorithm (with access to one set of oracles) runs a second algorithm (with access to a different set of oracles) as a subroutine. In order for the main algorithm to simulate the correct execution environment for the sub-algorithm, the main algorithm must simulate the oracles to which the sub-algorithm is expecting access. This is rather cumbersome to write in the typical $\mathcal{A}^{\mathcal{O}}(x)$ notation; hence, we introduce a new notation for this chapter and write $\mathcal{A}(x; \mathcal{O})$ for an algorithm which takes as input x and has access to an oracle $\mathcal{O}$.

If we are writing out the definition of an algorithm $\mathcal{B}$ that runs an algorithm $\mathcal{A}(x; \mathcal{O})$ as a subroutine, we will first detail the algorithm $\mathcal{B}$ and then detail a second algorithm $\mathcal{O}$ which explains how $\mathcal{B}$ responds to $\mathcal{A}$'s oracle queries. In other words, $\mathcal{B}$ will run the sub-algorithm $\mathcal{A}$ and use the sub-algorithm $\mathcal{O}$ to respond to $\mathcal{A}$'s oracle queries. This allows for a more compact and easily readable presentation of the main algorithm.

7.2 Preliminaries

In order to study the construction of secure hybrid signcryption schemes, it is highly instructive to first consider the basic KEM + DEM framework used to model hybrid encryption schemes. As a part of this, the necessary properties of data encapsulation mechanisms (DEMs) used as black-box components in hybrid schemes are defined.

7.2.1 The Hybrid Framework

To serve as a gentle introduction to the world of hybrid cryptography, it is instructive to discuss briefly the traditional KEM + DEM framework for hybrid encryption schemes [68]. This framework nicely illustrates the basic methodology employed and will be built upon later when discussing more complex constructions used for signcryption. We begin by defining the basic building blocks.

Definition 7.1 (KEM) A key encapsulation mechanism $KEM = $ (Setup, KeyGen, Encap, Decap) is a tuple of four algorithms:

- A probabilistic algorithm Setup that takes a security parameter 1^k as input, and returns some global information *param* that are common to all users of an instantiation of the scheme.
- A probabilistic algorithm KeyGen that takes the global information *param* as input and outputs a public/private keypair (sk, pk).

- A probabilistic algorithm Encap that takes a public key pk as input and outputs a pair (K, C), where K is a key and C is the encapsulation of K.
- A deterministic algorithm Decap that takes a private key sk and an encapsulation C as input and outputs either a key K or the unique error symbol $\perp$.

All variables may be represented as bitstrings of various lengths. In particular, the key K is a bitstring of a specific, fixed length determined by the security parameter. A KEM must be *sound*, in the sense that given a valid keypair (sk, pk) and a valid encapsulation $(K, C) \overset{R}{\leftarrow} \text{Encap}(pk)$, the output of $\text{Decap}(sk, C)$ will be K.

Definition 7.2 (DEM) A data encapsulation mechanism $DEM = (\text{Enc}, \text{Dec})$ is a tuple of two algorithms:

- A deterministic algorithm Enc that takes a key K and a message m as input and outputs a ciphertext C. We denote this $C \leftarrow \text{Enc}_K(m)$.
- A deterministic algorithm Dec that takes a key K and a ciphertext C as input and outputs either message m or the unique error symbol $\perp$. We denote this m or $\perp \leftarrow \text{Dec}_K(C)$.

The soundness criterion for a DEM is that the basic identity $m = \text{Dec}_K\big(\text{Enc}_K(m)\big)$ holds.

Given a KEM and DEM where the KEM outputs keys of suitable length for use with the DEM, a hybrid public-key encryption scheme (as defined in Sect. 1.3.3) can be constructed in a straightforward manner:

1. The Setup algorithm is run once to generate common information for all users.
2. Each user then runs KeyGen to generate their own public/private keypair.
3. When a sender S wants to transmit a message m to a receiver R, he computes $(K, C_1) \overset{R}{\leftarrow} \text{Encap}(pk_R)$ and encrypts the message as $C_2 \leftarrow \text{Enc}_K(m)$. The ciphertext $C \leftarrow (C_1, C_2)$ is then transmitted to R.
4. When the recipient R receives the ciphertext C from S, she extracts (C_1, C_2) from C, computes the symmetric key $K \leftarrow \text{Decap}(sk_R, C_1)$, and obtains the message $m \leftarrow \text{Dec}_K(C_2)$.

The above construction is a sound encryption scheme assuming the soundness of the KEM and DEM. Our main benefit of separating the encryption scheme into a KEM and a DEM is that the security of the components can be analyzed separately. Considering the basic building blocks instead of the entire scheme simplifies analysis and allows hybrid encryption schemes to be tailor-made, since choice of KEM and DEM can be made independently.

In order to build signcryption schemes instead of encryption schemes, it is tempting to start by modifying the basic specification of a KEM given in Definition 7.1 and changing as little as possible. As we will observe in Sect. 7.3.1 this leads us to Dent's basic framework for outsider-secure signcryption KEMs [71, 73]. Before we look at this, however, it is necessary to define what sort of security criteria we need the DEMs to fulfill in order to use them in building hybrid signcryption schemes.

7.2.2 Security Criteria for Data Encapsulation Mechanisms

Whereas the main goal of Sects. 7.3 and 7.4 will be to work out secure alternatives to KEMs that can be used to build efficient signcryption schemes, the DEM of Definition 7.2 shall largely be left alone. This has a perfectly reasonable explanation: When attempting to create a new type of public-key scheme based on models for hybrid encryption, our goal is best reached by altering the public-key component used. However, before we can start discussing hybrid signcryption schemes, we must first define which security properties we expect a secure DEM to fulfill.

As our requirements will differ in the case of insider-secure and outsider-secure signcryption, several different requirements will be given. In practice, all these requirements may be realized by a secure symmetric encryption algorithm (such as AES-CTR), possibly together with an authentication mechanism in form of a message authentication code (MAC) [68]. As in the case of regular (non-hybrid) signcryption, we distinguish between security criteria required for a scheme to provide confidentiality and criteria required to provide authenticity and integrity.

The standard notion of confidentiality in cryptography is that of indistinguishability (IND). In the particular case of data encapsulation mechanisms, the two notions that we are interested in are those of one-time IND-CPA security and one-time IND-CCA security, described in Sect. 1.3.4. As we shall see, almost paradoxically, we will require IND-CCA-secure DEMs for constructing outsider-secure signcryption schemes and IND-CPA-secure DEMs for constructing insider-secure signcryption schemes.

With respect to authenticity and integrity, we define a DEM to be integrally secure (INT-CCA) if there is no efficient adversary that can create valid ciphertexts C. This corresponds to the usual notion of unforgeability and gives a receiver faith that a valid ciphertext must have been generated legitimately. In practice, this is usually achieved by using a MAC. As we will see, INT-CCA security is only required for the outsider-secure hybrid constructions. The INT-CCA game between the challenger and adversary $\mathcal{A}$ is quite simple and runs as follows.

1. The challenger generates a random symmetric key K^* of appropriate length for the security parameter.
2. The adversary runs $\mathcal{A}$ on the input 1^k. When $\mathcal{A}$ terminates, it outputs a ciphertext C^*. During its execution, $\mathcal{A}$ may query an encryption oracle that for a given input message m outputs $\mathrm{Enc}_{K^*}(m)$ and a decryption oracle that for a given ciphertext C outputs $\mathrm{Dec}_{K^*}(C)$.

The adversary wins the game whenever $\mathrm{Dec}_K(C^*) \neq \perp$ and C^* was never output by the encryption oracle. The advantage of $\mathcal{A}$ is simply $Pr[\mathcal{A}$ wins].

Definition 7.3 (Unforgeable DEM) We say that a DEM is unforgeable (INT-CCA secure) if the advantage of any polynomial-time adversary in the INT-CCA game is negligible with respect to the security parameter k.

7.3 Hybrid Signcryption with Outsider Security

Signcryption schemes with outsider security are useful for communication between a set of trusted parties, as they are both more efficient with respect to computational cost and simpler to design and analyze than their insider-secure counterparts. The problem of constructing a framework for outsider-secure hybrid signcryption was first considered by Dent [71, 73] and can be solved by a fairly straightforward adaptation of the KEM/DEM construction for hybrid encryption discussed in Sect. 7.2.1. Although outsider-secure signcryption has largely been overlooked in the research literature, we believe that these schemes are useful and have practical applications. Our treatment closely follows Dent's original.

7.3.1 An Outsider-Secure Signcryption KEM

The main idea behind Dent's outsider-secure signcryption KEM [71, 73] is to use the traditional encryption KEM (described in Sect. 7.2.1) as a starting point and alter as little as possible to obtain something that behaves like as a signcryption scheme. This is reasonably straightforward: Instead of a single algorithm KeyGen, we should specify two algorithms, one used to generate sending ("signing") keys and a separate algorithm to generate keys for receiving ("decrypting") messages. Furthermore, the encapsulation algorithm must now take the private key of the sender *and* the public key of the receiver as input, and vice versa for the decapsulation algorithm. This leads directly to the following specification of an outsider-secure signcryption KEM (*SKEM*).

Definition 7.4 (Signcryption KEM) An (outsider-secure) signcryption KEM $SKEM = (\text{Setup}, \text{KeyGen}_S, \text{KeyGen}_R, \text{Encap}, \text{Decap})$ is a tuple of five algorithms.

- A probabilistic algorithm Setup that takes a security parameter 1^k as input and returns some global information *param* that are common to all users of an instantiation of the scheme.
- A probabilistic algorithm KeyGen_S that takes the global information *param* as input and outputs a public/private keypair (sk_S, pk_S) used for sending messages.
- A probabilistic algorithm KeyGen_R that takes the global information *param* as input and outputs a public/private keypair (sk_R, pk_R) used for receiving messages.
- A probabilistic algorithm Encap that takes the sender's private key sk_S and the receiver's public key pk_R as input, and outputs a pair (K, C), where K is a key and C is the encapsulation of K.
- A deterministic algorithm Decap that takes the sender's public key pk_S, the receiver's private key sk_R, and a key encapsulation C as input, and outputs either a symmetric key K or the unique error symbol $\perp$.

By combining the signcryption KEM with a standard DEM, we obtain a hybrid signcryption scheme in the obvious manner.

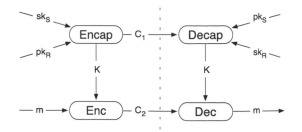

Fig. 7.1 Data flow in the outsider-secure signcryption KEM + DEM construction

Definition 7.5 (SKEM+DEM hybrid signcryption scheme) Suppose that (Setup, KeyGen$_S$, KeyGen$_R$, Encap, Decap) is a signcryption KEM and (Enc, Dec) is a DEM and that the keys produced by the signcryption KEM are of appropriate length for use with the DEM for all security parameters k. Then we can construct a hybrid signcryption scheme by using the Setup, KeyGen$_S$, and KeyGen$_R$ algorithms from the SKEM and defining the algorithms Signcrypt and Unsigncrypt as follows:

- The Signcrypt algorithm takes as input the private key of the sender sk_S, the public key of the receiver pk_R, and a message m. It computes $(K, C_1) \overset{R}{\leftarrow}$ Encap(sk_S, pk_R) and $C_2 \leftarrow$ Enc$_K(m)$ and outputs the signcryptext $C \leftarrow (C_1, C_2)$.
- The Unsigncrypt algorithm takes as input the public key of the sender pk_S, the private key of the receiver sk_R, and a signcryptext C. It parses C to obtain (C_1, C_2) and computes Decap(pk_S, sk_R, C_1). If Decap returned $\bot$, then the algorithm must output $\bot$ and halt. Otherwise, it computes Dec$_K(C_2)$. The output of Dec is either $\bot$ or a message m, in either case the algorithm outputs the result and halts.

The data flow between the Signcrypt and Unsigncrypt algorithms is illustrated in Fig. 7.1.

7.3.2 Security Criteria for Outsider-Secure Signcryption KEMs

The main advantage of the KEM + DEM construction paradigm is that we may analyze the security of the KEM and DEM separately, with no significant loss of concrete security. It is therefore necessary to give a precise specification of what it means for a signcryption KEM to be secure. To attain outsider security we require that the SKEM preserves the confidentiality of encapsulated keys, which is the same as the confidentiality requirement for encryption KEMs [68]. Additionally, a signcryption KEM must preserve the authenticity and integrity of the encapsulated key, to ensure that some third party may not alter the encapsulated key in any meaningful fashion. These security notions are expressed in the usual manner, by way of formal attack games.

With respect to confidentiality, we adapt the indistinguishability criterion to the signcryption KEM setting. More precisely, we want that any polynomial-time adversary $\mathcal{A}$ is unable to distinguish between a real key K_0 output by the Encap algorithm from a key K_1 drawn uniformly at random from the set of possible keys. For a given security parameter k, this may be expressed through the following game between the challenger and a two-stage adversary $\mathcal{A} = (\mathcal{A}_1, \mathcal{A}_2)$:

1. The challenger runs the appropriate algorithms to generate some global information $param$ and private/public keys for the sender and the receiver, denoted (sk_S, pk_S) and (sk_R, pk_R), respectively.
2. The adversary runs $\mathcal{A}_1$ on the input $(param, pk_S, pk_R)$. During its execution, $\mathcal{A}_1$ may query two oracles:

   - The encapsulation oracle $\mathcal{O}_{Encap}$ takes an arbitrary public receiving key pk as input and returns the result of computing $\text{Encap}(sk_S, pk)$.
   - The decapsulation oracle $\mathcal{O}_{Decap}$ takes an arbitrary public sending key pk and an encapsulation C as input and returns the result of computing $\text{Decap}(pk, sk_R, C)$.

   The algorithm terminates by outputting some state information $state$.

3. The challenger generates a valid encapsulation $(K_0, C^*) \xleftarrow{R} \text{Encap}(pk_S, sk_R)$, as well as a random key K_1 of the correct length. It then chooses a random bit $b \xleftarrow{R} \{0, 1\}$ and fixes the challenge encapsulation as (K_b, C^*).
4. The adversary runs $\mathcal{A}_2$ on the input $(K_b, C^*, state)$. During its execution, $\mathcal{A}_2$ may query the same oracles as before, with the restriction that it may not query the decapsulation oracle on the challenge encapsulation (pk_S, C^*). It terminates by returning a guess b' for the value of b.

The adversary wins the game if $b = b'$. The adversary's advantage is defined to be $|Pr[b = b'] - 1/2|$.

Definition 7.6 (Indistinguishable signcryption KEM) A signcryption KEM is said to be indistinguishable (IND-CCA2 secure) if the advantage of any polynomial-time adversary $\mathcal{A}$ in the IND-CCA2 game is negligible with respect to the security parameter k.

With respect to authenticity and integrity, Dent defines the security criterion in terms of indistinguishability of the real signcryption KEM and an *ideal* version of the same [71, 73]. This definition may seem somewhat unusual, as it is more common to see authenticity criteria specified in terms of an unforgeability requirement. However, an adversary creating forgeries of a signcryption KEM may in fact be used to distinguish said SKEM from an ideal one [71, 73]. As we will see, the definition using the notion of an ideal signcryption KEM turns out to be precisely what is needed to prove that our hybrid signcryption in Definition 7.5 is outsider secure. It also makes a nice parallel to the previous definition of IND-CCA2 security. For confidentiality, we needed the keys output by the encapsulation algorithm to be indistinguishable from random keys, the requirement for authenticity and integrity is that the entire signcryption KEM is indistinguishable from a random (i.e., ideal) one.

Given a signcryption KEM *SKEM* = (Setup, KeyGen$_S$, KeyGen$_R$, Encap, Decap) we define the corresponding ideal signcryption KEM to be the five-tuple of algorithms *Sim.SKEM* = (Sim.Setup, KeyGen$_S$, KeyGen$_R$, Sim.Encap, Sim.Decap), together with an internal state list *KeyList* containing key/encapsulation pairs. The simulated algorithms are defined as follows:

- The simulated setup algorithm Sim.Setup takes the security parameter 1^k as input and runs Setup to obtain the global information *param*. It then initializes *KeyList* as an empty list and returns *param*.
- The simulated encapsulation algorithm Sim.Encap takes the keys sk_S and pk_R as input. It then performs the following steps:

  1. Compute an encapsulation (K, C) using the real encapsulation algorithm Encap(sk_S,pk_R).
  2. Check whether there exists a pair (K', C) in *KeyList*. If this is the case, the algorithm returns K' and halts.
  3. Otherwise, the algorithm generates a new K' of appropriate length uniformly at random, adds (K', C) to *KeyList*, returns K', and halts.

- The simulated decapsulation algorithm Sim.Decap takes the keys pk_S and sk_R together with an encapsulation C as input. It then performs the following steps:

  1. Check whether there exists a pair (K, C) in *KeyList*. If this is the case, the algorithm returns K and halts.
  2. Otherwise, the algorithm runs the real decapsulation algorithm Decap $(pk_S$,sk_R,$C)$. If the decapsulation fails and outputs $\perp$, the algorithm returns $\perp$ and halts.
  3. If Decap did not return $\perp$, the algorithm generates a new K of appropriate length uniformly at random, adds (K, C) to *KeyList*, returns K, and halts.

It is clear from the above specification that the simulated signcryption KEM is self-consistent. Furthermore, it is "ideal" in the sense that we desire: an encapsulation C reveals *no* information about the encapsulated key K (since the key is chosen uniformly at random and independently of C). We say that the signcryption KEM is *left-or-right* secure (LoR-CCA) if there is no efficient algorithm to distinguish between the real and the idealized signcryption KEMs. For a given security parameter k, the LoR-CCA game proceeds as follows:

1. The challenger picks a bit $b \overset{R}{\leftarrow} \{0, 1\}$ at random.
2. The challenger generates global information *param*, either by running Setup if b was 0 or by running Sim.Setup if b was 1. The challenger then generates private/public keys for the sender and the receiver in the ordinary manner using KeyGen$_S$ and KeyGen$_R$.
3. The adversary runs $\mathcal{A}$ on the input (pk_S, pk_R). During its execution, $\mathcal{A}$ may query decapsulation and encapsulation oracles as specified in the previous IND-CCA2 game. However, the responses to $\mathcal{A}$'s queries are computed using the *real*

Encap and Decap algorithms if $b = 0$ and the *ideal* algorithms Sim.Encap and Sim.Decap if $b = 1$. $\mathcal{A}$ terminates by outputting a guess b' for the value of b.

The adversary wins the game if $b = b'$. The adversary's advantage is defined as $|Pr[b = b'] - 1/2|$.

Definition 7.7 (**LoR-CCA-secure signcryption KEM**) A signcryption KEM is said to be left-or-right (LoR-CCA) secure if the advantage of any polynomial-time adversary $\mathcal{A}$ in the LoR-CCA game is negligible with respect to the security parameter k.

Definition 7.8 (**Outsider-secure signcryption KEM**) A signcryption KEM is said to be *outsider secure* if it is both indistinguishable and left-or-right secure.

7.3.3 Security of the SKEM + DEM Construction

Having specified the security models in use for a signcryption KEM and DEM, it remains to show that the hybrid signcryption scheme of Definition 7.5 is an outsider-secure signcryption scheme satisfying the relevant security criteria defined in Chap. 3. The proof of this is quite straightforward and is quite similar to the original proof that hybrid *encryption* schemes are IND-CCA2 secure given in [68]. Since both security models for the signcryption KEMs are based on indistinguishability of certain attributes of the KEM from random in the view of the outside attacker, we state a well-known lemma used in the proofs. This can be thought of as a more general version of Lemma 1.1.

Lemma 7.1 (*Distinguisher lemma*) *Let G_0 and G_1 be two games. Suppose that an experimenter picks $b \overset{R}{\leftarrow} \{0, 1\}$ uniformly at random and proceeds to play G_b with a distinguisher algorithm that outputs a guess b' of the value of b. Then*

$$2\left|Pr[b = b'] - 1/2\right| = \left|Pr[b' = 0|b = 0] - Pr[b' = 0|b = 1]\right|. \tag{7.1}$$

The result follows from simple manipulation of conditional probabilities, see, for example, [71]. We proceed to prove that Dent's outsider-secure signcryption KEM can be used to build an outsider-secure hybrid signcryption scheme.

Theorem 7.1 (*Security of SKEM + DEM hybrid signcryption*) *Let SC be a hybrid signcryption scheme constructed from a signcryption KEM (Definition 7.4) and a DEM (Definition 7.2). If the signcryption KEM is IND-CCA2 secure and the signcryption DEM is one-time IND-CCA secure, then the hybrid signcryption scheme is multi-user outsider FSO/FUO-IND-CCA2 secure (Definition 3.1) with the bound*

$$\varepsilon_{SC,IND-CCA2} \leq 2\,\varepsilon_{SKEM,IND-CCA2} + \varepsilon_{DEM,IND-CCA} \tag{7.2}$$

where the ε values denote the maximal success probability of adversaries in the specified attack games. Furthermore, if the signcryption KEM is LoR-CCA secure *and the signcryption DEM is INT-CCA secure, then the hybrid signcryption scheme is multi-user outsider FSO/FUO-sUF-CMA secure (Definition 3.2) with the bound*

$$\varepsilon_{SC,sUF\text{-}CMA} \leq 2\,\varepsilon_{SKEM,LoR\text{-}CCA} + \varepsilon_{DEM,INT\text{-}CCA} \qquad (7.3)$$

Proof The proofs of the two statements are remarkably similar. In both cases, we proceed by modifying the original (FSO/FUO-IND-CCA2 or FSO/FUO-sUF-CMA) attack game for *SC* in a way that relates to the corresponding (IND-CCA2 or LoR-CCA) security criterion for the signcryption KEM. Lemma 7.1 is used to do this. Finally, we show that the adversary must break the (IND-CCA or INT-CCA) security of the DEM to gain any advantage in the modified game. We consider first the case of indistinguishability.

Let $\mathcal{A} = (\mathcal{A}_1, \mathcal{A}_2)$ be an adversary against the FSO/FUO-IND-CCA2 security of *SC*, G_0 be the regular FSO/FUO-IND-CCA2 game for outsider-secure sign-cryption as given by Definition 3.1, and X_0 the event that the adversary wins in G_0. Next we define a modified game G_1. The difference between G_0 and G_1 is that the challenge ciphertext is computed using a *random* symmetric key K_1. In other words, the challenge ciphertext $C^* = (C_1^*, C_2^*)$ is constructed by computing $(K_0, C_1^*) \xleftarrow{R} \mathrm{Encap}(sk_S, pk_R)$, drawing another key K_1 uniformly at random from the keyspace, and then using it to compute $C_2^* \leftarrow \mathrm{Enc}_{K_1}(m)$. In order to remain consistent, the challenger should also use K_1 to answer any unsigncryption oracle query of the form $\big(pk_S, (C_1^*, \cdot)\big)$. Hence, the difference between G_0 and G_1 lies solely in how the signcryption KEM operates. The two games correspond to the situations $b = 0$ and 1 in the IND-CCA2 game against the signcryption KEM.

Let X_1 be the event that $\mathcal{A}$ wins G_1. We argue that probability $|\mathrm{Pr}[X_0] - \mathrm{Pr}[X_1]|$ is bounded by $2\varepsilon_{SKEM,IND\text{-}CCA2}$, where $\varepsilon_{SKEM,IND\text{-}CCA2}$ is the advantage of a specific adversary $\mathcal{D}$ against the IND-CCA2 security of the signcryption KEM used to construct *SC*. The idea is that the distinguisher $\mathcal{D}$ plays either G_0 or G_1 with a regular adversary $\mathcal{A}$ against the full signcryption scheme, depending on the value of the hidden bit b which $\mathcal{D}$ is trying to determine. By Lemma 7.1, any non-negligible difference in the advantage of $\mathcal{A}$ can be leveraged by $\mathcal{D}$ to break the signcryption KEM, and the stated bound is obtained for the game transition.

Next, consider the probability that X_1 does in fact occur. We argue that this is the same as $\varepsilon_{DEM,IND\text{-}CCA}$. This follows from the way that G_1 is defined. The first part of the challenge C_1^* reveals no direct information about which message was signcrypted, since the symmetric key K_1 was chosen independently and uniformly at random. Thus, to gain a non-negligible advantage in G_2, the adversary must somehow learn something from the symmetric ciphertext C_2^*. The adversary is able to mount a chosen ciphertext attack, since decryption oracle queries of the form $\big(pk_S, (C_1^*, \cdot)\big)$ must be decrypted using K_1 to maintain consistency. More formally, we show by construction that an adversary $\mathcal{A}$ playing the game G_1 can be converted into an IND-CCA adversary $\mathcal{B}$ against the DEM with essentially the same advantage. A specification of such an adversary is shown in Fig. 7.3.

To summarize, we have shown that the difference $|\Pr[X_0] - \Pr[X_1]|$ is bounded by $2\varepsilon_{SKEM,IND-CCA2}$ while $Pr[X_1]$ itself is essentially equal to $\varepsilon_{DEM,IND-CCA}$, thus obtaining the stated bound.

For authenticity and integrity, the proof is highly similar in both approach and execution and will therefore not be specified in the same level of detail. Again we consider an adversary $\mathcal{A}$, this time attacking the FSO/FUO-sUF-CMA security of SC. Again, we let G_0 to be the regular FSO/FUO-sUF-CMA attack game given by Definition 3.2 and X_0 to be the event that $\mathcal{A}$ wins G_0. Our subsequent game G_1 is similar to G_0, but modified so that an *ideal* signcryption KEM is used instead of the regular one. It is straightforward to construct a new distinguisher similar to the one given in Fig. 7.2, which relates the difference between G_0 and G_1 to the advantage of a LoR-CCA adversary against the signcryption KEM. Furthermore, the advantage

$\mathcal{D}_1(param, pk_S, pk_R; \mathcal{O}_{Encap}, \mathcal{O}_{Decap})$:
  $(m_0, m_1, s) \xleftarrow{R} \mathcal{A}_1(param, pk_S, pk_R; \mathcal{O}_{SC}, \mathcal{O}_{USC})$.
  $state \leftarrow (m_0, m_1, s)$.
  Return state.

$\mathcal{D}_2(K^*, C_1^*, state; \mathcal{O}_{Encap}, \mathcal{O}_{Decap})$:
  Parse state as (m_0, m_1, s).
  $b \xleftarrow{R} \{0,1\}$.
  $C_2^* \leftarrow \text{Enc}_{K^*}(m_b)$.
  $C^* \leftarrow (C_1^*, C_2^*)$.
  $b' \xleftarrow{R} \mathcal{A}_2(C^*, s; \mathcal{O}_{SC}, \mathcal{O}_{USC})$.
  If $b = b'$ then return 1.
  Else return 0.

$\mathcal{O}_{SC}(pk, m)$:
  $(K, C_1) \xleftarrow{R} \mathcal{O}_{Encap}(pk)$.
  $C_2 \leftarrow \text{Enc}_K(m)$.
  $C \leftarrow (C_1, C_2)$.
  Return C.

$\mathcal{O}_{USC}(pk, C)$:
  $(C_1, C_2) \leftarrow C$.
  If $pk = pk_R$ and $C_1 = C_1^*$ then
    $K \leftarrow K^*$.
  Else if $\perp = \mathcal{O}_{Decap}(pk, C_1)$ then
    Return $\perp$ and halt.
  Else $K \leftarrow \mathcal{O}_{Decap}(pk, C_1)$.
  If $\perp = \text{Dec}_K(C_2)$ then
    Return $\perp$ and halt.
  Else $m \leftarrow \text{Dec}_K(C_2)$.
  Return m.

Fig. 7.2 A complete specification of the distinguisher algorithm $\mathcal{D}$ for the SKEM

$\mathcal{B}_1(1^k; \mathcal{O}_{Dec})$:
  $param \xleftarrow{R} \text{Setup}(1^k)$.
  $(sk_S, pk_S) \xleftarrow{R} \text{KeyGen}_S(param)$.
  $(sk_R, pk_R) \xleftarrow{R} \text{KeyGen}_R(param)$.
  $(m_0, m_1, s) \xleftarrow{R} \mathcal{A}(param, pk_S, pk_R; \mathcal{O}_{SC}, \mathcal{O}_{USC})$.
  $state \leftarrow (param, sk_S, pk_S, sk_R, pk_R, m_0, m_1, s)$.
  Return $(m_0, m_1, state)$.

$\mathcal{B}_2(C_2^*, state; \mathcal{O}_{Dec})$:
  Parse state as
    $(param, sk_S, pk_S, sk_R, pk_R, m_0, m_1, s)$.
  $(K, C_1^*) \xleftarrow{R} \text{Encap}(sk_S, pk_R)$.
  $C^* \leftarrow (C_1^*, C_2^*)$.
  $b \xleftarrow{R} \mathcal{A}_2(C^*, s; \mathcal{O}_{SC}, \mathcal{O}_{USC})$.
  Return b.

$\mathcal{O}_{SC}(pk, m)$:
  $(K, C_1) \xleftarrow{R} \text{Encap}(sk_S, pk)$.
  $C_2 \leftarrow \text{Enc}_K(m)$.
  $C \leftarrow (C_1, C_2)$.

$\mathcal{O}_{USC}(pk, C)$:
  $(C_1, C_2) \leftarrow C$.
  If $C_1 = C_1^*$ and $pk = pk_R$ then
    Return $\mathcal{O}_{Dec}(C_1)$.
  Else if $\perp = \text{Decap}(pk, sk_R, C_1)$ then
    Return $\perp$ and halt.
  Else $K \leftarrow \text{Decap}(pk, sk_R, C_1)$.
  If $\perp = \text{Dec}_K(C_2)$
    Return $\perp$ and halt.
  Else $m \leftarrow \text{Dec}_K(C_2)$.
  Return m.

Fig. 7.3 A complete specification of the distinguisher algorithm $\mathcal{B}$ for the DEM

of $\mathcal{A}$ in G_1 can be shown to be bounded by that of an INT-CCA adversary against the DEM, by a construction similar to that of Fig. 7.3. This concludes the proof. □

Although we have established that the combination of a signcryption KEM and DEM can be used to build outsider-secure hybrid signcryption schemes, more complex constructions are needed for insider security. This stems from the observation that there is no connection between the encapsulations generated by Encap and the actual message that is being signcrypted. In fact, the receiver can create a valid signcryptext for an arbitrary message m given a single valid signcryption $C = (C_1, C_2)$, by computing $K \leftarrow \text{Decap}(pk_S, sk_R, C_1)$ and computing a new value $C'_2 \leftarrow \text{Enc}_K(m)$. Hence the scheme is trivially forgeable by an inside attacker and has no way of providing non-repudiation. From this, we observe that in order to build insider-secure hybrid signcryption the signcryption KEM must somehow prevent the adversary from tampering with m or C_2.

7.3.4 Outsider-Secure Hybrid Signcryption in Practice

Outsider-secure signcryption has not been the target of much research since the distinction was first recognized by An et al. [10]. This is unfortunate, as it is possible to construct outsider-secure schemes that are simpler and more efficient than their insider-secure counterparts. These schemes would clearly be suitable for any real-world settings where insider attacks are not part of the threat model. The only known outsider-secure signcryption KEM was proposed by Dent in [71, 73]. It is extremely simple, has a low additional computational cost, and is based on the well-known ECIES encryption KEM [2, 101]. The ECISS[1]-KEM is specified in Fig. 7.4. In the two-user setting, this scheme has been proven to be secure (in the random oracle model), with respect to the computational Diffie–Hellman problem in the underlying group[2] [71, 73]. A tighter bound can be obtained by considering the security relative to the Gap Diffie–Hellman problem instead.

$\text{KeyGen}_S(param)$:
 $sk_S \xleftarrow{R} \mathbb{Z}_q^*$.
 $pk_S \leftarrow g^{sk_S}$.
 Return (sk_S, pk_S).

$\text{KeyGen}_R(param)$:
 $sk_R \xleftarrow{R} \mathbb{Z}_q^*$.
 $pk_R \leftarrow g^{sk_R}$.
 Return (sk_R, pk_R).

$\text{Encap}(sk_S, pk_R)$:
 $r \xleftarrow{R} \mathbb{Z}_q^*$.
 $C \leftarrow g^r$.
 $\kappa \leftarrow pk_R^{sk_S} \cdot g^r$.
 $K \leftarrow H(\kappa, pk_S, pk_R)$.
 Return (K, C).

$\text{Decap}(pk_S, sk_R, C)$:
 $\kappa \leftarrow pk_S^{sk_R} \cdot C$.
 $K \leftarrow H(\kappa, pk_S, pk_R)$.
 Return K.

Fig. 7.4 A complete specification of the ECISS-KEM

---

[1] ECISS stands for elliptic-curve integrated signcryption scheme.

[2] Note that the alternate scheme suggested without a security proof in [71] is insecure [92].

The ECISS scheme is a good example of how outsider-secure signcryption can be obtained at low additional cost compared to regular encryption and underlines the close relationship between outsider-secure signcryption KEMs and secure encryption KEMs. Comparing ECISS-KEM and ECIES-KEM, the only significant difference lies in how the input to the key derivation function H is computed. In the encryption-only scheme, the shared value is computed from the (receiver's) public key and the random value r as $pk^r = g^{sk \cdot r}$. For signcryption, the Diffie–Hellman value $pk_R^{sk_S} = pk_S^{sk_R} = g^{sk_S \cdot sk_R}$ is multiplied with g^r instead.

The original proof that ECISS-KEM is secure in the two-user model from [71] may readily be extended to the multi-user setting. However, to keep the reduction tight it is necessary to make the proof relative to the Gap Diffie–Hellman problem. One minor change to the original scheme is also required, namely that the public keys of the sender and receiver are included as input to the hash function. This has little practical significance, but enables us to keep sessions between different pairs of users distinct in the proof. As the proofs for IND-CCA2 and LoR-CCA security are almost identical, only the former will be shown here.

Theorem 7.2 *(Multi-user security of ECISS) The ECISS signcryption KEM is IND-CCA2 secure in the random oracle model, with respect to the Gap Diffie–Hellman problem. In particular, let A be an adversary that breaks the IND-CCA2 security of ECISS-KEM with advantage ε_{KEM}, while making at most q_E encapsulation and q_D decapsulation oracle queries. Then there exists an algorithm B solving the GDH problem whose advantage is given by*

$$\varepsilon_{\text{KEM}} \leq \varepsilon_{\text{GDH}} + \frac{q_E + q_D}{q}. \tag{7.4}$$

Proof Let B be an algorithm which tries to solve the Gap Diffie–Hellman problem (as defined in Sect. 4.1) in $\mathbb{G}$. The algorithm receives as input two random group elements g^a and g^b and will try to compute g^{ab} by using an adversary A against the ECISS signcryption KEM as a subroutine. During its execution, B may query a DDH oracle on triplets (g^x, g^y, g^z) which tests whether $g^{xy} = g^z$.

Our approach will be to use the challenge values g^a and g^b in place of the public keys pk_S and pk_R. This means that sk_S and sk_R will not be known to B and thus we have to be careful when simulating the encapsulation and decapsulation oracles. Partial consistency is maintained through our simulation of the key derivation function H as a random oracle and using the DDH oracle to verify that the correct relation between the public keys, C and κ, are maintained. The goal of B is to obtain values C and κ such that $C \cdot g^{ab} = \kappa$, in which case g^{ab} can be recovered.

We will use two lists to keep track of oracle queries by A. As opposed to [71], it will also be necessary to keep track of the public keys used in the oracle queries. Let *EncapList* be a list of tuples (pk_S, pk_R, C, K) and *HashList* be a list of tuples (pk, pk', κ, K). It is necessary to specify how B should respond to queries from A to the encapsulation, decapsulation, and random oracles, so that these responses are self-consistent and follow the correct distributions:

- For an encapsulation oracle query pk, $\mathcal{B}$ should first pick a random group element C. If there is an entry (pk_S, pk, C, K) in $EncapList$, then output the pair (C, K). Otherwise, if there is an entry (pk_S, pk, κ, K) in $HashList$ such that $(pk_S, pk, \kappa/C)$ is a DDH triple, output the pair (C, K). If neither is the case, then generate a random key K, store (pk_S, pk, C, K) in $EncapList$, and output the pair (C, K).

- On a decapsulation oracle query (pk, C), $\mathcal{B}$ must first check $EncapList$ for any previous entries (pk, pk_R, C, K). If such an entry is found, K must be output to maintain consistency. Otherwise, $HashList$ is checked for conforming entries (pk, pk_R, κ, K) such that $(pk_S, pk, \kappa/C)$ is a DDH triple, in which case K is returned. If no match is found in either list, then generate a random key K, store (pk, pk_R, C, K) in $EncapList$, and return K.

- Finally, on random oracle queries (κ, pk, pk'), one should first check $HashList$ whether the same query has been made before, in which case the same K should be returned. If this is not the case, $\mathcal{B}$ checks whether $EncapList$ contains any entries (pk, pk', C, K) such that $(pk, pk', \kappa/C)$ is a DDH triple, in which case K is returned. If no match is found in the list, a random key K is generated and $HashList$ is updated accordingly.

Note that it is simple for $\mathcal{B}$ to deal with the flexible oracle queries, since the information about which public keys are in use is embedded in every query. By using the public keys and the supplied DDH oracle, $\mathcal{B}$ is also able to maintain consistency between queries to the three oracles. A new entry is only added to $EncapList$ during an oracle query if the corresponding triplet of keys and encapsulation have not been used in a previous query to any of the oracles. Similarly, a new entry is added to $HashList$ only if the result has not been fixed (directly or indirectly) previously. Since all new encapsulations and keys are generated by sampling uniformly at random, the variables will also follow the correct distributions.

We now consider what happens when $\mathcal{B}$ plays the IND-CCA2 game for ECISS-KEM with $\mathcal{A}$. As previously stated, $\mathcal{B}$ uses the GDH challenge values g^x and g^y as the public keys pk_S and pk_R, generates $param$ from the description of the group, and runs $\mathcal{A}_1$ on $(param, pk_S, pk_R)$, while simulating the oracles as specified. Eventually $\mathcal{A}_1$ terminates, outputting some $state$. To generate a challenge, $\mathcal{B}$ first picks a group element C^* and a key K_0 uniformly at random and adds the value (pk_S, pk_R, C^*, K_0) to $EncapList$. After choosing another random key K_1 and a random bit b, $\mathcal{B}$ runs $\mathcal{A}_2$ on the parameters $(state, C^*, K_b)$. During the execution of $\mathcal{A}_2$, the oracles may be queried as before, with the restriction that the decapsulation query (pk_S, C^*) is forbidden. Eventually $\mathcal{A}_2$ will output some bit b', which is ignored by $\mathcal{B}$. Instead, $\mathcal{B}$ checks whether there are entries in (pk_S, pk_R, C, K) in $EncapList$ and (pk_S, pk_R, κ, K) in $HashList$ such that $(pk_S, pk_R, \kappa/C)$ is a DDH triple. In this case, κ/C is returned as the solution to the GDH problem; otherwise, a random group element is picked.

Analyzing the advantage of $\mathcal{B}$, we notice that the encapsulation and decapsulation algorithms are simulated perfectly at all times, except during the generation of the challenge C^*. With respect to C^* there are two things that may go wrong; either a previous oracle query made by $\mathcal{A}_1$ has already fixed a relation between pk_S, pk_R, C^*, and some K or a future encapsulation oracle query by $\mathcal{A}_2$ on pk_R may accidentally reveal the key associated with C^*. Under the assumption that $\mathcal{A}$ is only allowed to make a polynomial number of oracle queries, the probability that either of this happens is negligible and bounded above by $\frac{q_E + q_D}{q}$.

However, because K_0 and K_1 are sampled uniformly at random and independently of C^*, the only other way that $\mathcal{A}$ can learn anything about the value of b is to submit a query (κ^*, pk_S, pk_R) to the random oracle, where $\kappa^* / C^* = g^{sk_S \cdot sk_R} = g^{xy}$. But in this case $\mathcal{B}$ immediately obtains the solution to the Gap Diffie–Hellman problem instance.[3] Hence the advantage of $\mathcal{B}$ in the GDH game will be no worse than that of $\mathcal{A}$. This completes the proof. $\square$

7.4 Hybrid Signcryption with Insider Security

The problem of constructing a framework for insider-secure hybrid signcryption is significantly more complex than the outsider-secure setting, precisely due to the need to protect against insider-specific attacks. We briefly discuss why it appears necessary to use public-key signatures as a starting point, rather than encryption KEMs. Furthermore, we point out the shortcomings of Dent's proposed insider-secure signcryption KEM model [71, 72]. The main focus of the chapter is to present the concept of *signcryption tag-KEMs* [37] and how they avoid the main problems of Dent's model. Examples of schemes that fit the signcryption tag-KEM framework include a modified version of Zheng's signcryption scheme (as described in Sect. 3.3 and 4.3).

7.4.1 From Outsider to Insider Security

While outsider security is sufficient for communication between a trusted set of users, insider security is necessary for more general communication networks, where multiple users who may or may not trust each other wish to communicate in a secure fashion. It is also a necessary (though not sufficient) condition for creating signcryption schemes with non-repudiation functionality [130]—see Sect. 2.2.2. As we saw in Sect. 7.3.3, the model for hybrid signcryption proposed in Sect. 7.3 can never provide insider security, because there is no link between the key encapsulation and the message that is being signcrypted. The logical consequence of this is that any model for an insider-secure signcryption KEM must provide some form

---

[3] The way the oracles are simulated, $\mathcal{B}$ may also learn the target value from other queries involving pk_S and pk_R, but something other than the challenge.

of integrity service for the message that is being signcrypted, to verify that the relationship between message, key, and encapsulation has not been altered by the adversary. In effect, the encapsulation should provide a signature on all the relevant data for the specific message to be signcrypted, including the public keys of sender and receiver, the encapsulated symmetric key, and the message itself.

Recalling the semantics of a public-key signature scheme and pursuing this idea, it appears reasonable that the encapsulation algorithm should be changed to take the message m as input, as well as the public keys sk_S and pk_R. However, to *verify* the signature on m, it must first be decrypted. Hence it becomes necessary to specify *two* algorithms that are used to unsigncrypt a signcryptext: a decapsulation algorithm to recover the symmetric key K and a verification algorithm to verify that the "signature" part of the encapsulation is valid. On the positive side, it appears reasonable that the security requirement for the DEM can be relaxed to IND-CPA, since the insider-secure signcryption KEM must enforce the integrity of the message anyhow.

Following this intuitive approach yields the original insider-secure signcryption KEMs proposed by Dent [71, 73]. Unfortunately, it is not a particularly pleasant model to work with. One possible reason for this is the fact that it instantiates an example of the "encrypt-and-sign" paradigm, as discussed in Chap. 2 [10]. This means that special considerations have to be taken to avoid information about the signed message leaking through the key encapsulation. Specifically, the security criteria required of the signcryption KEM to provide confidentiality turn out to be quite awkward in Dent's model. To create an indistinguishable signcryption KEM one must consider two separate attack scenarios: one in which the adversary tries to distinguish a real key output by the encapsulation algorithm from a random key (similar to the IND-CCA2 requirement for outsider-secure signcryption KEMs in Sect. 7.3.2) and *another* in which the adversary tries to distinguish between encapsulations of two different messages. In the case of integrity, the standard criterion of strong existential unforgeability (of valid encapsulations) may be applied.

Another flaw of the intuitive approach followed above lies in the proof of the composition theorem for outsider-secure KEM + DEM. In Dent's original proof, the confidentiality of hybrid signcryption relies on the authenticity/integrity of the KEM as well as its confidentiality [71, 72]. This is not very intuitive and leads to poor concrete security: as shown by Bjørstad, the security bound for confidentiality of Zheng's signcryption scheme in the original scheme-specific proof [12, 13] is much tighter than the corresponding proof of security using the functionally equivalent signcryption KEM + DEM formulation [36]. Although Bjørstad suggests an alternate proof of confidentiality avoiding the need for unforgeability, this reimposes the requirement that the DEM must be IND-CCA and is therefore little better in practice. In short, the intuitive definition of an insider-secure signcryption KEM sketched in this section leads to a scheme that does not really simplify the analysis and typically achieves worse security results than a direct proof specific to the scheme under consideration. It follows that a different model is needed to make the concept of insider-secure hybrid signcryption useful.

7.4.2 Signcryption Tag-KEMs

A way to resolve the problems encountered in the previous section appeared in
early 2005, when Abe et al. proposed an alternate construction paradigm for hybrid
encryption, called *tag-KEMs* [4, 5]. The main idea of tag-KEMs is that the encapsulation algorithm is constructed in two steps: one in which the symmetric key is
generated and another where the key is encapsulated in some manner together with
an arbitrary string called a *tag*. As we shall see, the security requirement for tag-
KEMs also forces the key encapsulation to preserve the integrity of the tag. The
authors proceed to present a hybrid construction in which the symmetric ciphertext from the DEM is used as the tag and show that this yields an elegant hybrid
encryption scheme where the DEM only needs to be secure against passive attackers
(IND-CPA).

It is tempting to adapt the tag-KEM construction paradigm to the insider-secure
signcryption setting, precisely because our immediate goal is to design signcryption
KEMs that provide integrity services and only require an IND-CPA-secure DEM
to make the composition secure. In the hybrid signcryption setting this also acts
as an example of the "encrypt-then-sign" paradigm, since the "signature" part of
the encapsulation is made on the ciphertext tag instead of on the message itself. It is
not unreasonable to expect that such a construction will be more well-behaved under
formal analysis, since there is no longer any possibility that the signature component
can leak any information about the plaintext to an attacker.[4] Using Abe et al. [4, 5]
as inspiration, Bjørstad and Dent [37] give the following formal specification of the
tag-KEM construction for signcryption.

Definition 7.9 (Signcryption tag-KEM) A *signcryption tag-KEM SCTK* $=$
(Setup, KeyGen$_S$, KeyGen$_R$, Sym, Encap, Decap) is defined as a tuple of six algorithms:

- A probabilistic common parameter generation algorithm, Setup. It takes as input
  a security parameter 1^k and returns all the global information *param* needed by
  users of the scheme, such as choice of groups or hash functions.
- A probabilistic sender key generation algorithm KeyGen$_S$. It takes as input the
  global information *param* and outputs a public/private keypair (sk_S, pk_S) that is
  used to send signcrypted messages.
- A probabilistic receiver key generation algorithm KeyGen$_R$. It takes as input the
  global information *param* and outputs a public/private keypair (sk_R, pk_R) that is
  used to receive signcrypted messages.

---

[4] The alternate "sign-then-encrypt" construction might be even more appealing, because it keeps
the formal signature where it logically and semantically belongs: on the plaintext. However, it does
not appear to be practical to build a model for hybrid signcryption schemes instantiating this concept, due to the need to divide the signcryption KEM into separate "signature" and "encapsulation"
parts, and the complex information flows resulting from this.

- A probabilistic symmetric key generation algorithm Sym. It takes as input the private key of the sender sk_S and the public key of the receiver pk_R and outputs a symmetric key K together with internal state information ω.
- A probabilistic key encapsulation algorithm Encap. It takes as input some state information ω and an arbitrary tag τ, and returns an encapsulation C.[5]
- A deterministic decapsulation and verification algorithm Decap. It takes as input the sender's public key pk_S, the receiver's private key sk_R, an encapsulation C, and a tag τ. The algorithm returns either a symmetric key K or the unique error symbol $\bot$.

By combining the above signcryption tag-KEM with a DEM, we obtain a hybrid signcryption scheme as follows.

Definition 7.10 (SCTK+DEM hybrid signcryption scheme) Suppose that (Setup, KeyGen$_S$, KeyGen$_R$, Sym, Encap, Decap) is a signcryption tag-KEM and (Enc, Dec) a DEM and that the keys produced by the signcryption tag-KEM are of appropriate length for use with the DEM for all security parameters k. Then we can construct a hybrid signcryption scheme by using the Setup, KeyGen$_S$, and KeyGen$_R$ from the SCTK and defining the algorithms Signcrypt and Unsigncrypt as follows.

- The Signcrypt algorithm takes as input the private key of the sender sk_S, the public key of the receiver pk_R, and a message m. It performs the following steps:

  1. Compute Sym(sk_S, pk_R) to obtain a symmetric key K and state information ω.
  2. Compute Enc$_K(m)$ to produce a ciphertext C_2.
  3. Compute Encap(ω, C_2), using C_2 as the tag τ to produce the ciphertext C_1.
  4. Output the signcryptext $C \leftarrow (C_1, C_2)$ and halt.

- The Unsigncrypt algorithm takes as input the public key of the sender pk_S, the private key of the receiver sk_R, and a ciphertext C. It performs the following steps:

  1. Parse C to obtain its component parts C_1 and C_2.
  2. Compute $K \leftarrow$ Decap(pk_S, sk_R, C_1, C_2), using C_1 as the encapsulation and C_2 as the tag.
  3. If Decap returned $\bot$, output $\bot$, and halt. Otherwise, compute $m \leftarrow$ Dec$_K(C_2)$.
  4. Output m and halt.

---

[5] In principle, this algorithm can always be represented as a deterministic algorithm, which takes as input the appropriate amount of random bits embedded in ω as a string. In practice this is often the case, as random nonces may be chosen as part of Encap and used to create a random K, and then passed along to Sym as part of ω. However, from a theoretical point of view, if Encap is only *expected* polynomial time, the deterministic version will have an (arbitrarily small) probability of failing.

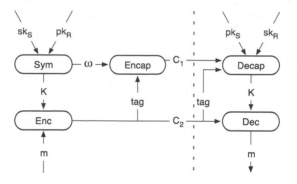

Fig. 7.5 Data flow in the insider-secure signcryption tag-KEM + DEM construction

The data flow between the `Signcrypt` and `Unsigncrypt` algorithms is illustrated in Fig. 7.5. Notice in particular how the symmetric ciphertext C_2 is used as the "tag" input to both `Encap` and `Decap`.

As it turns out, it is quite possible to express Zheng's signcryption scheme as a signcryption tag-KEM + DEM construction. However, it requires the trivial alteration of having the "signature" part of the scheme act on the symmetric ciphertext instead of the message itself. The resulting scheme is essentially the scheme of Gamage et al.—see Sect. 4.3.3. This is not expected to have any effect on the overall security of the scheme, an assumption that is verified independently by Bjørstad and Dent [37]. A concrete specification of the "Zheng signcryption tag-KEM" is given in Fig. 7.6. Since Zheng's scheme is known to be secure (in the random oracle model) [12, 13] this yields confidence that the signcryption tag-KEM construction is viable and useful, provided that a good generic security reduction can be made. As we shall see in Sects. 7.4.3 and 7.4.4 this is indeed the case.

7.4.3 Security Criteria for Signcryption Tag-KEMs

For the signcryption tag-KEM construction to be viable, we need clear and well-defined notions of what it means for a signcryption tag-KEM to be secure. Furthermore, these notions must be useful by themselves, so that it is possible to prove that suggested signcryption tag-KEMs fulfill them and admit an efficient security reduction for the generic hybrid signcryption scheme obtained by combining an SCTK with a DEM. As we observed in Sect. 7.4.1, this is not always achievable. However, in the signcryption tag-KEM setting we find intuitive and simple notions of security for both confidentiality and authenticity/integrity. We will define these security notions analogously with the main definitions given in Chap. 3, specifically the multi-user outsider model for confidentiality and the multi-user insider model for unforgeability. (Extensions to the other models given in Chap. 3 can be simply made using the techniques in this section.)

```
Setup(1^k)
   Pick a random large prime p with
      a k-bit prime q dividing p − 1.
   Pick g ∈ Z*_p of order q.
   Pick cryptographic hash functions:
      G : {0,1}* → K
      H : {0,1}* → Z_q
   param ← (p,q,g,G,H)
   Return param
```

```
KeyGen_S(param)
   x_S ←^R Z_q; y_S ← g^{x_S}
   sk_S ← (x_S,y_S); pk_S ← y_S
   Return (sk_S,pk_S)
```

```
KeyGen_R(param)
   x_R ←^R Z_q; y_R ← g^{x_R}
   sk_R ← (x_R,y_R); pk_R ← y_R
   Return (sk_R,pk_R)
```

```
Sym(param,sk_S,pk_R)
   Parse sk_S as (x_S,y_S); Parse pk_R as y_R
   If y_R ∉ ⟨g⟩ \ {1} then return ⊥
   x ←^R Z_q; κ ← y_R^x; K ← G(κ)
   bind ← pk_S||pk_R; ω ← (x_S,x,κ,bind)
   Return (K,ω)
```

```
Encap(ω,τ)
   Parse ω as (x_S,x,κ,bind)
   r ← H(τ||bind||κ)
   If r + x_S = 0 then return ⊥
   s ← x/(x_S + r)
   C ← (r,s)
   Return C
```

```
Decap(param,pk_S,sk_R,C,τ)
   Parse sk_R as (x_R,y_R); Parse pk_S as y_S
   If y_S ∉ ⟨g⟩ \ {1} then return ⊥
   Parse C as (r,s)
   If r ∉ Z_q or s ∉ Z_q
      Return ⊥
   κ ← (y_S g^r)^{s x_R}; K ← G(κ)
   bind ← pk_S||pk_R
   If H(τ||bind||κ) = r then return K
   Else return ⊥
```

Fig. 7.6 A complete specification of the Zheng signcryption tag-KEM (Zheng-SCTK). This scheme should be compared with the Gamage et al. specification in Sect. 4.3.3

A signcryption tag-KEM maintains confidentiality when it is impossible for an adversary to distinguish whether a given key K is embedded in an encapsulation C or not. This is the only requirement needed. However, as the adversary is allowed to specify the tag and may access flexible oracles, this is sufficient to ensure that the encapsulation is not malleable with respect to the tag. Since the symmetric key generation and encapsulation algorithms do not receive the unencrypted plaintext as input, the additional requirement of input indistinguishability is not necessary. For a given security parameter k, the IND-CCA2 game between challenger and a three-stage adversary $\mathcal{A} = (\mathcal{A}_1, \mathcal{A}_2, \mathcal{A}_3)$ runs as follows:

1. The challenger generates a set of global information $param \xleftarrow{R} \text{Setup}(1^k)$ and the key pairs $(sk_S, pk_S) \xleftarrow{R} \text{KeyGen}_S(param)$ and $(sk_R, pk_R) \xleftarrow{R} \text{KeyGen}_R(param)$ for the sender and the receiver.

2. The adversary runs $\mathcal{A}_1$ on the input $(param, pk_S, pk_R)$. During its execution, $\mathcal{A}_1$ is given access to flexible symmetric key generation, encapsulation, and decapsulation oracles:

   - The symmetric key generation oracle $\mathcal{O}_{Sym}$ takes a public key pk as input and runs $(K, \omega) \xleftarrow{R} \text{Sym}(sk_S, pk)$. It then stores the value of ω, hidden from the view of the adversary, and overwriting any previous value. The oracle outputs the key K.

- The key encapsulation oracle $\mathcal{O}_{Encap}$ takes a tag τ as input and checks whether there is a stored ω. If there is not, it outputs $\perp$. Otherwise it erases the value of ω from storage, computes $\mathrm{Encap}(\omega, \tau)$, and outputs the result.
- The decapsulation/verification oracle $\mathcal{O}_{Decap}$ takes a public sending key pk, an encapsulation C, and a tag τ as input. It then computes $\mathrm{Decap}(pk, sk_R, C, \tau)$ and outputs the result.

$\mathcal{A}_1$ terminates by outputting some state information $state_1$.

3. The challenger computes $(K_0, \omega^*) \overset{R}{\leftarrow} \mathrm{Sym}(sk_S, pk_R)$, generates a random symmetric key $K_1 \overset{R}{\leftarrow} \mathcal{K}$, where $\mathcal{K}$ is the output keyspace of the tag-KEM, and a random bit $b \overset{R}{\leftarrow} \{0, 1\}$.
4. The adversary runs $\mathcal{A}_2$ on the input $(state_1, K_b)$. During its execution, $\mathcal{A}_2$ may query the oracles as before. $\mathcal{A}_2$ terminates by outputting an arbitrary tag τ^* as well as any necessary state information $state_2$.
5. The challenger computes the challenge encapsulation $C^* \overset{R}{\leftarrow} \mathrm{Encap}\,(\omega^*, \tau^*)$.
6. The adversary runs $\mathcal{A}_3$ on the input $(C^*, state_2)$. During its execution, $\mathcal{A}_2$ may query the same oracles as before, with the restriction that (pk_S, C^*, τ^*) is not a valid query to the decapsulation oracle. $\mathcal{A}_3$ terminates by outputting a guess b' for the value of b.

The adversary wins the game if it is successful at guessing the hidden bit, i.e., $b = b'$. The advantage of $\mathcal{A}$ is defined as $|Pr[b = b'] - 1/2|$.

Definition 7.11 (Indistinguishable signcryption tag-KEM) A signcryption tag-KEM is said to be (multi-user outsider) indistinguishable (IND-CCA2) secure if the advantage of any polynomial-time adversary $\mathcal{A}$ in the IND-CCA2 game is negligible with respect to the security parameter k.

It is important to note the behind-the-scenes interaction between the symmetric key generation and encapsulation oracles in the IND-CCA2 game. This is done in order to let the adversary perform *completely* adaptive encapsulations without having access to the state information stored in ω (which may include nonces, private keys, random coins, and other information strictly internal to the execution of the signcryption tag-KEM).

With respect to the authenticity and integrity of signcryption tag-KEMs, we adapt the usual notion of strong existential unforgeability. The precise requirement is that an adversary should not be able to find encapsulation/tag pairs (C, τ) under some sender's key pk such that $\perp \neq \mathrm{Decap}(pk, sk_R, C, \tau)$. We let the adversary choose the receiving entity to which the adversary wishes to forge messages. The attack game corresponding to the sUF-CMA security of a signcryption tag-KEM runs as follows, for a given security parameter k:

1. The challenger generates a set of global information $param \overset{R}{\leftarrow} \mathrm{Setup}(1^k)$ and a sender keypair $(sk_S, pk_S) \overset{R}{\leftarrow} \mathrm{KeyGen}_S(param)$.

2. The adversary $\mathcal{A}$ is run on the input $(param, pk_S)$. During its execution, $\mathcal{A}$ has access to oracles for symmetric key generation and encapsulation corresponding to the sender's private key sk_S, as defined previously. $\mathcal{A}$ terminates by outputting a fixed receiver keypair (sk_R, pk_R), an encapsulation C, and a tag τ.

The adversary wins the game if $\perp \neq \mathtt{Decap}(pk_S, sk_R, C, \tau)$, provided that the encapsulation oracle never returned C when queried with the tag τ and the ω loaded from storage was not the result of a symmetric key oracle query on pk_R. The advantage of $\mathcal{A}$ is simply the probability $\Pr[\mathcal{A} \text{ wins}]$.

Definition 7.12 (Unforgeable signcryption tag-KEM) A signcryption tag-KEM is said to be (multi-user insider) strongly unforgeable (sUF-CMA secure) if the advantage of any polynomial-time adversary $\mathcal{A}$ in the sUF-CMA game is negligible with respect to the security parameter k.

Definition 7.13 (Secure signcryption tag-KEM) A signcryption tag-KEM is said to be *secure* if it is indistinguishable and unforgeable.

7.4.4 Security of the SCTK+DEM Construction

It remains to show that the combination of a secure signcryption tag-KEM and a secure DEM indeed yields a secure signcryption scheme. Although the original paper on signcryption tag-KEMs only investigated this in the two-user (ADR) model [37], later work has extended this to the multi-user (BSZ) model as well [200].

Theorem 7.3 (*Security of SCTK + DEM construction*) *Let SC be a hybrid signcryption scheme constructed from a signcryption tag-KEM and a DEM. If the signcryption tag-KEM is IND-CCA2 secure (Definition 7.9) and the DEM is IND-CPA secure, then SC is multi-user outsider FSO/FUO-IND-CCA2 secure (Definition 3.1) with the bound*

$$\varepsilon_{SC,IND\text{-}CCA2} \leq 2\,\varepsilon_{SCTK,IND\text{-}CCA2} + \varepsilon_{DEM,IND\text{-}CPA} \tag{7.5}$$

Furthermore, if the signcryption tag-KEM is sUF-CMA secure (Definition 7.12), then SC is multi-user insider FSO/FUO-sUF-CMA secure (Definition 3.2) with the bound

$$\varepsilon_{SC,sUF\text{-}CMA} \leq \varepsilon_{SCTK,sUF\text{-}CMA} \tag{7.6}$$

Proof We begin by proving the indistinguishability of the construction. The proof uses standard techniques and has a similar approach as the corresponding proof of security for encryption tag-KEMs [4, 5] and the proof of Theorem 7.1.

Let G_0 be the regular FSO/FUO-IND-CCA2 game for multi-user-secure signcryption, as described in Chap. 3. We modify G_0 so that the hybrid signcryption procedure uses a key drawn uniformly at random when computing the challenge signcryptext, instead of the actual key output by Sym. The resulting game is referred

$\mathcal{D}_1(param, pk_S, pk_R; \mathcal{O}_{Sym}, \mathcal{O}_{Encap}, \mathcal{O}_{Decap})$:
$\quad (m_0, m_1, s) \xleftarrow{R} \mathcal{A}_1(param, pk_R; \mathcal{O}_{SC}, \mathcal{O}_{USC})$.
$\quad state_1 \leftarrow (param, pk_S, pk_R, m_0, m_1, s)$.
$\quad$ Return $(state_1)$.

$\mathcal{D}_2(K^*, state_1; \mathcal{O}_{Sym}, \mathcal{O}_{Encap}, \mathcal{O}_{Decap})$:
$\quad b \xleftarrow{R} \{0, 1\}$.
$\quad C_2^* \leftarrow \text{Enc}_K(m_b)$.
$\quad state_2 \leftarrow (state_1, b, C_2^*)$.
$\quad$ Return $(C_2^*, state_2)$.

$\mathcal{D}_3(C_1^*, state_2; \mathcal{O}_{Decap})$:
$\quad$ Parse $state_2$ as
$\quad\quad ((param, pk_S, pk_R, m_0, m_1, s), b, C_2^*)$.
$\quad C^* \leftarrow (C_1^*, C_2^*)$.
$\quad b' \xleftarrow{R} \mathcal{A}_2(C^*, s; \mathcal{O}_{SC}, \mathcal{O}_{USC})$.
$\quad$ If $b = b'$, return 1.
$\quad$ Else return 0.

$\mathcal{O}_{SC}(pk, m)$:
$\quad K \xleftarrow{R} \mathcal{O}_{Sym}(pk)$.
$\quad C_2 \leftarrow \text{Enc}_K(m)$.
$\quad C_1 \xleftarrow{R} \mathcal{O}_{Encap}(C_2)$.
$\quad C \leftarrow (C_1, C_2)$.
$\quad$ Return C.

$\mathcal{O}_{USC}(pk, C)$:
$\quad$ Parse C as (C_1, C_2).
$\quad$ If $\perp = \mathcal{O}_{Decap}(pk, C_1, C_2)$ then
$\quad\quad$ Return $\perp$ and halt.
$\quad$ Else $K \leftarrow \mathcal{O}_{Decap}(pk, C_1, C_2)$.
$\quad m \leftarrow \text{Dec}_K(C_2)$.
$\quad$ Return m.

Fig. 7.7 A complete specification of the distinguisher algorithm $\mathcal{D}$ for the SCTK

to as G_1. Let X_0 and X_1 be the events that some adversary $\mathcal{A}$ guesses the correct key in G_0 and G_1, respectively. We bound $|\Pr[X_1] - \Pr[X_0]| \leq 2\,\varepsilon_{SCTK, IND\text{-}CCA2}$ by constructing a distinguisher algorithm $\mathcal{D} = (\mathcal{D}_1, \mathcal{D}_2, \mathcal{D}_3)$ that uses $\mathcal{A}$ to win the IND-CCA2 game against the underlying signcryption tag-KEM and applying Lemma 7.1. As can be seen from the specification in Fig. 7.7, $\mathcal{D}$ simulates the environment of $\mathcal{A}$ perfectly, playing either G_0 or G_1 depending on the hidden bit (which $\mathcal{D}$ is trying to find). This is precisely what is needed to apply Lemma 7.1.

A notable difference from the proof of Theorem 7.1 is that the random key introduced in G_1 is not needed to unsigncrypt oracle queries on the form $\left(pk_R, (C_1^*, C_2)\right)$. This is because of the way decapsulation works, where both the encapsulation and the tag must have an effect on the key.

Finally, the advantage of $\mathcal{A}$ in G_1 is easily seen to be the same as that of an adversary $\mathcal{B} = (\mathcal{B}_1, \mathcal{B}_2)$ performing a passive attack on the DEM. Such an adversary is specified in Fig. 7.8. We note that $\mathcal{B}$ wins the IND-CPA game by distinguishing whether the challenge ciphertext (which from the view of $\mathcal{B}$ has been encrypted with an unknown random key K) if and only if $\mathcal{A}$ can distinguish the correct signcryptext which it is being wrapped into by $\mathcal{B}$. A major difference from the proof of Theorem 7.1 is that the adversary is no longer *able* to make chosen ciphertext queries under the symmetric key used for the challenge, which is why we get away with passive (IND-CPA) security. This completes the proof of confidentiality.

Demonstrating the unforgeability of SC relative to the corresponding signcryption tag-KEM is simpler yet. Any valid forgery of SC requires that the adversary comes up with an encapsulation C_1 that acts as a signature on the ciphertext C_2. In the language of the signcryption tag-KEM, the adversary must in some way have constructed an encapsulation that acts as a signature on the ciphertext tag. This is precisely what it means to break the sUF-CMA security of a signcryption tag-KEM. Figure 7.9 gives the formal specification of an adversary $\mathcal{B}'$ that is able

$\mathcal{B}_1(1^k)$:
 $param \xleftarrow{R} \mathrm{Setup}(1^k)$.
 $(sk_S, pk_S) \xleftarrow{R} \mathrm{KeyGen}_S(param)$.
 $(sk_R, pk_R) \xleftarrow{R} \mathrm{KeyGen}_R(param)$.
 $(m_0, m_1, s) \xleftarrow{R} \mathcal{A}_1(param, pk_S, pk_R; \mathcal{O}_{SC}, \mathcal{O}_{USC})$.
 $state \leftarrow (param, sk_S, pk_S, sk_R, pk_R, m_0, m_1, s)$.
Return $(m_0, m_1, state)$.

$\mathcal{B}_2(C_2^*, state)$:
 Parse $state$ as
  $(param, sk_S, pk_S, sk_R, pk_R, m_0, m_1, s)$.
 $(K, \omega) \xleftarrow{R} \mathrm{Sym}(sk_S, pk_R)$.
 $C_1^* \xleftarrow{R} \mathrm{Encap}(\omega, C_2^*)$.
 $C^* \leftarrow (C_1^*, C_2^*)$.
 $b \xleftarrow{R} \mathcal{A}_2(s, C^*; \mathcal{O}_{SC}, \mathcal{O}_{USC})$.
Return b.

$\mathcal{O}_{SC}(pk, m)$:
 $(K, \omega) \xleftarrow{R} \mathrm{Sym}(pk, sk_R)$.
 $C_2 \leftarrow \mathrm{Enc}_K(m)$.
 $C_1 \xleftarrow{R} \mathrm{Encap}(\omega, C_2)$.
 $C \leftarrow (C_1, C_2)$.
 Return C.

$\mathcal{O}_{USC}(pk, C)$:
 Parse C as (C_1, C_2).
 If $\perp \leftarrow \mathrm{Decap}(pk, sk_R, C_1, C_2)$ then
  Return $\perp$ and halt.
 Else $K \leftarrow \mathrm{Decap}(pk, sk_R, C_1, C_2)$.
 $m \leftarrow \mathrm{Dec}_K(C_2)$.
 Return m.

Fig. 7.8 A complete specification of the distinguisher algorithm $\mathcal{B}$ for the DEM

$\mathcal{B}'(param, pk_S; \mathcal{O}_{Sym}, \mathcal{O}_{Encap})$:
 $(sk_R, pk_R, m, C) \xleftarrow{R} \mathcal{A}(param, pk_S; \mathcal{O}_{SC})$.
 Parse C as (C_1, C_2).
 Return (sk_R, pk_R, C_1, C_2).

$\mathcal{O}_{SC}(pk, m)$:
 $K \xleftarrow{R} \mathcal{O}_{Sym}(pk)$.
 $C_2 \leftarrow \mathrm{Enc}_K(m)$.
 $C_1 \xleftarrow{R} \mathcal{O}_{Encap}(C)$.
 $C \leftarrow (C_1, C_2)$.
 Return C.

Fig. 7.9 A complete specification of the forgery algorithm $\mathcal{B}'$ for the SCTK

to forge encapsulations for the signcryption tag-KEM, given a forger for the hybrid signcryption scheme SC.

To verify that $\mathcal{B}'$ indeed constitutes an efficient forgery algorithm, we note that it outputs a valid encapsulation (i.e., something that decapsulates to some message $m \neq \perp$) whenever $\mathcal{A}$ has outputted a valid forgery of SC. It is also a simple observation that $\mathcal{B}'$ simulates the runtime environment of $\mathcal{A}$ perfectly, since it does not make any independent actions and simply passes along oracle queries to the signcryption tag-KEM oracles.

The only remaining requirement is that the value C_1 had not been the end result of any pair of oracle queries $\mathcal{O}_{Sym}(pk_R)$ and $\mathcal{O}_{Encap}(C_2)$. The corresponding requirement of $\mathcal{A}$ is that the oracle simulated by $\mathcal{O}_{SC}$ did not respond with C on a query of (pk_R, m). Since decapsulation is deterministic, we note that C was only returned by $\mathcal{O}_{SC}$ if m was part of the query. Furthermore, $\mathcal{O}_{SC}$ will only respond with C if C_1 and C_2 were the output and input to $\mathcal{O}_{Encap}$. Finally, the public key pk_R is passed directly through $\mathcal{O}_{SC}$, so the only time it will be part of a query to $\mathcal{O}_{Sym}$ is if it was part of the signcryption oracle query from $\mathcal{A}$. We conclude that the two algorithms $\mathcal{A}$ and $\mathcal{B}'$ have identical advantages in their respective games. This completes the proof. $\square$

The proof of Theorem 7.3 also holds in alternate security models, from the two-user (ADR) models specified in Chap. 2 [37] and up to the full multi-user security models used here. It may also readily be extended to a general multi-user insider setting, where the adversary is allowed to pick the sending keys used in the indistinguishability game. As long as the same notion of security is applied to both the hybrid signcryption scheme and the underlying signcryption tag-KEM, the general reductions remain valid with the appropriate modifications.

7.4.5 Insider-Secure Hybrid Signcryption in Practice

As we have established, an insider-secure signcryption KEM needs to combine the key encapsulation functionality of a regular KEM with the authenticity-preserving and integrity-preserving features of a digital signature scheme. From prior experience with other hybrid schemes, an obvious approach would be to take a hybrid encryption scheme as a starting point and extend it to fulfill our additional requirements. However, this is harder than it seems. In fact, apart from trivial compositions combining KEMs and signature schemes, there are no known insider-secure hybrid signcryption schemes based on encryption KEMs.

The opposite approach is to start with a secure signature scheme and tweak it in such a way that it also acts as a KEM. One way to do this is to alter the computation of some internal value in such a way that it depends on the keys of both sender and receiver and using it to derive a symmetric key. This method has been more successful, with Zheng's original scheme [203] being the canonical example. But there is no general method known to generate efficient hybrid signcryption schemes from *arbitrary* signature schemes. However, most known insider-secure hybrid signcryption schemes apply exactly the same trick as Zheng's scheme (see Chaps. 4, 5, and 6).

The idea used by Zheng and the others applies to signature schemes that work in a very specific manner: to sign, one must pick a random nonce n, use it to compute a random group element g^n, which is hashed together with the message to be signed, whereupon some computations on the result based on the signer's private key are performed. To verify, the public key of the signer is used to reconstruct g^n from the signature data and verify that the output of the hash is correct. A signcryption scheme can therefore be created by modifying the first step to compute the randomizer as pk_S^n, requiring sk_S to reconstruct it from the g^n computed during normal verification. Although it has not been proven, it is conjectured that this construction works in general; all that is currently known is that it is secure (in the random oracle model) in several specific cases.

However, other efficient methods of constructing efficient insider-secure hybrid signcryption schemes from scratch are not known, and existing schemes that fit into the signcryption tag-KEM model are all based on variants of the Diffie–Hellman problem (see Chaps. 4 and 5). The scheme proposed by Malone-Lee (see Sect. 4.6.2) is of particular interest as it is an example of a hybrid signcryption scheme with non-repudiation, while the schemes proposed by Bjørstad and Dent (see Sect. 4.7) and by Libert and Quisquater (see Sect. 5.5) are of interest as they have particularly tight security reductions.

A rather different instantiation of signcryption tag-KEMs can be made by extending ordinary (non-hybrid) signcryption schemes that support transmission of associated plaintext data together with the signcryption [167]. In these schemes, the signcryption algorithm "binds" the associated data to the signcryptext, providing integrity protection for both. As we have seen previously in this chapter, this is *exactly* what we want. Intuitively, one may think of the plaintext label as the tag and use the regular signcryption scheme to signcrypt a symmetric key.

This construction is useful for precisely the same reasons that makes hybrid signcryption so appealing in the first place: it removes the restriction of non-hybrid schemes to small message spaces, which make them inefficient and slow for long messages. A hybrid construction using schemes with associated data was first suggested by Dodis et al. in [77], building on the theory of concealment schemes (discussed further in Chap. 8). Bjørstad and Dent [37] prove that signcryption tag-KEMs built in this manner yield the same scheme.

Formally, the syntax of a signcryption scheme with associated data differs from usual only in the ways the associated data are handled:

- The Signcrypt algorithm takes as additional input the associated data d, so that the syntax becomes $C \xleftarrow{R} \text{Signcrypt}(sk_S, pk_R, m, d)$.
- The Unsigncrypt algorithm also requires d as part of its input, hence $m \leftarrow \text{Unsigncrypt}(pk_S, sk_R, C, d)$.
- Signcryption and unsigncryption oracles are modified accordingly, so that the adversary may choose the value of d (or leave it empty) when making oracle queries.

The security criteria are also altered in the obvious manner, to ensure that the integrity of the associated data is maintained. With these alterations in mind, the construction of a signcryption tag-KEM is straightforward:

- The Sym algorithm takes sender and receiver keys sk_S and pk_R as input. It picks a symmetric key K uniformly at random, sets $\omega \leftarrow (sk_S, pk_R, K)$, and returns the pair (ω, K).
- The Encap algorithm takes state information ω and a tag τ as input. It parses $(sk_S, pk_R, K) \leftarrow \omega$, computes $C \xleftarrow{R} \text{Signcrypt}(sk_S, pk_R, K, \tau)$, and returns C.
- The Decap algorithm takes keys pk_S and sk_R, the signcryptext C, and tag τ as input. It uses the computes $K \leftarrow \text{Unsigncrypt}(pk_S, sk_R, C, \tau)$ and returns K.

It is quite straightforward to show that this construction is secure, and a proof will not be given here. The main intuition is that the signcryption tag-KEM acts as a wrapper for the underlying signcryption scheme in such a way that an adversary has very little opportunity to do anything "interesting." In the random oracle model, signcryption schemes using the common "hash-and-sign" approach can often be used in this manner by using the plaintext label as an additional input to the hash function.

Chapter 8
Concealment and Its Applications to Authenticated Encryption

Yevgeniy Dodis

8.1 Introduction

In this chapter we will study a recent cryptographic primitive called *concealment*, which was introduced by Dodis and An [75, 76] because of its natural applications to authenticated encryption. A concealment is a publicly known randomized transformation, which, on input m, outputs a *hider h* and a *binder b*. Together, h and b allow one to recover m, but separately (1) the hider h reveals "no information" about m, while (2) the binder b can be "meaningfully opened" by at most one hider h. While setting $b \leftarrow m$, $h \leftarrow \emptyset$ is a trivial concealment, the challenge is to make $|b| \ll |m|$, which we call a "non-trivial" concealment. We will examine necessary and sufficient assumptions for building various flavors of concealment and give simple, general, and efficient constructions of concealments.

We also discuss two main applications of concealments to the area of authenticated encryption. First, following [6, 75, 76], we show that concealment is the right cryptographic primitives to enable one to extend the domain of authenticated encryption. Specifically, let $\mathcal{AE}$ be an authenticated encryption scheme (either public-or symmetric-key)[1] designed to work on short messages. Using concealments, we can transform $\mathcal{AE}$ into a new authenticated encryption scheme $\mathcal{AE}'$ on longer messages as follows. To encrypt a longer message m, one uses a concealment scheme to get h and b and then outputs the authenticated ciphertext $\mathcal{AE}'(m) = \langle \mathcal{AE}(b), h \rangle$.

Second, the above paradigm leads to a very simple and general solution to the problem of *remotely keyed (authenticated) encryption* (RKAE) [39, 40], so far primarily studied in the symmetric-key setting. In this problem, one wishes to split

Y. Dodis (✉)
Cryptography Group, Department of Computer Science, New York University, New York, NY, USA
e-mail: dodis@cs.nyu.edu

---

[1] We note that authenticated encryption in the public-key setting is typically called *signcryption* [203, 204]. However, since all our applications of concealments will work, with minor adjustments, in both in the symmetric- and in the public-key settings, we will use the term *authenticated encryption* throughout.

A.W. Dent, Y. Zheng (eds.), *Practical Signcryption*, Information Security and Cryptography, DOI 10.1007/978-3-540-89411-7_8, © Springer-Verlag Berlin Heidelberg 2010

the task of high bandwidth authenticated encryption between a secure, but low bandwidth/computationally limited, device and an insecure, but computationally powerful, host. Following [75, 76], we show that the composition paradigm above gives a provably secure solution for RKAE: for an authenticated encryption of m, the host simply sends a short value b to the device (which stores the actual secret key for $\mathcal{AE}$), gets back $\mathcal{AE}(b)$, and outputs $\langle \mathcal{AE}(b), h \rangle$.

8.1.1 Domain Extension of Authenticated Encryption

We start by examining the natural question of securely extending the domain of authenticated encryption. Specifically, assume we have a secure authenticated encryption scheme $\mathcal{AE}$ (either symmetric- or public-key; see Footnote 1) which works on "short" messages. How then do we build a secure authenticated encryption scheme $\mathcal{AE}'$ for "long" messages out of $\mathcal{AE}$? (Throughout, we should interpret "short" as having very small length, like 256 bits; "long" stands for fixed, but considerably larger length, possibly on the order of gigabytes.) In the context of authenticated encryption, this question was formally studied by Dodis and An [75, 76] (whose work we closely follow here). However, domain extension clearly has rich history in the context of many other cryptographic primitives. We briefly review some of this work, since it will suggest the first solutions to our problem as well.

First, in the context of regular chosen plaintext secure (CPA secure) encryption, we can simply split the message into blocks and encrypt it "block-by-block." Of course, this solution multiplicatively increases the size of the ciphertext, so a lot of work has been developed into designing more efficient solutions. In the public-key setting, the classical "hybrid" encryption solution reduces the problem into that in the symmetric-key setting. Namely, one encrypts, using the public key, a short randomly chosen symmetric key τ and uses τ to symmetrically encrypt the actual message m. As for the symmetric-key setting, one typically uses one of many secure *modes of operations* on block ciphers (such as CBC mode; see [139]), which typically (and necessarily) add only one extra block of redundancy when encrypting a long message m. For authentication, a different flavor of techniques is usually used. Specifically, a common method is to utilize a *collision-resistant hash function* [69] H which maps a long input m into a short output such that it is hard to find a "collision" $H(m_0) = H(m_1)$ for $m_0 \neq m_1$. Then one applies the given authentication mechanism for short strings to $H(m)$ to authenticate the much longer m. This works, for example, for digital signatures (this is called "hash-then-sign"), message authentication codes (MACs), and pseudorandom functions (for the latter two, other methods are possible; see [8, 24, 25, 38] and the references therein).

8.1.1.1 First Solution Attempt

One way to use this prior work is to examine generic constructions of authenticated encryption using some of the above primitives and apply the above "compression" techniques to each basic primitive used. For example, in the symmetric-key setting we can take the "Encrypt-then-MAC" solution [26] for authenticated encryption, using the CBC mode for encryption and the CBC-MAC [25] for message authentication, and build a specific authenticated encryption on long messages using only a fixed-length block cipher. Even better, in this setting we could utilize some special purpose, recently designed modes of operation for *authenticated* encryption, such as IACBC [112] or OCB [168]. Similar techniques could be applied in the public-key setting using the "hybrid" technique for encryption, "hash-then-sign" for signatures, and any of the three generic signature/encryption compositions presented in Chaps. 2 and 3.

In other words, prior work already gives us some tools to build "long" authenticated encryption from other "short" primitives.

8.1.1.2 Why Examine This Problem Then?

The first reason is in its theoretical value. It is a very interesting structural question to design an elegant amplification from "short" to "long" authenticated encryption, without building the "long" primitive from scratch. For example, in the public-key setting especially, it is curious to see if there is a common generalization of such different looking methods as "hybrid" encryption and "hash-then-sign" authentication. Indeed, we shall see that this generalization yields a very elegant new primitive, certainly worth studying on its own. The second reason is that it gives one more *option* to designing "long-message" authenticated encryption. And having such an option may bring other advantages (e.g., efficiency, ease of implementation) depending on its application and implementation. Consider, for example, the public-key setting, where authenticated encryption is usually called *signcryption* [203, 204] (see Footnote 1). With any of the generic signature-encryption compositions described in Chap. 2, signcryption of a long messages will eventually reduce to a regular signature plus an encryption of some short message. With our paradigm, it will reduce to a single signcryption on a short message, which can potentially be faster than doing a separate signature and encryption. Indeed, this potential efficiency gain was the main motivation of Zheng [203, 204] to introduce signcryption in the first place!

Finally, our technique has important applications on its own. In particular, we show that it naturally leads to a very general, yet simple solution to the problem of *remotely keyed authenticated encryption* (RKAE) [39, 40, 125], discussed in Sect. 8.1.2. None of the other techniques we mentioned seem to yield a solution to this problem.

8.1.1.3 Main Construction and a New Primitive: Concealment

Following [75, 76], we seek to amplify a given "short" authenticated encryption scheme $\mathcal{AE}$ into a "long" authenticated encryption scheme $\mathcal{AE}'$ as follows. First, we somehow split the long message m into two parts $(h, b) \xleftarrow{R} T(m)$ using some transform T, where $|b| \ll |m|$, and then define $\mathcal{AE}'(m) = \langle \mathcal{AE}(b), h \rangle$. We investigate the question of which transformations T suffice in order to make $\mathcal{AE}'$ a "secure" authenticated encryption? The work of Dodis and An [75, 76] and Alt [6] completely characterizes these transformations T, which are called *concealments*. Specifically, they show that $\mathcal{AE}'$ is secure if and only if T is an "appropriate" concealment scheme, where "appropriate" depends on the exact setting we consider, as discussed later.

Intuitively, a concealment T has to be invertible and also satisfy the following properties: (1) the *hider* h reveals no information about m; (2) the *binder* b "commits" one to m in a sense that it is hard to find a valid (h', b) where $h' \neq h$. Property (2) has three formalizations leading to the notions of regular, relaxed, and super-relaxed concealment schemes. Super-relaxed concealments will turn out to be necessary and sufficient [6, 75, 76] for the symmetric-key setting and the so-called *outside-secure* public-key setting (see Chaps. 2 and 3). Relaxed concealments will be necessary and sufficient [6, 75, 76] for the stronger and more desirable *insider-secure* public-key setting (see Chaps. 2 and 3). Finally, regular concealments will be necessary and sufficient [75, 76] for the problem of RKAE (in either the symmetric-or the public-key settings). We also remark that concealments look very similar to *commitment schemes* at first glance, but there are few crucial differences, making these notions quite distinct. This comparison will be discussed in Sect. 8.2.

Finally, we are left with the question of constructing concealment schemes. First, we show that *non-trivial* (i.e., $|b| < |m|$) concealment schemes require the existence of one-way functions. Additionally, ensuring the regular binding property requires the existence of collision-resistant hash functions (CRHFs). From a positive perspective, we give a very efficient general construction of (all kinds of) concealments matching the necessary requirements stated above. Our construction uses any one-time-secure symmetric-key encryption (which can be built efficiently from pseudorandom generators or standard block ciphers) to ensure message hiding and a certain family of hash functions: almost universal hash functions (AUHFs) [185] for super-relaxed binding, universal one-way hash function (UOWHFs) [147] for relaxed binding, and collision-resistant hash functions (CRHFs) [69] for regular binding. When instantiated with standard components, our constructions have a binder b whose length is only proportional to the security parameter and is independent of the message length, while the length of the hider h is roughly equal to the length of the message. In fact, one special case of our construction looks very similar to the famous *Optimal Asymmetric Encryption Padding* (OAEP) [30], although without relying on random oracles!

To summarize, concealments are very natural cryptographic gadgets and can be efficiently built from standard assumptions. In particular, they give an efficient way to implement a "long" authenticated encryption scheme from a "short" one. Finally, we describe a powerful application of concealments and our amplification technique to the problem of RKAE, which deserves a separate introduction.

8.1.2 Remotely Keyed Authenticated Encryption

The problem of "remotely keyed encryption" (RKE) was first introduced by Blaze [39] in the symmetric-key setting. Intuitively, RKE is concerned with the problem of "high bandwidth encryption with low bandwidth smartcards." Essentially, one would like to store the secret key in a secure, but computationally bounded and low bandwidth, card, while a powerful host performs most of the operations for encryption/decryption using occasional access to the card. Of course, the communication between the host and the card should be minimal as well. The original work of Blaze lacked formal modeling of the problem, but inspired a lot of subsequent research. The first formal modeling of RKE was done by Lucks [125], who chose to interpret the question as that of implementing a remotely key *pseudorandom permutation* (or block cipher), which we will call an RK-PRP. Lucks' paper was further improved—both in terms of formal modeling and constructions— by an influential work of Blaze et al. [40]. For one thing, they observed that the PRP's length-preserving property implies that it *cannot* be semantically secure when viewed as encryption. Thus, in addition to RK-PRP, which they called a "length-preserving RKE," they introduced the notion of a "length-increasing RKE," which is essentially meant to be the notion of remotely keyed *authenticated* encryption, so we will call it RKAE. In other words, the informal notion of "RKE" was really formalized into two very distinct notions of RK-PRP and RKAE, none of which is really a plain encryption scheme. Blaze et al. [40] gave formal definitions and constructions of RKAE and RK-PRP, and Lucks [126] subsequently improved the RK-PRP constructions of [40].

While the RKAE definition of Blaze et al. [40] was an important first step towards properly formalizing this new notion (as opposed to the notion of RK-PRPs), their definition is convoluted and quite non-standard (it involves an "arbiter" who can fool any adversary). It looks nothing like the formal, universally accepted notion of regular (not remotely keyed) authenticated encryption [26, 33, 114]. Of course, there is a very objective reason for this, as the formal definition for authenticated encryption appeared *after* the work of [40]. Additionally, Blaze et al. perhaps tried to make their definition of "length-increasing RKE" look as close as possible to their definition of "length-preserving RKE" (i.e., RK-PRP). Still, we believe that the definition of RKAE should be based on the definition of regular authenticated encryption, rather than trying to mimic the definition of a somewhat related, but different concept. Thus, we will follow the work of Dodis and An [75, 76] who gave a simpler and more natural definition, which looks much closer to the definition of regular authenticated encryption. Additionally, Dodis and An [75, 76] naturally extend the whole concept of RKAE to the *public-key* setting, since it is equally applicable in this case too.[2] Notice, in the public-key setting the notion of RK-PRP makes no sense, which additionally justifies our choice to base our definition on that of regular authenticated encryption.

Another closely related work is that of Jakobsson et al. [107], who also effectively studied the problem of RKAE (despite calling it RKE even though authentication is considered as part of the requirement). We note that the definition of [107] looks much closer to the one of [75, 76]. However, there are still significant differences that make the latter notion stronger.[3] For example, Jakobsson et al. [107] do not support chosen ciphertext attack in its full generality (i.e., no card access is given to the adversary after the challenge is received) and also require the adversary

---

[2] In this chapter, though, we will concentrate on the more popular symmetric-key setting, only briefly mentioning the simple extension to the public-key setting.

[3] Except that both [107] and [40] insist on achieving some kind of pseudorandomness of the output. Even though our constructions achieve it as well, we feel this requirement is not crucial for any application of RKAE and was mainly put to make the definition look similar to RK-PRPs.

to "know" the messages corresponding to forged ciphertexts. We also mention that their main scheme uses an "OAEP"-like transform and their security analysis critically uses random oracles. As we show, using another (in fact, simpler) variant of OAEP for RKAE, we can eliminate random oracles from the analysis. Thus, a special case of our construction gives an equally simple and efficient scheme, which is provably secure in the standard model.

Finally, we mention the work of Joux et al. [110]. From our perspective, it showed that naive "remotely keyed" implementation of many natural block cipher modes of operations for (authenticated) encryption, such as CBC or IACBC, is completely insecure from the perspective of RKE/RKAE. In such naive implementations, the card stores the key to the block cipher, while the host does everything by itself except when it needs to evaluate the block cipher (or its inverse), in which case it calls the card. We notice that this means that to perform a single (authenticated) encryption/decryption, the host needs to adaptively access the card for a number of times proportional to the length of the (long) message. Perhaps not surprisingly, this gives too much power to the "blockwise-adaptive" adversary, allowing him to easily break the security of such naive RKE/RKAE implementations. In contrast, in our RKAE solutions the host accesses the card once and on a very short input, irrespective of the length of the message it actually processes. In fact, in one of the solutions of [75, 76] (see "extensions" paragraph below), the card only performs a single block cipher call per invocation!

Therefore, the work of Joux et al. [110] supports our prior claim that direct "long" authenticated encryption schemes, such as IACBC [112], do not appear to be naturally suited for RKAE, as they seem to be easily breakable by a simple "blockwise-adaptive" adversary.

8.1.2.1 RKAE Constructions

In addition to giving a simple and natural definition of RKAE, Dodis and An [75, 76] showed that our construction of "long-message" authenticated encryption from "short-message" authenticated encryption provides a very natural, general, and provably secure solution to the problem of RKAE. Recall, we had $\mathcal{AE}'(m) = \langle \mathcal{AE}(b), h \rangle$, where (h, b) was output by some transformation T, and $|b| \ll |m|$. This immediately suggests the following protocol for RKAE. The host computes (h, b) and sends short b to the card, which stores the secret key. The card computes short $c \xleftarrow{R} \mathcal{AE}(b)$ and sends it to the host, which outputs $\langle c, h \rangle$. Authenticated decryption is similar. Again, one can ask the question which transformations T will suffice to make this simple scheme secure. Not surprisingly, Dodis and An [75, 76] showed that concealment schemes were necessary and sufficient, even though in this case one needs the regular binding property of concealments and must utilize CRHFs. Overall, the above result gives a general and intuitively simple solution to the problem of RKAE. Also, it generalizes the previous "different looking" solutions of [40, 107], both of which can be shown to use some particular concealment and/or "short" authenticated encryption.

8.1.2.2 Extensions

All the techniques mentioned above naturally support authenticated encryption *with associated data* [167]. Intuitively, associated data allows one to "bind" a public label to the message, which does not need to be encrypted, but needs to be authenticated. Viewing the label as part of the message is a possible solution, but not the most efficient one, as was convincingly shown by [167]. As shown by Dodis and An [75, 76], these efficiency gains carry over to the questions studied in this chapter. However, we omit the details here and instead refer to [75, 76].

Also, we remark again that all our results apply to both the public- and the symmetric-key authenticated encryption. The only exception is the following extension from [75, 76] that makes sense only in the symmetric-key setting. They asked the question if one can replace the given "short" authenticated encryption $\mathcal{AE}$ by a (strong) pseudorandom permutation (i.e., a block cipher, since $\mathcal{AE}$ is applied on short inputs). This would enhance the practical usability of our composition even more. As shown by [75, 76], although arbitrary concealments are generally *not* enough to ensure the security of the enhanced scheme $\mathcal{AE}'$, some mild extra restrictions—enjoyed by the natural concealment constructions—make them sufficient for this purpose as well![4] Again, we refer to [75, 76] for more details.

8.2 Definition of Concealment

Intuitively, a concealment scheme efficiently transforms a message m into a pair (h, b) such that (1) (h, b) together reveal m; (2) the *hider h* reveals no information about m; and (3) the *binder b* "commits" one to m in a sense that it is hard to find a valid (h', b) where $h' \neq h$. A formal description is given below.

8.2.1 Syntax

A concealment scheme consists of three efficient algorithms: (Setup, Conceal, Open). The setup algorithm Setup(1^k), where k is the security parameter, outputs a public concealment key ck (possibly empty, but often consisting of public parameters). Given a message m from the corresponding message space $\mathcal{M}$, the randomized concealment algorithm Conceal$_{ck}(m)$ outputs a concealment pair (h, b), where h is the *hider* of m and b is the *binder* to m. For brevity, we will usually omit ck, writing $(h, b) \xleftarrow{R}$ Conceal(m). Sometimes we will write $h(m)$ (resp. $b(m)$) to denote the hider (resp. binder) part of a randomly generated (h, b). The deterministic open algorithm Open$_{ck}(h, b)$ outputs m if (h, b) is a "valid" pair for m (i.e., could have been generated by Conceal(m)) or $\perp$ otherwise. Again, we will usually write

---

[4] Unfortunately, the shortest length of the binder b which we can currently achieve is roughly 300 bits. This means that most popular block ciphers, such as AES, cannot be used in this setting. However, any block cipher with a 512-bit block seems to be more than sufficient.

$x \leftarrow \text{Open}(h, b)$, where $x \in \mathcal{M} \cup \{\perp\}$. The *correctness* property of concealment schemes says that $\text{Open}_{ck}(\text{Conceal}_{ck}(m)) = m$ for any m and ck.

8.2.2 Security of Concealment

Just like commitment schemes, concealment schemes have two security properties called *hiding* and *binding*. However, unlike commitment schemes, these properties apply to different parts of concealment, which makes a significant difference.

- *Hiding*. Even with knowledge of ck, it is computationally hard for the adversary $\mathcal{A}$ to come up with two messages $m_1, m_2 \in \mathcal{M}$ such that $\mathcal{A}$ can distinguish $h(m_1)$ from $h(m_2)$. That is, $h(m)$ reveals no information about m. Formally, for any probabilistic polynomial-time (PPT) adversary $\mathcal{A}$, which runs in two stages $\mathcal{A}_1$ and $\mathcal{A}_2$, we require that the probability below is at most $\frac{1}{2} + negl(k)$ (where $negl(k)$ denotes some negligible function of the security parameter k):

$$\Pr\left[\sigma = \tilde{\sigma} : \begin{array}{l} ck \xleftarrow{R} \text{Setup}(1^k), \ (m_0, m_1, \alpha) \xleftarrow{R} \mathcal{A}_1(ck), \ \sigma \xleftarrow{R} \{0, 1\}, \\ (h, b) \xleftarrow{R} \text{Conceal}_{ck}(m_\sigma), \ \tilde{\sigma} \xleftarrow{R} \mathcal{A}_2(h, \alpha) \end{array}\right]$$

where α is some state information. Sometime, we will write $h(m_0) \approx h(m_1)$ to indicate that $h(m_0)$ is computationally indistinguishable from $h(m_1)$.

- *Binding*. Even with knowledge of ck, it is computationally hard for the adversary $\mathcal{A}$ to come up with b, h, h', where $h \neq h'$ such that (b, h) and (b, h') are both valid concealment pairs (i.e., $\text{Open}_{ck}(h, b) \neq \perp$ and $\text{Open}_{ck}(h', b) \neq \perp$). Formally, for any PPT $\mathcal{A}$, the following probability is at most $negl(k)$:

$$\Pr\left[\begin{array}{l} h \neq h' \wedge \\ m, m' \neq \perp \end{array} : \begin{array}{l} ck \xleftarrow{R} \text{Setup}(1^k), \ (b, h, h') \xleftarrow{R} \mathcal{A}(ck), \\ m \leftarrow \text{Open}_{ck}(h, b), \ m' \leftarrow \text{Open}_{ck}(h', b) \end{array}\right]$$

That is, $\mathcal{A}$ cannot find a binder b which it can open with two different hiders.[5]

We immediately remark that setting $b \leftarrow m$ and $h \leftarrow \emptyset$ satisfies the definition above. Indeed, the challenge is to construct concealment schemes with $|b| \ll |m|$ (we call such schemes *non-trivial*). Since we must have $|b| + |h| \geq |m|$, achieving a very good concealment scheme implies that $|h| \approx |m|$.

As we shall see, for some applications of concealment two slightly weaker forms of binding will be enough. For the lack of better names, we call them *relaxed binding* and *super-relaxed binding*.

---

[5] We could have allowed $\mathcal{A}$ to find $h \neq h'$ as long as $(h, b), (h', b)$ do not open to distinct messages $m \neq m'$. However, we will find the stronger notion more convenient.

8.2.3 Relaxed Concealments

We consider *relaxed* concealment schemes, where the strict binding property above is replaced by the *relaxed binding* property, which states that $\mathcal{A}$ cannot find binder collisions for a *randomly generated* binder $b(m)$, even if $\mathcal{A}$ can choose m before learning $(h(m), b(m))$. Formally, for any PPT $\mathcal{A}$, which runs in two stages $\mathcal{A}_1$ and $\mathcal{A}_2$, the following probability is at most $negl(k)$:

$$\Pr\left[\begin{array}{l} h \neq h' \wedge \\ m' \neq \bot \end{array} : \begin{array}{c} ck \xleftarrow{R} \text{Setup}(1^k), \ (m, \alpha) \xleftarrow{R} \mathcal{A}_1(ck), \ (h, b) \xleftarrow{R} \text{Conceal}_{ck}(m), \\ h' \xleftarrow{R} \mathcal{A}_2(h, b, \alpha), \ m' \leftarrow \text{Open}_{ck}(h', b) \end{array}\right]$$

To justify this distinction, we will see later that non-trivial (regular) concealments will be equivalent to collision-resistant hash functions (CRHFs), while relaxed concealments can be built from universal one-way hash functions (UOWHFs). By the result of Simon [182], UOWHFs are strictly weaker primitives than CRHFs (in particular, they can be built from regular one-way functions [147]), which implies that relaxed concealments form a weaker cryptographic assumption than regular concealments.

8.2.4 Super-Relaxed Concealments

Finally, we will consider an even weaker form of binding. The *super-relaxed binding* property states that $\mathcal{A}$ cannot find binder collisions for a randomly generated binder $b = b(m)$ *without knowing the actual value b for which it is trying to find the collisions*. Formally, for any PPT $\mathcal{A}$, which runs in two stages $\mathcal{A}_1$ and $\mathcal{A}_2$, the following probability is at most $negl(k)$:

$$\Pr\left[\begin{array}{l} h \neq h' \wedge \\ m' \neq \bot \end{array} : \begin{array}{c} ck \xleftarrow{R} \text{Setup}(1^k), \ (m, \alpha) \xleftarrow{R} \mathcal{A}_1(ck), \ (h, b) \xleftarrow{R} \text{Conceal}_{ck}(m), \\ h' \xleftarrow{R} \mathcal{A}_2(h, \alpha), \ m' \leftarrow \text{Open}_{ck}(h', b) \end{array}\right]$$

The only difference with related concealments introduced earlier is that $\mathcal{A}_2$ does not get to see b. As we shall see, we will be able to achieve super-relaxed binding *unconditionally*, namely, without even relying on one-way functions (which were essential for relaxed and regular binding).

8.2.5 Comparison to Commitment

At first glance, concealment schemes look extremely similar to commitment schemes. Recall, commitments also transform m into a pair (c, d), where c is the "commitment" and d is the "decommitment." However, in this setting the commitment c is *both* the hider and the binder, while in our setting the hider and the binder are distinct. This seemingly minor distinction turns out to make a very big difference. For example, irrespective of parameter settings, commitments always imply the existence of one-way functions, while there are trivial concealments when $|b| = |m|$. On the other hand, when $|b| < |m|$, we will show that concealments require CRHFs, while quite non-trivial commitments can be built from one-way functions [146].

Not surprisingly, the two primitives have very different applications and constructions. In particular, commitments are not useful for our "domain extension" applications to authenticated encryption. Interestingly, though, commitments do have other applications to authenticated encryption. For example, in the Commit-then-Encrypt-and-Sign ($Ct\mathcal{E}\&\mathcal{S}$) paradigm [10] studied in Chap. 9 (see also Fig. 9.2), which uses commitments to build "parallel" authenticated encryption from regular signature and encryption schemes. Other more specialized applications of commitments to authenticated encryption are discussed in Chap. 6.

8.3 Constructing Concealment Schemes

In this section, we give very simple and general constructions of concealment schemes based on some "appropriate" family of hash functions (see below) and any symmetric one-time encryption scheme.

Our construction will be split into two phases. First, we show how to achieve hiding using a symmetric one-time encryption scheme and then we show how to use hash functions to add binding to any scheme which already enjoys hiding. We will conclude the section with the observation that all the assumptions we utilize in our constructions are not only sufficient but also necessary. Thus, our constructions are tight.

8.3.1 Achieving Hiding

We first show how to achieve the hiding property so that $|b| \ll |m|$. Recall that a symmetric encryption scheme $\mathcal{SE} = (\text{Enc}, \text{Dec})$ with keylength λ consists of an encryption algorithm Enc and a decryption algorithm Dec. Of course, if $\tau \xleftarrow{R} \{0, 1\}^{\lambda}$, we require that $\text{Dec}_{\tau}(\text{Enc}_{\tau}(m)) = m$. For our purposes we will need the most trivial and minimalistic notion of *one-time security*, as described in Sect. 1.3.4. For a randomly chosen symmetric key $\tau \in \{0, 1\}^{\lambda}$, we let $\text{Enc}_{\tau}(m_0) \approx \text{Enc}_{\tau}(m_1)$ denote that a PPT attacker cannot distinguish between the encryption of m_0 and m_1 in the one-time IND-CPA setting.

Of course, a regular one-time pad satisfies this notion. However, for our purposes we will want the secret key to be much shorter than the message: $|\tau| \ll |m|$. For the most trivial such scheme, we can utilize any pseudorandom generator (PRG) $G : \{0, 1\}^{k} \to \{0, 1\}^{n}$ where $k \ll n$. The secret key is a random $\tau \in \{0, 1\}^{k}$. To encrypt $m \in \{0, 1\}^{n}$, we compute $\text{Enc}_{\tau}(m) \leftarrow G(\tau) \oplus m$, and to decrypt c, we compute $\text{Dec}_{\tau}(c) \leftarrow G(\tau) \oplus c$. Of course, any stronger encryption scheme will suffice for our purposes too.

Now, let $b \leftarrow \tau$ and $h \overset{R}{\leftarrow} \mathrm{Enc}_\tau(m)$, so that $\mathrm{Open}(b, h) \leftarrow \mathrm{Dec}_b(h)$. It is easy to see that this scheme satisfies the hiding (but not yet the binding) property of concealment and also that $|b| \ll |m|$ if a good one-time secure encryption is used, such as the PRG-based scheme above.

Lemma 8.1 *If $\mathcal{SE}$ is a one-time IND-CPA secure encryption scheme, then the above concealment scheme satisfies hiding. Moreover, the scheme is non-trivial if and only if the key τ is shorter than the message m (which, by the result of [98], requires the existence of one-way functions).*

8.3.2 Achieving Binding

Next, we show how to add regular/relaxed/super-relaxed binding property using any family of collision-resistant/universal one-way/almost universal hash functions (CRHFs/UOWHFs/AUHFs). Recall that CRHFs/UOWHFs/AUHFs are defined by some family $\mathcal{H} = \{H\}$ of compressing functions for which no computationally bounded attacker can find, with non-negligible probability, a collision pair $x \neq x'$ such that $H(x) = H(x')$, where H is a function randomly chosen from $\mathcal{H}$. However,

- with CRHFs, we first select the function H and let the attacker find (x, x') based on H.
- with UOWHFs, the attacker selects x before seeing H and only then finds x' based on H.
- with AUHFs, the attacker has to select both (x, x') before seeing H.

We will comment on the known constructions of such hash families later, here only mentioning that AUHFs can be built unconditionally, the existence of UOWHFs is equivalent to the existence of one-way functions [169], while the existence of CRHFs seems to require strictly stronger computational assumptions than one-way functions [182]. Instead, now we see how to utilize such hash functions for our purposes of achieving the corresponding form of binding. In all the constructions we assume $\Pi = (\mathrm{Setup}, \mathrm{Conceal}, \mathrm{Open})$ already achieves hiding, and let $\mathcal{H} = \{H\}$ be some hash family whose input size is equal to the input size of the hider h of Π. Recall that in our schemes we will always have $|h| \approx |m|$, so we expect the input length of $\mathcal{H}$ to be roughly equal to the input length of our message m.

8.3.2.1 Regular Binding

Here we assume that $\mathcal{H} = \{H\}$ is a family of CRHFs. We turn the given "hiding" concealment Π into $\Pi' = (\mathrm{Setup}', \mathrm{Conceal}', \mathrm{Open}')$ which is a full-fledged concealment scheme as follows:

- $\mathrm{Setup}'(1^k)$: run $ck \overset{R}{\leftarrow} \mathrm{Setup}(1^k)$, $H \overset{R}{\leftarrow} \mathcal{H}$ and output $ck' \leftarrow \langle ck, H \rangle$.
- $\mathrm{Conceal}'(m)$: let $(h, b) \overset{R}{\leftarrow} \mathrm{Conceal}(m)$, $h' \leftarrow h$, $b' \leftarrow b \| H(h)$, and output $\langle h', b' \rangle$.

- Open$'(h', b')$: parse b' = as $b\|t$, output $\bot$ if $H(h') \neq t$, and output $m \leftarrow$ Open(h', b) otherwise.

Lemma 8.2 *If Π satisfies the hiding property and $\mathcal{H}$ is a CRHF, then Π' is a (regular) concealment scheme.*

Proof Since $h' = h$, we get hiding for free. As for binding, if some $\mathcal{A}$ outputs $b' = b\|t$ and $h_0 \neq h_1$ such that $H(h_0) = H(h_1) = t$, then, in particular, $\mathcal{A}$ outputs a collision (h_0, h_1) for $\mathcal{H}$, contradicting the collision resistance of $\mathcal{H}$. $\square$

As we can see, the output size of H directly contributes to the size of our binder b'. In practical constructions, this output size is proportional to the security parameter k and is independent of the input length n. Since the same is true for the key length of practical symmetric encryption schemes, we get that the size of the binder is optimally proportional to the security parameter k. For example, using AES-based encryption and SHA1-based hash function, $|b'| = 128 + 160 = 288$ bits.

8.3.2.2 Relaxed Binding

Here we assume that $\mathcal{H} = \{H\}$ is a family of UOWHFs. We turn the given "hiding" concealment Π into $\Pi'' = (\text{Setup}'', \text{Conceal}'', \text{Open}'')$ which is a full-fledged *relaxed* concealment scheme as follows:

- Setup$'' =$ Setup.
- Conceal$''(m)$: pick $H \leftarrow \mathcal{H}$, compute $(h, b) \overset{R}{\leftarrow}$ Conceal(m), set $h'' \leftarrow h$, $b'' \leftarrow b\|H(h)\|H$, and output $\langle h'', b'' \rangle$.
- Open$''(h'', b'')$: parse b'' as $b\|t\|H$, output $\bot$ if $H(h'') \neq t$, and output $m \leftarrow$ Open$''(h'', b)$ otherwise.

Lemma 8.3 *If Π satisfies the hiding property and $\mathcal{H}$ is a UOWHF, then Π'' is a relaxed concealment scheme.*

Proof Since $h'' = h$, we get hiding for free. As for binding, assume some $\mathcal{A}$ chooses m_0, gets back $b'' = b\|t\|H$ and h_0, and then successfully outputs $h_1 \neq h_0$ such that $H(h_0) = H(h_1) = t$. Since $h_0 = h(m_0)$ is computed independently of H, we can immediately turn this $\mathcal{A}$ into an attacker $\mathcal{A}'$ breaking the UOWHF security of $\mathcal{H}$. $\mathcal{A}_1'$ will use $\mathcal{A}_1$ to find m_0, will compute $(h_0, b) \overset{R}{\leftarrow}$ Conceal(m_0), and will output the message h_0 as the first colliding message. Upon learning random H, $\mathcal{A}_2'$ will run $\mathcal{A}_2$ on inputs $b'' \leftarrow b\|H(h_0)\|H$ and h_0 to produce the second colliding message $h_1 \neq h_0$. $\square$

We see that the construction is similar to the CRHF-based construction, except we pick a new hash function *for each call* and append it to the binder b''. This ensures that H is always selected independently of the input h to which it is applied, as required by the definition of UOWHFs. In theory, this shows that efficient *relaxed* concealments, unlike regular concealments, can be built from one-way functions (see Lemma 8.6). In practice, the message is less clear. On the one hand, the best theoretical constructions of UOWHFs (or even fixed-length UOWHFs) from one-way functions have key length roughly proportional to $O(k \log |m|)$ [32, 169, 179], which is slightly superlinear in the security parameter k when hashing long messages. For example, hashing 1 Gb message would require a binder of at least several kilobytes, which is less desirable. On the other hand, it might be much more reasonable to assume that a given "practical" hash family $\mathcal{H}$ is universal one way as opposed to collision resistant. For example, Halevi and Krawczyk [94] gave several efficient methods to construct UOWHFs with short keys (say, 160 bits) using building blocks which are not required (and unlikely) to be collision resistant. Thus, it seems reasonable that one might be able to construct a UOWHF family whose output *plus key size* might be comparable to (or perhaps only slightly larger than) the best reasonable output of a CRHF and yet rely on a provably weaker assumption!

8.3.2.3 Super-Relaxed Binding

To construct super-relaxed concealments, we use exactly the same construction Π'' as above, except we only need to assume that the hash family $\mathcal{H} = \{H\}$ is a family of AUHFs.

Lemma 8.4 *If Π satisfies the hiding property and $\mathcal{H}$ is a AUHF, then Π'' is a super-relaxed concealment scheme.*

Proof The proof is the same as of Lemma 8.3, except we observe that the attacker $\mathcal{A}$ never learns the value H when breaking the super-relaxed binding. This is because $\mathcal{A}$ is only given the value $h'' = h$ which does not include H. Thus, $\mathcal{A}$ effectively produces a collision pair (h_0, h_1) without having any information about H, contradicting the AUHF security of $\mathcal{H}$. □

It is known that one can construct AUHFs unconditionally. For example, the classical polynomial interpolation construction (see Bernstein [35] for some history) splits the n-bit message into blocks of size v, views each block as a coefficient of a degree n/v polynomial p over $GF[2^v]$, and then evaluates p at a random point x in $GF[2^v]$ (where this point x is the key for H). This construction achieves binding security level of $n/(v2^v)$,[6] and has the key and output size equal to v. For example, if the length of the message and the hider h is 1 Gb, to achieve security 2^{-80} it is sufficient to set $v = 106$. Thus, using this construction with AES-based encryption, the final length of the binder $b'' = \tau \| H(h) \| H$ is $128 + 106 + 106 = 340$ bits, which is quite reasonable for a 1 Gb message and is only 52 bits longer than the SHA1-based construction (for which we are required to assume the collision resistance of SHA1 and which certainly does not achieve even a "conditional" binding security level of 2^{-80}).

---

[6] Meaning that the maximal probability that two unequal messages collide under a random H is at most $\frac{n}{v2^v}$.

8.3.2.4 Collecting the Pieces Together

To summarize, we achieved the following constructions of concealment schemes. For the hider, all schemes set $h \stackrel{R}{\leftarrow} \mathrm{Enc}_\tau(m)$, where Enc is a one-time secure encryption scheme (such as $\mathrm{Enc}_\tau(m) = m \oplus G(\tau)$, where G is a PRG, or any block-cipher-based semantically secure encryption, such as CBC mode or CFB mode). For regular binding we set $b \leftarrow \tau \| H(h)$, where H is chosen from a family of CRHFs, while for the relaxed/super-relaxed binding we could make weaker assumptions by setting $b \leftarrow \tau \| H(h) \| H$ and assuming H is chosen from a family of UOWHFs/AUHFs. In particular, using the fact that the existence of CRHFs or UOWHFs implies the existence of one-way functions, and, hence, of one-time secure symmetric encryption, we get

Theorem 8.1 *The hiding property of regular/relaxed/super-relaxed concealment can be based on the existence of one-way functions (which is implied by the existence of CRHF). The binding property of regular/relaxed/super-relaxed concealments can be based on the existence of CRHF/one-way functions/no assumptions.*

As we will see in the next subsection, the above theorem is tight in terms of the minimal assumptions required.

8.3.2.5 Comparison with OAEP

Recall, the *Optimal Asymmetric Encryption Padding* (OAEP) [30] is a popular padding scheme used in designing various encryption and signature schemes based on trapdoor permutations. It picks a random value τ and sets $h \leftarrow G(\tau) \oplus m$, $b \leftarrow \tau \oplus H(h)$, where G and H are hash function (typically modeled as random oracles in the analysis). This construction is very similar to the particular concealment construction we had above, except we set $b \leftarrow \tau \| H(h)$. Namely, our construction is slightly more "redundant" in terms of the binder b. However, this "redundancy" is precisely makes it a secure concealment scheme. Indeed, OAEP decoding never outputs $\perp$, since it is a permutation over m and τ; thus, OAEP does not achieve any binding. What is interesting, though, is that our construction—which is so similar to the OAEP—does not need to assume G and H as random oracles in the analysis!

8.3.3 Necessity of Assumptions

We show that the assumptions of Lemmas 8.1, 8.2 and 8.3 (and hence those of Theorem 8.1) are not only sufficient, but also necessary. We start by showing that achieving non-trivial hiding requires one-way functions, as stated in Lemma 8.1.

Lemma 8.5 *If Π is non-trivial (i.e., $|b| < |m|$) and satisfies the correctness and hiding properties of concealment, then one-way functions exist.*

Proof We use the result of Impagliazzo and Luby [98] who showed that "non-trivial, one-time secure interactive encryption" (NOTE) implies the existence of one-way functions. Here NOTE refers to any interactive protocol between Alice and Bob, who are connected by a public channel P and a secure channel S such that (a) at the end of the protocol Alice transmits the message m to Bob; (b) Eve, who is passive and only observes all the communication over the public channel P, gets no information (in the usual sense of semantic security) about m; and (c) the total length of messages exchanged over the secure channel S (not observed by Eve) is strictly less than the length of the message m.

Thus, it suffices to show that non-trivial concealment satisfying correctness and hiding imply a NOTE scheme. But this is simple. Alice, on input m, runs the concealment scheme to obtain $(h, b) \xleftarrow{R} \text{Conceal}(m)$ and send b over the secure channel S and h over the public channel P. Bob can recover m from b and h (by correctness), the length of b is shorter than the length of m (by non-triviality of Π), and h observed by Eve reveals no information about m (by hiding). □

Next, we show the necessity of using CRHFs/UOWHFs to ensure the regular/relaxed binding of our constructions.

Lemma 8.6 *Let* $\Pi = (\text{Setup}, \text{Conceal}, \text{Open})$ *be a regular (resp. relaxed) concealment scheme where the binder b is shorter than the message m. Define a shrinking function family $\mathcal{H}$ by the following generation procedure: pick a random value r, run* $ck \xleftarrow{R} \text{Setup}(1^k)$*, and output* $\langle ck, r \rangle$ *as a description of a random function* $H \in \mathcal{H}$*. To evaluate such H on input m, run* $(h, b) \xleftarrow{R} \text{Conceal}_{ck}(m)$ *using the randomness r and set* $H(m) \leftarrow b$*. Then $\mathcal{H}$ is a family of CRHFs (resp. UOWHFs).*

Proof Assume Π is a regular concealment. Using the definition of H above, finding $m_0 \neq m_1$ such that $H(m_0) = H(m_1) = b$ implies finding $h_0 = h(m_0)$ and $h_1 = h(m_1)$ such that $\text{Open}_{ck}(h_0, b) = m_0 \neq \bot$, $\text{Open}_{ck}(h_1, b) = m_1 \neq \bot$, and $h_0 \neq h_1$ (since $m_0 \neq m_1$). But this clearly contradicts the binding property of concealment.

Now consider the relaxed concealment scenario, where the attacker has to choose m_0 beforehand. In this case, choosing a random $H \in \mathcal{H}$ involves choosing a random r. Thus, when evaluating $H(m_0)$, we effectively computed a *random* concealment $(h_0, b) \xleftarrow{R} \text{Conceal}_{ck}(m_0)$ and gave it to the adversary, as required by the definition of relaxed concealment. The rest of the proof is the same as for strong concealments. □

8.4 Applications to Authenticated Encryption

We now study applications of concealment to *authenticated encryption*. Recall, authenticated encryption provides means for private, authenticated communication between the sender and the receiver. Namely, an eavesdropper cannot understand anything from the transmission, while the receiver is sure that any successful transmission indeed originated from the sender and has not been "tampered with." The intuitive idea of using concealments for authenticated encryption is simple. If AuthEnc is an authenticated encryption scheme working on short $|b|$-bit messages, and $(h, b) \xleftarrow{R} \mathrm{Conceal}(m)$, we can define $\mathrm{AuthEnc}'(m) = \langle \mathrm{AuthEnc}(b), h \rangle$. Intuitively, sending the hider h "in the clear" preserves privacy due to the hiding property of concealments, while the authenticated encryption of the binder b provides authenticity due to the binding property. (The exact type of the required binding will depend on the particular setting, as explained later.)

We formalize this intuition by presenting two applications of the above paradigm. First, we argue that it indeed yields a secure authenticated encryption scheme on long messages from that on short messages and that this holds even if (super-) relaxed concealments are used. Second, we show that this paradigm also gives a very simple and general solution to *remotely keyed* authenticated encryption. Here, the full power of regular binding is needed.

We remark that our applications hold for both the symmetric- and the public-key notions of authenticated encryption (the latter is historically called *signcryption* [203, 204]). In terms of usability, long-message authenticated encryption is probably much more useful in the public-key setting, since signcryption is typically expensive. However, even in the symmetric-key setting our approach is very fast and should favorably compare with alternative direct solutions such as "Encrypt-then-MAC" [26]. For the remotely keyed setting, both public- and symmetric-key models seem equally useful and important. In fact, symmetric-key "remotely keyed encryption" is perhaps more relevant, since smartcards are currently much better suited for symmetric-key operations. Indeed, before Dodis and An [75, 76], prior work on "remotely keyed encryption" focused on the symmetric setting only.

8.4.1 Definition of Authenticated Encryption

We remark that formal modeling of authenticated encryption in the public-key setting is somewhat more involved than that in the symmetric-key setting due to issues such as multi-user security, "insider attacks", and "identity fraud" (see Chaps. 2 and 3). Therefore, we first give the details of the symmetric-key setting and then briefly sketch the changes required in the public-key setting.

8.4.1.1 Symmetric-Key Syntax

A symmetric-key authenticated encryption scheme consists of three algorithms: $\mathcal{AE} = (\mathrm{AuthKeyGen}, \mathrm{AuthEnc}, \mathrm{AuthDec})$. The randomized key generation algorithm $\mathrm{AuthKeyGen}(1^k)$, where k is the security parameter, outputs a shared secret key K and possibly a public parameter pub. Of course, pub can always be part of the secret key, but this might unnecessarily increase the secret storage. In the description below, all the algorithms (including the adversary's) can have access to pub, but we omit this dependence for brevity. The randomized *authencryption* (authenticate/encrypt) algorithm $\mathrm{AuthEnc}$ takes as input the key K and a message m from the associated message space $\mathcal{M}$, internally flips some coins, and outputs a ciphertext c; we write $c \xleftarrow{R} \mathrm{AuthEnc}_K(m)$ or $c \xleftarrow{R} \mathrm{AuthEnc}(m)$, omitting the key K for brevity. The deterministic *authdecryption* (verify/decrypt) algorithm $\mathrm{AuthDec}$

takes as input the key K, a ciphertext c from some ciphertext space $\mathcal{C}$, and outputs $m \in \mathcal{M} \cup \{\perp\}$, where $\perp$ indicates that the input ciphertext c is "invalid." We write $m \leftarrow \text{AuthDec}_K(c)$ or $m \leftarrow \text{AuthDec}(c)$ (again, omitting the key). We require that $\text{AuthDec}_K(\text{AuthEnc}_K(m)) = m$ for any $m \in \mathcal{M}$.

8.4.1.2 Symmetric-Key Security

Fix the sender S and the receiver R. Following the standard security notions [26], we define the attack models and goals of the adversary for both authenticity (i.e., sUF-CMA)[7] and privacy (IND-CCA2)[8] as follows. We first model our adversary $\mathcal{A}$. $\mathcal{A}$ has oracle access to the functionalities of both S and R. Specifically, it can mount a chosen message attack on S by asking S to produce a ciphertext C of an arbitrary message m, i.e., $\mathcal{A}$ has access to the *authencryption oracle* $\text{AuthEnc}_K(\cdot)$. Similarly, it can mount a chosen ciphertext attack on R by giving R any candidate ciphertext C and receiving back the message m (where m could be $\perp$), i.e., $\mathcal{A}$ has access to the *authdecryption oracle* $\text{AuthDec}_K(\cdot)$.[9] In other words, in all the definitions below $\mathcal{A}$ is given oracle access to both $\text{AuthEnc}_K(\cdot)$ and $\text{AuthDec}_K(\cdot)$.

To break the sUF-CMA security of the authenticated encryption scheme, $\mathcal{A}$ has to be able to produce a "valid" ciphertext C (i.e., $\text{AuthDec}_K(C) \neq \perp$), which was not returned earlier by the authencryption oracle.[10] Notice, $\mathcal{A}$ is not required to "know" $m = \text{AuthDec}_K(C)$ when producing C. The scheme is sUF-CMA secure if for any PPT $\mathcal{A}$, $\Pr[\mathcal{A} \text{ succeeds}] \leq negl(k)$.[11]

To break the IND-CCA2 security of the authenticated encryption scheme, $\mathcal{A}$ first has to come up with two messages m_0 and m_1. One of these messages m_σ (where σ is a random bit) will be authencrypted and the corresponding cipher-text $C^* \xleftarrow{R} \text{AuthEnc}_K(m_\sigma)$ will be given to $\mathcal{A}$. The task of $\mathcal{A}$ is then to guess the bit σ. To succeed in the CCA2 attack, $\mathcal{A}$ is only disallowed to ask R to authdecrypt the challenge C^*. The scheme is IND-CCA2 secure if for any PPT $\mathcal{A}$, $\Pr[\mathcal{A} \text{ succeeds}] \leq \frac{1}{2} + negl(k)$.

Remark 8.1 We also remark that IND-CPA security[12] is the same, except $\mathcal{A}$ is not given access to the authdecryption oracle. Moreover, in the symmetric-key setting it is known that IND-CPA+sUF-CMA security implies IND-CCA2 security [26]. However, since this implication does not hold in the public-key setting, discussed next, we do not follow this route in the symmetric-key setting.

---

[7] Meaning "strong unforgeability against chosen message attack."

[8] Meaning "indistinguishability against chosen ciphertext attack."

[9] Of course, since S and R share the same key and use the same algorithms, there is no need to allow for "another" chosen message attack on R or a chosen ciphertext attack on S.

[10] A slightly weaker notion of UF-CMA requires C to correspond to "new" message m not submitted to $\text{AuthEnc}_K(\cdot)$.

[11] Note that the definition does not prevent so-called reflection attacks, where a message produced by S is returned back to S as a valid message from R. Such attacks can (and should) be easily prevented by a higher level application.

[12] Meaning "indistinguishability against chosen plaintext attack."

8.4.1.3 Public-Key Syntax

For convenience, we will use almost the same syntax as before, with the following modifications. The key generation algorithm $\texttt{AuthKeyGen}(1^k)$ run by user U now outputs the public verification/encryption key pk_U and the secret signing/decryption key sk_U for U. The randomized *authencryption* (authenticate/encrypt) algorithm $\texttt{AuthEnc}$, run by the sender S to compose a ciphertext to the receiver R, takes as input the secret key sk_S of S, the public key pk_R of R, and a message m from the associated message space $\mathcal{M}$, internally flips some coins and outputs a ciphertext c; we write $c \xleftarrow{R} \texttt{AuthEnc}(pk_R, sk_S, m)$ or simply $c \xleftarrow{R} \texttt{AuthEnc}(m)$, when the identities of S and R are clear. The deterministic *authdecryption* (verify/decrypt) algorithm $\texttt{AuthDec}$ takes as input the secret key sk_R of R and the public key pk_S of S and outputs $m \in \mathcal{M} \cup \{\bot\}$, where $\bot$ indicates that the input ciphertext c is "invalid." We write $m \leftarrow \texttt{AuthDec}(sk_R, pk_S, c)$ or simply $m \leftarrow \texttt{AuthDec}(c)$ (again, omitting the keys of S and R, when clear). We require that $\texttt{AuthDec}(sk_R, pk_S, \texttt{AuthEnc}(pk_R, sk_S, m)) = m$ for any $m \in \mathcal{M}$.

8.4.1.4 Public-Key Security

The security is defined similarly to the symmetric-key setting, except there are several flavors now because the sender S and the receiver R now have different secret keys. We refer the reader to Chaps. 2 and 3 for the discussion of some of those flavors, here only discussing the distinction between *outsider security* and *insider security*. Informally, in the outsider security setting the attacker tries to break privacy or authenticity of two honest users S and R communicating between each other, by posing as a legitimate outsider party to either S or R. In contrast, in the insider security setting the attacker tries to break privacy or authenticity of an honest user U by "posing" as a valid sender or recipient to U. Thus, insider security is a stronger notion, but may not be required in some applications. We consider a full multi-user model for both outsider and insider security (as described in Chap. 3).

8.4.2 Authenticated Encryption of Long Messages

Assume $\mathcal{AE} = (\texttt{AuthKeyGen}, \texttt{AuthEnc}, \texttt{AuthDec})$ is a secure authenticated encryption on $|b|$-bit messages. We would like to build an authenticated encryption $\mathcal{AE}' = (\texttt{AuthKeyGen}', \texttt{AuthEnc}', \texttt{AuthDec}')$ on $|m|$-bit messages, where $|m| \gg |b|$. We start with the symmetric-key setting and later generalize to the public-key setting.

8.4.2.1 Symmetric-Key Setting

We will employ the following composition paradigm. The key K for $\mathcal{AE}'$ is the same as that for $\mathcal{AE}$. To authencrypt m, first split it into two pieces (h, b) (so that the transformation is invertible) and output $\texttt{AuthEnc}'_K(m) = \langle \texttt{AuthEnc}_K(b), h \rangle$.

The question we are asking is what are the necessary and sufficient conditions on the transformation $m \mapsto (h, b)$ so that the resulting authenticated encryption is secure? As shown by Alt [6], correcting the prior claim of Dodis and An [75, 76], the necessary and sufficient condition is to have the transformation above be a *super-relaxed concealment*.

More formally, assume $\Pi = (\texttt{Setup}, \texttt{Conceal}, \texttt{Open})$ satisfies the syntax, but not yet the security properties of a concealment scheme. We assume that $ck \xleftarrow{R} \texttt{Setup}(1^k)$ forms a public parameter pub of $\mathcal{AE}'$. We define $\mathcal{AE}'$ as stated above. Namely, $\texttt{AuthEnc}'(m)$ outputs $\langle \texttt{AuthEnc}(b), h \rangle$, where $(h, b) \xleftarrow{R} \texttt{Conceal}(m)$, and $\texttt{AuthDec}'(c, h)$ outputs $\texttt{Open}(h, \texttt{AuthDec}(c))$. Then

Theorem 8.2 *If $\mathcal{AE}$ is secure, then $\mathcal{AE}'$ is secure if and only if Π is a super-relaxed concealment scheme.*

Proof For one easy direction, we show that if Π does not satisfy the hiding property, then $\mathcal{AE}'$ cannot even be IND-CPA secure, let alone IND-CCA2 secure. Indeed, if some adversary $\mathcal{A}$ can find two messages m_0 and m_1 such that $h(m_0) \not\approx h(m_1)$, then obviously

$$\texttt{AuthEnc}'(m_0) \equiv (\texttt{AuthEnc}(b(m_0)), h(m_0))$$
$$\not\approx (\texttt{AuthEnc}(b(m_1)), h(m_1)) \equiv \texttt{AuthEnc}'(m_1),$$

contradicting IND-CPA security.

Similarly, if Π does not satisfy the super-relaxed binding property, then $\mathcal{AE}'$ cannot be sUF-CMA secure. Indeed, assume some concealment adversary $\mathcal{A}$ can produce m such that when $(h, b) \xleftarrow{R} \texttt{Conceal}(m)$ is generated and h is given to $\mathcal{A}$, $\mathcal{A}$ can find (with non-negligible probability ε) a value $h' \neq h$ such that $\texttt{Open}(h', b) \neq \bot$. We build a forger $\mathcal{A}'$ for $\mathcal{AE}'$ using $\mathcal{A}$. $\mathcal{A}'$ gets m from $\mathcal{A}$ and asks its authencryption oracle the value $\mathcal{AE}'(m)$. $\mathcal{A}'$ gets back (h, c), where c is a valid authencryption of b and (h, b) is a random concealment pair for m. $\mathcal{A}'$ gives h to $\mathcal{A}$ and gets back (with probability ε) the value $h' \neq h$ such that $\texttt{Open}(h', b) \neq \bot$. But then (h', c) is a valid authencryption (with respect to $\mathcal{AE}'$) different from (h, c), contradicting the sUF-CMA security of $\mathcal{AE}'$.

The other (interesting) direction was formally proven in [6, 75, 76]. Here, we only give an informal intuition. For sUF-CMA security, by the assumed sUF-CMA security of $\mathcal{AE}$, the only way $\mathcal{A}$ can break sUF-CMA security of $\mathcal{AE}'$ is by "reusing" some prior ciphertext $c = \texttt{AuthEnc}(b)$ returned (together with h) by the authencryption oracle. Since $\mathcal{AE}$ is semantically secure, the value c does not give $\mathcal{A}$ any more information about b than $\mathcal{A}$ can deduce from h alone.[13] Thus, if $\mathcal{A}$ outputs a forgery (c, h'), for some $h' \neq h$, then $\mathcal{A}$ effectively broke the super-relaxed binding property of Π. The IND-CCA2 security is proven similarly. First, the sUF-CMA security above implies that only IND-CPA security of $\mathcal{AE}'$ needs to be proven [26]. The latter trivially follows from the IND-CPA security of $\mathcal{AE}$ and the hiding property of Π. $\square$

---

[13] The formalization of this claim is somewhat subtle; see [6].

8.4.2.2 Public-Key Setting

We generalize the above composition paradigm as follows. The new authenticated encryption scheme $\mathcal{AE}'$ for user U will utilize the same public/secret-key pair (pk_U, sk_U) as the original authenticated encryption scheme $\mathcal{AE}$. To authencrypt m from S to R, first split it into two pieces (h, b) (so that the transformation is invertible) and output $\texttt{AuthEnc}'(pk_R, sk_S, m) \xleftarrow{R} \langle \texttt{AuthEnc}(pk_R, sk_S, b), h \rangle$. As earlier, we ask what are the necessary and sufficient conditions on the transformation $m \mapsto (h, b)$ so that the resulting public-key authenticated encryption is secure? We get a slightly different answer depending on whether we are interested in the outsider or the insider security. As shown by Alt [6] (slightly correcting the prior claim of [75, 76]), the necessary and sufficient condition for outsider/insider security is to have the transformation above be a *super-relaxed/relaxed concealment*.

Theorem 8.3 *If $\mathcal{AE}$ is secure, then $\mathcal{AE}'$ is outsider/insider secure if and only if Π is a super-relaxed/relaxed concealment scheme.*

Proof The outsider security proof is essentially identical to the symmetric-key setting considered in Theorem 8.2, because the outsider public-key security is very similar to the symmetric-key security. The only difference is that the IND-CCA2 security is no longer implied by the sUF-CMA and IND-CPA security, so it has to be proven directly. However, it still follows from the outsider security of $\mathcal{AE}$ and the super-relaxed binding property of Π. Indeed, the only way to break the IND-CCA2 security of $\mathcal{AE}'$ without breaking one for $\mathcal{AE}$ is to "reuse" the challenge ciphertext $c^* = \texttt{AuthEnc}(b^*)$ with some hider $h \neq h^*$ and, moreover, to do so without having "any information" about the actual binder b^* (due to the privacy of $\mathcal{AE}$). However, the latter contradicts the super-relaxed binding of Π.

As for the insider security, we only sketch why *relaxed* binding is required, referring to [6, 75, 76] for the actual proof why it is in fact *sufficient* to "lift" both the IND-CCA2 and sUF-CMA proofs of security from the outsider to the insider security setting. The reason is because, when trying to forge a ciphertext from the target user U to some receiver R, the attacker $\mathcal{A}$ can know the secret key sk_R of R. More precisely, if Π does not satisfy the relaxed binding property, then $\mathcal{AE}'$ cannot be sUF-CMA secure. Indeed, assume some concealment adversary $\mathcal{A}$ can produce m such that when $(h, b) \xleftarrow{R} \texttt{Conceal}(m)$ is generated and (h, b) is given to $\mathcal{A}$, $\mathcal{A}$ can find (with non-negligible probability ε) a value $h' \neq h$ such that $\texttt{Open}(h', b) \neq \bot$. We build a forger $\mathcal{A}'$ (attacking user U) for $\mathcal{AE}'$ using $\mathcal{A}$. First, $\mathcal{A}'$ honestly generates keys (sk_R, pk_R) for some receiver R. Then, $\mathcal{A}'$ gets m from $\mathcal{A}$ and asks its authencryption oracle the value $\texttt{AuthEnc}'(pk_R, m)$. $\mathcal{A}'$ gets back (h, c), where c is a valid authencryption of b and (h, b) is a random concealment pair for m. Using sk_R, $\mathcal{A}$ retrieves the value b from c (this is the key difference from the outsider setting), gives (h, b) to $\mathcal{A}$, and gets back (with probability ε) the value $h' \neq h$ such that $\texttt{Open}(h', b) \neq \bot$. But then (h', c) is a "fresh" (different from (h, c)) authencryption of some valid message from U to R, contradicting the sUF-CMA security of $\mathcal{AE}'$.

Fortunately, it was shown by Dodis and An [75, 76] that ensuring relaxed binding not only prevents the above attack but is actually enough to argue both insider privacy and confidentiality (provided, of course, that one starts with an insider-secure authenticated encryption $\mathcal{AE}$). □

8.4.3 Remotely Keyed Authenticated Encryption

Similar to the previous section, we first consider the symmetric-key setting and then briefly sketch the extension to the public-key setting.

8.4.3.1 Symmetric-Key Syntax

A one-round remotely keyed authenticated encryption (RKAE) scheme consists of seven efficient algorithms: $\mathcal{RK} = $ (KeyGen, StartEnc, CardEnc, FinishEnc, StartDec, CardDec, FinishDec) and involves two parties called the *host* and the *card*. The host is assumed to be powerful, but insecure (subject to break-in by an adversary), while the card is secure but has limited computational power and low bandwidth. The randomized key generation algorithm KeyGen(1^k), where k is the security parameter, outputs a secret key K and possibly a public parameter *pub*. In the description below, all the algorithms (including the adversary's) can have access to *pub*, but we omit this dependence for brevity. This key K is stored in the card. The process of authenticated encryption is split into the following three steps. First, on input m, the host runs probabilistic algorithm StartEnc(m) and gets (b, α). The value b should be short, as it will be sent to the card, while α denotes the state information that the host needs to remember. We stress that StartEnc involves no secret keys and can be run by anybody. Next, the card receives b and runs probabilistic algorithm CardEnc$_K(b)$ using its secret key K. The resulting (short) value c will be sent to the host. Finally, the host runs another randomized algorithm FinishEnc(c, α) and outputs the resulting ciphertext C as the final authencryption of m. Again, FinishEnc involves no secret keys. The sequential composition of the above three algorithms induces an authenticated encryption algorithm, which we will denote by AuthEnc$'_K$.

Similarly, the process of authenticated decryption is split into three steps as well. First, on input C, the host runs deterministic algorithm StartDec(C) and gets (u, β). The value u should be short, as it will be sent to the card, while β denotes the state information that the host needs to remember. We stress that StartDec involves no secret keys and can be run by anybody. Next, the card receives u and runs deterministic algorithm CardDec$_K(u)$ using its secret key K. The resulting (short) value v will be sent to the host. We note that one possible value for v will be $\perp$, meaning that the card found some inconsistency in the value of u. Finally, the host runs another randomized algorithm FinishDec(v, β) and outputs the resulting plaintext m if $v \neq \perp$ or $\perp$, otherwise. Again, FinishDec involves no secret keys. The sequential composition of the above three algorithms induces an authenticated decryption algorithm, which we will denote by AuthDec$'_K$. We also call the value C *valid* if AuthDec$'_K(C) \neq \perp$.

The correctness property states for any m, AuthDec$'$(AuthEnc$'(m)$) $= m$.

8.4.3.2 Security of RKAE

As we pointed out, RKAE in particular induces a regular authenticated encryption scheme, if we combine the functionalities of the host and the card. Thus, at the very least we would like to require that the induced scheme $\mathcal{AE}' = (\text{KeyGen}, \text{AuthEnc}', \text{AuthDec}')$ satisfies the IND-CCA2 and sUF-CMA security properties of regular authenticated encryption. Of course, this is not a sufficient guarantee in the setting of RKAE. Indeed, such security only allows the adversary oracle access to the *combined* functionality of the host and the card. In the setting of RKAE, the host is anyway insecure, so the adversary should have *oracle access to the functionality of the card*. Specifically, we allow our adversary $\mathcal{A}'$ to have oracle access to the card algorithms $\text{CardEnc}_K(\cdot)$ and $\text{CardDec}_K(\cdot)$.

Just like regular authenticated encryption, RKAE has security notions for privacy and authenticity, which we denote by RK-IND-CCA and RK-sUF-CMA, respectively.

To break the RK-sUF-CMA security of RKAE, $\mathcal{A}'$ has to be able to produce "one more forgery" when interacting with the card. Namely, $\mathcal{A}'$ tries to output $t + 1$ valid ciphertexts $C_1 \ldots C_{t+1}$ after making at most t calls to $\text{CardEnc}_K(\cdot)$ (where t is any polynomial in k). Again, we remark that $\mathcal{A}'$ is not required to "know" the plaintext values $m_i = \text{AuthDec}'_K(C_i)$. The scheme is RK-sUF-CMA secure if for any PPT $\mathcal{A}'$, $\Pr[\mathcal{A}' \text{ succeeds}] \leq negl(k)$. We note that this is the only meaningful authenticity notion in the setting of RKAE. This is because the values $c \xleftarrow{R} \text{CardEnc}_K(b)$ returned by the card have no "semantic" meaning of their own. So it makes no sense to require $\mathcal{A}'$ to produce a new "valid" string c. On the other hand, it is trivial for $\mathcal{A}'$ to compute t valid ciphertexts $C_1 \ldots C_t$ with t oracle calls to CardEnc, by simply following to honest authencryption protocol on arbitrary messages $m_1 \ldots m_t$. Thus, security against "one more forgery" is the most ambitious goal we can try to meet in the setting of RKAE.

To break the RK-IND-CCA security of RKAE, $\mathcal{A}'$ first has to come up with two messages m_0 and m_1. One of these will be authencrypted at random, the corresponding ciphertext $C^* \xleftarrow{R} \text{AuthEnc}_K(m_\sigma)$ (where σ is a random bit) will be given to $\mathcal{A}'$ and $\mathcal{A}'$ has to guess the value σ. To succeed in the CCA2 attack, $\mathcal{A}'$ is only disallowed to call the card authdecryption oracle $\text{CardDec}_K(\cdot)$ on the well-defined value u^*, where we define $\text{StartDec}(C^*) = (u^*, \beta^*)$. This value is uniquely defined as StartDec is a deterministic algorithm. This restriction is to prevent $\mathcal{A}'$ from trivially authdecrypting the challenge. The scheme is RK-IND-CCA secure if for any PPT $\mathcal{A}'$, $\Pr[\mathcal{A}' \text{ succeeds}] \leq \frac{1}{2} + negl(k)$. We briefly remark that RK-IND-CPA security is the same, except we do not give $\mathcal{A}'$ access to the card authdecryption oracle.

8.4.3.3 Canonical RKAE

A natural implementation of RKAE would have the card perform regular authenticated encryption/decryption on short messages, while the host should do the special preprocessing to produce the short message for the card from the given long message. Specifically, in this case we start from some auxiliary authenticated encryption $\mathcal{AE} = (\texttt{AuthKeyGen}, \texttt{AuthEnc}, \texttt{AuthDec})$ which works on "short" $|b|$-bit messages and require that $\texttt{CardEnc} = \texttt{AuthEnc}$ and $\texttt{CardDec} = \texttt{AuthDec}$. Moreover, we would like the card to authdecrypt the same value c that it produced during authencryption. In our prior notation, $u = c$ and $v = b$, where $c \xleftarrow{R} \texttt{AuthEnc}_K(b)$. Finally, it is natural to assume that the host outputs c as part of the final (long) ciphertext. Putting these together, we come up with the following notion of *canonical* RKAE.

First, the host runs $\texttt{StartEnc}(m)$, which we conveniently rename $\texttt{Conceal}(m)$, and produces (h, b), where h will be part of the final ciphertext and b is "short." Then it sends b to the card and gets back $c \xleftarrow{R} \texttt{AuthEnc}_K(b)$. Finally, it outputs $C = \langle c, h \rangle$ as the resulting authencryption of m. Similarly, to authdecrypt $C = \langle c, h \rangle$, it sends c to the card, gets $b = \texttt{AuthDec}_K(c)$, and outputs $\texttt{FinishDec}(h, b)$, which we conveniently rename $\texttt{Open}(h, b)$. Thus, the canonical RKAE is fully specified by a "short" authenticated encryption $\mathcal{AE}$ and a triple $\Pi = (\texttt{Setup}, \texttt{Conceal}, \texttt{Open})$ (where $\texttt{Setup}$ is run at key generation and outputs a publicly available key pub).

The natural question we address is what security properties of $\texttt{Conceal}$ and $\texttt{Open}$ are needed in order to achieve a secure canonical RKAE (provided the auxiliary $\mathcal{AE}$ is secure)? As shown by Dodis and An [75, 76], the necessary and sufficient condition is to employ a secure (regular) concealment scheme. We remark that the final *induced* scheme $\mathcal{AE}'$ we construct is *exactly* the composition scheme we discussed in Sect. 8.4.2. However, in that application the entire authenticated encryption was performed honestly—in particular, b was chosen by properly running $\texttt{Conceal}(m)$—so that (super-)relaxed concealments were sufficient. Here, an untrusted host can ask the card to authencrypt any value b it wishes, so we need the full binding power of concealments.

Theorem 8.4 *If $\mathcal{AE}$ is secure and a canonical $\mathcal{RK}$ is constructed from $\mathcal{AE}$ and Π, then $\mathcal{RK}$ is secure if and only if Π is a (regular) concealment scheme.*

Proof The proof of this result is very similar to that of Theorem 8.2 and is omitted. We only mention why regular binding is necessary. If $\mathcal{A}$ can come up with a triple (b, h, h') such that $\texttt{Open}(h, b) \neq \perp$, $\texttt{Open}(h', b) \neq \perp$, and $h \neq h'$, then we can construct $\mathcal{A}'$ breaking the RK-sUF-CMA security of $\mathcal{AE}'$ as follows. $\mathcal{A}'$ asks the card to authencrypt the value b, gets back the ciphertext c, and outputs two valid ciphertexts $\langle c, h \rangle \neq \langle c, h' \rangle$. $\square$

8.4.3.4 Comparison to Previous RKAEs

We briefly compare our scheme with those of [40, 107]. First, both schemes could be put into our framework by extracting appropriate concealment schemes. In fact, the concealment we extract from [40] is essentially the same as our construction with $b \leftarrow \tau \| H(h)$ and $h \xleftarrow{R} \texttt{Enc}_\tau(m)$ (they model one-time encryption slightly differently, but this is a minor difference)! On the other hand, instead of applying arbitrary authenticated encryption to the value of b, they build a very specific one based on block ciphers and pseudorandom functions. To summarize, the construction of [40] is quite good and efficient, but focuses on a specific ad hoc implementations for both concealment and authenticated encryption. We believe that our generality provides many more options, as well as gives better understanding toward designing RKAE, since our general description is much simpler than the specific scheme of [40]. As for the scheme of [107], one can also extract an "OAEP"-like concealment out of it, making it a special case of our framework too. However, the specific choices made by the authors make it very hard to replace the random oracles by some provable implementation. On the other hand, our "OAEP"-like construction (based on a PRG and a CRHF) is equally simple, but achieves provable security without the random oracles.

8.4.3.5 Using A Block Cipher in Place of $\mathcal{AE}$

So far we considered schemes of the form $\langle \text{AuthEnc}(b), h \rangle$, where AuthEnc is an authenticated encryption of short messages. While authenticated encryption is gaining popularity, in the symmetric-key setting block ciphers are much more popular. Moreover, a secure block cipher—formally known as a (strong) pseudorandom permutation—is "almost" a secure authenticated encryption. The only difference being that it does not provide semantic security (but gives at least one-wayness). Therefore, in the symmetric setting it is natural to consider constructions of the form $\text{AuthEnc}'(m) \leftarrow \langle P_K(b), h \rangle$, where we replace the "inner" authenticated encryption AuthEnc by a block cipher P. This is especially relevant in the setting of RKAE, where the above scheme would mean that the card is simply an implementation of a block cipher! As shown by Dodis and An [75, 76], while general concealments might not be enough for such a replacement, the main scheme from Sect. 8.3 works in the cases of interest! Below we assume that all the messages are fixed length.

Specifically, consider the scheme with $h \xleftarrow{R} \text{Enc}_\tau(m)$ and $b \leftarrow \tau \| H(h)$, where H is collision resistant and Enc is one-time secure. Assume also that H is *preimage resistant*—meaning that it is hard to find a preimage $v \in H^{-1}(r)$ of a random value r. We note that any CRHF family $\mathcal{H} = \{H\}$ with $|H(h)| < |h| - \omega(\log k)$ must be preimage resistant. However, preimage resistance is usually required anyway when constructing practical hash functions. Finally, assume Enc is *key-one-way*, meaning that for *any* message m, it is hard to recover the key τ from the ciphertext $\text{Enc}_\tau(m)$. Once again, this property holds for the PRG-based scheme $\text{Enc}_\tau(m) \leftarrow G(\tau) \oplus m$ as long as $|m| = |G(\tau)| > |\tau| + \omega(\log k)$ and also for standard block-cipher-based schemes, such as CBC. Then, the following result from [75, 76] holds:

Theorem 8.5 *If (P, P^{-1}) is a strong pseudorandom permutation, Enc is one-time secure and key-one-way, and H comes from a family of preimage-resistant CRHFs, then $\text{AuthEnc}'_K(m) = \langle c, h \rangle$, with $c \leftarrow P_K(\tau \| H(h))$ and $h \xleftarrow{R} \text{Enc}_\tau(m)$, gives rise to a secure RKAE.*[14]

---

[14] Clearly, this also means that this is a secure way to build a "long" authenticated encryption from a *single call* to a block cipher. In fact, preimage resistance of H and key-one-wayness of Enc are not needed in this case.

8.4.3.6 Extension to the Public-Key Setting

This extension (with the exception of replacing authenticated encryption by a block cipher, which makes no sense in the public-key setting) is pretty straightforward. In fact, unlike the question of domain extension studied in Sect. 8.4.2, no new subtleties arise in the public-key setting. Namely, when building "long" authenticated encryption from a "short" authenticated encryption, regular concealments are necessary and sufficient to maintain either insider or outsider security.

Chapter 9
Parallel Signcryption

Josef Pieprzyk and David Pointcheval

9.1 Introduction

The primary motivation for signcryption was the gain in efficiency when both encryption and signing need to be performed. These two cryptographic operations may be done sequentially either by first encrypt and then sign ($\mathcal{E}t\mathcal{S}$) or alternatively, by first sign and then encrypt ($\mathcal{S}t\mathcal{E}$). Further gains in efficiency can be achieved if encryption and signature are carried out in parallel ($\mathcal{E}\&\mathcal{S}$). More importantly, however, is that these efficiency gains are complemented by gains in security, i.e., we may use relative weak encryption and signature schemes in order to obtain a "stronger" signcryption scheme. The reader is referred to Chaps. 2 and 3 for a discussion of the different "strengths" of security model (e.g., outsider vs. insider adversaries, two-user vs. multi-user setting).

9.2 Concept of Parallel Signcryption

Efficiency and security are the two main requirements for cryptographic algorithms. Striking the balance between the two requirements is the real challenge. New ever-growing Internet applications such as distance learning, video streaming, e-commerce, e-government, e-health, etc., heavily rely on sophisticated protocols whose explicit goals are the fast, reliable, and secure delivery of large volumes of data.

Cryptographic protocols can be sped up by

- designing new, faster secure cryptographic algorithms—this option is not always available as once an algorithm becomes a standard or has been incorporated into the protocol: the designers are stuck with it for some time,

J. Pieprzyk (✉)
Department of Computing, Center for Advanced Computing – Algorithms and Cryptography, Macquerie University, Sydney, Australia
e-mail: josef@comp.mq.edu.au

A.W. Dent, Y. Zheng (eds.), *Practical Signcryption*, Information Security and Cryptography, DOI 10.1007/978-3-540-89411-7_9,
© Springer-Verlag Berlin Heidelberg 2010

- parallelizing operations required by the cryptographic algorithms—this approach can be applied at the level of a single algorithm (parallel thread implementation) and/or at the level of the protocol (parallel execution of the protocol components).

Privacy and authenticity are two basic security goals. As already discussed in the motivation for signcryption, there are many applications that require both goals to be achieved simultaneously. However, the main problem considered initially was the design of encryption and signature so that their concatenation maximizes savings of computing resources. Our goal here is to achieve the lower bound in terms of time necessary to perform authenticated encryption and decryption, or

$$\text{time(parallel Encrypt\& Sign)} \approx \max\{\text{time(Encrypt), time(Sign)}\}$$
$$\text{and}$$
$$\text{time(parallel Decrypt\& Verify)} \approx \max\{\text{time(Decrypt), time(Verify)}\}$$

At best, one would expect that parallel encryption and signing will consume roughly the same time as the most time-consuming operation (either signing or encryption for the signcryption operation and either verifying or decrypting for the unsigncryption operation).

The parallel encryption and signing methodology was introduced by An et al. [10]—see Chap. 2 for a detailed discussion of their results. Independently, the concept was also developed by Pieprzyk and Pointcheval [160]. Both works can be seen as generalizations of the signcryption concept introduced by Zheng [203, 204]. An et al. [10] developed a security model for parallel signcryption and present the commit-then-encrypt-and-sign ($\mathcal{CtE\&S}$) scheme that uses three cryptographic blocks: a commitment scheme, a public key encryption scheme, and a signature scheme (as described in Chap. 6). The solution given by Pieprzyk and Pointcheval [160] implements the commitment part very efficiently using secret sharing. It also shows how to combine encryption and signing so that they strengthen each other and can be executed in parallel.

9.3 Overview of Constructions

A trivial implementation of parallel signcryption could be as simple as applying encrypt and sign operations to the same message in parallel. This, of course, does not work as the signature may reveal the message (see Chap. 2).

A classical solution could be the well-known *envelope technique* (see Fig. 9.1) that first defines a secret session key. This key is encrypted under the public key and is used, in parallel, to encrypt, under a symmetric encryption, a message and a signature on it. If one assumes that the symmetric encryption has a negligible cost (some may disagree with this claim), then this allows parallel encryption and signing. For unsigncryption, the recipient first decrypts the session key and then extracts the message and the signature. Only when all that operations have been completed,

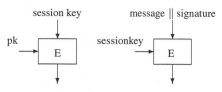

Fig. 9.1 Envelope technique

can one verify the signature. Therefore, decryption and verification cannot be done in parallel.

The commit-then-encrypt-and-sign ($\mathcal{CtE\&S}$) [10] is a little bit better. It is shown in Fig. 9.2. The signcryption algorithm first commits to the message m, computing the actual committed value c and the decommitment d (see Sect. 6.4.2). It then encrypts d in e and signs c getting s. The unsigncryption algorithm can unsign-crypt the ciphertext (e, c, s) by first verifying (c, s) and decrypting e into d. The decommitment d finally helps to recover m (by opening c). However, the opening algorithm may not be as efficient as required.

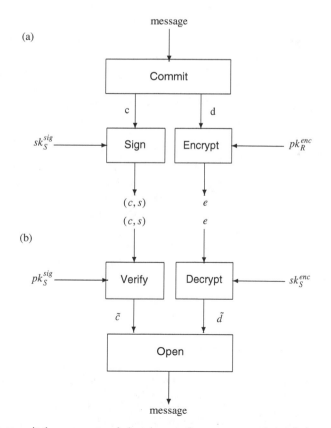

Fig. 9.2 The commit-then-encrypt-and-sign signcryption **a** encrypt and sign, **b** decrypt and verify

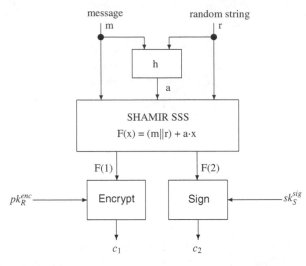

Fig. 9.3 Generic signcryption

The two constructions presented in this chapter are in the same vein as those presented in Chap. 6. They apply an efficient commitment scheme (proven secure in the random oracle model [29]) which allows for weak assumptions about the underlying encryption and signature schemes. The commitment scheme is based on a $(2, 2)$ Shamir secret sharing scheme (see Fig. 9.3). In a (k, n) Shamir secret sharing scheme, a secret is shared among n parties. Any k parties out of n can recover the secret while any group of less than k parties has no information about the secret. The (k, n) Shamir secret sharing scheme [176] simply exploits Lagrange interpolation of polynomials of degree $k - 1$.

As we use a $(2, 2)$ Shamir secret sharing, we need a linear polynomial whose coefficients are strongly related to the message m in a randomized way. For a random string r, the constant coefficient is $(m\|r)$ and the linear coefficient is $h(m\|r)$, where h is a hash function returning values from $\mathbb{Z}_p$. The polynomial, over $\mathbb{Z}_p$, evaluated at two points produces two shares. One of the shares is encrypted and the other is authenticated (in parallel). The perfectness of Shamir secret sharing guarantees that knowledge of one of the shares provides no information (in the information-theoretic sense) about the constant coefficient (the secret), and consequently no information about the message m.

9.4 Generic Parallel Signcryption

9.4.1 Description of the Scheme

The signcryption scheme uses the following building blocks:

- an encryption scheme $\mathcal{E} = (\texttt{EncKeyGen}, \texttt{Encrypt}, \texttt{Decrypt})$,
- a signature scheme $\mathcal{S} = (\texttt{SigKeyGen}, \texttt{Sign}, \texttt{Verify})$,
- a large $(k + 1)$-bit prime p, which defines the field $\mathbb{Z}_p$ with $p \geq 2^k$,

- a hash function $h : \mathbb{Z}_p \rightarrow \mathbb{Z}_p$,
- two integers k_1 and k_2 that are two security parameters such that $k = k_1 + k_2$.

We will use a signature scheme with message recovery (see Sect. 1.3.2). This means that the verification algorithm Verify takes as input a signature s and a public key pk^{sig}. It outputs either a message m indicating that the signature is valid for message m or the error symbol $\perp$.

The signcryption scheme is defined by the following collection of algorithms:

- KeyGen(1^k) : Compute $(sk^{sig}, pk^{sig}) \overset{R}{\leftarrow} \text{KeyGen}_S(1^k) \overset{\text{def}}{=} \text{SigKeyGen}(1^k)$ and $(sk^{enc}, pk^{enc}) \overset{R}{\leftarrow} \text{KeyGen}_R(1^k) \overset{\text{def}}{=} \text{EncKeyGen}(1^k)$. The sender keys are

$$(sk_S, pk_S) \overset{\text{def}}{=} (sk^{sig}, pk^{sig})$$

and the receiver keys are

$$(sk_R, pk_R) \overset{\text{def}}{=} (sk^{enc}, pk^{enc})$$

We now consider two users, the sender with keys (sk_S, pk_S) and the receiver with keys (sk_R, pk_R).

- Signcrypt(sk_S, pk_R, m): Given a message $m \in \{0, 1\}^{k_1}$ that needs to be encrypted and signed:

  1. Choose a random integer $r \in \{0, 1\}^{k_2}$ and compute $a = h(m\|r) \in \mathbb{Z}_p$, where $(m\|r) \in \{0, 1\}^k \subseteq \mathbb{Z}_p$.
  2. Form an instance of a $(2, 2)$ Shamir secret sharing scheme over $\mathbb{Z}_p$ with the polynomial $F(x) = (m\|r) + ax \bmod p$. Define two shares $s_1 \leftarrow F(1)$ and $s_2 \leftarrow F(2)$ in $\mathbb{Z}_p$.
  3. Calculate in parallel $c_1 \leftarrow \text{Encrypt}(pk_R, s_1)$ and $c_2 \leftarrow \text{Sign}(sk_S, s_2)$. The ciphertext (c_1, c_2) is dispatched to the receiver R.

- Unsigncrypt($pk_S, sk_R, (c_1, c_2)$):

  1. Perform decryption and signature verification in parallel:

$$t_1 \leftarrow \text{Decrypt}(sk_R, c_1)$$

and

$$t_2 \leftarrow \text{Verify}(pk_S, c_2)$$

Note that both the Decrypt and Verify algorithms return integers in $\mathbb{Z}_p$ unless a failure occurs. Indeed, it is possible that Decrypt returns $\perp$ if it decides that the ciphertext is invalid. Similarly, Verify returns a message (as the signature scheme is assumed to have message recovery) or $\perp$ if the signature is invalid. In case of at least one failure, the decryption and verifying algorithm Unsigncrypt returns $\perp$ and stops.

2. Given the two points $(1, t_1)$ and $(2, t_2)$, use the Lagrange interpolation and find the polynomial $\tilde{F}(x) = a_0 + a_1 x \bmod p$ for which these two points are solutions (i.e., compute $a_0 = 2t_1 - t_2$ and $a_1 = t_2 - t_1$).

3. Check whether $a_1 = h(a_0)$ or equivalently if $t_2 - t_1 = h(2t_1 - t_2)$. If the check holds, extract m from a_0 (as $a_0 = (m \| r)$) and return m. Otherwise, output $\perp$.

9.4.2 Security Analysis

The original research of Pieprzyk and Pointcheval [160] proved the following theorem:

Theorem 9.1 *If the encryption scheme is* IND-CCA2 *and the signature scheme is* sUF-RMA, *then the generic parallel signcryption scheme is* IND-CCA *and* UF-CMA *secure in the outsider security model for the two-user setting.*

The security model in this theorem is unfortunately weak, i.e., outsider security for the two-user setting, without FSO/FUO. However, the multi-user setting with FSO/FUO is covered if both ID_S and ID_R are included in the hash value, i.e., $a = h(ID_S \| ID_R \| m \| r)$. Furthermore, in the case of a deterministic signature, one even gets insider security:

Theorem 9.2 *If the encryption scheme is* IND-CCA2 *and the signature scheme is deterministic and* UF-RMA, *then the generic parallel signcryption scheme, as modified above, is* FSO/FUO-IND-CCA2 *and* FSO/FUO-UF-CMA *secure in the insider security model for the multi-user setting.*

More precisely, we are going to prove the two following results.

Lemma 9.1 *Suppose there exists an insider adversary $\mathcal{A}$ against* FSO/FUO-UF-CMA *security of the generic parallel signcryption scheme, in the multi-user setting, with advantage $Adv_{Signcrypt}^{UF-CMA}(k)$ whose running time is bounded by t and asks at most q_h queries to the random oracle h and q_{sc} queries to the signcryption oracle. Then, there exists an adversary $\mathcal{B}$ against the* UF-RMA *security of the signature scheme with advantage $Succ_{Sign}^{UF-RMA}(k)$ whose running time is bounded by $t' \leq t + q_{sc}(\tau + O(1))$, where τ denotes the maximal running time of the encryption and signing algorithms, and that asks at most q_{sc} queries to its signature oracle, for which*

$$Adv_{Signcrypt}^{UF-CMA}(k) \leq Succ_{Sign}^{UF-RMA}(k) + 2q_{sc} \times \frac{q_h + q_{sc}}{2^{k_2}}.$$

Lemma 9.2 *Suppose there exists an insider adversary $\mathcal{A}$ against* FSO/FUO-IND-CCA2 *of the generic parallel signcryption scheme, in the multi-user setting, with* *advantage $Adv_{Signcrypt}^{IND-CCA2}(k)$ whose running time is bounded by t and who asks at most q_h queries to the random oracle h and q_{usc} queries to the unsigncryption oracle. Then there exists an attacker $\mathcal{B}$ against the IND-CCA2 security of the encryption scheme with advantage $Adv_{Encrypt}^{IND-CCA2}(k)$ whose running time is bounded by t' and that makes at most q_{usc} queries to the unsigncryption oracle, where $t' \leq t + q_{usc}(\tau + O(1))$ and τ denotes the maximum running time of the decryption and verification algorithms, and*

$$Adv_{Signcrypt}^{IND-CCA2}(k) \leq 2 \times Adv_{Encrypt}^{IND-CCA2}(k) + \frac{q_h + q_{usc}}{2^{k_2-1}}$$

if the signature scheme is deterministic.

We prove the above lemmas in the random oracle model. When a random oracle h is called, we have two possibilities. One possibility is that the query has been already asked. In this case the answer has already been defined by the simulation and the same answer has to be given. The second possibility is that the query has not been asked. In this case, a random value in $\mathbb{Z}_p$ is given. Of course, one has to be careful when defining an answer of a random oracle as the following conditions have to be satisfied:

- this answer must not have already been defined and
- the answer must be uniformly distributed.

Furthermore, we denote by q_H the number of answers defined for h. This number will be easily upper bounded by $q_h + q_{sc} + q_{usc}$ in the following simulations.

Proof (of Lemma 9.1) Assume that after q_{sc} queries to the oracle $\mathtt{Signcrypt}$, an adversary $\mathcal{A}$ outputs a new ciphertext (c_1, c_2), which is valid with probability $Adv_{Signcrypt}^{UF-CMA}(k)$. We use the adversary to perform an existential forgery (under a random message attack) against the signature scheme $\mathcal{S}$. For this proof, we consider the multi-user insider security model. Hence, the attacker knows the public key pk_S of the target sender ID_S^* and has access to the signcryption oracle under sk_S.

We first design a simulator $\mathcal{B}$ which has access to a list of message–signature pairs, produced by the signing oracle under sk_S (the messages are assumed to have been randomly drawn from $\mathbb{Z}_p$ and not chosen by the adversary). It is given the private/public keys (sk_R, pk_R) produced by the adversary, for the encryption scheme, and is also provided with the public key pk_S of the signature scheme. Any query m by $\mathcal{A}$ to the oracle $\mathtt{Signcrypt}$ under sk_S, for any recipient ID_R, can be simulated using a new valid message–signature pair (M, S), for the signature scheme. Indeed, M is defined to be s_2 and S is defined to be c_2. Then, one chooses a random r. Since

$$s_2 = (m\|r) + 2h(ID_S^*\|ID_R\|m\|r) \bmod p = M$$

one needs to define the random oracle at the point $(ID_S^*\|ID_R\|m\|r)$ (unless it has already been done, which then raises the event BADH). So we get

$$h(ID_S^* \| ID_R \| m \| r) \leftarrow \frac{M - (m \| r)}{2} \bmod p$$

and therefore

$$s_1 \leftarrow (m \| r) + h(ID_S^* \| ID_R \| m \| r) = \frac{M + (m \| r)}{2} \bmod p$$

Using the public key of the encryption scheme for the recipient ID_R, one can encrypt s_1 to obtain c_1. The pair (c_1, c_2) is a valid ciphertext of m.

Finally, the adversary $\mathcal{A}$ returns a ciphertext (c_1, c_2) for a new message m', for ID_R^* from ID_S^*, which is valid with probability $Adv_{Signcrypt}^{UF-CMA}(k)$. With the public key of the signature scheme, one can extract the message s_2 from c_2. By definition, (s_2, c_2) is an existential forgery for the signature scheme. Indeed, one just has to check whether it is a really new signed message. If this is not a new signed message, then s_2 has already been signed by the oracle Signcrypt for $m \| r$, where

$$s_2 = (m \| r) + 2h(ID_S^* \| ID_R \| m \| r) \bmod p$$

Note that s_2 is uniquely defined in the list of the queries asked to the random oracle h unless one has found a collision for the function

$$G : (x, y) \mapsto x + 2h(ID_S^* \| y \| x) \bmod p$$

among the q_{sc} values given by the simulation and the q_H answers obtained by the adversary (either directly from queries or implicitly defined by the simulation). Because of the randomness of the random oracle h, this is upper bounded by $q_{sc} \cdot q_H / 2^k$.

Furthermore, one has to be sure that everything looks like in a real attack from the adversary $\mathcal{A}$ point of view. However, when one defines a value for h, it may have already been defined (event BADH). Because of the randomness of r, the probability of such an event is less than $q_H / 2^{k_2}$ for each simulation of the oracle Signcrypt.

Finally, the probability for $\mathcal{B}$ to produce an existential forgery against the signature scheme is greater than

$$Adv_{Sign}^{UF-RMA}(k) \geq Adv_{Signcrypt}^{UF-CMA}(k) - q_{sc} \cdot q_H \times \left(\frac{1}{2^{k_2}} + \frac{1}{2^k} \right)$$

$$\geq Adv_{Signcrypt}^{UF-CMA}(k) - 2q_{sc} \cdot q_H \times \left(\frac{1}{2^{k_2}} \right)$$

Furthermore, one can easily see that $q_H \leq q_h + q_{sc}$, hence the result. □

Proof (of Lemma 9.2) Assume that an adversary $\mathcal{A}$ has made q_{usc} queries to the oracle Unsigncrypt. $\mathcal{A}$ also has chosen a pair of messages m_0 and m_1 and has received a ciphertext (c_1^*, c_2^*) under (sk_S, pk_R) of either m_0 or m_1. The unknown message is denoted by m_b, where b is the bit the adversary wishes to find out. The adversary outputs a bit d which is equal to b with advantage ε such that $\Pr[d = b] = 1/2 + \varepsilon$.

We work with the multi-user insider security model. The attacker receives a target receiver ID_R^* public key pk_R and has access to the unsigncryption oracle under sk_R.

We design a simulator $\mathcal{B}$ which is given the public key pk_R of the encryption scheme and has access to the decryption oracle Decrypt (under sk_R).

Any call by $\mathcal{A}$ to the oracle Unsigncrypt under sk_R, from any sender ID_S, can be simulated using the decryption oracle Decrypt access. Indeed, for a query (c_1, c_2), one first asks the query c_1 to the oracle Decrypt and obtains s_1. Thanks to the public key of the signature scheme, one can get s_2 from c_2. This is enough to check the validity of the ciphertext (c_1, c_2) and to decrypt it. We will see later if this simulation is always possible.

Let us first show how one generates the challenge ciphertext. When $\mathcal{B}$ receives the pair of messages m_0 and m_1 from $\mathcal{A}$, it randomly chooses two random integers r_0 and r_1 to produce two new messages for the encryption scheme, namely

$$M_0 \leftarrow (m_0 \| r_0) + h(ID_S^* \| ID_R^* \| m_0 \| r_0) \bmod p$$
$$M_1 \leftarrow (m_1 \| r_1) + h(ID_S^* \| ID_R^* \| m_1 \| r_1) \bmod p$$

$\mathcal{B}$ receives the ciphertext c_1^* of M_b and has to guess the bit b, with the help of $\mathcal{A}$. For that, it chooses a random bit b' (hoping it to be equal to b) and defines

$$s_2^* \leftarrow (m_{b'} \| r_{b'}) + 2h(ID_S^* \| ID_R^* \| m_{b'} \| r_{b'}) \bmod p$$

Then, it signs it using the private key sk_S of the signature scheme and gets c_2^*. Next it sends the pair (c_1^*, c_2^*) as a ciphertext of m_b (for the unknown bit b). Finally, the adversary $\mathcal{A}$ ends its attack, returning a bit d to $\mathcal{B}$ and $\mathcal{B}$ forwards it as its final answer.

The simulation of $\mathcal{A}$'s unsigncryption queries by $\mathcal{B}$ works fine for any query (c_1, c_2) with $c_1^* \neq c_1$, as shown above. The above simulation breaks for queries (c_1^*, c_2), as the decryption oracle is prevented to be queried for the challenge ciphertext c_1^* while the oracle Unsigncrypt accepts queries as long as $c_1 \neq c_1^*$, or $c_2 \neq c_2^*$, or $ID_S \neq ID_S^*$. If $\mathcal{A}$ submits an unsigncryption oracle query of them (c_1^*, c_2) then the simulator $\mathcal{B}$ returns $\perp$. The event that $\mathcal{B}$ rejects an unsigncryption oracle (c_1^*, C_2) which is actually valid is called BADD. Later, we will show that this happens with a negligible probability.

Now, we study the advantage of the simulator $\mathcal{B}$ in breaking IND-CCA2 of the encryption scheme, which is

$$
\begin{aligned}
Adv_{Encrypt}^{IND-CCA2}(k) &= \Pr[d = b] - \tfrac{1}{2} \\
&\geq \Pr[d = b \wedge \neg \text{BADD}] - \tfrac{1}{2} \\
&\geq \Pr[d = b \mid \neg \text{BADD}] - \Pr[\text{BADD}] - \tfrac{1}{2} \\
&= \tfrac{1}{2} \cdot \Pr[d = b \mid b = b' \wedge \neg \text{BADD}] + \tfrac{1}{2} \cdot \Pr[d = b \mid b \neq b' \wedge \neg \text{BADD}] \\
&\quad - \Pr[\text{BADD}] - \tfrac{1}{2}
\end{aligned}
$$

Let us now examine each term. First note that, when $b' = b$, the simulated challenge (c_1^*, c_2^*) is identical to a real challenge:

$$\varepsilon = \Pr[d = b \mid b' = b] - 1/2$$
$$\leq \Pr[d = b \mid b' = b \wedge \neg \text{BADD}] + \Pr[\text{BADD}] - 1/2$$

Let us now focus on the second term in the inequality (when $b' \neq b$), by defining AskH to be the event that the adversary $\mathcal{A}$ either asks $(ID_S^* \| ID_R^* \| m_0 \| r_0)$ or $(ID_S^* \| ID_R^* \| m_1 \| r_1)$ to the random oracle h. It is equal to

$$\Pr[d = b \mid b' \neq b \wedge \neg \text{BADD}]$$
$$\geq \Pr[d = b \mid b' \neq b \wedge \neg \text{BADD} \wedge \neg \text{AskH}]$$
$$\times \Pr[\neg \text{AskH} \mid b' \neq b \wedge \neg \text{BADD}]$$

Clearly, in the case that $b' \neq b$, the adversary may have some information (in the theoretical sense) about

$$M_b = (m_b \| r_b) + h(ID_S^* \| ID_R^* \| m_b \| r_b) \bmod p$$
$$s_2^* = (m_{b'} \| r_{b'}) + 2h(ID_S^* \| ID_R^* \| m_{b'} \| r_{b'}) \bmod p$$

However, without the event AskH, the hash values perfectly hide the first part and therefore the answer of $\mathcal{A}$ is independent of b (a random variable):

$$\Pr[d = b \mid b' \neq b \wedge \neg \text{BADD} \wedge \neg \text{AskH}] = \frac{1}{2}$$

On the other hand, as we have said above, the value $h(ID_S^* \| ID_R^* \| m_i \| r_i)$ perfectly hides $(m_i \| r_i)$, for $i = 0, 1$, and therefore one cannot get any information about the random values r_0 and r_1 without a guess. The event AskH happens with the probability less than $2q_H / 2^{k_2}$. We therefore conclude

$$\Pr[\neg \text{AskH} \mid b' \neq b \wedge \neg \text{BADD}] \geq 1 - 2q_H / 2^{k_2}$$

Finally, let us examine the probability $\Pr[\text{BADD}]$ of a wrong decryption reject: $c_1 = c_1^*$ but $c_2 \neq c_2^*$ or $ID_S \neq ID_S^*$. Since this should be a valid signature, c_2 is the signature of some element s_2 and c_1 is the encryption of M_b such that $s_2 - M_b = h(ID_S \| ID_R^* \| 2M_b - s_2)$.

Because of the random oracle h, the probability to find such a pair (ID_S, s_2) is less than $q_H / 2^k$, except the constructed pair (ID_S^*, s_2^*). But since the signature scheme is deterministic, then $c_2 = c_2^*$ and $ID_S = ID_S^*$, and such a query cannot be asked to the unsigncryption oracle. As a consequence,

$$\Pr[\text{BADD}] \leq \frac{q_H}{2^k}$$

Now we collect all the terms and get

$$Adv_{Encrypt}^{IND-CCA2}(k) \geq \frac{1}{2}\left(\varepsilon - \Pr[\text{BADD}] + \frac{1}{2}\right)$$

$$+ \frac{1}{2}\left(\frac{1}{2}\Pr[\neg A\text{SKH}|b' \neq b \wedge \neg\text{BADD}]\right) - \Pr[\text{BADD}] - \frac{1}{2}$$

$$\geq \frac{\varepsilon}{2} - \frac{3}{2}\Pr[\text{BADD}] - \frac{q_H}{2^{k_2+1}}$$

$$\geq \frac{1}{2}Adv_{Signcrypt}^{IND-CCA2}(k) - \frac{3 \cdot q_H}{2 \cdot 2^k} - \frac{q_H}{2 \cdot 2^{k_2}}$$

This concludes the proof, since $q_H \leq q_h + q_{usc}$. $\quad\square$

From the efficiency point of view, this generic scheme is almost optimal since on the sender side, only one hash value and two additions are required before the parallel encryption and signature processes. The process needed on the receiver side reaches the same kind of optimality. However, the security requirements of the basic schemes, the encryption scheme $\mathcal{E}$ and the signature scheme $\mathcal{S}$, are very strong. Indeed, the encryption scheme is required to be semantically secure against chosen-ciphertext attack and the signature scheme must already prevent existential forgeries.

9.5 Optimal Parallel Signcryption

Adding a kind of OAEP technique [30], we can improve the generic scheme, in the sense that we can weaken the security requirements of the basic primitives. The new proposal just requires the encryption scheme to be deterministic and one way against chosen-plaintext attack, which is a very weak security requirement—even the plain RSA encryption scheme [165] achieves it under the RSA assumption. The signature scheme is required to prevent universal forgeries under the random message attack—the plain RSA signature scheme achieves this security level.

9.5.1 Description of the Scheme

The scheme is illustrated in Fig. 9.4. The building blocks are

- an encryption scheme $\mathcal{E} = (\text{EncKeyGen}, \text{Encrypt}, \text{Decrypt})$,
- a signature scheme $\mathcal{S} = (\text{SigKeyGen}, \text{Sign}, \text{Verify})$,
- a large k-bit prime p, which defines the field $\mathbb{Z}_p$, with $p \geq 2^k$,
- two integers k_1 and k_2 that are security parameters such that $k = k_1 + k_2$,
- hash functions

$$f : \{0, 1\}^k \to \{0, 1\}^k, g : \{0, 1\}^k \to \{0, 1\}^k \text{ and } h : \{0, 1\}^* \to \{0, 1\}^{k_2}$$

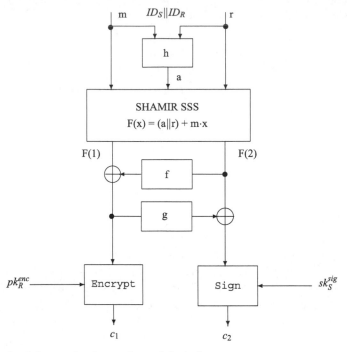

Fig. 9.4 Optimal signcryption (encryption and signing)

The signcryption scheme works as follows:

- KeyGen(1^k) : Compute $(sk^{sig}, pk^{sig}) \xleftarrow{R} \text{KeyGen}_S(1^k) \overset{\text{def}}{=} \text{SigKeyGen}(1^k)$ and $(sk^{enc}, pk^{enc}) \xleftarrow{R} \text{KeyGen}_R(1^k) \overset{\text{def}}{=} \text{EncKeyGen}(1^k)$. The sender keys are

$$(sk_S, pk_S) \overset{\text{def}}{=} (sk^{sig}, pk^{sig})$$

and the receiver keys are

$$(sk_R, pk_R) \overset{\text{def}}{=} (sk^{enc}, pk^{enc})$$

We now consider two users, the sender with the keys (sk_S, pk_S) and the receiver with the keys (sk_R, pk_R).

- Signcrypt(sk_S, pk_R, m): Given a message $m \in \mathbb{Z}_p$ that needs to be encrypted and signed:

1. Choose a random integer $r \in \{0, 1\}^{k_1}$ and compute $a = h(ID_S \| ID_R \| m \| r)$.
2. Form an instance of a $(2, 2)$ Shamir secret sharing scheme over $\mathbb{Z}_p$ with the polynomial $F(x) = (a \| r) + mx \bmod p$. Define two shares $s_1 \leftarrow F(1)$ and $s_2 \leftarrow F(2)$.

3. Compute the transform $r_1 \leftarrow s_1 \oplus f(s_2)$ and $r_2 \leftarrow s_2 \oplus g(r_1)$.
4. Calculate (in parallel) $c_1 \leftarrow \texttt{Encrypt}(pk_R, r_1)$ and $c_2 \leftarrow \texttt{Sign}(sk_S, r_2)$. The ciphertext (c_1, c_2) is then dispatched to the receiver R.

- $\texttt{Unsigncrypt}(pk_S, sk_R, (c_1, c_2))$:

  1. Perform decryption and signature verification in parallel so

$$u_1 \leftarrow \texttt{Decrypt}(sk_R, c_1)$$

and

$$u_2 \leftarrow \texttt{Verify}(pk_S, c_2)$$

  Note that both the $\texttt{Decrypt}$ and $\texttt{Verify}$ algorithms return integers in $\mathbb{Z}_p$ unless some failure occurs. It is possible that $\texttt{Decrypt}$ returns $\perp$ if it decides that the ciphertext is invalid. Similarly, $\texttt{Verify}$ returns a message (as we are using a signature with message recovery) or $\perp$ if the signature is invalid. In the case of a failure, the $\texttt{Unsigncrypt}$ algorithm returns $\perp$ and stops.
  2. Compute the inversion $t_2 \leftarrow u_2 \oplus g(u_1)$ and $t_1 \leftarrow u_1 \oplus f(t_2)$.
  3. Knowing two points $(1, t_1)$ and $(2, t_2)$, use the Lagrange interpolation and find the polynomial $\tilde{F}(x) = a_0 + a_1 x \bmod p$, where $a_0 = 2t_1 - t_2$ and $a_1 = t_2 - t_1$.
  4. Extract r from a_0 and check whether $h(ID_S \| ID_R \| a_1 \| r) \| r = a_0 \bmod p$. If the check holds, return a_1 as m. Otherwise, return $\perp$.

9.5.2 Security Analysis

The following theorem characterizes the security of the optimal parallel signcryption. (Recall that the universal forgery notion for a signature scheme is discussed in Sect. 1.3.2.)

Theorem 9.3 *If the encryption scheme is deterministic and* OW-CPA *secure and the signature scheme is deterministic and* uUF-RMA *secure, then the optimal parallel signcryption scheme is* FSO/FUO-IND-CCA2 *and* FSO/FUO-UF-CMA *secure in the insider security model for the multi-user setting.*

More precisely, one can prove the two following results.

Lemma 9.3 *Consider an insider adversary $\mathcal{A}$ against the* FSO/FUO-UF-CMA *security of the optimal parallel signcryption scheme, in the multi-user setting, with advantage $Adv_{Signcrypt}^{UF-CMA}(k)$ whose running time is bounded by t and who makes at most q_h queries to the random oracle h, q_g queries to the random oracle g, and q_{sc} queries to the signcryption oracle. Then there exists an attacker $\mathcal{B}$ against the* uUF-RMA *security of the signature scheme with advantage $Adv_{Sign}^{uUF-RMA}(k)$ whose running time is bounded by $t' \leq t + q_{sc}(\tau + O(1))$, where τ denotes the* *maximal running time of the encryption and signing algorithms, and that makes at most $q_h + q_{sc}$ queries to the signing oracle, for which*

$$Adv_{Signcrypt}^{UF-CMA}(k) \le (q_h + q_{sc}) \times Adv_{Sign}^{uUF-RMA}(k) + \frac{(q_g + q_h + q_{sc})^2 + 2}{2^{k_2}}$$

Lemma 9.4 *Consider an insider adversary $\mathcal{A}$ against the* FSO/FUO-IND-CCA2 *security of the generic parallel signcryption scheme, in the multi-user setting, with advantage $Adv_{Signcrypt}^{IND-CCA2}(k)$ whose running time is bounded by t and which makes at most q_h queries to the random oracle h and q_{usc} queries to the unsigncryption oracle. Then there exists an attacker $\mathcal{B}$ against the* OW-CPA *security of the public key encryption scheme with advantage $Adv_{Encrypt}^{OW-CPA}(k)$ and whose running time is bounded by $t' \le t + q_{usc}(\tau + O(1))$, where τ denotes the maximal running time of the decryption and verification algorithms, for which*

$$Adv_{Signcrypt}^{IND-CCA2}(k) \le Adv_{Encrypt}^{OW-CPA}(k) + \frac{q_h}{2^{k_1}} + \frac{q_{usc}}{2^{k_2}}$$

The proofs are similar to the proofs of Lemmas 9.1 and 9.2. Again, we are in the random oracle model, and the functions f, g, and h are modeled by random oracles. The number of queries to these oracles is q_f, q_g, and q_h, respectively. Furthermore, we denote by q_F, q_G, and q_H the number of answers defined for f, g, and h, respectively.

Proof (of Lemma 9.3) Assume that after q_{sc} queries to oracle `Signcrypt`, an adversary $\mathcal{A}$ outputs a new ciphertext (c_1, c_2), which is valid with the probability $Adv_{Signcrypt}^{UF-CMA}(k)$. We use this adversary to perform a universal forgery that produces a new signature on a designated random message μ (under a known random message attack) against the signature scheme $\mathcal{S}$. Since we are dealing with the insider security model, the adversary has a target sender ID_S^* in mind and he/she knows the sender public key pk_S. The adversary has access to the signcryption oracle under sk_S. Now we design a simulator $\mathcal{B}$, which has access to a list of message–signature pairs, produced by the signing oracle (the messages are assumed to have been randomly drawn from $\mathbb{Z}_p$ and not chosen by the adversary). It is given the private/public keys (sk_R, pk_R) produced by the adversary, for the encryption scheme of the target receiver ID_R^*. Note that a valid ciphertext must satisfy the equality $h(ID_S \| ID_R \| m \| r) \| r = a_0 \bmod p$. Therefore, the probability of getting a valid ciphertext (from ID_S^* to ID_R^*) without asking $h(ID_S^* \| ID_R^* \| m \| r)$ is at most 2^{-k_2}. The query $(ID_S^* \| ID_R^* \| m \| r)$ must have been asked to the oracle h with a probability greater than $Adv_{Signcrypt}^{UF-CMA}(k) - 2^{-k_2}$. It is provided with the public key pk_S of ID_S^* for the signature scheme. It is furthermore given a list of q_H message–signature (M, S) pairs, where messages are randomly chosen. $\mathcal{B}$ simulates $\mathcal{A}$ in the following way (where any query to a random oracle is answered randomly, if nothing else is specified). The simulation of the h-oracle is performed as followed, after having chosen a random index $i \in \{1, \ldots, q_H\}$ and initialized a counter j to be 0. The index i will designate the critical query we expect to be involved in the forgery:

- For any new query $(ID_S^* \| ID_R \| m \| r)$ asked to h (by the adversary or by our simulation of Signcrypt—see below), we increment the counter j. If $j \neq i$, a new valid message–signature pair (M, S) is taken from the list.
- Then, one chooses a random ρ, defines $h(ID_S \| ID_R \| m \| r) \leftarrow \rho$, and sets

$$s_1 \leftarrow \rho \| r + m \bmod p \quad s_2 \leftarrow \rho \| r + 2m \bmod p \quad r_1 \leftarrow s_1 \oplus f(s_2)$$

- One eventually defines $g(r_1) \leftarrow s_2 \oplus M$, which is a random value, since M is randomly distributed. (Note that for the i-th query to h, we use the designated message μ instead of M, expecting it to be involved in the forgery.) It may fail if $g(r_1)$ has already been defined. However, because of the *fresh* random choice of ρ, this occurs with a probability at most $q_G/2^{k_2}$ for each fresh h-query.

For the i-th query to h, one simply chooses a random output.

In other words, any query m by $\mathcal{A}$ to the oracle Signcrypt can be simulated, thanks to the above simulation of h (except for the i-th query to h). Indeed, for answering a Signcrypt-query m from ID_S^* to ID_R, one simply chooses a random r, asks for $h(ID_S^* \| ID_R \| m \| r)$, using the above simulation. Except for the i-th query to h, the signature S involved in the pair (M, S) used for the h simulation is a signature c_2 of $r_2 = M$. Using the public key of the receiver ID_R, one can encrypt r_1 in order to obtain c_1. The pair (c_1, c_2) is a valid ciphertext of m. If there is a signcrypt query related to the i-th h-query, we are stuck, we then simply stop the simulation: this i-th query cannot be involved in the forgery, because of the determinism of the process.

Finally, the adversary $\mathcal{A}$ produces a new ciphertext (c_1, c_2), from ID_S^* to ID_R^*, which is valid with the probability greater than $Adv_{Signcrypt}^{UF-CMA}(k)$, unless the above simulation of h fails when trying to assign $h(ID_S \| ID_R \| m \| r) \leftarrow \rho$. Such a failure happens with the probability upper bounded by $q_H q_G/2^{k_2}$. Simulation indeed fails if it fails for any of the messages (the number of messages is q_H).

As we have already mentioned, if a forgery is not related to a specific h-oracle query, then the probability of success is $1/2^{k_2}$. Hence, with probability at least $Adv_{Signcrypt}^{UF-CMA}(k) - (q_G q_H + 1)/2^{k_2}$, we have that the forgery is related to a specific h-oracle query. With the probability $1/q_H$, otherwise we abort the simulation, this ciphertext is involved in the i-th query to the h-oracle and consequently c_2 is a valid signature of μ. Either this is a new signature or it was already involved in a ciphertext (c_1', c_2') to ID_R' produced by Signcrypt. In the latter case, since $c_2 = c_2'$, this implies that $c_1 \neq c_1'$ or $ID_R^* \neq ID_R'$. If $ID_R' = ID_R^*$, then $c_1' \neq c_1$ and, thus, because of the determinism of the encryption scheme, it means that $u_1 \neq u_1'$, and then the redundancy may hold with the probability at most $1/2^{k_2}$. If $ID_R \neq ID_R^*$, then again the redundancy may hold with the probability at most $1/2^{k_2}$.

Finally, the probability for $\mathcal{B}$ to produce a new valid signature of μ is greater than

$$Adv_{Sign}^{uUF-RMA}(k) \geq \frac{1}{q_H} \times \left(Adv_{Signcrypt}^{UF-CMA}(k) - \frac{q_G q_H + 2}{2^{k_2}} \right)$$

Furthermore, one can easily see that $q_G = q_g + q_H$, where $q_H \leq q_h + q_{sc}$. $\square$

Proof (of Lemma 9.4) As we are dealing with the insider security model FSO/FUO-IND-CCA2 in the multi-user setting, the adversary has a target receiver ID_R^* in mind. The adversary knows the receiver public key pk_R and has access to the Unsigncrypt oracle under sk_R. Further, we assume that an adversary $\mathcal{A}$ observed q_{usc} queries to the Unsigncrypt oracle. $\mathcal{A}$ also has chosen a pair of messages m_0 and m_1 and a key pair (sk_S, pk_S) for ID_S. It receives a ciphertext (c_1^*, c_2^*) under (sk_S, pk_R) of either m_0 or m_1. The unknown message is denoted by m_b, where b is the bit the adversary wishes to find out. The adversary $\mathcal{A}$ outputs a bit d which is equal to b with the advantage ε, i.e., $\Pr[d = b] = 1/2 + \varepsilon$. In the following, we use a $*$ for all the internal values used in computing the challenge signcryption.

Let us first remark that because of the randomness of the random oracles f and g, and since $r_1^* \leftarrow s_1^* \oplus f(s_2^*)$ and $r_2^* \leftarrow s_2^* \oplus g(r_1^*)$, to get any information about the bit b (and thus about the encrypted and signed message), the adversary must have got some information about the internal values s_1^* and s_2^* from either the ciphertext or from the plaintext. The former case is only possible if the adversary asks for r_1^* to the oracle g (otherwise it has no information about either s_2^* or s_1^* and thus has no information about the polynomial F, and consequently no information about r^*). The event that the adversary $\mathcal{A}$ has asked the oracle g for r_1^* is denoted by AskG. The latter case means that the adversary has asked either $h(ID_S^* \| ID_R^* \| m_0 \| r^*)$ or $h(ID_S^* \| ID_R^* \| m_1 \| r^*)$. This event is denoted by AskR. Consequently, $\Pr[d = b \mid \neg(\text{AskG} \vee \text{AskR})] = 1/2$, and thus

$$
\begin{aligned}
\varepsilon &= Adv_{Signcrypt}^{IND-CCA2}(k) \\
&= \Pr[d = b] - 1/2 \\
&= \Pr[d = b \wedge (\text{AskG} \vee \text{AskR})] + \Pr[d = b \wedge \neg(\text{AskG} \vee \text{AskR})] - 1/2 \\
&= \Pr[d = b \mid \text{AskG} \vee \text{AskR}] \cdot \Pr[\text{AskG} \vee \text{AskR}] \\
&\qquad + \Pr[d = b \mid \neg(\text{AskG} \vee \text{AskR})] \cdot \Pr[\neg(\text{AskG} \vee \text{AskR})] - 1/2 \\
&\leq \Pr[\text{AskG} \vee \text{AskR}] + \Pr[\neg(\text{AskG} \vee \text{AskR})]/2 - 1/2 \\
&\leq \Pr[\text{AskG} \vee \text{AskR}] \\
&\leq \Pr[\text{AskG}] + \Pr[\text{AskR} \mid \neg \text{AskG}] \\
&\leq \Pr[\text{AskG}] + \frac{q_h}{2^{k_1}}
\end{aligned}
$$

This last inequality comes from the fact that if AskG does not occur then the adversary has no knowledge of r_1^* and so AskR can only occur by guessing this value.

If AskG occurs, then the plaintext r_1^* of c_1^* has to appear in the queries asked to g. For each query asked to g, one runs the deterministic encryption algorithm and therefore can find the plaintext of a given c_1^*. So we may use the adversary $\mathcal{A}$ to break OW-CPA of the encryption scheme (EncKeyGen, Encrypt, Decrypt). To complete the proof, we have to show how we can simulate all the oracles available to the adversary $\mathcal{A}$. We thus design a simulator $\mathcal{B}$ which receives the private/public keys (sk_S, pk_S) for the signature scheme, from the adversary $\mathcal{A}$, and it is also given the public key pk_R of the encryption scheme. The simulator $\mathcal{B}$ works as follows:

- $\mathcal{B}$ is given a ciphertext c^* (of a random message) to decrypt under the encryption scheme $\mathcal{E}$ and then runs $\mathcal{A}$.
- When $\mathcal{B}$ receives the pair of messages m_0 and m_1 from $\mathcal{A}$, it sets $c_1^* \leftarrow c^*$ and randomly chooses r_2^* that it can sign using the private key of the signature scheme to produce c_2^*. It therefore sends the pair (c_1^*, c_2^*) as a ciphertext of m_b (for some bit b). Finally, the adversary $\mathcal{A}$ follows the attack in which it cannot detect the above simulation of the challenge from a real challenge unless the event ASKG happens, which breaks OW-CPA.
- Before simulating the oracle Unsigncrypt, let us explain how one deals with h-queries. Indeed, a list Λ_h is managed. For any query $h(ID_S\|ID_R\|m\|r)$, one anticipates the signcryption:

$$H = h(ID_S\|ID_R\|m\|r) \quad a_0 = H\|r \quad t_1 = a_0+m \bmod p \quad t_2 = a_0+2m \bmod p$$

  Then, $u_1 = t_1 \oplus f(t_2)$ and $u_2 = t_2 \oplus g(u_1)$ (using the canonical simulations of f and g, which are new random elements for new queries). Eventually, one stores $(m, r, H, u_1, u_2, t_1, t_2)$ in the list Λ_h.
- Any call by $\mathcal{A}$ to the oracle Unsigncrypt under pk_R can be simulated using the queries–answers of the random oracles. Indeed, to a query (c_1, c_2), one first gets u_2 from c_2, thanks to the public key of the signature scheme ($u_2 = $ Verify(pk_S, c_2)). Then, one looks up into Λ_h for tuples $(m, r, H, u_1, u_2, t_1, t_2)$. Then, one checks whether one of the u_1 is really encrypted in c_1 under pk_R, thanks to the deterministic property of the encryption. If no tuple is found, the simulator outputs $\perp$, considering it is a wrong ciphertext. Otherwise, the simulator returns m as the plaintext.

For all the ciphertexts correctly constructed (with $s_2 = t_2$ asked to f, $r_1 = u_1$ asked to g and $(ID_S\|ID_R^*\|m\|r)$ asked to h), the simulation gets back the message. However, the adversary may produce a valid ciphertext without asking $h(ID_S\|ID_R^*\|m\|r)$ required by the above simulation. In that sole case, the simulation may not be perfect.

First, let us assume that $(ID_S\|ID_R^*\|m\|r)$ has not been asked to h:

- If $(ID_S\|ID_R^*\|m\|r) \neq (ID_S^*\|ID_R^*\|m_b\|r^*)$ (the tuple involved in the challenge ciphertext) then $H \leftarrow h(ID_S\|ID_R^*\|m\|r)$ is totally random. The probability that $H\|r$ is equal to a_0 is less than 2^{-k_2} and so $\perp$ is the correct response except with probability 2^{-k_2}.
- In the case where $(ID_S\|ID_R^*\|m\|r) = (ID_S^*\|ID_R^*\|m_b\|r^*)$, since the process to produce r_1 and r_2 is deterministic, $r_1 = r_1^*$ and $r_2 = r_2^*$, the same as in the challenge ciphertext. We remind that both the encryption scheme and the signature scheme are deterministic. Then $c_1 = c_1^*$ and $c_2 = c_2^*$, which is not possible.

Therefore, the probability that the simulation wrongly rejects a valid ciphertext is less than 2^{-k_2}.

If all the decryption simulations are correct (no occurrence of the event BADD), we have seen that with a good probability the plaintext c_1^*, and thus of c^*, appears in the queries asked to g, which is immediately detected thanks to the deterministic property of the encryption scheme so

$$\Pr[\text{ASKG} \mid \neg\text{BADD}] \geq \Pr[\text{ASKG}] - \Pr[\text{BADD}] \geq \left(\varepsilon - \frac{q_h}{2^{k_1}}\right) - \frac{q_{usc}}{2^{k_2}}$$

$\square$

Part IV
Extensions of Signcryption

Chapter 10
Identity-Based Signcryption

Xavier Boyen

10.1 Introduction

The notion of identity-based (IB) cryptography was proposed by Shamir [177] as a specialization of public key (PK) cryptography which dispensed with the need for cumbersome directories, certificates, and revocation lists.

We recall that in the traditional public key (or asymmetric key) cryptography model some mechanism must be used in order to bind a particular public key to its owner; often, this mechanism involves a trusted certificate authority (CA), whose role is to issue certificates, which are digital signatures that bind a user's public key to his/her real name. Such a system is called a public key infrastructure (PKI), and an apt metaphor for it is that of a phone book bearing the authentic seal of the phone authority.

By contrast, the distinguishing characteristic of IB cryptography lies in its ability to use any string as a public key, such as the real name of a person. Because of this, IB systems implement an automatic directory with implicit binding, without the need for costly certification and public key publication steps. Although public keys can be computed by anyone from public information, the corresponding private key can only be extracted by a trusted authority called the private key generator (PKG). The PKG has custody of a master secret, which allows it to compute any private key in the IB system. The PKG can be thought of as an identity-based analog to the CA at the helm of a traditional public key infrastructure.

10.1.1 Identity-Based Cryptography

In his original description, Shamir had already envisioned the use of IB cryptography for the purposes of signature and encryption. Although IB signatures could

X. Boyen (✉)
Chair of Cryptography and Information Security, Montefiore Institute, Universite de Liege, Liege, Belgium
e-mail: xb@boyen.org

A.W. Dent, Y. Zheng (eds.), *Practical Signcryption*, Information Security and Cryptography, DOI 10.1007/978-3-540-89411-7_10, © Springer-Verlag Berlin Heidelberg 2010

be constructed based on the techniques known at the time, it was only much later that a solution for IB encryption became known [45, 46]. In both types of scheme, individual users authenticate with the PKG in order to obtain their private key, in person or over a secure channel. The keys may then be used as follows:

> IB signature (IBS): For signing, a private key can be used by its owner to create IB signatures: these signatures can be verified from the public parameters of the IB system only and are binding on the signer's name without requiring a certificate chain.
>
> IB encryption (IBE): In the case of encryption, the private key will be used to decrypt any message encrypted under the recipient's proper name (and the IB system's public parameters): the originator need not look up the recipient's key, and indeed the recipient need not even know her private key at the time the ciphertext is created.

We note that in actual implementations, identity-based keys for signature and encryption are likely to be distinct and incompatible; however, the abstract key generation process is the same in both instances.

Many refinements to Shamir's model have been proposed in recent years. For key generation, Boneh and Franklin [45, 46] suggested that systems could take advantage of the flexibility in users' public keys by appending validity periods to the names of the individuals, in order to enforce a more frequent rotation of keys and lessen or eliminate the need for revocation lists. Another refinement is the combination of IB signature and IB encryption into a single IB signcryption operation [51], for both performance and security reasons.

> IB signcryption (IBSC): Consider two parties, Alice and Bob, with unique names in some common IB system (controlled by the same PKG). Using her private key, Alice may signcrypt a message addressed to a recipient named Bob. Using his private key, Bob can decrypt the ciphertext and authenticate the sender as Alice.

On top of this basic functionality, there may be advantages to using an IB signcryption primitive that features a number of additional security properties. For instance, Bob may wish to obtain from the decryption process a cleartext signature by Alice stripped of its encryption: this requires that the process of *unsigncryption* be separable into a pair of independent decryption/verification algorithms (we shall call such an IBSC scheme a two-layer or *detachable* IBSC scheme). Additionally, it is often desirable to have some guarantee of anonymity, which is that no outsider should be able to recognize the parties involved in a signcrypted transmission.

The reader will notice that there are many similarities between the security properties that one can obtain from an identity-based signcryption scheme and certain non-ID-based signcryption schemes from pairings discussed in Chap. 5. In the next section we outline certain features specific to ID-based cryptography.

10.1.2 Advantages and Disadvantages

Identity-based cryptosystems differ substantially from their PKI counterparts in a number of respects. Before we turn our attention to IB signcryption per se, it is useful to review some of the main implications of identity-based private key generation. See also Paterson and Price [157] for further discussion on the advantages and disadvantages of identity-based cryptography.

10.1.2.1 Simplicity of Deployment

A substantial benefit of identity-based encryption over traditional public key systems is that the sender need not obtain the recipient's certified public key prior to initiating a secure communication. The recipient need not generate these keys ahead of time in the first place or even archive them on the client side since the PKG can always regenerate lost keys as needed. As a result, the number of flows of interactions between the various parties is reduced and key management tends to be greatly simplified, especially on the users' side.

10.1.2.2 Expiration vs. Revocation

As a side effect of the simplified key management that IB cryptography has to offer, the issue of compromise and revocation can be dealt with differently and more simply. Rather than deal with the long-lived keys and revocation lists typical of PKI, it is common in IB systems to eschew explicit revocation altogether and instead make the keys sufficiently short-lived that they will expire naturally shortly after any compromise. Boneh and Franklin [45, 46] propose appending a time-dependent common component, such as the number of weeks since a predetermined time in the past, to all static identities. To revoke a user, the PKG will simply stop issuing her new keys. This approach of using medium-lived keys is practical with IB systems, but not in traditional PKI, due to the higher complexity of the PKI key generation and certification process. Generally, medium-sized keys all but eliminate the need for revocation lists, unless revocation must occur with a shorter latency than any practical lifespan of the identity-based keys would allow.

Revocation lists are orthogonal to the IB model and can be used in conjunction with IB cryptography if necessary. However, it is generally an advantage not to push revocation lists to the edges of the networks (the users) and instead deal with revocation centrally, at the PKG level. Another advantage of this is that the list of revoked users need not be made public.

10.1.2.3 Compactness of Signatures

For signatures, the advantages of IB cryptography are less obvious, since IB signatures are functionally equivalent to regular PKI signatures with full certificate chains to the root CA; the main difference is that certificate chains are likely to occupy much more space than an IB signature. The benefit of identity-based signatures is thus one of compactness. This benefit will carry over to identity-based signcryption, provided that the ciphertext can be stripped of the encryption layer to expose a plaintext with a regular IB signature.

IB signatures are also useful in cases where an IB encryption system is already in use, and the keys and infrastructure can be shared. In the context of IB signcryption, it is natural to seek to reuse the same infrastructure and keys for the signature and the encryption functionalities.

10.1.2.4 Concentration of Trust

The main criticism facing IB cryptography stems from the high level of trust that is bestowed upon the PKG, which has to be trusted at least to the same extent as a CA is trusted in the traditional model. Indeed, an untrustworthy PKG will have the power to forge signatures in the name of any user of the system, as well as the ability to decrypt all of their private communications. One difference is that an abuse of trust by a CA in a PKI is detectable by the afflicted party, whereas in an ID-based infrastructure there is more potential for a malicious PKG to remain undetected.

The single point of failure that constitutes the PKG can be partially alleviated by splitting the master secret among several PKGs under the jurisdiction of several independent authorities, using threshold techniques as explained in [45, 46]. Additionally, one can reduce the window of vulnerability from compromise of the PKG by instituting a policy whereby the public parameters are periodically changed, and all expired master secrets beyond a certain age are permanently purged from the system, which would effectively limit the interval during which any IB private key can be issued.

10.1.2.5 Proof of Possession

A small potential benefit of identity-based cryptography, over public key infrastructures, is that public key certification in the latter requires the registrant to submit a *proof of possession* of the corresponding private key, in addition to proper authentication credentials, or else security can be doubted. There is no analogous step in identity-based key extraction, which may result in one fewer point of failure.

10.1.2.6 Mandatory Key Escrow

A direct consequence of PKG-issued private keys is that the PKG acts as a mandatory key escrow. In certain circumstances this is not desirable, such as when the users of the system are individuals acting on their own behalf. In other settings the existence of a mandatory key escrow is indeed very desirable, as in corporate environments or in any case where the private key holders are members of a larger organization: the PKG then acts as an easy-to-administer and hard-to-circumvent central key escrow system, which ensures continuity of decryption by the company in the event that employees part with the organization without surrendering their keys. In general, this is a greater concern for encryption than for signatures.

10.1.3 From IBE to Signcryption

Although the idea of IB cryptography dates from 1984 [177], only an IB signature scheme was actually constructed at the time, based on conventional algebraic methods in composite-order RSA groups. One had to wait until 2000 and 2001 to see the apparition of practical IB encryption (IBE) schemes. One such IBE construction, due to Cocks [64], is based on the quadratic residuosity problem in traditional composite-order RSA groups. A more efficient approach was independently proposed in Sakai et al. [171] and Boneh and Franklin [45, 46], based on the mathematical notion of a bilinear pairing constructed on certain types of elliptic curves (see Chap. 5). Among these, Boneh and Franklin [45, 46] were the first to define a rigorous security model for IBE and prove the security of their construction in that model. The work of Sakai et al. [171] can be more appropriately described as an IB key exchange protocol that uses IB public and private keys similar to the Boneh–Franklin system. The difference is that key agreement requires secret keys on both sides and thus requires both parties to be enrolled in the system.

Pairings had made their appearances earlier in cryptology, first in the cryptanalysis of certain elliptic-curve systems with the MOV attack [138] and later in constructive cryptography with the creation of a tripartite key exchange protocol [109]. Also, and although IB signatures had been known long ago, it was soon realized that pairings opened the door to simpler and more efficient constructions than those already known. Among the first and most influential pairing-based IBS schemes, we mention Paterson [156], Hess [96], and Cha and Cheon [57].

10.1.3.1 Combining IBE with IBS

A natural question therefore is how to combine IB signatures or authentication with IB encryption. A direct approach would be to invoke such black-box combination techniques as discussed in Chap. 2, starting from any IBE and IBS primitive. This is based on the observation that the identity-based character of the primitives being combined does not interfere with the security of the combination, provided that their respective keys are independent.

The first real strides toward efficient IBSC constructions were, however, nongeneric. They included an authenticated key agreement scheme [59], an authenticated IBE system [127], and two IB signcryption schemes from [129, 122] with differing security properties. Such combined systems were typically more efficient than what could be achieved by using black-box combination techniques.

10.1.3.2 Alternative IB Paradigms

In parallel, over the years one has seen the development of several alternative approaches to IBE from pairings, with sometimes quite different characteristics and applications. We follow the nomenclature introduced in [52].

The *full-domain hash* IB family is that of the celebrated original Boneh–Franklin scheme and its many derivatives. It has many advantages, such as simplicity of principle and implementation. Its main drawback is its unavoidable reliance on the random oracle model for all security reductions. The *commutative blinding* family is by far the largest. It originates in Boneh and Boyen's first IBE scheme (called BB-1) from [41]. It is more complex, but more efficient and empirically much more flexible, having been extended in many ways, e.g., to support parallel hierarchies [43], attributes [93], or wildcards [3]. The *exponent inversion* family is also quite well known. Its earliest instance in the random-oracle model is the Sakai–Kasahara [170] scheme and in the standard model the Boneh–Boyen [41] second scheme (called BB-2). Members of this family are often very efficient, but tend to require stronger complexity assumptions, and there are only few known extensions [52]. Gentry's [88] tight IBE scheme arguably belongs to this family.

Whereas in the past 5 years much of the activity in IB cryptography happened in the commutative blinding paradigm, most known IBSC constructions still follow the original full-domain hash framework (perhaps because of the simple and very convenient IBS primitives it supports). For this reason, the concrete IBSC schemes we discuss here are all based on the Boneh–Franklin full-domain hash paradigm.

10.1.4 Specifying an IBSC System

In this chapter, we study the question of combining IBE and IBS in a practical and secure way into a unified IBSC system with good security properties. Indeed, it is of great practical interest to be able to use the same IB infrastructure for signing and encrypting, while reaping efficiency gains over generic approaches in the process.

To this end, we aim to exploit similarities between IBE and IBS and elaborate a dual-purpose IBSC scheme based on a shared infrastructure. On the one hand, a unified system built on a shared infrastructure should bring us efficiency rewards. On the other hand, care must be taken to ensure that no hidden weakness arises from the combination, which is always a risk if the same parameters and keys are used. The questions we must address can be summarized as follows:

- Can IBE and IBS be practiced in conjunction, sharing infrastructure, parameters, and keys, with greater efficiency than black-box constructions?
- How can such a combination be done in a secure manner?
- What emerging security properties can be gained from the combination?

We will address these questions in a two-prong approach, first by defining a stringent security model for IBSC and then by studying an actual construction that fulfills the security model. Both the model and the construction are borrowed from Boyen [51].

10.1.4.1 Security Models for IBSC

Following [51], we define a five-prong security model that any unified IBSC system should satisfy. At the core, our model must capture the strong notions of security commonly accepted in public key cryptography, adapted for IBSC: indistinguishability of the ciphertext under adaptive chosen-ciphertext attacks and existential unforgeability of the signature under chosen-message attacks. In both cases, we specifically consider "insider" adversaries (see Chaps. 2 and 3).

Additionally, we propose three new security notions for IBSC: ciphertext authentication, anonymity, and unlinkability. Although less conventional, these security notions are highly desirable in practice: they serve to convince the legitimate recipient that the ciphertext itself is authentic and hide its origin and destination to any eavesdropper or man-in-the-middle impersonator (see also Chap. 5 for the related notions for non-identity-based signcryption).

10.1.4.2 Two-layer Detachable IBSC Design

After establishing the model, we construct a compliant IBSC scheme following a two-layer design. It consists of an inner randomized IBS component, on top of which is grafted a simplified deterministic IBE which "reuses" the randomness of the inner layer. This results in more compact ciphertexts than a generic composition of IBE and IBS. The two-layer design also allows the ciphertext to be stripped of its encryption in order to expose a signature on the decrypted message that anyone can verify. Here, the two-layer design is furthermore well suited for multi-recipient encryption of the same message, because the recipient-specific encryption header can be detached in such a way to allow the signature layer and the bulk message encryption to be shared across all recipients.

We remark that an efficient and generic approach for constructing "hybrid" signcryption schemes was recently proposed in [37], based on an underlying tag-KEM, a.k.a. key encapsulation mechanism with labels (see Chap. 7).

10.1.5 Concrete IBSC from Pairings

For concreteness, at the end of this chapter we shall study the IBSC construction of Boyen [51], which uses the properties of bilinear pairings to achieve a detachable sign-then-encrypt combination. In the nomenclature of [52], it is based on the full-domain hash IB paradigm of Boneh and Franklin and has proofs of security under the bilinear Diffie–Hellman (BDH) assumption [45, 46] in the random oracle model [29]. This scheme was selected because it satisfies the strongest and most useful notions of security for IBSC. Its construction borrows elements from the Boneh–Franklin IBE [45, 46] and the Cha–Cheon IBS [57], but achieves better performance than their generic combination.

We mention that a variation of the Boyen scheme [51] has been subsequently proposed by Chen and Malone-Lee [60]. The latter version is slightly more efficient but eschews some of the security properties of the original scheme, which is why we will focus on the original construction. We also note that several other IBSC systems have been proposed over the years [18, 122, 129, 136, 145, 170]; some of these are even more efficient than the two schemes we just mentioned, but at the expense of one or another important security property.

10.2 The Identity-Based Signcryption Primitive

An *identity-based signcryption* scheme, or IBSC, comprises four algorithms:
Setup, Extract, Signcrypt, and Unsigncrypt. In a (two-layer) IBSC with
detachable signature, the signcryption/unsigncryption algorithms are the composition of explicit subroutines: Signcrypt = Encrypt ∘ Sign and Unsigncrypt =
Verify ∘ Decrypt.

In summary, Setup generates random instances of the common public parameters and master secret; Extract computes the private key corresponding to a given
public identity string; Signcrypt produces a signature for a given message and
private key, and then encrypts the signed plaintext for a given identity (note that
the encryption routine may specifically require the signature as input); Decrypt
decrypts a ciphertext using a given private key; Verify checks the validity of a given
signature for a given message and identity. Messages are arbitrary strings in $\{0, 1\}^*$.

It is useful to decompose Signcrypt into Sign and Encrypt, even if the latter
can only be applied on the output of the former. We shall need this finer level of
granularity when discussing efficient multi-recipient signcryption in particular. With
this convention, the functions that compose a generic IBSC scheme are as follows:

- Setup(1^k): On input 1^k, produces a pair (msk, mpk) (where msk is a randomly
  generated master secret and mpk the corresponding common public parameters,
  for the security parameter k).
- Extract(mpk, msk, ID): On input ID, computes a private key sk (corresponding
  to the identity ID under (msk, mpk)).
- Signcrypt(mpk, ID_S, ID_R, sk_S, m): The sequential application of

  - Sign(mpk, ID_S, sk_S, m): On input (ID_S, sk_S, m), outputs a signature s (for
    sk_S, under mpk), and some ephemeral state data r.
  - Encrypt(mpk, ID_R, sk_S, m, s, r): On input (ID_R, sk_S, m, s, r), outputs an
    anonymous ciphertext C (containing the signed message (m, s) encrypted for
    the identity ID_R under mpk).

- Unsigncrypt($mpk, sk_R, \hat{C}$): The sequential application of

  - Decrypt($mpk, sk_R, \hat{C}$): On input $(sk_R, \hat{C})$, outputs a triple $(\hat{ID}_S, \hat{m}, \hat{s})$ (con-
    taining the purported sender identity and signed message obtained by decrypt-
    ing $\hat{C}$ by the private key sk_R under mpk).
  - Verify($mpk, ID_S, \hat{m}, \hat{s}$): On input $(\hat{ID}_S, \hat{m}, \hat{s})$, outputs $\top$ "true" or $\bot$ "false"
    (indicating whether $\hat{s}$ is a valid signature for the message $\hat{m}$ by the identity
    $\hat{ID}_S$, under mpk).

As mentioned, we shall often view the sequential application of Sign and Encrypt
as a single function, called Signcrypt, which for all purposes may be monolithic. However, we insist on keeping a formal separation between the Decrypt
and Verify algorithms that constitute the function Unsigncrypt. The separation
is necessary in order to allow the authenticity of the plaintext message to be verifiable by third parties, without requiring the recipient's decryption key. The two-step

unsigncryption process produces a decrypted message–signature pair as an intermediate output that is no longer bound to the recipient and is thus verifiable by anyone.
Of course, if both operations are performed in lockstep, we may refer to them as a
single Unsigncrypt function.

We have the following consistency constraints.

Definition 10.1 For master secret and common parameters $(msk, mpk) \xleftarrow{R}$
Setup(1^k), any identities ID_S and ID_R, and matching private keys $sk_S \xleftarrow{R}$
Extract(mpk, msk, ID_S) and $sk_R \xleftarrow{R}$ Extract(mpk, msk, ID_R), we require for
consistency that, $\forall m \in \{0, 1\}^*$:

$$
\left.
\begin{aligned}
(s, r) &\xleftarrow{R} \text{Sign}(mpk, ID_S, sk_S, m) \\
C &\xleftarrow{R} \text{Encrypt}(mpk, ID_R, sk_S, m, s, r) \\
(\hat{ID}_S, \hat{m}, \hat{s}) &\leftarrow \text{Decrypt}(mpk, sk_R, \hat{C})
\end{aligned}
\right\}
\implies
\begin{aligned}
\hat{ID}_S &= ID_S \\
\hat{m} &= m \\
\text{Verify}(mpk, ID_S, \hat{m}, \hat{s}) &= \top
\end{aligned}
$$

We omit the parameters mpk and msk when understood from context.

Identity Roles for Signature and Encryption

To reduce the number of keys that need to be handed out by the PKG, it is desirable
to allow the same user private key, extracted from a given identity, to be used alternatively as a signing key in a sender role and as a decryption key in a recipient role.
This corresponds to the notion of one-key signcryption (see Chap. 3). The drawback
of this approach, compared to two-key signcryption, is that it may complicate the
security reduction. Furthermore, it may also be necessary for technical reasons to
disallow the same identity from assuming both the sender and the recipient roles at
once in the same ciphertext: This is the *irreflexivity requirement*.

If for some reason a "signcrypt-to-self" functionality is desired in a one-key system subject to the irreflexivity requirement, it can be emulated by making available
to every user an additional "self"-identity for the sole purpose of signcrypting to
oneself. A less economical option is to duplicate each identity into a signing identity
and a decryption identity, in essence downgrading the one-key system to a two-
key system, at the cost of doubling the number of private keys to be extracted and
stored.

Notational Convention

In the sequel we consider one-key signcryption by default. For clarity, we adopt the
convention of using the subscripts "S" for the sender and "R" for the recipient.

10.3 Security Definitions

We define a number of notions of security for identity-based signcryption.

Fundamental Properties

Our first two notions are the usual security notions for confidentiality and non-repudiation/origin authentication, adapted to the context of IBSC. Following the taxonomy of Chap. 2, in both cases we consider the strongest type of attacker, the "insider," which has access to all private keys except that of the party being attacked.

More precisely, when defining *message confidentiality*, we assume that the adversary may obtain any private key other than that of the targeted recipient and has an oracle that decrypts any valid ciphertext other than the challenge: this is an insider chosen-ciphertext attack in the terminology of Chap. 2.

When defining *signature non-repudiation*, we correspondingly assume that the forger has access to any private key other than that of the signer and can query an oracle that signs and encrypts any message but the challenge: This adversary therefore mounts an insider chosen-message existential forgery attack in the terminology of Chap. 2.

Peripheral Properties

We also define the complementary notions of *ciphertext authentication* and *ciphertext unlinkability*, which allow the legitimate recipient to privately authenticate that he was indeed the intended recipient of a particular ciphertext, but not prove this to a third party. This is important because the message (and its universally verifiable signature) does not necessarily specify who the intended recipient is; only the ciphertext does so unequivocally by virtue of being encrypted under a particular identity. Ciphertext authentication and unlinkability are not trivial to combine with non-repudiation and confidentiality, and we note, for example, that most IBSC schemes proposed in the literature do not achieve all four properties at once. Ciphertext authentication was introduced by Lynn [127] in the context of authenticated IBE and ciphertext unlinkability was defined by Boyen [51].

Another natural property to demand is *ciphertext anonymity* [51], which is the requirement that no third party should be able to discover whom a ciphertext originates from or is addressed to, without the recipient's private key. As for confidentiality, it is possible to define anonymity against insider attacks, where the adversary has access to the sender's signing key: this is the notion we shall consider. We note that the anonymity requirement only guarantees security against attacks that focus on the cryptographic aspect of IBSC; in practice, it will be equally important that the ciphertext conveyance mechanism from sender to recipient does not betray their identities, e.g., from a traffic analysis attack on the communication network. Ciphertext anonymity has recently become an active subject of inquiry in other areas of IBE; see, for example, [1, 44, 53].

Omitted Properties

A couple of additional properties of IBSC schemes have also been put forward in the literature; these properties are redundant or conflict with the above, so we will not define them explicitly.

One redundant property is that of *forward secrecy*, suggested in the context of IBSC first by Libert and Quisquater [122] and also by Nalla and Reddy [145], and later formalized by McCullagh and Barreto [136]. All these papers define forward secrecy as the infeasibility of recovering the message from an IBSC ciphertext, even under exposure of the private key of the sender. Since it is essentially the notion of semantic security under insider attacks defined in Chap. 2, forward secrecy is implied by our model and we will not need to consider it explicitly.

One incompatible property that has been put forward is that of *transferable verification*; see, for example, Libert and Quisquater [122] and McCullagh and Barreto [136]. Transferable verification requires that the ciphertext itself, and not just the decrypted message, be publicly verifiable under a weakened notion of authenticity that excludes knowledge of the message: transferable verification ensures that anyone, including third parties, can ascertain the true originator of a ciphertext (but not its content or the intended recipient).[1]

The main objection against transferable verification is that it violates intuitive expectations of secrecy, because the sender is compelled to broadcast her identity to everyone, in the clear and without repudiation. Transferable verification thus conflicts with ciphertext unlinkability. For these reasons, transferable verification is not necessarily needed or desirable for security; rather, it should be accepted only after due consideration of its ramifications.

Summary of the IBSC Security Notions

The five distinct IBSC security properties that we seek are thus the following:

1. *Insider message confidentiality* (Sect. 10.3.1): Guarantees the secrecy, or semantic security, of the message among the communicating parties, against any attacker, even if the sender's private key is subsequently exposed. This implies *forward secrecy*.
2. *Insider signature non-repudiation* (Sect. 10.3.2): Provides universal verifiability that a decrypted message was written by the signer. The signature remains binding even if the correct recipient's private key is exposed. As usual, non-repudiation implies message authentication and integrity.
3. *Ciphertext unlinkability* (Sect. 10.3.3): Allows the sender to disavow creating a ciphertext for any given recipient, even though he/she remains bound to any validly signed message it contains. In other words, it allows a sender to claim that her signed message was re-encrypted for another recipient.
4. *Ciphertext authentication* (Sect. 10.3.4): Guarantees to the legitimate recipient, alone, that the ciphertext and the signed message it contains were crafted by the same entity. This property also implies ciphertext integrity and, in particular,

---

[1] We remark that, among the three generic signcryption methods studied by Zheng [203, 204], "encrypt-then-sign" ($\mathcal{E}t\mathcal{S}$) entails transferable verification, "sign-then-encrypt" ($\mathcal{S}t\mathcal{E}$) forbids it, and "encrypt-and-sign" ($\mathcal{E}\&\mathcal{S}$) can go either way.

reassures the recipient that the communication was secured end to end and was not re-encrypted along the way.

5. *Insider ciphertext anonymity* (Sect. 10.3.5): Makes the ciphertext appear anonymous (hiding both the sender and the recipient identities) to anyone who does not possess the recipient decryption key. This remains true even if the sender's signing key is exposed.

These properties (including the redundant forward secrecy) were first achieved together in the IBSC construction of Boyen [51]. Subsequently, Chen and Malone-Lee [60] made the scheme computationally more efficient by sacrificing ciphertext unlinkability.

10.3.1 Message Confidentiality

Message confidentiality against adaptive chosen-ciphertext attacks is defined in terms of the following game, played between a challenger and an adversary. We combine signature and encryption into a dual-purpose oracle, to allow Encrypt to access the ephemeral random state data r from Sign. We give the adversary access to a decryption oracle which differs from an unsigncryption oracle in that it returns messages and signatures for correctly formed ciphertexts, rather than just messages.

1. *Start*: The challenger runs the Setup procedure for a given value of the security parameter k and provides the common public parameters mpk to the adversary, keeping the secret msk for itself.
2. *Phase 1*: The adversary makes a number of queries to the challenger, in an adaptive fashion (i.e., one at a time, with knowledge of the previous replies). The following queries are allowed:

   - *Signcryption queries* in which the adversary submits a message and two distinct identities, and obtains a ciphertext containing the message signed in the name of the first identity and encrypted for the second identity.
   - *Decryption queries* in which the adversary submits a ciphertext and an identity, and obtains the identity of the sender, the decrypted message, and a valid signature, provided that (1) the decrypted identity of the sender differs from that of the specified recipient and (2) the signature verification condition Verify $= \top$ is satisfied; otherwise, the oracle only indicates that the ciphertext is invalid for the specified recipient.
   - *Private key extraction queries* in which the adversary submits any identity of its choice and obtains the corresponding private key.

3. *Selection*: At some point, the adversary returns two distinct messages m_0 and m_1 (assumed to be of equal length), a signer identity ID_S, and a recipient identity ID_R, on which it wishes to be challenged. The adversary must have made no private key extraction query on ID_R.

4. *Challenge*: The challenger flips $b \overset{R}{\leftarrow} \{0, 1\}$, computes $sk_S \overset{R}{\leftarrow} \texttt{Extract}(ID_S)$,
   $(s, r) \overset{R}{\leftarrow} \texttt{Sign}(ID_S, sk_S, m_b)$, $C^* \overset{R}{\leftarrow} \texttt{Encrypt}(ID_R, sk_S, m_b, s, r)$, and returns
   the ciphertext C as challenge to the adversary.
5. *Phase 2*: The adversary adaptively issues a number of additional signcryption,
   decryption, and extraction queries, under the additional constraint that it not ask
   for the private key of ID_R or the decryption of C^* under ID_R.
6. *Response*: The adversary returns a guess $\hat{b} \in \{0, 1\}$ and wins if $\hat{b} = b$.

It is emphasized that the adversary is allowed to know the private key sk_S corresponding to the signing identity. The resulting notion is that of *insider security* for
confidentiality, also called forward secrecy.

This game is very similar to the IND-ID-CCA attack defined in [45, 46]; we call
it an IND-IBSC-CCA attack.

Definition 10.2 An identity-based signcryption (IBSC) scheme is said to be semantically secure against adaptive chosen-ciphertext insider attacks, or *IND-IBSC-CCA
secure*, if no randomized polynomial-time adversary has a non-negligible advan-
tage in the above game. In other words, the advantage $Adv_{\mathcal{A}}(k) = |\Pr[\hat{b} = b] - \frac{1}{2}|$
of every randomized polynomial-time IND-IBSC-CCA adversary $\mathcal{A}$ is a negligible
function of the security parameter k.

We remark that the model requires the decryption oracle to perform a validity
check before returning a decryption result, even though Decrypt does not specify
it. This requirement does not weaken the model since the verification function is
public and allows for stronger security results. We similarly ask that the oracles
enforce the irreflexivity requirement, e.g., by refusing to produce or decrypt ciphertexts addressed to their sender.

10.3.2 Signature Non-repudiation

Signature non-repudiation is formally defined in terms of the following game,
played between a challenger and an adversary.

1. *Start*: The challenger runs the Setup procedure for a given value of the security
   parameter k and provides the common public parameters mpk to the adversary,
   keeping the secret msk for itself.
2. *Query*: The adversary makes a number of queries to the challenger. The attack
   may be conducted adaptively and allows the same queries as in the confidentiality game of Sect. 10.3.1, namely signcryption queries, decryption queries, and
   private key extraction queries.
3. *Forgery*: The adversary returns a recipient identity ID_R and a ciphertext C.
4. *Outcome*: The adversary wins the game if the ciphertext C decrypts, under the
   private key of ID_R, to a signed message $(ID_S, \hat{m}, \hat{s})$ that satisfies $ID_S \neq ID_R$ and
   $\texttt{Verify}(ID_S, \hat{m}, \hat{s}) = \top$, where we also require that (1) no private key extraction
   query was made on ID_S and (2) no signcryption query was made that involved $\hat{m}$,

ID_S, and some recipient $ID_{R'}$, and resulted in a ciphertext C' whose decryption under the private key of $ID_{R'}$ is the claimed forgery $(ID_S, \hat{m}, \hat{s})$.

Such a model is very similar to the usual notion of existential unforgeability against chosen-message attacks [163]; we call it an sUF-IBSC-CMA attack.

Definition 10.3 An IBSC scheme is said to be existentially signature-unforgeable against chosen-message insider attacks, or *sUF-IBSC-CMA secure*, if no probabilistic, polynomial-time adversary has a non-negligible advantage in the forgery game above. That is, the advantage $Adv_{\mathcal{A}}(k) = \Pr[\text{Verify}(mpk, ID_S, \hat{m}, \hat{s}) = \top]$ of every randomized polynomial-time sUF-IBSC-CMA adversary $\mathcal{A}$ is a negligible function of the security parameter k.

In the above experiment, the adversary is allowed to obtain the private key sk_R for the forged message recipient ID_R, which corresponds to the stringent requirements of *insider security* for authentication (see Chaps. 2 and 3). There is one important difference: in Chaps. 2 and 3, unforgeability and non-repudiation apply to the ciphertext itself, which is the only sensible choice in the context of a signcryption model with a monolithic "unsigncryption" function. Here, given our two-step Decrypt/Verify specification, we define sUF-IBSC-CMA with a notion of non-repudiation that concentrates on the decrypted message and its signature, which is more intuitively desirable and does not preclude ciphertext unlinkability (see Sect. 10.3.3).

10.3.3 Ciphertext Unlinkability

Ciphertext unlinkability is the property that makes it possible for Alice to deny having sent a given ciphertext to Bob, even if the ciphertext decrypts (under Bob's private key) to a message bearing Alice's signature. In other words, the signature should only be a proof of authorship of the plaintext message; not that the ciphertext was addressed to a particular recipient.

Ciphertext unlinkability allows Alice, e.g., as a news correspondent in a hostile area, to stand behind the content of her reporting, but conceals any detail regarding the particular channel, method, place, or time of communication, lest subsequent forensic investigations be damaging to her sources. When used in conjunction with the multi-recipient technique of Sect. 10.4.4, ciphertext unlinkability also allows her to make exact copies of her writings to additional recipients without anyone being able to prove that she made those copies.

We do not present a formal experiment for this property. A sufficient condition for this property is that, given a plaintext message signed by Alice, anyone should be able to create from it a valid ciphertext addressed to himself with an identical distribution as the corresponding signcryption from Alice.

Definition 10.4 An IBSC scheme is said to be ciphertext unlinkable if there exists a polynomial-time algorithm EncryptToSelf that, given an identified signed message (ID_S, m, s) such that $\text{Verify}(ID_S, m, s) = \top$, and a private key $d_R \xleftarrow{R}$

Extract(ID_R), assembles a ciphertext C that is computationally indistinguishable from a genuine encryption of (m, s) by ID_S for ID_R.

As mentioned earlier, ciphertext unlinkability is the reason why we considered the notion of (plaintext) signature unforgeability in Sect. 10.3.2, instead of the usual notion of ciphertext unforgeability as studied in the signcryption model discussed in Chaps. 2 and 3. Indeed, if the ciphertext itself were unforgeable it would not be unlinkable.

Note also that ciphertext unlinkability only makes sense in a detachable signcryption model as in this chapter, as opposed to the monolithic model of Zheng [203, 204] used by Malone-Lee [129] and by Libert and Quisquater [122]. Indeed, if part of the ciphertext itself is needed to verify the authenticity of the plaintext, ciphertext indistinguishability is lost as soon as the recipient is compelled to expose the validity of the signature. Ciphertext unlinkability is thus a property that is unattainable in the monolithic signcryption model.

10.3.4 Ciphertext Authentication

Ciphertext authentication is, in a sense, complementary to ciphertext unlinkability. Whereas unlinkability required that the recipient be unable to prove the origin of a given ciphertext to a third party, authentication allows the recipient to positively authenticate the same ciphertext as originating from Alice: it just cannot prove it to anyone else. Technically, we define ciphertext authentication as the requirement that the legitimate recipient be able to match the origin of a ciphertext with that of the signed message it contains.

A useful application is to convince the recipient that the ciphertext remained encrypted throughout the entire transmission (because it would not pass the test if it had been re-encrypted in transit). In particular, a ciphertext properly authenticated in this model cannot have been the target of a (successful, active) man-in-the-middle interception. We define ciphertext authentication in terms of the following game:

1. *Start*: The challenger runs the Setup procedure for a given value of the security parameter k and provides the common public parameters mpk to the adversary, keeping the secret msk for itself.
2. *Query*: The adversary makes a number of queries to the challenger as in the confidentiality game of Sect. 10.3.1, namely signcryption queries, decryption queries, and private key extraction queries.
3. *Forgery*: The adversary returns a recipient identity ID_R and a ciphertext C.
4. *Outcome*: The adversary wins the game if C decrypts, under the private key of ID_R, to a signed message $(ID_S, \hat{m}, \hat{s})$ such that $ID_S \neq ID_R$ and that satisfies Verify($ID_S, \hat{m}, \hat{s}$) $= \top$, provided that (1) no private key extraction query was made on either ID_S or ID_R and (2) C did not result from a signcryption query with sender and recipient identities ID_S and ID_R.

We contrast the above experiment, which is a case of "outsider" security for authentication on the whole ciphertext, with the scenario for signature non-repudiation, which required insider security on the signed plaintext only. We call the above experiment an AUTH-IBSC-CMA attack.

Definition 10.5 An IBSC scheme is said to be existentially ciphertext-unforgeable against chosen-message outsider attacks, or *AUTH-IBSC-CMA secure*, if no randomized polynomial-time adversary has a non-negligible advantage in the preceding game. That is, the advantage $Adv_{\mathcal{A}}(k) = \Pr[\text{Verify}(ID_S, \hat{m}, \hat{s}) = \top]$ of every randomized polynomial-time sUF-IBSC-CMA adversary $\mathcal{A}$ is a negligible function of the security parameter k.

10.3.5 Ciphertext Anonymity

Ciphertext anonymity is the last property we define. It requires that the ciphertext leak no knowledge about its originator or its intended recipient to a polynomially bounded adversary. (Naturally, the ciphertext must be decipherable by the intended recipient without that information.)

   Ciphertext anonymity against adaptive chosen-ciphertext attacks is defined as follows:

1. *Start*: The challenger runs the Setup procedure for a given value of the security parameter k and provides the common public parameters mpk to the adversary, keeping the secret msk for itself.
2. *Phase 1*: The adversary is allowed to make adaptive queries of the same types as in the confidentiality game of Sect. 10.3.1, i.e., signcryption queries, decryption queries, and private key extraction queries.
3. *Selection*: At some point, the adversary returns a message m, two sender identities ID_{S_0} and ID_{S_1}, and two recipient identities ID_{R_0} and ID_{R_1}, on which it wishes to be challenged. The adversary must have made no private key extraction query on either ID_{R_0} or ID_{R_1}.
4. *Challenge*: The challenger flips two random coins $b', b'' \xleftarrow{R} \{0, 1\}$, computes $sk \xleftarrow{R} \text{Extract}(ID_{S_{b'}})$, $(s, r) \xleftarrow{R} \text{Sign}(ID_{S_{b'}}, sk, m)$, $C \xleftarrow{R} \text{Encrypt}(ID_{R_{b''}}, sk_S, m, s, r)$, and gives the ciphertext C to the adversary.
5. *Phase 2*: The adversary adaptively issues a number of additional signcryption, decryption, and extraction queries, under the additional constraint that it not ask for the private key of either ID_{R_0} or ID_{R_1} or the decryption of C under ID_{R_0} or ID_{R_1}.
6. *Response*: The adversary returns two guesses $\hat{b}', \hat{b}'' \in \{0, 1\}$ and wins the game if $(\hat{b}', \hat{b}'') = (b', b'')$.

This game is the same as for confidentiality, except that the adversary is challenged on the identities instead of the message; it is an insider attack. We call it an ANON-IBSC-CCA attack.

Definition 10.6 An IBSC scheme is said to be ciphertext-anonymous against adaptive chosen-ciphertext insider attacks, or *ANON-IBSC-CCA secure*, if no randomized polynomial-time adversary has a non-negligible advantage in the above game. In other words, the advantage $Adv_{\mathcal{A}}(k) = |\Pr[\hat{b} = b] - \frac{1}{4}|$ of every randomized polynomial-time ANON-IBSC-CCA adversary $\mathcal{A}$ is a negligible function of the security parameter k, where $b = (b', b'')$ and $\hat{b} = (\hat{b}', \hat{b}'')$.

We emphasize that anonymity only pertains to the ciphertext, against non-recipients and is thus consistent with both non-repudiation (Sect. 10.3.2) and authentication (Sect. 10.3.4). To illustrate the difference between unlinkability and anonymity, we note that the authenticated IBE scheme of Lynn [127] is unlinkable, since any ciphertext can be created by its recipient rather than its sender, but not anonymous, since the sender identity must be known prior to decryption in order to decrypt.

An analogous notion of ciphertext anonymity exists for traditional public key cryptography (see the discussion in Chap. 5).

10.4 A Concrete IBSC Scheme

In this section we construct two efficient identity-based signcryption schemes; both are based on the two-layer detachable design and satisfy the full complement of security properties presented in Sect. 10.3. Both constructions make use of the Boneh–Franklin setup, which we recall next.

10.4.1 The Boneh–Franklin Framework

We give a brief summary of the Boneh–Franklin system for identity-based cryptography based on bilinear pairings on elliptic curves. Its setup and private key generation algorithms will be used in the IBSC construction.

We recall the notion of a bilinear map group from Sect. 5.2. In this chapter, we treat the bilinear pairing and the algebraic group over which it is defined as abstract mathematical objects satisfying the properties summarized in a few definitions to follow.

Let $\mathbb{G}_1$ and $\mathbb{G}_T$ be two cyclic groups of prime order p written in multiplicative notation (and using 1 to denote their respective neutral elements).

Definition 10.7 A *bilinear pairing* is an efficiently computable, non-degenerate map $e : \mathbb{G}_1 \times \mathbb{G}_1 \to \mathbb{G}_T$ such that, for all $x, y \in \mathbb{G}_1$ and all $a, b \in \mathbb{Z}$, we have $e(x^a, y^b) = e(x, y)^{ab}$. The group $\mathbb{G}_1$ is called a bilinear map group; the group $\mathbb{G}_T$ is the target group.

Definition 10.8 The (computational) *bilinear Diffie–Hellman (BDH) problem* in a bilinear map group as above is described as follows: given $g, g^a, g^b, g^c \in \mathbb{G}_1$, where g is a generator and $a, b, c \xleftarrow{R} \mathbb{Z}_p$ are chosen at random, compute $e(g, g)^{abc}$. The advantage of an algorithm $\mathcal{B}$ at solving the BDH problem is defined as $Adv_{\mathcal{B}}(k) = \Pr[\mathcal{B}(g, g^a, g^b, g^c) = e(g, g)^{abc}]$.

Definition 10.9 Let $\mathcal{G}$ be a polynomial-time randomized function that, on input 1^k, returns the description of a bilinear pairing $e : \mathbb{G}_1 \times \mathbb{G}_1 \to \mathbb{G}_T$ between two groups $\mathbb{G}_1$ and $\mathbb{G}_T$ of prime order p. A BDH parameter generator $\mathcal{G}$ satisfies the *bilinear Diffie–Hellman assumption* if there is no probabilistic, polynomial-time algorithm $\mathcal{B}$ that solves the BDH problem in time at most polynomial in k and with advantage at least inverse polynomial in k. The probability space is that of the randomly generated parameters $(\mathbb{G}_1, \mathbb{G}_T, p, e)$, the BDH instances (g, g^a, g^b, g^c), and the randomized executions of $\mathcal{B}$.

Using a BDH parameter generator, the Boneh–Franklin IBE scheme defines four operations: two operations used by the PKG (for setup and key extraction) and two used by the individual users (for encryption and decryption). We will make use of the two PKG algorithms (as defined below):

bfSetup: On input a security parameter $k \in \mathbb{N}$: obtain $(\mathbb{G}_1, \mathbb{G}_T, p, e) \overset{R}{\leftarrow} \mathcal{G}(1^k)$ from the BDH parameter generator; pick a random generator $g \overset{R}{\leftarrow} \mathbb{G}_1$ and a random exponent $msk \overset{R}{\leftarrow} \mathbb{Z}_p$, set $g^{msk} \in \mathbb{G}_1$; and specify a hash function $H_0 : \{0, 1\}^* \to \mathbb{G}_1$. Output the common public parameters $mpk = (\mathbb{G}_1, \mathbb{G}_T, p, e, g, g^{msk}, H_0)$ and the master secret msk.

bfExtract: On input $ID \in \{0, 1\}^*$: hash the given identity into a public element $i_{ID} \leftarrow H_0(ID) \in \mathbb{G}_1$ and output $d_{ID} \leftarrow (i_{ID})^{msk} \in \mathbb{G}_1$ as the private key sk_{ID}.

10.4.2 Fully Secure IBSC Construction

Table 10.1 details the algorithms of the scheme.

Although Sign and Encrypt are described separately, the latter can only be run on the output of the former; together they constitute the atomic identity-based Signcrypt operation.

Recall also that Decrypt and Verify together define the Unsigncrypt operation, but those can be used separately.

10.4.2.1 Principle of Operation

The Setup and Extract functions are based on the original Boneh–Franklin IBE system [45, 46]. Sign and Verify implement the IBS of Cha and Cheon [57]. Encrypt and Decrypt are specially crafted to interface with the IBS layer and reuse its randomness.

In brief, Sign implements a randomized IBS whose signatures comprise a commitment j to some random r chosen by the sender and a closing v that depends on r and the message m. Encrypt superimposes two layers of (expansionless)

Table 10.1 The identity-based signcryption (IBSC) scheme introduced by Boyen [51]

Setup

Input: security parameter $k \in \mathbb{N}$
Method:
Create Boneh–Franklin parameters $\mathbb{G}_1, \mathbb{G}_T, p, e, g, g^{msk}$ and secret msk as in `bfSetup`
Specify five independent cryptographic hash functions (H_0 as in `bfSetup`):
$H_0 : \{0, 1\}^* \to \mathbb{G}_1$
$H_1 : \mathbb{G}_1 \times \{0, 1\}^* \to \mathbb{Z}_p$
$H_2 : \mathbb{G}_T \to \{0, 1\}^{\lceil \log p \rceil}$
$H_3 : \mathbb{G}_T \to \mathbb{Z}_p$
$H_4 : \mathbb{G}_1 \to \{0, 1\}^k$
Output: the public system parameters $(\mathbb{G}_1, \mathbb{G}_T, p, e, g, g^{msk}, k, H_0, H_1, H_2, H_3, H_4)$ and corresponding master secret $msk \in \mathbb{Z}_p$

Extract

Input: master secret msk and identity string $ID \in \{0, 1\}^*$
Output: private key $d_{ID} \leftarrow H_0(ID)^{msk} \in \mathbb{G}_1$, as in `bfExtract`

Signcrypt = Sign + Encrypt	Unsigncrypt = Decrypt + Verify
Sign	Decrypt
Input: private key d_S of some ID_S, plaintext message m	*Input:* pvt. key d_R of recipient ID_R, anonymous ciphertext $(\hat{x}, \hat{y}, \hat{z})$
Method:	*Method:*
$i_S \leftarrow H_0(ID_S)$ (so $d_S = (i_S)^{msk}$)	$i_R \leftarrow H_0(ID_R)$
Randomly sample $r \xleftarrow{R} \mathbb{Z}_p$	$\hat{w} \leftarrow e(\hat{x}, d_R)$
$j \leftarrow (i_S)^r \in \mathbb{G}_1$	$\hat{v} \leftarrow H_2(\hat{w}) \oplus \hat{y}$
$h \leftarrow H_1(j, m) \in \mathbb{Z}_p$	$(\hat{ID}_S, \hat{m}) \leftarrow \text{Dec}_{H_4(\hat{v})}(\hat{z})$
$v \leftarrow (d_S)^{r+h} \in \mathbb{G}_1$	$\hat{i}_S \leftarrow H_0(\hat{ID}_S)$
Output: signature (j, v) and auxiliary data (m, r, ID_S, i_S, d_S)	$\hat{u} \leftarrow e(\hat{i}_S, d_R)$
	$\hat{k} \leftarrow H_3(\hat{u})$
Encrypt	$\hat{j} \leftarrow \hat{x}^{\hat{k}^{-1}}$
Input: recipient ID_R, signature data $(ID_S, i_S, d_S, j, v, m, r)$ as above	*Output:* purported plaintext $\hat{m}$, signature $(\hat{j}, \hat{v})$, and sender $\hat{ID}_S$
Method:	Verify
$i_R \leftarrow H_0(ID_R)$	*Input:* message $\hat{m}$, signature $(\hat{j}, \hat{v})$, and sender $\hat{ID}_S$ to verify
$u \leftarrow e(d_S, i_R) \in \mathbb{G}_T$	*Method:*
$k \leftarrow H_3(u) \in \mathbb{Z}_p$	$\hat{i}_S \leftarrow H_0(\hat{ID}_S)$
$x \leftarrow j^k \in \mathbb{G}_1$	$\hat{h} \leftarrow H_1(\hat{j}, \hat{m})$
$w \leftarrow u^{kr} \in \mathbb{G}_T$	Test $e(g, \hat{v}) \overset{?}{=} e(g^{msk}, (\hat{i}_S)^{\hat{h}} \hat{j})$
$y \leftarrow H_2(w) \oplus v$	*Output:* $\top$ if equality holds; else $\bot$
$z \leftarrow \text{Enc}_{H_4(v)}((ID_S, m))$	
Output: ciphertext (x, y, z)	

Here, $\text{Enc}_{key}(data)$ and $\text{Dec}_{key}(data)$ are the encryption and decryption functions of a deterministic symmetric cipher assumed semantically secure under passive attacks (for one-time keys), e.g., the "XOR" operation with the key used as a one-time pad. All hash functions are modeled as random oracles

deterministic encryption. The inner layer encrypts j into x using a minimalist authenticated IBE built from an implicit identity-based key agreement. The outer layer concurrently determines the value w that encrypts to the same x under a kind of anonymous IBE, derandomized to rely on the entropy already present in x. Bulk encryption uses a deterministic symmetric cipher with a one-time key.

It is helpful to observe that the exponentiations $\star^r$ and $\star^k$ used in Sign for commitment and in Encrypt for authenticated encryption, as well as the key extraction $\star^{msk}$, and the bilinear pairing $e(\star, i_R)$ that intervenes in the determination of w, all commute. The legitimate recipient derives its ability to decrypt x from the capacity to perform all of the above operations (either explicitly or implicitly), in a specific order, which is different from the order in which the sender performed the corresponding operations, but gives the same result.

10.4.2.2 Consistency and Security

The next theorem establishes that the scheme behaves as expected when operated by honest parties.

Theorem 10.1 *The IBSC scheme of Table 10.1 is consistent.*

Proof First, we show that the decryption of a honest ciphertext is correct. Observe that if $(\hat{x}, \hat{y}, \hat{z}) = (x, y, z)$, it follows that $\hat{w} = e(i_S^{rk}, i_R^{msk}) = e(i_S^{msk}, i_R)^{rk} = w$ (in $\mathbb{G}_T$), and thus $\hat{v} = v$ and $(\hat{ID}_S, \hat{m}) = (ID_S, m)$; we also have $\hat{u} = e(\hat{i}_S, i_R)^{msk} = u$ (in $\mathbb{G}_T$), hence $\hat{k} = k$ (in $\mathbb{Z}_p$), and thus $\hat{j} = (j^k)^{\hat{k}^{-1}} = j$ (in $\mathbb{G}_1$).

Next, we show that the decrypted message/signature pair will pass the verification test. Indeed, if $(\hat{m}, \hat{ID}_S, \hat{j}, \hat{v}) = (m, ID_S, j, v)$, we have $e(g, \hat{v}) = e(g, i_S)^{msk\,(r+h)} = e(g^{msk}, (\hat{i}_S)^h (\hat{i}_S)^r) = e(g^{msk}, (\hat{i}_S)^h \hat{j})$ (in $\mathbb{G}_T$), as required.

We now state without proof the security theorems corresponding to the five security properties given in Sect. 10.3. We refer the reader to the full version of [51] for the proofs.

Theorem 10.2 *Let $\mathcal{A}$ be a polynomial-time IND-IBSC-CCA attacker that has advantage at least ε and makes at most q_i queries to the random oracles H_i, $i = 0, 1, 2, 3, 4$. Then, there exists a polynomial-time algorithm $\mathcal{B}$ that solves the bilinear Diffie–Hellman problem with advantage at least $\varepsilon/(q_0\,q_2)$.*

Theorem 10.3 *Let $\mathcal{A}$ be an sUF-IBSC-CMA attacker that makes at most q_i queries to the random oracles H_i, $i = 0, 1, 2, 3, 4$, and at most q_{sc} queries to the signcryption oracle. Assume that, within a time span at most t, $\mathcal{A}$ produces a successful forgery with probability at least $\varepsilon = 10\,(q_{sc} + 1)\,(q_{sc} + q_1)/2^k$, for a security parameter k. Then, there exists an algorithm $\mathcal{B}$ that solves the bilinear Diffie–Hellman problem in expected time at most $120686\,q_0\,q_1\,t/\varepsilon$.*

Theorem 10.4 *There exists a deterministic polynomial-time EncryptToSelf algorithm that, given an identifier ID_S, a signed plaintext (m, j, v) issued by ID_S, and a private key d_R for an identity ID_R, creates a ciphertext (x, y, z) identical to the ciphertext that Encrypt would produce from (m, j, v) for identity ID_R. In particular, (x, y, z) decrypts to (m, j, v) under d_R with probability 1.*

Theorem 10.5 *Let $\mathcal{A}$ be a polynomial-time AUTH-IBSC-CMA attacker with advantage at least ε that makes at most q_i queries to the random oracles H_i, $i = 0, 1, 2, 3, 4$. Then, there exists a polynomial-time algorithm $\mathcal{B}$ that solves the BDH problem with advantage at least $2\varepsilon / (q_0 (q_0 - 1) (q_1 q_2 + q_3))$.*

Theorem 10.6 *Let $\mathcal{A}$ be a polynomial-time ANON-IBSC-CCA attacker that has advantage at least ε and makes at most q_i queries to the random oracles H_i, $i = 0, 1, 2, 3, 4$. Then, there exists a polynomial-time algorithm $\mathcal{B}$ that solves the bilinear Diffie–Hellman problem with advantage at least $3\varepsilon / (q_0 (q_0 - 1) (q_1 q_2 + 2 q_2 + q_3))$.*

10.4.3 A Performance/Security Trade-Off

It is possible to optimize the previous scheme in various ways if one accepts to relax certain of its security properties.

For example, Chen and Malone-Lee [60] show how to achieve a 30% speed-up by removing some of the blinding and unblinding from the encryption and decryption functions, at the cost of dropping the unlinkability requirement.

We briefly describe the changes as follows:

- Sign is unchanged.
- Encrypt is simplified by dropping the computation of $x = j^k$ and outputting j instead, and using a hash of u^r instead of u^{kr} to blind (v, ID_S, m) in the output.
- Decrypt is likewise simplified by computing $\hat{u}^k = e(\hat{j}, d_R)$ instead of $\hat{w}$ and using it to unblind $(\hat{v}, I\hat{D}_S, \hat{m})$. The second pairing previously used to recover $\hat{j}$ is no longer necessary since $\hat{j}$ is now given in the ciphertext.
- Verify is unchanged. It takes the decrypted quadruple $(\hat{m}, \hat{j}, \hat{v}, I\hat{D}_S)$ as input.

With this modification, the resulting scheme is no longer unlinkable because the "decrypted" signature component $\hat{j}$, required by Verify, can be matched with the "encrypted" ciphertext component j, exposed by Encrypt.

10.4.4 Signcrypting for Multiple Recipients

It is often desirable to sign and encrypt the same message for multiple recipients. In this case, and especially if the message is a large data file, it is natural to ask whether the bulk of the signcryption can be performed once, with each recipient receiving identical ciphertexts except for some small recipient-specific header file.

In the scheme (as well as in the relaxed version), signcrypting the same message m for a set of n recipients $ID_{R_1}, \ldots, ID_{R_n}$ is easily achieved by carrying out the Sign operation once (which establishes the randomization parameter r), followed by an application of the Encrypt operation for each recipient identity, based on the same intermediate values.

Since the message m and the randomization parameter r are invariant for all the Encrypt instances, it is easy to see that the z component of the ciphertext also remains the same. Thus, the multi-recipient composite ciphertext is easily assembled from one instance of $(x_i, y_i) \in \mathbb{G}_1 \times \mathbb{G}_1$ for each recipient R_i, plus a single instance of $z \in \{0, 1\}^*$ to be shared by all. Thus, a multi-recipient ciphertext is compactly encoded in the form $C \leftarrow ((x_1, y_1), \ldots, (x_n, y_n), z)$. Since z is the only ciphertext component whose length depends on the message, this encoding results in a substantial economy of space.

Chapter 11
Key Establishment Using Signcryption Techniques

Alexander W. Dent

11.1 Introduction

Possibly the most useful branch of public key cryptography is key establishment. After all, it is the problem of symmetric key distribution that prompted Diffie and Hellman to propose the notion of public key cryptography in the first place [74]. The basic idea behind a key establishment protocol is that two (or more) parties should exchange cryptographic messages in such a way that, at the end of the protocol, they both know a shared key—typically a bitstring of a fixed length that can be used with a symmetric cryptosystem. It is imperative that no party other than those actively participating in the key establishment protocol (and perhaps one or more trusted third parties) can obtain any information about this shared secret key. We also usually require that, at the end of a successful protocol execution, each party is convinced of the identity of the other party. Hence, the basic security notions we require from a key establishment protocol are those of confidentiality and entity authentication.

Key establishment can generally be broken down into two categories: *key transport protocols* and *key agreement protocols*. A key transport protocol is a protocol in which one party randomly generates a shared key and securely transports that key to another party. This can be very simple and efficient, but in some applications the fact that only one of the two parties contribute to the key generation process may be seen as a drawback. This is particularly true if the two parties do not trust each other! However, in other applications, this can be an advantage; for example, if one party is a low power device that cannot reliably contribute to the key generation process. The other category is that of key agreement protocols. These are protocols in which both parties contribute equally to the choice of key that is finally established, and

A.W. Dent (✉)
Information Security Group, Royal Holloway, University of London, Egham TW20 OEX, Surrey, UK
e-mail: a.dent@rhul.ac.uk

A.W. Dent, Y. Zheng (eds.), *Practical Signcryption*, Information Security and Cryptography, DOI 10.1007/978-3-540-89411-7_11,
© Springer-Verlag Berlin Heidelberg 2010

no one party has the ability to choose the key value. Key agreement protocols are typically more complicated than key transport protocols.

As we have mentioned, a key establishment protocol typically requires confidentiality protection and entity authentication. The entity authentication requirement bears further examination. A good key establishment protocol assures each party of the identities of all the other parties currently engaging in a protocol execution. This requires two assurances: that the messages that they are receiving come from a named individual (origin authentication) and that the messages that they are receiving have been recently generated (freshness). It is easy to see that a signcryption scheme can provide confidentiality protection and origin authentication, but does not contain an implicit assurance of freshness.

The basic requirements of confidentiality protection and entity authentication can prevent most attacks against a key establishment protocol. For example, the confidentiality protection requirement should prevent an attacker from discovering any information about the key that the protocol establishes (sometimes known as the *session key*). The freshness requirement should prevent an attacker from being able to replay old messages and force a party to re-use an old (and therefore potentially compromised) session key. The origin authentication requirement should prevent an attacker from being able to establish a key with a party on the mistaken assumption that the attacker is someone else. Thus our set of basic requirements prevent most reasonable types of attack; however, there are a few specific attacks that are worth further consideration. Most notably, we need to consider *forward secrecy*.

Attacks against forward secrecy involve an attacker trying to compromise an old session between two parties. The basic requirement is that an attacker should be unable to determine the session key that was established in a previous execution of the key establishment protocol, even if the attacker manages to get hold of the long-term private keys of both parties. Hence, the key remains secret against attacks that are made in the future—this is why the security property is known as forward secrecy even though it refers to attacks made against past sessions. This is a useful property for a key establishment protocol to have, but again it is not necessary for all applications and may be computationally more expensive than other protocols.

Although signcryption seems like an excellent candidate to provide the basic security notions of confidentiality and authentication required by a key establishment protocol, there are comparatively few such protocols. Signcryption-based key establishment protocols have been proposed by Zheng and Imai [205, 208], Dent [73], Kim and Youm [116], Bjørstad and Dent [37], and Gorantla et al. [92]. Only Gorantla et al. present a security proof for their key establishment scheme. We discuss these proposals (plus a simple key transport protocol) and try to establish a security proof for the Bjørstad and Dent scheme.

Key establishment protocols are difficult and subtle cryptographic operations. Unfortunately, we will not have space in this chapter to survey the whole field. A good introduction to the design and analysis of entity authentication and key establishment protocols is given by Boyd and Mathuria [50].

11.2 Formal Security Models for Key Establishment

11.2.1 Motivation

Several attempts have been made to provide formal security models for key establishment. The first model was proposed by Dolev and Yao [79] and was designed for the automated checking of key establishment protocols. It treated any cryptographic operation as a perfect "black-box" operation and can therefore not guarantee security. Another model, termed the CK model, was developed by Bellare et al. [23] and Canetti and Krawczyk [55]. This approach is modular and allows for easier design of new protocols; however, it tends to produce less efficient protocols and is not really suitable for analyzing existing protocols. A third model is known as the universal composability model and was developed by Canetti [54] and Canetti and Krawczyk [56]. Here, security is proven by showing that the protocol is indistinguishable from an ideally functioning protocol. This provides a strong guarantee of security, but tends to involve complex proofs. A good analysis of these different approaches is given by Boyd [49].

We choose to use the approach initially put forward by Bellare and Rogaway [28] and subsequently revised by Bellare et al. [27] and Choo et al. [63]. There are several reasons for choosing this model. First, it is particularly suitable for examining existing protocols rather than for the construction of new protocols (unlike the modular CK model). Second, it provides reasonable security guarantees. It does not provide the strong guarantees of the universal composability model of Canetti, which shows that the protocol is secure under all conditions, but it does show that the protocol is secure against any reasonable attacker when used in any reasonable environment. Lastly, the proof techniques used with the Bellare–Rogaway approach are similar to the techniques used elsewhere in this book (unlike the Canetti or Dolev–Yao approaches).

The idea behind the Bellare–Rogaway security model is to give the attacker complete control over the network by which a series of legitimate parties communicate. The attacker can examine any message as it is sent across the network, alter messages, delete messages, delay messages, inject entirely new messages, or replay old messages. In order that the attacker has some network traffic to view, he can also force any party in the network begin a key establishment protocol with any other party in the network and all parties must respond correctly to any message that they receive. The attacker also has the ability to reveal the session key that was computed in a successfully completed execution of the protocol and corrupt parties to learn their long-term private keys. This models the case where the attacker is a legitimate member of the network and/or can obtain a party's long-term private key through bribery, intimidation, or theft. We believe that this models the abilities of an attacker in any reasonable system.

So, we have now modeled the attacker's ability to interact with the network, but we have not considered what it means for a protocol to be secure. In order to model security, the attacker at some point chooses a successfully completed execution of the protocol which has resulted in the establishment of a shared secret key about which the attacker *should have* no information. The attacker is then given either that shared secret key (with probability 1/2) or a completely random key (with probability 1/2). It is the attacker's job to guess whether the key that they have been given is real or random. The idea is that if no reasonable attacker can tell the difference between a real key and a random key, then, as far as the attacker can tell, any cryptographic operations computed using the shared secret key might as well have been computed using a random key that is unrelated to any of the messages that the attacker saw during the key establishment protocol.

11.2.2 Sessions

The formal security model is going to talk about the security of a session belonging to an entity. The notion of a session is very important, as we wish to deal with situations where one entity can be communicating with another entity in multiple ways or for multiple purposes. Each of these communications is a session and knowledge of the session key for one session should not help an attacker determine the session key for another session. In other words, we wish to model a situation where (for example) a user is communicating with a server through both a HTTPS protocol and an SFTP protocol. These are separate sessions despite the fact that they are both passing data between the same entities. Knowledge of the session key used to encrypt data in the HTTPS session should not help an attacker break the SFTP session.

More precisely, we will talk about entity A having a session with entity B under the session identity (SID) sid. This is the session belonging to entity A for the purposes of sending and receiving messages from entity B and identified from the complete list of open sessions that these two entities share by the use of unique session identity sid. Therefore, a full communication consists of two sessions: the session entity A has with entity B under session identity sid and the session entity B has with entity A under the same session identity sid. However, since we are going to give an attacker the ability to send messages to A that purport to come from entity B, the fact that entity A has an open session with entity B under session identity sid does not mean that entity B has to hold a corresponding session with entity A.

Furthermore, even if the A holds an open session with B under session identity sid and B holds an open session with A under session identity sid, this does not mean that the messages that A has sent have necessarily been delivered to B unaltered or vice versa. We introduce the idea of a *matching conversation* to describe a situation where messages are passed faithfully between A and B. Two sessions are a matching conversation if they both agree on the identities of the participants, they both agree on the session identity, and the only messages that are passed between them are the messages output by their partner (and these are passed in the correct order).

Note that a session is uniquely identified by three things: (1) the identity of the owner of the session (entity A), (2) the identity of the corresponding party (entity B), and (3) the session identity (sid).

11.2.3 The Formal Security Model

Let $\mathcal{A}$ be any probabilistic, polynomial-time attacker. We suppose that the protocol involves entities with identities defined in some namespace S. Hence, we refer to actions taken by an entity A with an identity $ID_A \in S$. We assume that the identity ID_A uniquely identifies A from the set of all possible entities. $\mathcal{A}$ has access to the network via the following series of oracles:

- Query(ID_A): This oracle allows the attacker to obtain the legitimate public information about the entity A, including their public key values.
- Send(ID_A, ID_B, sid, m): This mimics the effects of entity A sending the message m to entity B using the session with session identity sid. Hence, the oracle will return the response of entity B to this message.

  There are a couple of subtleties in the use of this oracle. First, the attacker may choose to send a special message symbol λ. This query Send(ID_A, ID_B, sid, λ) forces entity A to initiate the key establishment protocol with entity B. If the protocol allows the session identity to be chosen by an outside agent, then this is supplied as sid; otherwise, sid should be the empty string.

  Second, if the attacker chooses to send a message Send(ID_A, ID_B, sid, m) for which entity B does not have an existing session with entity A under session identity sid, then the oracle responds as entity B would respond as if it received the first message in a fresh session of the key establishment protocol.

  Third, if Send(ID_A, ID_B, sid, m) causes entity B to terminate its involvement in a protocol (either because the protocol has been violated or because the protocol has been successfully completed) then the oracle will not only provide the correct response but also inform the attacker that the protocol has *terminated* and whether the protocol execution was *successful* or *unsuccessful*. After a protocol has terminated for a party, further Send(ID_A, ID_B, sid, m) queries do not elicit a response.

  Lastly, it is worth noting that session identities do not have to remain fixed during protocol execution. As each party sends a message, it is possible for the session identity to change providing that both parties can always recognize to which session an identity refers. Indeed, many protocols define the session identity to be the concatenation of all messages that have been sent so far in a particular protocol execution (along with the identities of the participants).

- Expire(ID_A, ID_B, sid): This allows a session identity to be re-used by indicating that the original session with that identity has now expired. If an attacker calls the oracle Expire(ID_A, ID_B, sid) then entity B assumes that the protocol execution with entity A using session identity sid has been terminated. Thus, any subsequent $\texttt{Send}(ID_A, ID_B, sid, m)$ queries will be handled as if this were the beginning of a new protocol execution.

- $\texttt{Reveal}(ID_A, ID_B, sid)$: This allows the attacker to determine the secret shared key that entity B has computed in the session sid with entity A. It can only be used if entity B has *successfully terminated* a protocol execution with session identity sid and if entity B believes that the protocol execution was undertaken with entity A. It returns the session key for that session.

- $\texttt{Corrupt}(ID_B)$: This allows an attacker to corrupt a legitimate party. It is meant to model insider attacks and attacks in which the attacker can coerce parties into revealing their private information. There is some debate about whether this should involve the attacker learning all of the secret information held by a party (including internal state variables) or just the party's long-term private keys. We will only consider the simpler case where the oracle returns the long-term private key of entity B. This models attacks in which the attacker can corrupt a registration authority to learn private keys, or the private key distribution service, but cannot corrupt the key establishment device itself to learn internal state variables. Thus, security proofs in this model only guarantee security in situations where the attacker cannot learn the value of these variables.

- $\texttt{Test}(ID_A, ID_B, sid)$: This oracle may only be queried once and can only be used if entity B has *successfully terminated* the session with session identity sid and if it believes that the session is established with entity A. The oracle randomly chooses a bit $b \xleftarrow{R} \{0, 1\}$. If $b = 0$ then the oracle responds with the session key for that session. If $b = 1$ then the oracle responds with a randomly generated key of the same length as the session key.

  Note that the attacker is only attempting to determine the key held by entity B (in the session with identity sid that it believes that it has completed with entity A). We do not require that entity A has successfully terminated the protocol or that entity A has even undertaken a protocol execution with entity B under the session identity sid.

The attacker's aim is to guess the value of b used in the $\texttt{Test}$ query. Of course, there are trivial ways in which an attacker can succeed in this task; for example, the attacker could use a $\texttt{Reveal}$ query to obtain the correct value of the session key or use a $\texttt{Corrupt}$ query to learn the long-term secret of one the parties and then impersonate that party in the protocol execution that is to be tested. We wish to exclude these trivial attacks and, by doing so, we introduce a formal notion of freshness:

Definition 11.1 (Freshness) A protocol execution that entity B believes it has undertaken with entity A and using session identity sid is *fresh* if

1. entity B has successfully terminated the protocol execution,
2. the attacker has not queried the $\texttt{Reveal}$ oracle on the input (ID_A, ID_B, sid) unless the attacker has called the $\texttt{Expire}(ID_A, ID_B, sid)$ oracle,

3. the attacker has not queried the Reveal oracle on the input (ID_B, ID_A, sid) unless the attacker has called the Expire(ID_B, ID_A, sid) oracle,
4. the attacker has not queried the Corrupt oracle on either ID_A or ID_B.

Again, we stress that this definition is about the state of the key held by entity B. We do not require that A has successfully terminated the protocol or that A has even undertaken a protocol execution with B under the session identity sid. (Although we do require that if A has undertaken the protocol, then the attacker may not make a Reveal query to A to learn the key value.)

Definition 11.2 (Security of a key establishment protocol) A key establishment protocol is said to be secure if every probabilistic, polynomial-time attacker $\mathcal{A}$ has negligible advantage in winning the following game:

1. The challenger generates the system parameters *param* for the protocol at a given security level k.
2. The attacker executes $\mathcal{A}$ on the input $(1^k, param)$. The attacker may query any of the oracles described above. The attacker terminates by outputting a guess b' for b.

The attacker is said to win the game if $b = b'$ and the test session remains fresh (i.e., the attacker does not make a Corrupt query on either of the participants of the test session or a Reveal query on the test session before making an Expire query). The attacker's advantage is defined to be

$$Adv_{\mathcal{A}}(k) = |\Pr[\mathcal{A} \text{ wins}] - 1/2| \qquad (11.1)$$

11.2.4 Entity Authentication

As we discussed in the introduction to this chapter, most key establishment protocols are supposed to reassure a party of the identity of all the other parties with which they have established a shared key. At first glance, the security model we have introduced does not appear to model attacks against the entity authentication requirements for a key establishment protocol. After all, the model appears to be only concerned with whether an attacker can distinguish a real key from a random key, a test traditionally associated with assessing confidentiality protection. However, many different types of entity authentication attack are included in this model by virtue of the way in which the model defines freshness.

Consider, for example, an attack against the origin authentication property of a protocol. In such an attack, entity B is typically convinced that they have established a key with entity A under a session identity sid, when in fact they have established a key with entity A' under the session identity sid'. Suppose the attacker makes the query Test(ID_A, ID_B, sid) and receives back either the key that B has established or a random key. The attacker can easily determine whether it has been given the real key or not by making a Reveal($ID_B, ID_{A'}, sid'$) query. This query does not contradict the definition of freshness, which forbids Reveal(ID_A, ID_B, sid)

and Reveal(ID_B, ID_A, sid) queries, and is therefore perfectly legal. Hence, the existence of an attack against origin authentication implies that the protocol is not secure in the given security model.

We may use a similar trick to demonstrate that the attacker may not replay old messages. Suppose B successfully concludes the key establishment protocol with A with the session identity sid. If a replay attack is possible, then the attacker can make the query Test(ID_A, ID_B, sid) and then force the session to expire using the Expire(ID_A, ID_B, sid) query. The attacker can then replay the messages to set up a new session with the same session key. This session can be the subject of a Reveal(ID_A, ID_B, sid) query and so the attacker can learn the correct value of the key for the test session.

11.2.5 Forward Secrecy

Forward secrecy is the idea that a session key should remain secure even if a party's long-term private key is later compromised. These attacks can easily be modeled using the Bellare–Rogaway model by allowing the attacker to query the Corrupt oracle after making the Test query; however, our model explicitly excludes these types of attack by demanding that the test session remains fresh throughout the attack game. This is purposefully done. While forward secrecy is a useful property of a key establishment scheme, it is not required by many applications and can degrade efficiency. None of the signcryption-based key establishment protocols that we will examine have forward secrecy.

11.2.6 Key Compromise Impersonation Attacks

Another interesting type of attack against the entity authentication properties of a key establishment protocol is a *key compromise impersonation* attack. In this scenario, the attacker corrupts an entity and then tries to impersonate a different entity to the corrupted entity. We may define resistance to key impersonation attacks by saying that a (possibly corrupt) party will only ever terminate successfully in a session with an uncorrupted party if there exists a matching conversation for that session. Most key establishment protocols based on signcryption techniques automatically resist key compromise attacks if the signcryption scheme is secure against unforgeability attacks made by an insider.

11.2.7 Notation

We will use the following notation in this chapter. Let A and B be two parties who wish to establish a shared key, let ID_A and ID_B be digital representations of their identities in some commonly agreed format, and let (sk_A, pk_A) and (sk_B, pk_B) be their public/private key pairs. We assume that A and B wish to establish the common key K_{AB} of length ℓ_k and that all nonces are of length ℓ_n. A nonce produced by an entity A will typically be denoted N_A.

11.3 Key Transport

A key transport protocol is a protocol in which one party generates a key and securely forwards this key to one or more recipient parties. It is simple to construct a secure key establishment protocol that combines a public key encryption scheme and a digital signature scheme, and several such protocols are contained within the ISO/IEC standard for key establishment [100]. As an example, consider Key Transport Mechanism 4 from ISO/IEC 11770-3:

1. B generates a random number (nonce) N_B and send this to B.
2. A generates a random key K_{AB} and (optionally) a nonce N_A. B sends

$$ID_B, N_A, N_B, \texttt{Encrypt}(pk_B, ID_A \| K_{AB}),$$
$$\texttt{Sign}(sk_A, ID_B \| N_A \| N_B \| \texttt{Encrypt}(pk_B, ID_A \| K_{AB}))$$

to B where $\texttt{Encrypt}_B$ denotes public key encryption under the public key of B and $\texttt{Sign}_A$ denotes a digital signature created using the private key of A.
3. B checks whether the message contains the nonce N_B, the correct identity ID_B and checks that the signature verifies (using the public key of A). If so, B decrypts the ciphertext and checks that the identity ID_A is correctly included. If so, B accepts the key K_{AB}. Otherwise, if any of the checks fail, then B rejects the key and terminates.

The message flows for this protocol are summarized in Table 11.1. The use of the nonce N_A is optional and is included to maintain consistency with other protocols. It is also worth noting that the sending of ID_B and N_B in the second message is redundant and can be omitted.

It is immediately clear that the Encrypt-then-Sign approach of the key transport mechanisms of ISO/IEC 11770-3 can be replaced with a signcryption algorithm. The resulting protocol is given in Table 11.2. The protocol not only is more efficient that the original protocol (which requires separate signing and encryption operations) but also arguably has better security properties. These better security properties arise from the fact that the signature in the original protocol only guarantees that A knows the ciphertext $\texttt{Encrypt}_B(ID_B, K_{AB})$ whereas the signcryptext attests to the fact that A knows the underlying key K_{AB}. This is conceptually stronger.

Table 11.1 ISO/IEC 11770-3 Key Transport Mechanism 4

1. $B \rightarrow A : N_B$
2. $A \rightarrow B : ID_B, N_A, N_B, \texttt{Encrypt}(pk_B, ID_A \| K_{AB}),$
   $ \texttt{Sign}(sk_A, ID_B \| N_A \| N_B \| \texttt{Encrypt}(pk_B, ID_A \| K_{AB}))$

Table 11.2 ISO/IEC 11770-3 Key Transport Mechanism 4 using signcryption

1. $B \rightarrow A : N_B$
2. $A \rightarrow B : ID_B, N_A, N_B, \texttt{Signcrypt}(sk_A, pk_B, ID_A \| ID_B \| N_A \| N_B \| K_{AB}))$

However, these protocols are vulnerable to very simple impersonation attacks. An attacker can impersonate another entity B simply by sending A a message N_B that purports to be from B. In this situation, A will generate a fresh key K_{AB} and messages that allow B to recover the key, and then terminate successfully. The attacker will then destroy these messages, leaving A under the impression that it now shares a key with B, while B is completely unaware of any protocol interaction. These attacks are trivial examples of key compromise impersonation attacks that do not even require the compromise of A's key. They can easily be avoided if B is required to prove knowledge of the key K_{AB} to A before A will successfully terminate. This requires an extra message to be sent from A to B. It is worth noting, however, that these attacks are unidirectional—it is not possible to impersonate the entity A to B even if A's long-term private key is compromised. This is because of the unforgeability properties of the signcryption scheme.

The ISO/IEC 11770-3 standard contains six key transport mechanisms. Four of these mechanisms use a Sign-then-Encrypt or Encrypt-then-Sign approach to provide authenticated encryption (see Chap. 2). We believe that all of these Sign-then-Encrypt and Encrypt-then-Sign operations could be replaced with signcryption operations with no loss of security and considerable efficiency gains.

11.4 Key Establishment Based on Zheng's Signcryption Scheme

Zheng and Imai [205, 208] have extended these basic key transport protocols in the specific case where the underlying signcryption scheme is the original Zheng signcryption scheme (see Sects. 3.3 and 4.3). These protocols make efficiency savings by observing two things: first, that there is no need to include identifiers in the message field if the protocol automatically identifies the participants and, second, there is no need to include the nonce in the message field if the generated key depends upon the nonce. Both of these improvements reduce the length of the message that needs to be encrypted and, thus, save computation time. This led to the development of the two protocols shown in Tables 11.3 and 11.4.

Note that in the DKTUN protocol, A has complete control over the key value; while in the IKTUN protocol, A only has a limited form of key control (assuming that the hash function is one-way). In the IKTUN protocol, A may not choose the value of the shared key K_{AB} directly, but may repeatedly choose values for k until K_{AB} is of a useful form. On average, one would expect A to have to choose 2^s different values of k in order to fix s bits of information in K_{AB}. This is a common trade-off in key agreement protocols and was first noted by Mitchell et al. [142]. Again, both of these protocols are susceptible to impersonation attacks in which an attacker masquerades as B in the protocol by sending a nonce value to A. It does not seem possible for an attacker to impersonate A.

Table 11.3 Zheng's DKTUN (Direct Key Transport Using a Nonce) protocol

A		B
$K_{AB} \xleftarrow{R} \{0,1\}^{\ell_k}$	$\xleftarrow{\quad N_B \quad}$	$N_B \xleftarrow{R} \{0,1\}^{\ell_n}$
$k \xleftarrow{R} \mathbb{Z}_q$		
$(k_1, k_2) \leftarrow hash_1(pk_B^k)$		
$c \leftarrow \text{Enc}_{k_1}(K_{AB})$		
$r \leftarrow hash_2(k_2, K_{AB}, N_B)$		
$s \leftarrow k/(r + sk_A) \bmod q$	$\xrightarrow{\quad c,r,s \quad}$	$(k_1, k_2) \leftarrow hash_1((pk_A \cdot g^r)^{s \cdot sk_B})$
		$K_{AB} \leftarrow \text{Dec}_{k_1}(c)$
		Accept K_{AB} if $hash_2(k_2, K_{AB}, N_B) = r$

Table 11.4 Zheng's IKTUN (Indirect Key Transport Using a Nonce) protocol

A		B
$k \xleftarrow{R} \mathbb{Z}_q$	$\xleftarrow{\quad N_B \quad}$	$N_B \xleftarrow{R} \{0,1\}^{\ell_n}$
$(K_{AB}, k_2) \leftarrow hash_1(pk_B^k)$		
$r \leftarrow hash_2(k_2, K_{AB}, N_B)$		
$s \leftarrow k/(r + sk_A) \bmod q$	$\xrightarrow{\quad r,s \quad}$	$(K_{AB}, k_2) \leftarrow hash_1((pk_A \cdot g^r)^{s \cdot sk_B})$
		Accept K_{AB} if $hash_2(k_2, K_{AB}, N_B) = r$

Zheng and Imai [205, 208] also propose a key agreement protocol based on two (almost) independent executions of the DKTUN protocol. The protocol is given in Table 11.5. It should be noted that the DKEUN protocol, as it stands, is not a key agreement protocol. Since B has complete knowledge of K_A when choosing K_B, B can arrange the shared key value K_{AB} to be any value of his choice by setting $K_B = K_{AB} \oplus K_A$. This can be avoided by setting the shared key to be $K_{AB} = hash'(K_A, K_B)$, where $hash'$ is an independent hash function, although even this protocol would be subject to the Mitchell et al. [142] attack previously mentioned. This protocol does not appear to be vulnerable to the impersonation attacks to which the simpler protocols are vulnerable, nor does it appear to be vulnerable to key compromise impersonation attacks.

Kim and Youm [116] propose a similar, yet simplified protocol. The protocol is given in Table 11.6. Unlike the Zheng DKEUN protocol, this protocol is subject to an impersonation attack. The attack requires the attacker to observe the first message (c, r, s) from a legitimate protocol execution and then replay it. This causes B to successfully terminate without a partner. It is also slightly worrying, from a conceptual point of view, that the secret value k_1 is used for two separate purposes: it is used as a random seed for the blinding factor $hash_2(ID_A, ID_B, k_1)$ and it is also used to "select" a hash function when computing the checksum value $\delta \leftarrow hash_4(k_1, \sigma)$.

11.5 Key Agreement Based on Signcryption KEMs

The idea of formalizing public key encryption to an asymmetric *key encapsulation mechanism (KEM)* and a symmetric *data encapsulation mechanism (DEM)* was first put forward by Cramer and Shoup [68]. Since the KEM allows one user to

Table 11.5 Zheng's DKEUN (Direct Key Exchange Using a Nonce) protocol

A		B
$K_A \xleftarrow{R} \{0, 1\}^{\ell_k}$	$\xleftarrow{N_B}$	$N_B \xleftarrow{R} \{0, 1\}^{\ell_n}$
$k \xleftarrow{R} \mathbb{Z}_q$		
$(k_1, k_2) \leftarrow hash_1(pk_B^k)$		
$c \leftarrow Enc_{k_1}(K_A)$		
$r \leftarrow hash_2(k_2, K_A, N_B)$		
$s \leftarrow k/(r + sk_A) \bmod q$	$\xrightarrow{c, r, s}$	$(k_1, k_2) \leftarrow hash_1((pk_A \cdot g^r)^{s \cdot sk_B})$
		$K_A \leftarrow Dec_{k_1}(c)$
		Accept K_A if $hash_2(k_2, K_A, N_B) = r$
		$K_B \xleftarrow{R} \{0, 1\}^{\ell_k}$
		$k' \xleftarrow{R} \mathbb{Z}_q$
		$(k_1', k_2') \leftarrow hash_1(pk_A^{k'})$
		$c' \leftarrow Enc_{k_1'}(K_B)$
		$r' \leftarrow hash_2(k_2', K_B, K_A)$
		$s' \leftarrow k'/(r' + sk_B) \bmod q$
$(k_1', k_2') \leftarrow hash_1((pk_B \cdot g^{r'})^{s' \cdot sk_A})$	$\xleftarrow{c', r', s'}$	$K_{AB} \leftarrow K_A \oplus K_B$
$K_B \leftarrow Dec_{k_1'}(c')$		
Accept K_B if		
$\quad hash_2(k_2', K_B, K_A) = r'$		
$K_{AB} \leftarrow K_A \oplus K_B$		

Table 11.6 Kim and Youm's SAKE protocol

A		B
$k \xleftarrow{R} \mathbb{Z}_q$		
$(k_1, k_2) \leftarrow hash_1(pk_B^k)$		
$c \leftarrow hash_2(ID_A, ID_B, k_1) \cdot g^k$		
$r \leftarrow hash_3(k_2, c)$		
$s \leftarrow k/(r + sk_A) \bmod q$	$\xrightarrow{c, r, s}$	$(k_1, k_2) \leftarrow hash_1((pk_A \cdot g^r)^{s \cdot sk_B})$
		Accept c if $hash_3(k_2, c) = r$
		$k' \xleftarrow{R} \mathbb{Z}_q$
		$\mu \leftarrow g^{k'}$
		$\sigma \leftarrow (c/hash_2(ID_A, ID_B, k_1))^{k'}$
		$\delta \leftarrow hash_3(k_1, \sigma)$
$\sigma \leftarrow \mu^k$	$\xleftarrow{\mu, \delta}$	$K_{AB} \leftarrow hash_4(\sigma)$
Accept σ if $hash_3(k_1, \sigma) = \delta$		
$K_{AB} \leftarrow hash_4(\sigma)$		

securely generate and transport a symmetric key to another user, it is tempting to think that KEMs provide a good basis for building key establishment protocols; however, while KEMs and key establishment protocols are often based on the same techniques, a KEM is only required to transport a key in a confidential manner. The KEM does not provide any entity authentication or freshness guarantees.

11.5.1 Key Agreement Based on Signcryption KEMs

Dent [73] has suggested that signcryption KEMs are a more appropriate choice for constructing a key establishment protocol. A signcryption KEM (with outsider security—see Chap. 7) can provide both confidentiality protection and origin authentication. Dent [73] proposed a simple protocol to add freshness guarantees via the use of a MAC value computed on a nonce (see Sect. 1.3.5). The protocol is given in Table 11.7. We note that the Dent protocol is subject to the same simple impersonation against A that many of the other protocols in this chapter have also been vulnerable. In this attack, A is given an adversarially generated nonce N_B and terminates successfully after outputting (C, tag) despite the fact that B has no matching conversation. More interestingly, as Dent's proposed protocol only required the use of an outsider-secure signcryption KEM, the protocol does not guarantee security against key compromise impersonation attacks that allow us to impersonate an entity A to B (see Sect. 11.2.6). This attack takes advantage of the fact that an outsider-secure signcryption KEM may allow an attacker to forge a valid encapsulation given the recipient's private key. We use this to launch attack against the party B in the protocol by forging the signcryptext C and the MAC value tag.

Note that this protocol allows the session identity sid to be chosen by the outside application that is using the key establishment protocol: the protocol does not choose or alter the given session identity in any way. This will be true for almost all of the key establishment protocols described in this Chapter—the only exception being the Gorantla et al. protocol discussed below.

Gorantla et al. [92] prove a series of interesting results about one-pass key agreement protocols (i.e., protocols which consist of a single message passed from A to B). First, they prove that any secure one-pass key agreement protocol provides an outsider-secure signcryption KEM (see Sect. 7.3) and use this result to give a new outsider-secure signcryption KEM based on the HMQV protocol [118]. Second, they show that any outsider-secure signcryption KEM can be used as a one-pass key agreement protocol. The construction is given in Table 11.8.

Table 11.7 Key establishment using a signcryption KEM

A		B
$(K_{AB}, C) \xleftarrow{R} Encap(sk_A, pk_B)$	$\xleftarrow{N_B}$	$N_B \xleftarrow{R} \{0, 1\}^{\ell_n}$
$\tau = (N_B, sid)$		
$tag \leftarrow MAC_{K_{AB}}(N_B)$	$\xrightarrow{C, tag}$	$K_{AB} \leftarrow Decap(pk_A, sk_B, C)$
		Accept K_{AB} if $MAC_{K_{AB}}(N_B) = tag$

Table 11.8 Key establishment using a signcryption KEM

A		B
$(K_{AB}, C) \xleftarrow{R} Encap(sk_A, pk_B)$	$\xrightarrow{C}$	$K_{AB} \leftarrow Decap(pk_A, sk_B, C)$

Theorem 11.1 *If a signcryption KEM is outsider secure (see Sect. 7.3.2) then the Gorantla et al. key establishment protocol is secure in a security model in which the attacker makes no* Expire *queries and in which the session identity is defined to be the ciphertext C.*

More formally, if there exists an attacker $\mathcal{A}$ against the key establishment protocol with advantage $Adv_{\mathcal{A}}^{KEP}(k)$ that makes at most q_{query} queries to the Query *oracle and at most q_{send} queries to the* Send *oracle, then there exists an attacker $\mathcal{B}$ against the LoR security of the signcryption KEM with advantage $Adv_{\mathcal{B}}^{LoR}(k)$ and an attacker $\mathcal{B}'$ against the outsider FEO/FUO-IND-CCA2 security of the signcryption KEM with advantage $Adv_{\mathcal{B}'}^{IND}(k)$ such that*

$$Adv_{\mathcal{A}}^{KEP} \leq \frac{1}{q_{query}^2}Adv_{\mathcal{B}}^{LoR}(k) + \frac{1}{q_{query}^2 q_{send}}Adv_{\mathcal{B}'}^{IND}(k) \qquad (11.2)$$

Initially, it may appear as if the Gorantla et al. protocol is insecure as it does not provide freshness guarantees. It is certainly possible to replay ciphertexts from A to B. The proof of security is made possible by a technical detail in the security model: the definition of C as the session identity and the inability of the attacker to expire sessions. These combine to mean that the attacker cannot re-submit a ciphertext C to entity B as this would involve sending a new message to a completed session (with session identity C). Hence, replay attacks are forbidden. This "trick" of avoiding replays by defining the session identity to be the concatenation of all messages sent in the protocol is widely used in the cryptographic literature. In practice, however, this translates to a requirement that entity B remembers all valid ciphertexts C that have been submitted to it as part of the key establishment protocol and rejects any attempt to re-use an old ciphertext. This may require large amounts of memory storage and may significantly increase the processing time for the protocol. Hence, it is unlikely to be useful for general security applications.

Lastly, we note that the results of Gorantla et al. are slightly more stronger than is proven in Theorem 11.1. The authors actually prove the theorem using a weaker notion of unforgeability than left-or-right security (see the discussions on the subject of unforgeability in Sect. 7.3.2) in which the attacker wins if it can produce a valid encapsulation C from A to B which has not been produced by A. This notion of security is implied by left-or-right security but is strictly weaker than it.

11.5.2 Key Agreement Based on Signcryption Tag-KEMs

Bjørstad and Dent [37] extended the idea of using signcryption KEMs to build key establishment protocols to give a generic protocol in which the nonce value was directly involved in the computation of the shared key via a signcryption tag-KEM (see Chap. 7). The protocol that Bjørstad and Dent propose runs as follows:

1. B generates a nonce $N_B \overset{R}{\leftarrow} \{0, 1\}^{\ell_n}$ of an agreed length and sends N_B to A.
2. A computes $(K_{AB}, \omega) \overset{R}{\leftarrow} Sym(sk_A, pk_B)$ and $C \overset{R}{\leftarrow} Encap(\omega, \tau)$ where τ is the unique tag given by $\tau = (N_B, sid)$. A accepts K_{AB} as the shared key and sends C to B.

Table 11.9 Key establishment using a signcryption tag-KEM

A		B
$(K_{AB}, \omega) \overset{R}{\leftarrow} Sym(sk_A, pk_B)$	$\overset{N_B}{\longleftarrow}$	$N_B \overset{R}{\leftarrow} \{0, 1\}^{\ell_n}$
$\tau = (N_B, sid)$		
$C \overset{R}{\leftarrow} Encap(\omega, \tau)$	$\overset{C}{\longrightarrow}$	$\tau = (N_B, sid)$
		$K_{AB} \leftarrow Decap(pk_A, sk_B, C, \tau)$

3. B computes the key $K_{AB} \leftarrow Decap(pk_A, sk_B, C, \tau)$ using the tag $\tau = (N_B, sid)$ and accepts this as the shared key if $K_{AB} \neq \perp$.

This protocol is summarized in Table 11.9. Since a signcryption tag-KEM is a simpler mechanism than a signcryption scheme, it is hoped that this protocol will provide a simple and flexible method to provide key establishment. It is of particular use in situations where signcryption tag-KEMs are also being used to provide authenticated encryption directly.

We note that this protocol is still vulnerable to the simple impersonation attack discussed in which an attacker masquerades as entity B to A. It does not appear to be vulnerable to simple impersonation or key compromise impersonation attacks in which the attacker masquerades as A to B. Furthermore, this protocol is provably secure in the security model of Sect. 11.2.3. The formal proof is given in Sect. 11.5.3, but the proof basically works in three steps:

1. We show that it is practically impossible for an attacker to find two legitimate sessions that have the same nonce or guess the value of a nonce used in a particular session in advance. Both of these situations lead to trivial attacks against the scheme and both can be prevented by insisting that ℓ_n be sufficiently large so that the number of possible nonces far exceeds the number of possible sessions.
2. We show that if an entity B successfully terminates a session, then there must be a matching conversation from the entity A with the same session identity. Since entity B only terminates after receiving a valid encapsulation for the tag $\tau = (N_B, sid)$ and every nonce that B generates must be different, any encapsulation that causes B to successfully terminate must either be from a matching conversation or must be a forgery. Since it is practically impossible to forge an encapsulation, we deduce that the encapsulation must have come from a matching conversation.
3. We show that an attacker that distinguishes between a real or random key in the Test session is actually deciding whether that key is random or the key one would obtain if one decapsulated C. Since the signcryption tag-KEM is IND-CCA2 secure, this is not possible. Hence, the key establishment protocol is secure.

It is interesting to note that if one instantiates the key establishment protocol given by Bjørstad and Dent [37] with the Zheng-based signcryption tag-KEM given in the same paper, then the resulting protocol (shown in Table 11.10) is strikingly similar to the IKTUN protocol given by Zheng and Imai [205, 208] and discussed in Sect. 11.4.

Table 11.10 Key establishment using Zheng's signcryption tag-KEM

A		B
$k \xleftarrow{R} \mathbb{Z}_q$	$\xleftarrow{N_B}$	$N_B \xleftarrow{R} \{0,1\}^{\ell_n}$
$k_1 \leftarrow pk_B^k$		
$r \leftarrow hash_1(N_B \| sid \| pk_A \| pk_B \| k_1)$		
$s \leftarrow k/(r + sk_A)$		
$K_{AB} \leftarrow hash_2(k_1)$	$\xrightarrow{r,s}$	$k_1 \leftarrow (pk_A \cdot g^r)^{s \cdot sk_B}$
		Accept k_1 if
		$\quad hash_1(N_B \| sid \| pk_A$
		$\quad \| pk_B \| k_1) = r$
		$K_{AB} \leftarrow hash_2(k_1)$

11.5.3 Security Proof for the Bjørstad–Dent Protocol

In this section we present the formal security proof for the Bjørstad–Dent key establishment protocol. The proof is somewhat complex and may be omitted on a first reading of this chapter.

Theorem 11.2 *Let* $(Setup, KeyGen_S, KeyGen_R, Sym, Encap, Decap)$ *be a signcryption tag-KEM scheme and let* $\mathcal{A}$ *be an attacker against the key establishment protocol using this signcryption tag-KEM that makes at most* q_{query} *queries to the* Query *oracle,* q_{send} *queries to the* Send *oracle, and has advantage* $Adv_{\mathcal{A}}^{KEP}(k)$.

Then there exists an attacker $\mathcal{B}$ *against the unforgeability of the signcryption tag-KEM with advantage* $Adv_{\mathcal{B}}^{forge}(k)$ *and an attacker* $\mathcal{B}'$ *against the IND-CCA2 property of the signcryption tag-KEM in the multi-user model with an advantage* $Adv_{\mathcal{B}'}^{SCTK}(k)$ *such that*

$$Adv_{\mathcal{B}'}^{SCTK}(k) + \frac{1}{q_{send}} Adv_{\mathcal{B}}^{forge}(k) \geq \frac{1}{q_{send} q_{query}^2} \left\{ Adv_{\mathcal{A}}^{KEP}(k) - \frac{q_{send}^2}{2^{\ell_n - 1}} \right\} \quad (11.3)$$

Proof Let $\mathcal{A}$ be any polynomial-time attacker against the key establishment protocol. By definition, $\mathcal{A}$ has advantage $Adv_{\mathcal{A}}^{KEP}(k)$ in breaking the key establishment protocol in the model given in Sect. 11.2.3. Our proof works in two stages. First, we alter the model in which $\mathcal{A}$ runs in a series of successive steps and at each step deduce a lower bound for the advantage that $\mathcal{A}$ has in this new security model. Second, we show that the advantage that $\mathcal{A}$ has in this altered security model is directly related to the advantage that another attacker $\mathcal{B}'$ has in breaking the IND-CCA2 security of the signcryption tag-KEM. Thus, we will be able to conclude that the key establishment protocol is secure whenever the signcryption tag-KEM is secure.

We will prove this result using some basic techniques of game hopping [34, 180]. We will propose a sequence of security models (games) in which $\mathcal{A}$ will be run. Let W_i be the probability that $\mathcal{A}$ wins the Game i and let Adv_i be $\mathcal{A}$'s advantage in Game i.

Game 1: This is the normal security for a key establishment protocol (as described in Sect. 11.2.3). Hence, $Adv_1 = Adv_{\mathcal{A}}^{KEP}(k)$.

Game 2: In this game we change very slightly the way that we determine whether $\mathcal{A}$ wins the game or not. We change the game so that if $\mathcal{A}$ causes an entity B to start two sessions (with $\mathtt{Send}(ID_A, ID_B, sid, \lambda)$ commands) that output the same nonce, then the attacker is automatically deemed to have lost the game. In particular, this means that the test session must use a nonce value that is different from those used in any other session.[1]

Let E be the event that this occurs and note that $Pr[E] \leq q_{send}^2/2^{\ell_n}$. Note also that Game 1 and Game 2 are identical unless E occurs. The following is a well-established lemma in game hopping theory:

Lemma 11.1 *Let A, B, and E be events in the same probability space for which* $A \wedge \neg E = B \wedge \neg E$. *Then* $|Pr[A] - Pr[B]| \leq Pr[E]$.

Hence, we have that $|\mathrm{Pr}[W_1] - \mathrm{Pr}[W_2]| \leq \mathrm{Pr}[E]$ and so that

$$Adv_2 \geq Adv_1 - q_{send}^2/2^{\ell_n} \tag{11.4}$$

Game 3 We have now prevented the possibility of the attacker being able to break the scheme because B outputs the same nonce twice. We must also show that it is not possible for the attacker to guess a nonce in advance, as this also leads to an attack.[2] We therefore declare an attacker to have immediately lost the game if it begins a session with entity B (with a $\mathtt{Send}(ID_A, ID_B, sid, \lambda)$ query) that outputs a nonce that has previously been input to the start of a session with an entity A (with a $\mathtt{Send}(ID_B, ID_A, sid, N)$ query). Let E be the event that this occurs and note that $\mathrm{Pr}[E] \leq q_{send}^2/2^{\ell_n}$. Hence, by Lemma 11.1, we have that

$$Adv_3 \geq Adv_2 - q_{send}^2/2^{\ell_n}$$

---

[1] We note that if an attacker can arrange for two sessions to have the same nonce, then this attacker can break the scheme. The attacker starts a series of new sessions between A and B using a single session identity sid. If the nonce that B outputs is fresh (i.e., different from all previous nonces) then the attacker passes this nonce to B, who outputs an encapsulation. The attacker then reveals the session key for this session; records the nonce, encapsulation, and key; expires both A and Bs sessions; and repeats the process. If the nonce that is output is not fresh, then the attacker finds the corresponding encapsulation with the same nonce from his records and submits this to B as A's response. The attacker makes this the test session; however, the attacker already knows this session key from the earlier reveal query.

[2] In this attack, $\mathcal{A}$ generates $q_{send}/2$ distinct nonces, queries an entity A with each nonce using the $\mathtt{Send}$ oracle, stores the associated encapsulation C, obtains the session key for each session using the $\mathtt{Reveal}$ oracle, and then expires the session. Each key is stored with the appropriate encapsulation and nonce. $\mathcal{A}$ then starts $q_{send}/2$ distinct sessions with an entity B. If the entity outputs a nonce different to any of those generated in the first phase, then the attacker expires the session. If B outputs a nonce which is the same as one that the attacker generated in the first phase, then the attacker responds using the appropriate encapsulation and declares this to be the $\mathtt{Test}$ session. Since the attacker already knows the key associated with the encapsulation, the attacker can trivially win the game.

Game 4: We now attempt to guess the identity of the identities who will act as A and B in the test session. Since we assume that the namespace S is too large for us to guess the names of these entities directly, we instead guess which query to the Query oracle will be about these entities. (Note that we are making the assumption that A will always query the Query oracle on the identities that it intends to use in the test session.) If we guess incorrectly, then game immediately halts and the attacker is declared to have won with probability exactly 1/2 (i.e., with no advantage).

To guess the identity of A and B, the game randomly chooses values $i_A, i_B \in \{1, 2, \ldots, q_{query}\}$ where q_{query} is maximum number of queries that A may make to the Query oracle. We define A^* to be the entity about which the i_A-th query is made and B^* to be the entity about which the i_B-th query is made. If the attacker does not choose A^* to act as A and B^* to act as B in the test session, then the game immediately halts and A is assumed to have output a random value $b' \xleftarrow{R} \{0, 1\}$ as its guess for b. Hence, in this case, A will win with probability 1/2.

Note that the probability that the game correctly guesses A^* and B^* is $1/q_{query}^2$ and that the event that this happens is independent of any of A's actions (including whether A wins Game 3 or not). Let E be this event. We have that

$$Adv_4 = |\Pr[W_4] - 1/2| \tag{11.5}$$
$$= |\Pr[W_4|E]\Pr[E] + \Pr[W_4|\neg E]\Pr[\neg E] - 1/2| \tag{11.6}$$
$$= |\Pr[W_4|E]\Pr[E] + \Pr[\neg E]/2 - 1/2| \tag{11.7}$$
$$= |\Pr[W_4|E]\Pr[E] - \Pr[E]/2| \tag{11.8}$$
$$= |\Pr[W_3|E]\Pr[E] - \Pr[E]/2| \tag{11.9}$$
$$= |\Pr[W_3]\Pr[E] - \Pr[E]/2| \tag{11.10}$$
$$= \Pr[E] \cdot |\Pr[W_3] - 1/2| \tag{11.11}$$
$$= \Pr[E] \cdot Adv_3 \tag{11.12}$$
$$= Adv_3/q_{query}^2 \tag{11.13}$$

Equation (11.9) derives from the fact that Game 3 and Game 4 are identical if E occurs. Equation (11.10) derives from the fact that W_3 and E are independent. Hence, $Adv_4 = Adv_3/q_{query}^2$.

Game 5: We now consider the test session. Since the owner of the test session must successfully terminate, there are two possibilities:

- A^* is the owner of the test session—i.e., the attacker defines the test session using the query $\mathrm{Test}(ID_{B^*}, ID_{A^*}, sid^*)$. In this case, A^* will have received a nonce N^*, output an encapsulation C^* and terminated successfully. In this situation, we cannot be sure that the nonce that A^* received is the same nonce as B^* sent nor even that B^* output a nonce for use in this session at all.
- B^* is the owner of the test session—i.e., the attacker defines the test session using the query $\mathrm{Test}(ID_{A^*}, ID_{B^*}, sid^*)$. In this case, B^* will have initially output a random nonce $N_{B^*}^*$ (different from any other nonce used in the game), received

an encapsulation C^*, successfully recovered a key from C^*, and successfully terminated.

It is this second case with which we are concerned now. We claim that if the encapsulation C^* was not produced by entity A^* using the nonce N^*_{B*} and the session identity sid^*, then it is highly unlikely for B^* to have terminated successfully. In other words, B^* is unlikely to successfully terminate the test session unless A^* holds a matching conversation. This is because, if these circumstances do not hold, then C^* is a forged encapsulation and we know that forgeries are practically impossible due to the security properties of the signcryption tag-KEM (see Chap. 7).

Let E be the event that B^* successfully terminates in the test session but that A^* does not have a session with a matching conversation. If E occurs, then the game aborts and assumes that $\mathcal{A}$ has lost. If E does not occur, then the game continues as normal; hence, $W_5 \land \neg E = W_4 \land \neg E$. By Lemma 11.1, we have

$$|\Pr[W_5] - \Pr[W_4]| \leq \Pr[E]$$

and so we can conclude that $Adv_5 \geq Adv_4 - Pr[E]$.

It therefore remains to bound $Pr[E]$. We do this by noting several things. First, we must have that the nonce used in the test session must not have been output by B^* prior to the test session (due to the restriction given in Game 1) and cannot have been input to A^* before it was output by B^* (due to the restriction given in Game 2). Thus, since there exists no matching conversation, A^* cannot have output the encapsulation C^* computed using the tag $\tau^* = (N^*_{B*}, sid^*)$ at any point before the Test query is made.

We are now in a position to describe the attacker $\mathcal{B}$ against the unforgeability of the signcryption tag-KEM. Recall that in a signcryption tag-KEM there, an entity has two key pairs. A complete set of key pairs for an entity A compromises of a pair of sender keys $(sk^S_A, pk^S_A) \xleftarrow{R} \text{KeyGen}_S(param)$ that are used when A wishes to send messages and a pair of receiver keys $(sk^R_A, pk^R_A) \xleftarrow{R} \text{KeyGen}_R(param)$ that are used when A wishes to receive messages. Recall further that in the security model for unforgeability, $\mathcal{B}$ takes as input the global parameters $param$ and a sender public key pk^S_*.

$\mathcal{B}$ runs as follows. First, it generates random integers $i_A, i_B \xleftarrow{R} \{1, 2, \ldots, q_{query}\}$. We will arrange that pk^S_* to be the sender public key for A^*. $\mathcal{B}$ runs the attacker $\mathcal{A}$ on the input $(param, 1^k)$. During its execution, $\mathcal{A}$ has access to the following oracles (which are simulated for $\mathcal{A}$ by $\mathcal{B}$):

- Query(ID_A): If this is not the i_A-th query to this oracle, then the oracle generates key pairs $(sk^S_A, pk^S_A) \xleftarrow{R} KeyGen_S(param)$ and $(sk^R_A, pk^R_A) \xleftarrow{R} KeyGen_R(param)$ and returns the public keys (pk^S_A, pk^R_A). The private keys are stored for later use.

    If this is the i_A-th query to the oracle, then the oracle sets $pk^S_A \leftarrow pk^S_*$ (the challenge public key), computes the receiver keys $(sk^R_A, pk^R_A) \xleftarrow{R} KeyGen_R(param)$, and returns the public keys (pk_A^S, pk_A^R). The receiver private key is stored for later use.

- Send(ID_A, ID_B, sid, m): If this query does not have $B = A^*$ (i.e., if B is not required to simulate A^*'s output) then B can answer any query using its knowledge of the private keys.

    If $B = A^*$ and the query relates to either the first or the third message in the protocol (i.e., the queries in which A^* will be acting as B in the protocol execution), then B can answer any query using knowledge of A^*'s private receiver key.

    If $B = A^*$ and the query relates to the second message in the protocol (i.e., the query is one in which A^* will be acting as A in the protocol execution), then B can compute A^*'s response using the flexible encapsulation oracle.

Note that in all of these cases, if a session terminates successfully, then we are able to compute the session key for that session. These keys are stored for later use.

- Expire(ID_A, ID_B, sid): This oracle forces a session to expire. B simply makes a note of the session expiration and responds to further Send queries as if they were part of a new session.
- Reveal(ID_A, ID_B, sid): The oracle returns the key of the successfully terminated session (apart from the test session). This is easily done as we will have calculated the session key each party computes in any session that has successfully concluded; hence, we simply return this session key value.
- Corrupt(ID_A): If $A \neq A^*$ then B can return the private key values for A that were generated during the Query query. If $A = A^*$ then B must have guessed the identity of A^* incorrectly (i.e., A^* will not be acting as A in the test session) and so B aborts the simulation and outputs $\perp$.
- Test(ID_A, ID_B, sid): If A queries this oracle for any session which does not have A^* acting as A and B^* acting as B, then B aborts the simulation and outputs $\perp$.

    If the test session is against A^*, then B aborts and outputs $\perp$.

    If the test session is against B^* and the encapsulation C^* that B^* receives does not come from a matching conversation with A^*, then B aborts the simulation and outputs C^* as a forgery.

    Otherwise B aborts and outputs $\perp$.

If A terminates and outputs a bit b, then B outputs $\perp$.

Note that B successfully simulates all the oracles available to A in Game 4 and Game 5 (up until the point that A makes a Test query). Note further that if E occurs (i.e., the test session is against B^* and involves an encapsulation C^* which has not been output by A^* in a matching conversation), then B outputs C^* as a forgery. Since A^* cannot have output an encapsulation C^* computed using the tag τ^*, we know that the encapsulation C^* cannot have been returned by the signcryption tag-KEM's encapsulation oracle. Hence, if E occurs, then C^* is a valid forgery, which implies that

$$\Pr[E] \leq Adv_{\mathcal{B}}^{\texttt{forge}}(k)$$

and so that $Adv_5 \geq Adv_4 - Adv_{\mathcal{B}}^{\texttt{forge}}(k)$.

Game 6: We are now in a very strong position. We know that the game has guessed the identities of A^* and B^* in the test session. Furthermore, we know that the encapsulation C^* used in the test session is the encapsulation output by A^* regardless of whether the test session targets A^* or B^*. In this game, we attempt to guess which of A^*'s sessions will correspond to the test session, i.e.,

- if the test session is against A^*, then we attempt to guess the test session,
- if the test session is against B^*, then we attempt to guess the matching conversation that A^* has for the test session.

We do this by selecting a random value $j \xleftarrow{R} \{1, 2, \ldots, q_{send}\}$. This value will correctly identify the test session with probability $1/q_{send}$ and the event that the correct session is identified is independent of any of $\mathcal{A}$'s actions. Hence, by the same arguments as in Game 4, we have that

$$Adv_6 = Adv_5/q_{send}$$

The reduction: We are now in a position to relate the advantage of the attacker $\mathcal{A}$ in Game 6 to that of an attacker $\mathcal{B}'$ (which we will construct) against the IND-CCA2 properties of the signcryption tag-KEM (see Chap. 7). The assumption that the signcryption tag-KEM is secure in the IND-CCA2 model will then allow us to conclude that the key establishment protocol is secure. The proof is similar to that given in Game 5.

Recall that in the IND-CCA2 security model for a multi-user signcryption tag-KEM, the game chooses a public key pk_*^R which is to be used when computing the challenge encapsulation. The attacker $\mathcal{B}'$ takes as input the global parameter information *param* and the receiver's public key pk_*^R as input.

The algorithm $\mathcal{B}'$ takes as input the receiver public key pk_*^R and the global information *param* for the system. $\mathcal{B}'$ picks random values $i_A, i_B \xleftarrow{R} \{1, 2, \ldots, q_{query}\}$ and $j \xleftarrow{R} \{1, 2, \ldots, q_{send}\}$ and runs the attacker $\mathcal{A}$ on the input *param*. $\mathcal{B}'$ answers $\mathcal{A}$'s oracle query as follows:

- Query(ID_B): If this is not the i_B-th query to this oracle, then the oracle generates key pairs $(sk_B^S, pk_B^S) \xleftarrow{R} KeyGen_S(param)$ and $(sk_B^R, pk_B^R) \xleftarrow{R} KeyGen_R(param)$ and returns the public keys (pk_B^S, pk_B^R). The private keys are stored for later use.
  If this is the i_B-th query to this oracle, then $\mathcal{B}'$ sets $pk_{B*}^R = pk_*^R$ (the challenge key), generates a sender key pair $(sk_{B*}^S, pk_{B*}^S) \xleftarrow{R} KeyGen_S(param)$, and returns the public keys (pk_{B*}^S, pk_{B*}^R).
- Send(ID_A, ID_B, sid, m): If this query does not relate to the j-th session and the entity B^* is not acting as B in the session, then the response of this oracle can easily be computed using knowledge of the private keys for A and B.

If this query does not relate to the j-th session and the entity B^* is acting as B in the session, then the response for a message $\text{Send}(ID_A, ID_{B^*}, sid, m)$ can be computed using the flexible decapsulation oracle. Note that due to the restrictions we have placed on the nonces output by B^* in Game 1 mean that B' will never make an illegal decapsulation oracle query on (C^*, τ^*).

Furthermore, note that for any session that terminates successfully, except for the test session, the above response will result in B' computing the correct shared secret key K_{AB}. This is stored for later use.

The situation is more complicated when dealing with the j-th session. If the j-th session is not a session owned by A^* and in communication with B^*, then B' aborts the simulation and outputs a random bit $b' \xleftarrow{R} \{0, 1\}$. Otherwise, B' arranges for the response to be the challenge encapsulation. B' does this by requesting a key K^* from the IND-CCA2 game, then outputting the tag $\tau^* = (N^*_{B^*}, sid^*)$ to the IND-CCA2 game and receiving back a challenge encapsulation C^* for that tag. B' returns C^* to $\mathcal{A}$.

- $\text{Expire}(ID_A, ID_B, sid)$: This oracle forces a session to expire. B simply makes a note of the expiry of the session and responds to further $\text{Send}(ID_A, ID_B, sid, m)$ queries as if they were part of a new session.
- $\text{Reveal}(ID_A, ID_B, sid)$: This oracle returns the key of a successfully terminated session (apart from the test session). Note that, except in the case of the test session, this key will have been successfully computed and stored as the result of an earlier Send query. Hence, B' returns this stored key value. If $\mathcal{A}$ makes a Reveal query on the test session, then we must have incorrectly guessed the test session and so B' aborts the simulation and outputs a random bit $b' \xleftarrow{R} \{0, 1\}$.
- $\text{Corrupt}(ID_B)$: If $B \neq B^*$ then B' can return the correct private key values (sk_B^S, sk_B^R) from the list of key values it generated earlier. If $B = B^*$ then we must have incorrectly guessed the identity B^* and so B' aborts the simulation and outputs a random bit $b' \xleftarrow{R} \{0, 1\}$.
- $\text{Test}(ID_A, ID_B, sid)$: If this query refers to any session other than the session corresponding to the j-th session (i.e., if the test query targets A^* then the session should be the j-th session; if the test query targets B^* then the session should be the matching conversation to the j-th session) then we have incorrectly guessed the test session and B' terminates by outputting a random guess $b' \xleftarrow{R} \{0, 1\}$ for b. Otherwise, B' returns K^* (the challenge key obtained from the jth session) to $\mathcal{A}$.

$\mathcal{A}$ eventually terminates and outputs a guess b' for b. At this point, B' also outputs the bit b' and terminates.

B' accurately simulates the oracles available to $\mathcal{A}$ in Game 6. Furthermore, if $\mathcal{A}$ successfully wins Game 6, then B' wins the IND-CCA2 signcryption tag-KEM game. Hence,

$$Adv_{B'}^{\text{SCTK}}(k) \geq Adv_6$$

and so

$$Adv_{\mathcal{B}'}^{\text{SCTK}}(k) + \frac{1}{q_{send}} Adv_{\mathcal{B}}^{\text{forge}}(k) \geq \frac{1}{q_{send}q_{query}^2}\left\{Adv_{\mathcal{A}}^{\text{KEP}}(k) - \frac{q_{send}^2}{2^{\ell_n-1}}\right\}$$

Hence, the theorem holds.   □

It is worth pointing out that it is likely that the efficiency of this reduction can be improved by a more advanced proof. In particular, we believe that the reduction can be improved to

$$Adv_{\mathcal{B}'}^{\text{SCTK}}(k) \geq \frac{1}{q_{send}q_{query}}\left\{Adv_{\mathcal{A}}^{\text{KEP}}(k) - \frac{q_{send}^2}{2^{\ell_n}}\right\} - \frac{1}{q_{send}} Adv_{\mathcal{B}}^{\text{forge}}(k)$$

11.6 Key Establishment Based on Timestamps

This chapter has concentrated on key establishment protocols that assure freshness using nonces; however, freshness can be guaranteed in other ways. One other common method for assuring freshness is the use of timestamps. A timestamp is simply a piece of data recording the time and date that a message was created. Any entity that receives such a message can then verify that it is fresh by checking the time and date attached to that message. Obviously, it transmitted in an integrity protected form or it can be altered by an attacker (which leads to a variety of dangers including replay attacks).

The are a number of practical problems that need to be solved before timestamps can be used effectively to provide freshness guarantees. One major problem is that both the sender and the receiver must have securely synchronized clocks. Furthermore, even if two entities have precisely synchronized clocks, due to the time taken to forward a message from one entity to another, any message sent between these entities will contain a slightly delayed timestamp. Thus, parties have to agree a window within which they accept that a timestamp is fresh and a mechanism to prevent replays within that window. (Typically, this mechanism is simply to record all messages that are received within the window, but this may require significant memory resources.)

However, timestamp-based key establishment protocols do have one major advantage: they typically require less messages to be sent in the protocol exchange. This is because parties do not have to exchange nonces before commencing the main part of the protocol execution. We can adapt all of the protocols in this chapter to the use of timestamps. We use TS_A to be the timestamp produced by entity A. Tables 11.11 and 11.12 present the timestamp versions of Zheng and Imai's key establishment protocols described in Sect. 11.4. It is unclear if these protocols are optimal: for example, the requirement that TS_A is encrypted in the IKTUTS (Table 11.12) is unnecessary as this may be easily guessable by an attacker. Table 11.13 presents the timestamp version of the Bjørstad and Dent key establishment protocol described in Sect. 11.5.

Table 11.11 Zheng's DKTUTS (Direct Key Transport Using a Timestamp) protocol

A	B
$K_{AB} \xleftarrow{R} \{0, 1\}^{\ell_k}$	
$k \xleftarrow{R} \mathbb{Z}_q$	
$(k_1, k_2) \leftarrow hash_1(pk_B^k)$	
$c \leftarrow \text{Enc}_{k_1}(K_{AB}, TS_A)$	
$r \leftarrow hash_2(k_2, K_{AB}, TS_A)$	
$s \leftarrow k/(r + sk_A) \bmod q \quad \xrightarrow{c, r, s}$	$(k_1, k_2) \leftarrow hash_1((pk_A \cdot g^r)^{s \cdot sk_B})$
	$(K_{AB}, TS_A) \leftarrow \text{Dec}_{k_1}(c)$
	Accept K_{AB} if TS_A is fresh
	$hash_2(k_2, K_{AB}, N_B) = r$

Table 11.12 Zheng's IKTUTS (Indirect Key Transport Using a Timestamp) protocol

A	B
$k \xleftarrow{R} \mathbb{Z}_q$	
$(k_1, k_2) \leftarrow hash_1(pk_B^k)$	
$c \leftarrow \text{Enc}_{k_1}(TS_A)$	
$r \leftarrow hash_2(k_2, TS_A)$	
$s \leftarrow k/(r + sk_A) \bmod q$	
$K_{AB} \leftarrow hash_3(k_1, k_2, TS_A) \quad \xrightarrow{c, r, s}$	$(k_1, k_2) \leftarrow hash_1((pk_A \cdot g^r)^{s \cdot sk_B})$
	$TS_A \leftarrow \text{Dec}_{k_1}(c)$
	$K_{AB} \leftarrow hash_3(k_1, k_2, TS_A)$
	Accept K_{AB} if TS_A is fresh
	$hash_2(k_2, TS_A) = r$

Table 11.13 Key establishment using a signcryption tag-KEM and timestamps

A	B
$(K_{AB}, \omega) \xleftarrow{R} Sym(sk_A, pk_B)$	
$\tau = (TS_A, sid)$	
$C \xleftarrow{R} Encap(\omega, \tau) \quad \xrightarrow{TS_A, C}$	$\tau = (TS_A, sid)$
	$K_{AB} \leftarrow Decap(pk_A, sk_B, \tau)$
	Accept K_{AB} if TS_A is fresh

Chapter 12
Applications of Signcryption

Yang Cui and Goichiro Hanaoka

Signcryption can provide improvements on efficiency for public-key cryptographic protocols over more traditional cryptographic mechanisms that offer security functions separately. Notably, applying signcryption in protocols where message confidentiality, integrity, and authenticity are all required is expected to result in protocols with better performance than when traditional public-key encryption and signatures are used. While a broad range of applications of signcryption can be found in the literature, it has become clear that signcryption is particularly effective when

- a sender and a receiver rely on public-key encryption and digital signature for communication security, and
- the verification of the sender's identity is only required by the receiver.

In the following sections, we investigate the effectiveness of signcryption in practical applications.

12.1 Application Fields of Signcryption

From a cryptographic point of view, signcryption provides a general method for initializing a confidential and authenticated channel in an efficient way, as was already discussed in Chap. 11. In the underlying channel, signcryption is used not only to establish a secure, shared session key among two communication parties but also to assure the sender's identity in a way that is more efficient than a straightforward composition of public-key encryption and digital signature.

The shared secret key between the parties makes possible an unlimited number of applications. Among these applications, one can first think of the following three:

- secure and authenticated key establishment,
- secure multicasting, and
- authenticated key recovery.

Y. Cui (✉)
National Institute of Advanced Industrial Science and Technology (AIST), Research Center for Information Security (RCIS), Tokyo, Japan
e-mail: y-cui@aist.go.jp

A.W. Dent, Y. Zheng (eds.), *Practical Signcryption*, Information Security and Cryptography, DOI 10.1007/978-3-540-89411-7_12,
© Springer-Verlag Berlin Heidelberg 2010

Furthermore, one can think of a diverse array of network environments ranging from mobile ad hoc networks to asynchronous transfer mode (ATM) networks, where computational resources and communication bandwidth are scarce and as a result signcryption may offer desirable solutions. Consider ATM networks, which serve as a data transport mechanism for high-speed networks including conventional wide area networks (WAN). A characteristic of ATM is that data is transported in a cell or packet of fixed size, of 53 bytes (a 48-byte payload together with a 5-byte cell header). With such a relatively small cell size, it is impossible to use conventional public-key cryptographic techniques to embed key agreement materials in a single cell. The signcryption methodology enjoys the merit of a compact size ciphertext and can be employed to solve this problem. Similarly, for a mobile ad hoc network, as mobile terminals typically have very limited energy supply and computational powers, if computationally expensive public-key encryption and signature are employed separately, then these mobile terminals will run out of power very quickly. Signcryption provides a power-saving security solution for mobile ad hoc networks.

A number of signcryption-based security protocols have been proposed for aforementioned networks and similar environments. These include

- secure ATM networks,
- secure routing in mobile ad hoc networks,
- secure voice over IP (VoIP) solutions,
- encrypted email authentication by firewalls,
- secure message transmission by proxy, and
- mobile grid web services.

In addition to the above applications, signcryption has various applications in electronic commerce, where its security properties are most useful. Looking from an application-oriented point of view, a great amount of electronic commerce can take advantage of signcryption to provide efficient security solutions for

- electronic payment,
- electronic toll collection system,
- secure and authenticated transactions using smart cards, etc.

As we consider these applications, we will pay particular attention to improvements in operation speed and message overhead that can be obtained by using the signcryption methodology in place of applying conventional confidentiality and integrity protection mechanisms.

12.2 Example Applications of Signcryption

In this section, we will select some concrete schemes and proposals from the aforementioned list of applications and provide more details of performance benefits from using signcryption. Specifically, we investigate the following applications of signcryption: secure multicasting over the Internet [134], authenticated key recovery [151], secure ATM networks [208], secure routing in mobile ad hoc networks [154], encrypted e-mail authentication by firewalls [86], and improved secure electronic transaction (SET) [95]. A brief investigation of the uses of signcryption with voice over IP network systems (VoIP) will also be included. This inevitably leaves out many other interesting applications, including secure networking and routing [87, 115], secure message transmission [85], mobile grid web services [155], and Electronic Fund Transfer (EFT) [175]. The reader is directed to the relevant references for further technical details on these applications.

12.2.1 Secure Multicasting Over the Internet

Multicast is an important network addressing method, which sends information to a group of destinations at once. Different from broadcast which, delivers information to all the members in a network, multicast transmits information to a set of chosen destinations only. In an open network such as the Internet, multicast security services often start with session key distribution for users of the chosen destinations.

In [134], Matsuura et al. proposed a multicast key distribution protocol using signcryption. The goal of the proposed protocol is to obtain a secure and authenticated key delivery service which is scalable and compact.

Traditionally the Internet Group Management Protocol (IGMP) [105] is used to multicast packets for the final delivery between a local router (which forwards and routes packets) and a member belonging to its sub-network. On the other hand, for a sparsely distributed network, the most scalable techniques use a shared-tree approach, such as the protocol-independent multicast-sparse mode (PIM-SM) [106] and the core-based tree (CBT) routing protocol [104]. The latter is more scalable and has fewer entries in routing tables.

Matsuura et al. made use of the core-based tree (CBT) [104] routing protocol and multiple key distribution centers (KDCs), which are more practical and flexible than a single trusted key distribution center, to achieve a scalable routing scheme. They took advantage of signcryption to significantly reduce the communication cost and computation time delay of the CBT protocol.

A (trusted) key distribution center (KDC) aims to issue a key to valid users in the network. However, security in the network cannot, and should not, rely wholly on a single KDC. Instead, a group key distribution center (GKDC) has been proposed as a practical solution for key distribution over the Internet. This requires a KDC in each local group which has its own public and private signing key pair. CBT can be viewed as a routing protocol that employs GKDCs. Valid users, when looking to access services across groups, need to join the new group and receive a distributed key before accessing the services.

In a conventional CBT routing protocol, public-key encryption and signature are used in succession to guarantee the secrecy of transferred packets and the identity of the sender, respectively. More precisely, in the join request step, a host employs a public-key encryption scheme to compute a ciphertext with the public key of the next GKDC and then receives a signature from the GKDC to which the host currently belongs. There may be some intermediate GKDCs (routers) between the destination GKDC and the sender host, thus the join request should be sent to its neighbor GKDC and relayed to next hop, and so on. Conversely, in the join acknowledgment step, the destination GKDC verifies the identity of the host. It then signs key materials and encrypts them with its neighbor's public key. Next, the neighbor decrypts the ciphertext and verifies the signature, then re-encrypts and re-signs the keying materials with the public key of the next hop before finally returning it to the host. During this repeated encryption, decryption, and signing process, signcryption can be applied in place of separate encryption and signing, whereby saving both communication bandwidth and computational time, as we will show in the following.

12.2.1.1 Performance Comparison

Since the most popular public-key signature and encryption algorithms are RSA and ElGamal, whose security relies on the factoring and discrete log assumptions, respectively, the comparison of signcryption and the underlying cryptographic algorithms is provided among these popular schemes.

We use four notations in our comparison: *RSA*, *ElGamal*, *SC_E*, and *SC_R* which are defined as follows:

- *RSA*: This scheme is composed of a RSA signature [91] and a standard RSA encryption. (For simplicity, only the textbook RSA encryption is considered; performance for more advanced RSA-based schemes can only be worse than that of the textbook RSA.)
- *ElGamal*: This scheme is composed of a shortened ElGamal signature (DSS) [149] and a textbook ElGamal encryption.
- *SC_R*: This scheme is composed of a RSA signature in addition to Zheng's original signcryption scheme [203].
- *SC_E*: This scheme is composed of a shortened ElGamal signature (DSS) in addition to Zheng's signcryption scheme.

All the above techniques can be used in modified CBT-based protocols. Note that in the modified CBT routing protocol proposed in [134], the processes of join request and join acknowledgment typically need Encrypt-then-Sign. (For a discussion on differences between Encrypt-then-Sign and Sign-then-Encrypt, please refer to Chap. 3.) An independent signature scheme is used in the routing protocol, which is the reason why all the above techniques have a separate signature scheme.

12.2.1.2 Computational Cost

Computational cost for the RSA and ElGamal algorithms is mostly concentrated on modular exponentiations and modular multiplications. For the RSA cryptosystem with a public composite n, let $|n|$ be the binary length of n. The main cost occurring in the decryption and signing processes includes two regular modular exponentiations:

- One for decryption, together with an encryption with a very small public exponent (requiring relatively small computational overhead).
- One for signature generation, together with signature verification with a very small public exponent (requiring relatively small computational overhead).

These operations usually take $1.5|n|$ modular multiplications using the "square-and-multiply" method. With the help of the Chinese Remainder Theorem (CRT), which achieves the fastest known implementation of RSA, the aforementioned cost could be reduced to $1.5|n|/4 = 0.375|n|$ modular multiplications [66, 203]. It is considered to be the primary cost for computation for the *RSA*-based protocol.

    With ElGamal, it requires

- one modular exponentiation for signature generation,
- two modular exponentiations for signature verification,
- two modular exponentiations for encryption, and
- one modular exponentiation for decryption.

The corresponding cost of *ElGamal* for exponentiation calculation can be represented by the following numbers of modular multiplications: $1.5|q|$, $1.75|q|$, $3|q|$, and $1.5|q|$ [134], where q is the order of the subgroup used in the ElGamal algorithm.

    On the other hand, the cost of signcryption-based schemes can be estimated as follows:

- one modular exponentiation for signcryption,
- two modular exponentiations for unsigncryption,

which lead to $1.5|q|$ and $1.75|q|$ modular multiplications, respectively.

    To achieve a similar security level, n and q are set to 1,536 and 176. (We refer to [121] for a more precise analysis on the key sizes of RSA and elliptic curve cryptography.) It is shown by experimental results [134] that, assuming that there are two hops between the host and the destination, when the cost of the key distribution protocol using *ElGamal* is set to 1, then the protocol using SC_E takes 0.87, *RSA* takes 0.80, and SC_R takes 0.745. Clearly, the protocol implemented with SC_R is the most efficient from a computational point of view.

12.2.1.3 Communication Overhead

As for communication bandwidth overhead, from Table 12.1, it is easy to see that protocols using signcryption have a significant saving, especially in the join-acknowledgment process of a CBT-based routing protocol. It is interesting to note that the SC_E protocol affords the smallest communication overhead.

Table 12.1 Communication overhead of *SC_E* by the ratios to *RSA*, *ElGamal*, and *SC_R* [134]

	Join request process (%)	Join acknowledgment process (%)
vs. *RSA*	17.2	15.0
vs. *ElGamal*	100.0	39.7
vs. *SC_R*	17.2	22.5

12.2.2 Authenticated Key Recovery

A key recovery system is a scheme in which a third party, called the "data recovery agency (DRA)," is able to recover a plaintext from a ciphertext without the help of a sender or a recipient. Various key recovery systems have been discussed in [70, 195].

In a typical key recovery system, as shown in Fig. 12.1, a sender transfers an encrypted message with a data recovery field (DRF) attached to it. Within the DRF, a session key that is used to encrypt the message is stored after being encrypted with the public key of the key recovery agent (KRA). Typically the KRA can only decrypt the session key, with no access to the ciphertext. The DRA can ask the KRA to help decrypt the encrypted session key that will in turn allow the DRA to recover the encrypted message. Note that the KRA only returns the session key in DRF after successfully verifying the identity of and request from the DRA, and the DRA cannot recover the message directly by himself. This provides a way to recover the encrypted message from the ciphertext without the help of the sender or the receiver.

A necessary condition for successful recovery is the assurance of correctness of DRF, that is, if the sender prepares a bogus DRF, then the key recovery system must fail. With a typical key recovery system, this condition is not met, as the DRF is not authenticated. As a result a bogus DRF could be forged by a malicious entity. To address this issue, an authenticated DRF can be used to ensure the integrity and authenticity of the data and can serve as undeniable evidence that the sender has indeed sent the corresponding DRF. Signcryption can be used to construct the DRF with authenticity and confidentiality together while requiring a smaller overhead compared to conventional schemes. Unfortunately, this does not completely solve the problem as the sender could still send a bogus DRF. However, if the signcryption

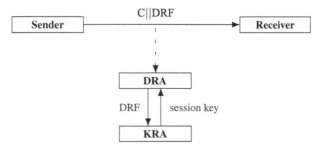

Fig. 12.1 Key recovery system

scheme has public verifiability, then all parties will be able to check that a DRF corresponding to correct sender has been included and then the malicious sender can be pursued by KRA for failing to adhere to the key recovery protocols.

12.2.2.1 Computational Cost

Table 12.2 shows the computational cost of various implementations of a key recovery system. It can be seen that, among the schemes with both confidentiality and authenticity, signcryption does represent the most efficient implementation.

More precisely, Zheng's signcryption scheme SCS1 [203, 204] saves one modular exponentiation relative to RSA Sign-then-Encrypt and two modular exponentiations relative to "Schnorr signature + ElGamal encryption" (see Sects. 3.3 and 4.3). This immediately leads to a big saving of computation, since modular exponentiations are a dominant issue in computational cost. In the following, let us consider a 1,024-bit RSA modulus n, a large prime p and a large q, such that $q|p-1$. A generator of the subgroup with order q modulo p is chosen. A typical setting is $|p| = 1024$ and $|q| = 160$.

In Table 12.2, EXP denotes the number of exponentiations, MUL that of multiplication, DIV that of division, and HASH that of hash computation. For the purpose of comparison with both RSA-based and ElGamal-based schemes, we also include in the table the costs of RSA and ElGamal encryption schemes. Due to differences in sizes of exponents, a direct comparison of computational costs of RSA and ElGamal by merely counting the number of exponentiations can be misleading. A more accurate approach is to evaluate the number of multiplications required. Similar to the analysis in Sect. 12.2.1, one RSA modular exponentiation can be completed in $0.375|n|$ multiplications and one ElGamal modular exponentiation is $1.5|q|$. Therefore, the signcryption-based scheme requires the least computational cost and saves the computational cost by

$$(0.375|n| - 1.5|q|)/0.375|n| = 37.5\%$$

where typically $|n| = 1,024$ and $|q| = 160$. On the other hand, compared to "Schnorr signature + ElGamal encryption," two less exponentiations are required which leads to a 66.7% saving in computational cost.

Table 12.2 Comparison of computational cost for a key recovery system [151]

	Type	Computational cost EXP+MUL+DIV+HASH
RSA enc.	Encryption	1+0+0+0
ElGamal enc.	Encryption	2+0+0+0
RSA sig. then enc.	Signature+Encryption	2+0+0+1
Schnorr sig.+ElGamal enc.	Signature+Encryption	3+1+0+1
SCS1 [203, 204]	Signcryption	1+0+1+2

12.2.2.2 Communication Overhead

In Table 12.3, we compare the computational overhead of the different implementations using typical security parameters. We set $|n| = |p| = 1,024$, $|q| = 160$, the length of keyed hash function's output to be $|KeyHash(\cdot)| = 128$ and the length of session key to be $|k_{session}| = 128$.

Using the signcryption scheme SCS1 by Zheng [203, 204] results in a very small message overhead. More precisely, compared to an RSA encryption-based key recovery system, signcryption saves the bandwidth by

$$\frac{|n| - (|KeyHash(\cdot)| + |q| + |k_{session}|)}{|n|} = 59.4\%$$

12.2.3 Secure ATM Networks

The asynchronous transfer mode (ATM) protocol is a packet switching protocol in which data traffic is encoded into a fixed-size cell, with 384 bits of payload data and 40 bits of header information. The ATM protocol works in the data link layer, which is layer 2 in the open systems interconnection basic reference model (OSI) [212]. The data link layer receives services from the fundamental physical layer (layer 1) and provides services to upper layers. ATM differs from other technologies like Internet protocol (IP) principally in that it has a fixed-size cell. It is used in wide area networks (WANs) and asymmetric digital subscriber lines (ADSLs).

ATM is designed as a protocol with high transportation speed and low latency, to transfer real-time video and audio, etc. The small and fixed size cell is helpful in reducing the latency of transportation. This specific requirement of ATM cell's size poses interesting challenges in terms of data confidentiality and authenticity, especially using conventional public-key cryptography. We note that some encryption schemes such as ElGamal can be built with a compact overhead of 161 bits, on an elliptic curve over a finite field $GF(2^{160})$. However, it does not work well in ATM networks. It is because that the remaining $384 - 161 = 223$ bits are not adequate to transmit a key with a digital signature. Furthermore, if we consider the higher IND-CCA2 level of security (discussed in Sect. 1.3.3), then even more ciphertext overhead is required. As a result, elliptic curve cryptography technology alone cannot provide an appropriate solution for confidentiality and authenticity in ATM networks.

Table 12.3 Comparison of communication cost for a key recovery system [151]

	Type	Communication overhead
RSA enc.	Encryption	$\|n\|$
ElGamal enc.	Encryption	$\|p\| + \|k_{session}\|$
RSA sig. then enc.	Signature+Encryption	$\|n\| + \|n\|$
Schnorr sig.+ElGamal enc.	Signature+Encryption	$\|hash(\cdot)\| + \|q\| + \|p\| + \|k_{session}\|$
SCS1 [203, 204]	Signcryption	$\|KeyHash(\cdot)\| + \|q\| + \|k_{session}\|$

While it is possible to encrypt and sign key materials and then transport the resultant ciphertext in several cells, due to buffering it may lead to a longer latency that is not acceptable in certain high-speed applications.

Signcryption techniques can be used to provide key establishment in short packets suitable for use in ATM protocols. Consider the key establishment protocols with timestamps proposed by Zheng and Imai [205, 208] described in Sect. 11.4. If we assume that r and s are 80- and 160-bit long, respectively, and the timestamp is 32-bit long, then the direct construction of Table 11.3 can be used to encrypt a 64-bit key, as the ciphertext size is 336-bit long. However, a 128-bit session key leads to a 400-bit ciphertext, which is beyond the limit of the ATM cell size. The indirect construction of Table 11.4 can be used to encrypt a 128-bit session key and results in a ciphertext of 368 bits in length, which can be comfortably placed in an ATM cell that has 384 bits for payload.

12.2.4 Secure Routing for Mobile Ad Hoc Networks

A mobile ad hoc network (MANET), widely employed in military and emergency communication systems, is a network of devices that interact but do not have a fixed network topology. Typically, it is a collection of small portable devices that communicate wirelessly. It is common to assume that these devices are only equipped with restricted power and limited computational resources. These restrictions are part of the reason why there are currently few secure routing protocols that can be efficiently employed in large-scale MANETs. A protocol for secure routing has to be compact to satisfy the restricted bandwidth requirements and be sufficiently fast to tolerate the dynamically changing topology of MANET. The constrained computation power and low energy of mobile terminals also prohibit the direct use of expensive cryptographic tools, such as multiparty computations.

To cope with the underlying problems, efficiency of cryptographic solutions is crucial and highly desired. Among the proposed secure routing protocols for MANETs, an ID-based signcryption routing protocol called ISMANET [154] is shown to achieve fairly good performance, compared to those based on conventional (separate) signature and encryption algorithms.

ID-based cryptography was first proposed by Shamir [177] in 1984. ID-based signcryption was developed by Malone-Lee et al. [129, 122, 51] and is extensively discussed in Chap. 10. It has a significant advantage in that, unlike conventional signcryption schemes, it does not require certificates for public keys. A further advantage is that recipients can request their private keys *after* receiving the data from the sender. These properties are useful in a dynamic MANET environment.

Figure 12.2 shows the flow of ISMANET protocol, which takes advantage of ID-based techniques and signcryption mechanisms. The former avoids the requirement of certification of public keys and the latter reduces the computational and communication cost. The proposed protocol is based on the AODV routing protocol [158].

The basic AODV routing process consists of two steps, route request (RREQ) and route reply (RREP), to determine unicast routes to destinations within the MANET. In [154], a slightly modified protocol using ID-based signcryption has been described, where a sender first broadcasts RREQ packets with its identity ID_S, and key material T to all its neighbors. These intermediate nodes verify the packets, if the packets are valid then transfer them to the destination. As the destination node receives the packets, it will return RREP packets to determine the unicast routes, if the packets from ID_S have been verified. The RREQ packets contain the fields including routing information, such as source address, broadcast ID, destination address, etc. Similarly, RREP packets contain the destination address, the source address and hop counters which define the unicast routes.

As in Fig. 12.2, a signcrypted part will provide authenticity to the packets. The protocol makes use of the ID-based signcryption scheme proposed by Libert and Quisquater [122]. $SC_S[\cdot]$ and $SC_D[\cdot]$ are the identity-based signcryption schemes employed by source and destination, respectively. The user's public key is computed from its ID by using a publicly known hash function. Therefore, it is convenient to compute the public key from its corresponding ID without the help of a trusted authority, which is especially useful since the trusted authority is difficult to maintain in MANET. While on the other hand, the private key can be retrieved beforehand or at a later stage.

T is generated as the signcryption text as in [122], in addition to a distributed key generation process in [154], which works in a threshold manner to prevent key compromise.

When the signcrypted packets are verified by intermediate node X (Intermediate in Fig. 12.2), a temporary T_X is computed similarly and added to the packets. In reverse, the destination returns its reply if it successfully verifies T, T_X, and $SC_S[H(RREQ||ID_S||T)]$. A small change is that the destination unicasts its packet in the reverse way, including authentication information for intermediate nodes.

12.2.4.1 Performance of ID-Based Signcryption Routing Protocol

Compared to two conventional secure routing protocols for MANETs, ARAN [172] and SRP [153], this ID-based signcryption scheme (ISMANET) is advantageous in

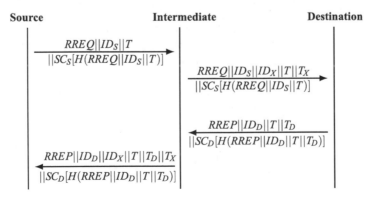

Fig. 12.2 Routing request and reply protocol

both computational cost and communication overhead. ARAN and SRP are secure routing protocols for ad hoc networks based on RSA and elliptic curve cryptography (ECC), respectively. Table 12.4 shows that ISMANET has the best performance in terms of computational cost among three protocols. Performance details by simulations are given by Park and Lee [154].

12.2.5 Encrypted and Authenticated E-mail by Firewalls

Firewalls are widely used in networks to filter network traffic according to specified rules and criteria, and are especially useful for blocking malicious intrusion from external networks. Firewalls can work well at several layers in an OSI seven layer network [212], including the data link layer (layer 2), network layer (layer 3), and the application layer (layer 7). In the data link layer (layer 2), firewalls are able to filter data traffic according to frame contents. In the network layer (layer 3), firewalls can be run according to more complicated rules, such as packet addresses, port addresses, and packet header. In the application layer (layer 7), filtering is defined by the rules specified by an end user.

Signcryption can be used to send a message (from a sender to a receiver) with confidentiality and integrity protection. One notices that when a signcrypted message passes through a firewall between the sender and the receiver, it may present a problem. This is because the firewall cannot examine the contents of the signcrypted message, nor can it determine the authenticity of the message (as origin authentication is only guaranteed for the receiver). To address this problem, a signcryption scheme that offers public verifiability (see Sect. 4.3.3) can be used, whereby a firewall can check the authenticity of the message without having to decrypt the message first.

Note that it is very important to verify the authenticity of the network traffic without the help of the receiver, as firewalls are only intermediaries on the communication routes. Gamage et al. [86] proposed a variant of signcryption enjoying public verifiability (see Sect. 4.3.3). A scheme by Bao and Deng [15] also has public verifiability although it does not offer confidentiality (see Sect. 4.3.2).

Table 12.4 Comparison of ISMANET, ARAN, and SRP [154]

Scheme	ISMANET	ARAN	SRP
Key distribution	Public key (ID-based signcryption)	Public key (RSA)	Public key (ECC)
Key management	Distributed	Centralized	Centralized
Intermediate node authentication	Yes	No	No
Certification	No need	Need	Need*
Communication overhead	Low	High	Low
Computational cost	Low	High	High
Cost in computation and communication	≈ Cost(signcrypt)	Cost(signature)+ Cost(encryption)	≈Cost(encryption)

12.2.5.1 Cost Advantages Due to Signcryption

From a computational point of view, Gamage et al.'s signcryption scheme (see Sect. 4.3.3) requires four modular exponentiations, while Zheng's original signcryption scheme (see Sect. 4.3.1) requires three modular exponentiations, although the latter cannot be used to authenticate encrypted message by firewalls. Table 12.5 shows that Gamage et al.'s signcryption scheme can achieve a 39% saving in computation compared to the combination of DSA signature and ElGamal encryption, which typically requires six modular exponentiations in total. Note that the number in parentheses takes into account a technique that can be used to compute the product of two modular exponentiations in time roughly equal to 1.17 regular modular exponentiations [139, p. 618].

Hence, we can see that Gamage et al.'s signcryption scheme requires the same amount of communication overhead as that of Zheng's original signcryption scheme, which is, as we have seen previously in the Chapter, considered advantageous over a conventional Sign-then-Encrypt method.

12.2.6 Signcryption in Secure VoIP

A voice over IP (VoIP) system is a system for transmitting voice data and real-time images over packet-switched IP networks. These systems have recently been highlighted for their attractive cost-saving features. Using voice transmission over IP networks, instead of public switched telephone networks (PSTN), makes long-distance phone calls cheaper and provides a more flexible structure for a variety of services. Examples of VoIP services include Microsoft's Windows NetMeeting and Apple Macintosh iChat.

Along with these desirable properties, however, VoIP also introduces a range of new security issues and these issues apparently contributed to a lag in sales in the US market, according to a recent investigation by a market research firm called In-Stat [99]. These security issues include

- legal issues,
- the narrow margin left for security in the system architecture, which is latency sensitive and has a low tolerance for packet loss,
- the more complicated network architecture of Internet relative to conventional PSTN, requiring new technologies to protect VoIP systems.

Unlike a conventional PSTN, where intercepting conversations implies physical access to telephones lines, VoIP has more vulnerable points that could be penetrated

Table 12.5 Computational cost saving on firewalls for modified signcryption over DSA [86]

Operation mode	Cost savings
Signcryption with message recovery	5/6 (4.17/5.17) 17% (19%)
Signcryption with verification only	4/6 (3.17/5.17) 33% (39%)

by an intruder. In addition, VoIP is also more sensitive to the delay of transmission, which makes security countermeasures more difficult. Typically, an upper bound of 150 ms delay is appropriate for acceptable voice quality at the receiver end. Note that voice encoding typically takes 1–30 ms and it takes about 100 ms to transmit data across the North American continent. As a result there are only about 20–50 ms left for all security-related operations [150, p. 19]. Meanwhile, it is important to remember that a typical payload in a VoIP system is 10–50 bytes, which is quite small. Security techniques such as TLS and IPsec cannot be readily adapted to protect VoIP. As a result, in the strict performance environment required by VoIP, current technology does not provide physical wire security comparable to PSTN networks.

From the above discussions, we can see that the complicated security issues involved in implementing a VoIP system require an elaborate but efficient security solution. As VoIP is implemented over IP networks, security answers should adapt to a variety of Internet mechanisms, such as multicasting, firewalls, and perhaps even wireless networks. We have already shown that in these situations signcryption can be used to improve performance.

For authenticated key distribution in VoIP systems, public-key encryption or Diffie–Hellman key agreement has been advocated for use in the secure real-time protocol (SRTP) [150, p. 17]. We argue that signcryption should instead be employed, providing protection for confidentiality and authenticity with a smaller computational and communication overhead.

H323 is a family of widely adopted standards [103, 150] for audio and video communication over packetized networks by the International Telecommunication Union (ITU). H323 includes a series of protocols supporting a suite of media control policies. Among them, H235v2 provides a security solution for the H323 suite. In H235v2, a hybrid security profile is used to establish an authenticated key between two entities during their initial handshake [150, p. 32]. The authenticated key establishment process makes use of a Diffie–Hellman key agreement and an RSA signature; the efficiency and bandwidth of this system can clearly be improved by making use of a signcryption-based key establishment protocol (see Chap. 11).

Finally, in bandwidth-restricted VoIP networks, which typically have a payload of 10–50 bytes, it is cumbersome to use both public-key encryption and digital signature in short packets. As we have analyzed in Sect. 12.2.3, signcryption can work well in ATM networks which have a 384-bit (48-byte) fixed-size payload. Furthermore, as has been extensively discussed in the previous sections, communication cost would be greatly reduced by using a signcryption scheme.

12.2.7 Applications to Electronic Payment

Signcryption finds a natural application in electronic payment protocols in which both confidentiality and non-repudiation are essential. We focus our attention on improving the *Secure Electronic Transaction* (SET) [132, 133] protocol with signcryption [95].

12.2.7.1 An Overview of SET

The payment model on which SET is based consists of three participants: a card-holder, a merchant, and a payment gateway. The card holder (C) initiates a payment with the merchant (M). The merchant then has to authorize the payment; the payment gateway acts as the front end to the existing financial network, and through this the card issuer can be contacted to explicitly authorize each and every transaction that takes place. In the SET protocol, there are a total of 32 different types of messages [132, 133]. Among the messages, the most important ones, and the messages transmitted at the highest frequency, are the following six: PInitReq, PInitRes, PReq, PRes, AuthReq, and AuthRes. Other messages are used mainly for administrative purposes, such as creating certificates, canceling messages registration, error handling, etc. Hence these messages are transmitted with significantly less frequency than the six messages mentioned above, which in turn implies that any attempt to improve the efficiency of SET must focus on the six main messages. The flow of the six main messages is shown in Fig. 12.3.

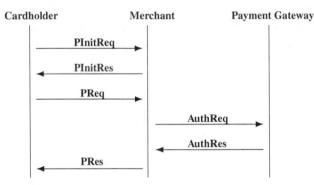

Fig. 12.3 Flows of the main SET messages

Next we discuss in detail the functions of the six dominant messages. A few frequently used notations are summarized in Table 12.6. To simplify our discussion, addition information such as request and response will be denoted by a nonce with a specified format.

The SET protocol starts with purchase initialization (PInitReq and PInitRes). Purchase request (PReq) is then executed conforming to the structure described in Table 12.7. In PReq, PI and OI are destined for different entities but sent in the same cryptographic envelope. They share a signature, called a dual signature [132, 133],

Table 12.6 Notations

$\text{Encrypt}(m, pk)$	Encrypt m using a public encryption key pk
$\text{Enc}_K(m)$	Encrypt m by using the symmetric encryption key K
$\text{Sign}(m, sk)$	Sign m using a signing key sk
$H(t)$	Hash of t
sk_C^{sig}	Cardholder's private signing key
pk_P^{enc}	Payment gateway's public encryption key

Table 12.7 Structure of PReq

Message	Message factor
PReq	{PI, OI}
PI	{$\texttt{Encrypt}((K, \text{PANData, nonce}), pk_P^{enc})$,
	$\texttt{Enc}_K(\text{PI-OILink}, H(\text{PANData,nonce}))$,
	Dual signature}
OI	{OIData, $H(\text{PIData})$}
PANData	Primary account number data
PIData	Purchase instruction data
OIData	Order information data
PI-OILink	{PIData(except PANData), $H(\text{OIData})$}
Dual signature	$\texttt{Sign}(H(H(\text{PIData}), H(\text{OIData})), sk_C^{sig})$

which can be verified by either entity. The structure of the dual signature used in SET is illustrated in Table 12.7.

After receiving PReq, the merchant verifies it (especially, the dual signature). If it is valid, he produces an authentication request (AuthReq) message and sends it to the payment gateway (P). Upon receiving AuthReq, the payment gateway verifies it. If successful, the payment gateway sends authentication response (AuthRes) back to the merchant. Finally, the protocol is finished with purchase response (PRes) produced by the merchant.

12.2.7.2 Some Remarks for Applying Signcryption

As is well known, signcryption executes two different procedures simultaneously, and there are often problems in the implementations of dual security systems. In SET, the problem of straightforwardly applying signcryption is as follows: signcryption does not provide efficient message linking though this functionality is very often required in SET. For example, in PReq the relationship between the information for the payment and that for the order must be guaranteed. Namely, PIData and OIData are linked with each other in the message. In the conventional SET, this requirement is fulfilled by the dual signature. However, it is difficult to provide the functionality of the dual signature using signcryption for the above reason, although a dual signature can be verified by both the merchant and the payment gateway, a signcrypted message cannot (assuming usual computational costs). Therefore, straightforward applications of signcryption is not be appropriate for SET. Hence, we need to slightly modify signcryption to provide the functionality of message linking. This signcryption-based SET is called *LITESET*.[1]

12.2.7.3 Conventional Set vs. Signcryption-Based Set

Under the Gap Diffie–Hellman assumption and a gap version of the discrete logarithm assumption [152], Zheng's signcryption scheme [203, 204] has been proven secure against chosen ciphertext and chosen message attacks [12, 13] (see

---

[1] Though SET is no longer supported by VISA and Mastercard, this performance-enhanced protocol LITESET provides a proof of concept and a possible choice for future electronic payments.

Table 12.8 Computational cost for message generation of main messages [95]

Message	SET	LITESET [95]	Saving (%)
PInitReq	–	–	–
PInitRes	384	240	37.5
PReq	401	480	−19.7
AuthReq	401	240	40.1
AuthRes	802	480	40.1
PRes	384	240	37.5
Total	2, 372	1680	29.2

Sect. 4.3.1). This scheme is used in the LITESET protocol, ensuring that the security level of LITESET is the same as the conventional SET with RSA-OAEP [30] and RSA-PSS [31]. We focus our comparison on RSA-based SET and LITESET (which is built on discrete-logarithm-based signcryption). The analysis can be easily extended to elliptic curve versions of SET and LITESET.

As explained in Sect. 12.2.1, the computational cost depends mainly on modulo exponentiations in encryption or signature generation. Hence, the number of modulo multiplications in modulo exponentiation can be used to benchmark computational cost. We estimate the number of modulo multiplications by using "square-and-multiply" and "simultaneous multiple exponentiation." Namely, the number of modulo multiplications for one y^r is $1.5 \cdot |q|$ and for $(y_0 \cdot y_1{}^{r_0})^{r_1}$ it is equal to $\frac{7}{4} \cdot |q|$, where y, y_0, and y_1 are elements of a group with order q over the finite field $GF(p)$, and r, r_0, and r_1 are elements of $\mathbf{Z}_q$. In the conventional SET, 1,024-bit RSA composite is used. To achieve the same security level, $|q| = 160$ bits and $|p| = 1024$ bits should be chosen for LITESET [203, 204]. Table 12.8 shows the costs of message generation for the six main messages, where the unit of cost is modulo multiplication. We notice that the computational costs are saved by approximately 30%. Although difficult to quantify, a further advantage of LITESET lies in the fact that it requires less certificate verifications thanks to a reduced number of public-key certificates required for signcryption.

12.2.7.4 Message Overhead

Expanded bits by signature and encryption are considered as message overhead. Table 12.9 shows the message overhead of the six main messages. We can see that message overhead is saved by over 60% for each message.

Table 12.9 Message overhead of main messages [95]

Message	Conventional scheme	This scheme [95]	Saving (%)
PInitReq	–	–	–
PInitRes	1,024 bit	320 bit	68.7
PReq	2,008 bit	720 bit	64.1
AuthReq	4,056 bit	640 bit	84.2
AuthRes	4,256 bit	480 bit	88.7
PRes	1,024 bit	320 bit	68.7
Total	12,368 bit	2,480 bit	79.9

References

1. M. Abdalla, M. Bellare, D. Catalano, E. Kiltz, T. Kohno, T. Lange, J. Malone-Lee, G. Neven, P. Paillier, and H. Shi. Searchable encryption revisited: Consistency properties, relation to anonymous IBE, and extensions. *Journal of Cryptology*, 21(3):350–391, 2008.
2. M. Abdalla, M. Bellare, and P. Rogaway. The oracle Diffie-Hellman assumptions and an analysis of DHIES. In D. Naccache, editor, *Progress in Cryptology – CT-RSA 2001*, volume 2020 of *Lecture Notes in Computer Science*, pages 143–158. Springer, 2001.
3. M. Abdalla, D. Catalano, A. W. Dent, J. Malone-Lee, G. Neven, and N. P. Smart. Identity-based encryption gone wild. In M. Bugliesi, B. Preneel, V. Sassone, and I. Wegener, editors, *Automata, Languages and Programming – ICALP 2006 (Part II)*, volume 4052 of *Lecture Notes in Computer Science*, pages 300–311. Springer, 2006.
4. M. Abe, R. Gennaro, and K. Karosawa. Tag-KEM/DEM: A new framework for hybrid encryption. *Journal of Cryptology*, 21(1):97–130, 2008.
5. M. Abe, R. Gennaro, K. Karosawa, and V. Shoup. Tag-KEM/DEM: A new framework for hybrid encryption and a new analysis of Kurosawa–Desmedt KEM. In R. Cramer, editor, *Advance in Cryptology – Eurocrypt 2005*, volume 3494 of *Lecture Notes in Computer Science*, pages 128–146. Springer, 2005.
6. S. Alt. Authenticated hybrid encryption for multiple recipients. Available from `http://eprint.iacr.org/2006/029`, 2006.
7. J. H. An. Authenticated encryption in the public-key setting: Security notions and analyses. Available from `http://eprint.iacr.org/2001/079`, 2001.
8. J. H. An and M. Bellare. Constructing VIL-MACs from FIL-MACs: Message authentication under weakened assumptions. In M. Wiener, editor, *Advances in Cryptology – Crypto '99*, volume 1666 of *Lecture Notes in Computer Science*, pages 252–269. Springer, 1999.
9. J. H. An and M. Bellare. Does encryption with redundancy provide authenticity? In B. Pfitzmann, editor, *Advances in Cryptology – Eurocrypt 2001*, volume 2045 of *Lecture Notes in Computer Science*, pages 512–528. Springer, 2001.
10. J. H. An, Y. Dodis, and T. Rabin. On the security of joint signatures and encryption. In L. Knudsen, editor, *Advances in Cryptology – Eurocrypt 2002*, volume 2332 of *Lecture Notes in Computer Science*, pages 83–107. Springer, 2002.
11. J. Baek, B. Lee, and K. Kim. Secure length-saving ElGamal encryption under the computational Diffie-Hellman assumption. In E. Dawson, A. Clark, and C. Boyd, editors, *Proceedings of the 5th Australasian Conference on Information Security and Privacy (ACISP 2000)*, volume 1841 of *Lecture Notes in Computer Science*, pages 49–58. Springer, 2000.
12. J. Baek, R. Steinfeld, and Y. Zheng. Formal proofs for the security of signcryption. In D. Naccache and P. Paillier, editors, *Public Key Cryptography (PKC 2002)*, volume 2274 of *Lecture Notes in Computer Science*, pages 80–98. Springer, 2002.
13. J. Baek, R. Steinfeld, and Y. Zheng. Formal proofs for the security of signcryption. *Journal of Cryptology*, 20(2):203–235, 2007.

A.W. Dent, Y. Zheng (eds.), *Practical Signcryption*, Information Security and Cryptography, DOI 10.1007/978-3-540-89411-7
© Springer-Verlag Berlin Heidelberg 2010

14. J. Baek and Y. Zheng. Simple and efficient threshold cryptosystem from the gap Diffie-Hellman group. In *Proceedings of the IEEE Global Telecommunications Conference – GLOBECOM 2003*, volume 3 of pages 1491–1495. IEEE Communications Society, 2003.

15. F. Bao and R. H. Dong. A signcryption scheme with signature directly verifiable by public key. In H. Imai and Y. Zheng, editors, *Public Key Cryptography – PKC '98*, volume 1431 of *Lecture Notes in Computer Science*, pages 55–59. Springer, 1998.

16. M. Barbosa and P. Farshim. Certificateless signcryption. In *Proceedings of the 2008 ACM Symposium on Information, Computer and Communications Security – ASIA CCS 2008*, pages 369–372. ACM Press, 2008.

17. P. S. L. M. Barreto, H. Y. Kim, B. Lynn, and M. Scott. Efficient algorithms for pairing-based cryptosystems. In M. Yung, editor, *Advances in Cryptology – Crypto 2002*, volume 2442 of *Lecture Notes in Computer Science*, pages 354–368. Springer, 2002.

18. P. S. L. M. Barreto, B. Libert, N. McCullagh, and J.-J. Quisquater. Efficient and provably-secure identity-based signatures and signcryption from bilinear maps. In B. Roy, editor, *Advances in Cryptology – Asiacrypt 2005*, volume 3788 of *Lecture Notes in Computer Science*, pages 515–532. Springer, 2005.

19. P. S. L. M. Barreto, B. Lynn, and M. Scott. On the selection of pairing-friendly groups. In M. Matsui and R. Zuccherato, editors, *Selected Areas in Cryptography – SAC 2003*, volume 3006 of *Lecture Notes in Computer Science*, pages 17–25. Springer, 2003.

20. P. S. L. M. Barreto and N. McCullagh. Pairing-friendly elliptic curves of prime order. In B. Preneel and S. Tavares, editors, *Selected Areas in Cryptography – SAC 2005*, volume 3897 of *Lecture Notes in Computer Science*, pages 319–331. Springer, 2005.

21. M. Bellare, A. Boldyreva, A. Desai, and D. Pointcheval. Key-privacy in public-key encryption. In C. Boyd, editor, *Advances in Cryptology – Asiacrypt 2001*, volume 2248 of *Lecture Notes in Computer Science*, pages 566–582. Springer, 2001.

22. M. Bellare, A. Boldyreva, and S. Micali. Public-key encryption in a multi-user setting: Security proofs and improvements. In B. Preneel, editor, *Advances in Cryptology – Eurocrypt 2000*, volume 1807 of *Lecture Notes in Computer Science*, pages 259–274. Springer, 2000.

23. M. Bellare, R. Canetti, and H. Kraczyk. A modular approach to the design and analysis of authentication and key exchange protocols. In *Proceedings of the 30th Symposium on the Theory of Computing – STOC 1998*, pages 419–428. ACM Press, 1998.

24. M. Bellare, R. Canetti, and H. Krawczyk. Keying hash functions for message authentication. In N. Koblitz, editor, *Advances in Cryptology – Crypto '96*, volume 1109 of *Lecture Notes in Computer Science*, pages 1–15. Springer, 1996.

25. M. Bellare, J. Killian, and P. Rogaway. The security of the cipher block chaining message authentication code. *Journal of Computer and System Sciences*, 61(3):362–399, 2000.

26. M. Bellare and C. Namprempre. Authenticated encryption: Relations among notions and analysis of the generic composition paradigm. In T. Okamoto, editor, *Advances in Cryptology – Asiacrypt 2000*, volume 1976 of *Lecture Notes in Computer Science*, pages 531–545. Springer, 2000.

27. M. Bellare, D. Pointcheval, and P. Rogaway. Authenticated key exchange secure against dictionary attacks. In B. Preneel, editor, *Advances in Cryptology – Eurocrypt 2000*, volume 1807 of *Lecture Notes in Computer Science*, pages 139–155. Springer, 2000.

28. M. Bellare and P. Rogaway. Entity authentication and key distribution. In D. R. Stinson, editor, *Advances in Cryptology – Crypto '93*, volume 773 of *Lecture Notes in Computer Science*, pages 232–249. Springer, 1993.

29. M. Bellare and P. Rogaway. Random oracles are practical: A paradigm for designing efficient protocols. In *Proceedings of the 1st ACM Conference on Computer and Communications Security*, pages 62–73. ACM Press, 1993.

30. M. Bellare and P. Rogaway. Optimal asymmetric encryption. In A. De Santis, editor, *Advances in Cryptology – Eurocrypt '94*, volume 950 of *Lecture Notes in Computer Science*, pages 92–111. Springer, 1994.

31. M. Bellare and P. Rogaway. The exact security of digital signatures—how to sign with RSA and Rabin. In U. Maurer, editor, *Advances in Cryptology – Eurocrypt '96*, volume 1070 of *Lecture Notes in Computer Science*, pages 399–416. Springer, 1996.

32. M. Bellare and P. Rogaway. Collision-resistant hashing: Towards making UOWHFs practical. In B. S. Kaliski Jr., editor, *Advances in Cryptology – Crypto '97*, volume 1294 of *Lecture Notes in Computer Science*, pages 470–484. Springer, 1997.

33. M. Bellare and P. Rogaway. Encode-then-encipher encryption: How to exploit nonces or redundancy in plaintexts for efficient cryptography. In T. Okamoto, editor, *Advances in Cryptology – Asiacrypt 2000*, volume 1976 of *Lecture Notes in Computer Science*, pages 317–330. Springer, 2000.

34. M. Bellare and P. Rogaway. The security of triple encryption and a framework for code-based game-playing proofs. In S. Vaudenay, editor, *Advances in Cryptology – Eurocrypt 2006*, volume 4004 of *Lecture Notes in Computer Science*, pages 409–426. Springer, 2006.

35. D. J. Bernstein. The Poly1305-AES message-authentication code. In H. Gilbert and H. Handschuh, editors, *Fast Software Encryption – FSE 2005*, volume 3557 of *Lecture Notes in Computer Science*, pages 32–49. Springer, 2005.

36. T. E. Bjørstad. Provable security of signcryption. Master's thesis, Norwegian University of Technology and Science, 2005. Available from `http://www.ii.uib.no/$\sim$tor/pdf/msc_thesis.pdf`.

37. T. E. Bjørstad and A. W. Dent. Building better signcryption schemes with tag-KEMs. In M. Yung, Y. Dodis, A. Kiayas, and T. Malkin, editors, *Public Key Cryptography – PKC 2006*, volume 3958 of *Lecture Notes in Computer Science*, pages 491–507. Springer, 2006.

38. J. Black, S. Halevi, H. Krawczyk, T. Krovetz, and P. Rogaway. UMAC: Fast and secure message authentication. In M. Wiener, editor, *Advances in Cryptology – Crypto '99*, volume 1666 of *Lecture Notes in Computer Science*, pages 216–233. Springer, 1999.

39. M. Blaze. High-bandwidth encryption with low-bandwidth smartcards. In D. Gollmann, editor, *Fast Software Encryption – FSE '96*, volume 1039 of *Lecture Notes in Computer Science*, pages 33–40. Springer, 1996.

40. M. Blaze, J. Feigenbaum, and M. Naor. A formal treatment of remotely keyed encryption. In K. Nyberg, editor, *Advances in Cryptology – Eurocrypt '98*, volume 1403 of *Lecture Notes in Computer Science*, pages 251–265. Springer, 1998.

41. D. Boneh and X. Boyen. Efficient selective-ID secure identity based encryption without random oracles. In C. Cachin and J. Camenisch, editors, *Advances in Cryptology – Eurocrypt 2004*, volume 3027 of *Lecture Notes in Computer Science*, pages 223–238. Springer, 2004.

42. D. Boneh and X. Boyen. Short signatures without random oracles. In C. Cachin and J. Camenisch, editors, *Advances in Cryptology – Eurocrypt 2004*, volume 3027 of *Lecture Notes in Computer Science*, pages 56–73. Springer, 2004.

43. D. Boneh, X. Boyen, and E.-J. Goh. Hierarchical identity based encryption with constant size ciphertext. In R. Cramer, editor, *Advance in Cryptology – Eurocrypt 2005*, volume 3494 of *Lecture Notes in Computer Science*, pages 440–456. Springer, 2005.

44. D. Boneh, G. Di Crescenzo, R. Ostrovsky, and G. Persiano. Public key encryption with keyword search. In C. Cachin and J. Camenisch, editors, *Advances in Cryptology – Eurocrypt 2004*, volume 3027 of *Lecture Notes in Computer Science*, pages 506–522. Springer, 2004.

45. D. Boneh and M. Franklin. Identity-based encryption from the Weil pairing. In J. Kilian, editor, *Advances in Cryptology – Crypto 2001*, volume 2139 of *Lecture Notes in Computer Science*, pages 213–229. Springer, 2001.

46. D. Boneh and M. Franklin. Identity-based encryption from the Weil pairing. *SIAM Journal on Computing*, 32(2):586–615, 2003.

47. D. Boneh, B. Lynn, and H. Shacham. Short signatures from the Weil pairing. In C. Boyd, editor, *Advances in Cryptology – Asiacrypt 2001*, volume 2248 of *Lecture Notes in Computer Science*, pages 514–532. Springer, 2001.

48. D. Boneh, B. Lynn, and H. Shacham. Short signatures from the Weil pairing. *Journal of Cryptology*, 17(4):297–319, 2004.

49. C. Boyd. Design of secure key establishment protocols: Successes, failures and prospects. In A. Canteaut and K. Viswanathan, editors, *Progress in Cryptology – Indocrypt 2004*, volume 3348 of *Lecture Notes in Computer Science*, pages 1–13. Springer, 2004.

50. C. Boyd and A. Mathuria. *Protocols for Authentication and Key Establishment*. Springer, 2003.

51. X. Boyen. Multipurpose identity-based signcryption: A Swiss army knife for identity-based cryptography). In D. Boneh, editor, *Advances in Cryptology – Crypto 2003*, volume 2729 of *Lecture Notes in Computer Science*, pages 383–399. Springer, 2003.

52. X. Boyen. General *ad hoc* encryption from exponent inversion IBE. In M. Naor, editor, *Advances in Cryptology – Eurocrypt 2007*, volume 4515 of *Lecture Notes in Computer Science*, pages 394–411. Springer, 2007.

53. X. Boyen and B. Waters. Anonymous hierarchical identity-based encryption (without random oracles). In C. Dwork, editor, *Advances in Cryptology – Crypto 2006*, volume 4117 of *Lecture Notes in Computer Science*, pages 290–307. Springer, 2006.

54. R. Canetti. Universally composable security: A new paradigm for cryptographic protocols. In *Proceedings of the 42nd Symposium on Foundations of Computer Science – FOCS 2001*, pages 136–145. IEEE Computer Society, 2001.

55. R. Canetti and H. Krawczyk. Analysis of key-exchange protocols and their uses for building secure channels. In B. Pfitzmann, editor, *Advances in Cryptology – Eurocrypt 2001*, volume 2045 of *Lecture Notes in Computer Science*, pages 453–474. Springer, 2001.

56. R. Canetti and H. Krawcyzk. Universally composable notions of key exchange and secure channels. In L. Knudsen, editor, *Advances in Cryptology – Eurocrypt 2002*, volume 2332 of *Lecture Notes in Computer Science*, pages 337–351. Springer, 2002.

57. J. C. Cha and J. H. Cheon. An identity-based signature from gap Diffie-Hellman groups. In Y. G. Desmedt, editor, *Public Key Cryptography – PKC 2003*, volume 2567 of *Lecture Notes in Computer Science*, pages 18–30. Springer, 2003.

58. D. Chaum and H. van Antwerpen. Undeniable signatures. In G. Brassard, editor, *Advances in Cryptology – Crypto '89*, volume 435 of *Lecture Notes in Computer Science*, pages 212–216. Springer, 1989.

59. L. Chen and C. Kudla. Identity based authenticated key agreement protocols from pairings. In *Proceedings of the 16th IEEE Computer Security Foundations Workshop – CSFW 2003*, pages 219–233. IEEE Computer Society, 2003.

60. L. Chen and J. Malone-Lee. Improved identity-based signcryption. In S. Vaudenay, editor, *Public Key Cryptography – PKC 2005*, volume 3386 of *Lecture Notes in Computer Science*, pages 362–379. Springer, 2005.

61. J. H. Cheon. Security analysis of the strong Diffie-Hellman problem. In S. Vaudenay, editor, *Advances in Cryptology – Eurocrypt 2006*, volume 4004 of *Lecture Notes in Computer Science*, pages 1–11. Springer, 2006.

62. B. Chevallier-Mames. An efficient CDH-based signature scheme with a tight security reduction. In V. Shoup, editor, *Advances in Cryptology – Crypto 2005*, volume 3621 of *Lecture Notes in Computer Science*, pages 511–526. Springer, 2005.

63. K.-K. R. Choo, C. Boyd, and Y. Hitchcock. Examining indistinguishability-based proof models for key establishment protocols. In B. Roy, editor, *Advances in Cryptology – Asiacrypt 2005*, volume 3788 of *Lecture Notes in Computer Science*, pages 585–604. Springer, 2005.

64. C. Cocks. An identity based encryption scheme based on quadratic residues. In B. Honary, editor, *Cryptography and Coding – Proceedings of the 8th IMA International Conference*, volume 2260 of *Lecture Notes in Computer Science*, pages 360–363. Springer, 2001.

65. D. Coppersmith. Evaluating logarithms in $GF(2^n)$. In *Proceedings of the 16th Annual ACM Symposium on Theory of Computing – STOC 1984*, pages 201–207. ACM Press, 1984.

66. D. Coppersmith. Finding a small root of a univariate modular equation. In U. Maurer, editor, *Advances in Cryptology – Eurocrypt 1996*, volume 1070 of *Lecture Notes in Computer Science*, pages 155–165. Springer, 1996.

67. J.-S. Coron, M. Joye, D. Naccache, and P. Paillier. Universal padding schemes for RSA. In M. Yung, editor, *Advances in Cryptology – Crypto 2002*, volume 2442 of *Lecture Notes in Computer Science*, pages 226–241. Springer, 2002.

68. R. Cramer and V. Shoup. Design and analysis of practical public-key encryption schemes secure against adaptive chosen ciphertext attack. *SIAM Journal on Computing*, 33(1): 167–226, 2004.

69. I. B. Damgård. Collision free hash functions and public key signature schemes. In D. Chaum and W. L. Price, editors, *Advances in Cryptology – Eurocrypt '87*, volume 304 of *Lecture Notes in Computer Science*, pages 203–216. Springer, 1987.

70. D. E. Denning and D. K. Branstad. A taxonomy for key escrow encryption systems. *Communications of the ACM*, 39(3):34–40, 1996.

71. A. W. Dent. Hybrid cryptography. Available from http://eprint.iacr.org/2004/210/, 2004.

72. A. W. Dent. Hybrid signcryption schemes with insider security (extended abstract). In C. Boyd and J. Gonzalez, editors, *Proceedings of the 10th Australasian Conference in Information Security and Privacy – ACISP 2005*, volume 3574 of *Lecture Notes in Computer Science*, pages 253–266. Springer, 2005.

73. A. W. Dent. Hybrid signcryption schemes with outsider security (extended abstract). In J. Zhou and J. Lopez, editors, *Proceedings of the 8th International Conference on Information Security – ISC 2005*, volume 3650 of *Lecture Notes in Computer Science*, pages 203–217. Springer, 2005.

74. W. Diffie and M. E. Hellman. New directions in cryptography. *IEEE Transactions on Information Theory*, 22(6):644–654, 1976.

75. Y. Dodis and J. H. An. Concealment and its application to authenticated encryption. In E. Biham, editor, *Advances in Cryptology – Eurocrypt 2003*, volume 2656 of *Lecture Notes in Computer Science*, pages 312–329. Springer, 2003.

76. Y. Dodis and J. H. An. Concealment and its application to authenticated encryption. Full version. Available from http://people.csail.mit.edu/~dodis/academic.html, 2003.

77. Y. Dodis, M. J. Freedman, S. Jarecki, and S. Walfish. Optimal signcryption from any trapdoor permutation. Available from http://eprint.iacr.org/2004/020, 2004.

78. Y. Dodis, M. J. Freedmen, S. Jarecki, and S. Walfish. Versatile padding schemes for joint signature and encryption. In *Proceedings of the 11th ACM Conference on Computer and Communications Security – ACM CCS 2004*, pages 344–353. ACM Press, 2004.

79. D. Dolev and A. Yao. On the security of public-key protocols. *IEEE Transactions on Information Theory*, 29(2):198–208, 1983.

80. S. Duan, Z. Cao, and R. Lu. Robust ID-based threshold signcryption scheme from pairings. In *Proceedings of the 3rd International Conference on Information Security*, volume 85 of *ACM International Conference Proceeding Series*, pages 33–37. ACM Press, 2004.

81. T. ElGamal. A public key cryptosystem and a signature scheme based on discrete logarithms. In G. R. Blakley and D. Chaum, editors, *Advances in Cryptology – Crypto '84*, volume 196 of *Lecture Notes in Computer Science*, pages 10–18. Springer, 1984.

82. G. Frey and H.-G. Rück. A remark concerning m-divisibility and the discrete logarithm in the divisor class group of curves. *Mathematics of Computation*, 62(206):865–874, 1994.

83. E. Fujisaki and T. Okamoto. How to enhance the security of public-key encryption at minimal cost. In H. Imai and Y. Zheng, editors, *Public Key Cryptography*, volume 1560 of *Lecture Notes in Computer Science*, pages 53–68. Springer, 1999.

84. E. Fujisaki and T. Okamoto. Secure integration of asymmetric and symmetric encryption schemes. In M. Wiener, editor, *Advances in Cryptology – Crypto '99*, volume 1666 of *Lecture Notes in Computer Science*, pages 535–554. Springer, 1999.

85. C. Gamage, J. Leiwo, and Y. Zheng. An efficient scheme for secure message transmission using proxy-signcryption. In *Proceedings of the 22nd Australasian Computer Science Conference – ACSC '99*, pages 420–431. Australian Computer Science, Springer, New York, 1999.

86. C. Gamage, J. Leiwo, and Y. Zheng. Encrypted message authentication by firewalls. In H. Imai and Y. Zheng, editors, *Public Key Cryptography – PKC '99*, volume 1560 of *Lecture Notes in Computer Science*, pages 69–81. Springer, 1999.

87. C. Gamage and Y. Zheng. Secure high speed networking with ABT and signcryption. Unpublished manuscript, 1997.

88. C. Gentry. Practical identity-based encryption without random oracles. In S. Vaudenay, editor, *Advances in Cryptology – Eurocrypt 2006*, volume 4004 of *Lecture Notes in Computer Science*, pages 445–464. Springer, 2006.

89. M. Girault, G. Poupard, and J. Stern. On the fly authentication and signature schemes based on groups of unknown order. *Journal of Cryptology*, 19(4):463–487, 2006.

90. S. Goldwasser and S. Micali. Probabilistic encryption. *Journal of Computer Systems Science*, 38(2):270–299, 1984.

91. S. Goldwasser, S. Micali, and R. Rivest. A digital signature scheme secure against adaptive chosen-message attacks. *SIAM Journal on Computing*, 12(2):281–308, April 1988.

92. M. C. Gorantla, C. Boyd, and J. M. González Nieto. On the connection between signcryption and one-pass key establishment. In S. D. Galbraith, editor, *Cryptography and Coding – Proceedings of the 11th IMA International Conference*, volume 4887 of *Lecture Notes in Computer Science*, pages 277–301. Springer, 2007.

93. V. Goyal, O. Pandey, A. Sahai, and Brent Waters. Attribute-based encryption for fine-grained access control of encrypted data. In R. N. Wright, S. De Capitani di Vimercati, and V. Shmatikov, editors, *Proceedings of the 13th ACM Conference on Computer and Communications Security – ACM CCS 2006*, pages 89–98. ACM Press, 2006.

94. S. Halevi and H. Krawczyk. Strengthening digital signatures via randomized hashing. In C. Dwork, editor, *Advances in Cryptology – Crypto 2006*, volume 4117 of *Lecture Notes in Computer Science*, pages 41–59. Springer, 2006.

95. G. Hanaoka, Y. Zheng, and H. Imai. Improving the Secure Electronic Transaction protocol by using signcryption. *IEICE Transactions on Fundamentals of Electronics, Communications and Computer Sciences*, E84-A(8):2042–2051, 2001.

96. F. Hess. Exponent group signature schemes and efficient identity based signature schemes based on pairings. Available from http://eprint.iacr.org/2002/012, 2002.

97. H. Imai and S. Hirakawa. A new multilevel coding method using error-correcting codes. *IEEE Transactions on Information Theory*, 23(3):371–377, 1977.

98. R. Impagliazzo and M. Luby. One-way functions are essential for complexity based cryptography. In *Proceedings of the 30th Symposium on Foundations of Computer Science – FOCS '89*, pages 230–235. IEEE Computer Society, 1989.

99. In-Stat. US Businesses Lag In Securing VoIP, 2008. Available from http://www.instat.com/.

100. International Organization for Standardization. *ISO/IEC 11770–3, Information technology — Security techniques — Key management — Part 3: Mechanisms using asymmetric techniques*, 1999.

101. International Organization for Standardization. *ISO/IEC 18033–2, Information technology — Security techniques — Encryption algorithms — Part 2: Asymmetric Ciphers*, 2006.

102. International Organization for Standardization. *ISO/IEC WD 29150, IT security techniques — Signcryption*, 2008.

103. International Telecommunication Union. *ITU-T H323 — Infrastructure of audiovisual services – Systems terminal equipment for audiovisual services — Packet-based multimedia communications systems*, 2006.

104. Internet Engineering Task Force. *RFC 2189: Core Based Trees (CBT version 2) Multicast Routing – Protocol Specification*, 1997.

105. Internet Engineering Task Force. *RFC 3376: Internet Group Management Protocol, Version 3*, 2002.

106. Internet Engineering Task Force. *RFC 4601: Protocol Independent Multicast – Sparse Mode (PIM-SM): Protocol Specification (Revised)*, 2006.

107. M. Jakobsson, J. P. Stern, and M. Yung. Scramble all, encrypt small. In L. Knudsen, editor, *Fast Software Encryption – FSE '99*, volume 1636 of *Lecture Notes in Computer Science*, pages 95–111. Springer, 1999.

108. I. R. Jeong, H. Y. Jeong, H. S. Rhee, D. H. Lee, and J. I. Lim. Provably secure encrypt-then-sign composition in hybrid signcryption. In P. J. Lee and C. H. Lim, editors, *Information Security and Cryptology – ICISC 2002*, volume 2587 of *Lecture Notes in Computer Science*, pages 16–34. Springer, 2002.

109. A. Joux. A one round protocol for tripartite Diffie-Hellman. In W. Bosma, editor, *Algorithmic Number Theory – ANTS IV*, volume 1838 of *Lecture Notes in Computer Science*, pages 385–393. Springer, 2000.

110. A. Joux, G. Martinet, and F. Valette. Blockwise-adaptive attackers: Revisiting the (in)security of some provably secure encryption models: CBC, GEM, IACBC. In M. Yung, editor, *Advances in Cryptology – Crypto 2002*, volume 2442 of *Lecture Notes in Computer Science*, pages 17–30. Springer, 2002.

111. A. Joux and K. Nguyen. Separating decision DiffieHellman from computational DiffieHellman in cryptographic groups. *Journal of Cryptology*, 16(4):239–248, 2003.

112. C. S. Jutla. Encryption modes with almost free message integrity. In B. Pfitzmann, editor, *Advances in Cryptology – Eurocrypt 2001*, volume 2045 of *Lecture Notes in Computer Science*, pages 529–544. Springer, 2001.

113. J. Katz and N. Wang. Efficiency improvements for signature schemes with tight security reductions. In *Proceedings of the 10th ACM conference on Computer and Communications Security – ACM CCS 2003*, pages 155–164. ACM Press, 2003.

114. J. Katz and M. Yung. Unforgeable encryption and chosen ciphertext secure modes of operation. In B. Schneier, editor, *Fast Software Encryption – FSE 2000*, volume 1978 of *Lecture Notes in Computer Science*, pages 284–299. Springer, 2000.

115. E. Kim, K. Nahrstedt, L. Xiao, and K. Park. Identity-based registry for secure interdomain routing. In *Proceedings of the 2006 ACM Symposium on Information, Computer and Communications Security – ASIA CCS 2006*, pages 321–331. ACM Press, 2006.

116. R.-H. Kim and H.-Y. Youm. Secure authenticated key exchange protocol based on EC using signcryption scheme. In *IEEE International Conference on Hybrid Information Technology – ICHIT '06*, volume 2, pages 74–79. IEEE Computer Society, 2006.

117. H. Krawczyk. The order of encryption and authentication for protecting communications (or: How secure is SSL?). In J. Kilian, editor, *Advances in Cryptology – Crypto 2001*, volume 2139 of *Lecture Notes in Computer Science*, pages 310–331. Springer, 2001.

118. H. Krawczyk. HMQV: A high-performance secure Diffie-Hellman protocol. In V. Shoup, editor, *Advances in Cryptology – Crypto 2005*, volume 3621 of *Lecture Notes in Computer Science*, pages 546–566. Springer, 2005.

119. H. Krawczyk and T. Rabin. Chameleon signatures. In *Proceedings of the Network and Distributed Systems Symposium – NDSS 2000*, pages 143–154. 2000.

120. A. K. Lenstra. Key lengths. In H. Bidgoli, editor, *Handbook of Information Security*. Wiley, 2005.

121. A. K. Lenstra and E. R. Verheul. Selecting cryptographic key sizes. *Journal of Cryptology*, 14(4):255–293, 2001.

122. B. Libert and J.-J. Quisquater. New identity based signcryption schemes from pairings. In *Proceedings of the IEEE Information Theory Workshop*, pages 155–158. IEEE Information Theory Society, 2003.

123. B. Libert and J.-J. Quisquater. Efficient signcryption with key privacy from gap diffie-hellman groups. In F. Bao, R. Deng, and J. Zhou, editors, *Public Key Cryptography – PKC 2004*, volume 2947 of *Lecture Notes in Computer Science*, pages 187–200. Springer, 2004.

124. B. Libert and J.-J. Quisquater. Improved signcryption from q-Diffie-Hellman problems. In C. Blundo and S. Cimato, editors, *Security in Communication Networks – SCN 2004*, volume 3352 of *Lecture Notes in Computer Science*, pages 220–234. Springer, 2004.

125. S. Lucks. On the security of remotely keyed encryption. In E. Biham, editor, *Fast Software Encryption – FSE '97*, volume 1267 of *Lecture Notes in Computer Science*, pages 219–229. Springer, 1997.

126. S. Lucks. Accelerated remotely keyed encryption. In L. Knudsen, editor, *Fast Software Encryption – FSE '99*, volume 1636 of *Lecture Notes in Computer Science*, pages 112–123. Springer, 1999.

127. B. Lynn. Authenticated identity-based encryption. Available from http://eprint.iacr.org/2002/072, 2002.

128. C. Ma. Efficient short signcryption scheme with public verifiability. In H. Lipmaa, M. Yung, and D. Lin, editors, *Information Security and Cryptology – Inscrypt 2006*, volume 4318 of *Lecture Notes in Computer Science*, pages 118–129. Springer, 2006.

129. J. Malone-Lee. Identity-based signcryption. Available from http://eprint.iacr.org/2002/098, 2002.

130. J. Malone-Lee. Signcryption with non-interactive non-repudiation. *Designs, Codes and Cryptography*, 37(1):81–109, 2005.

131. J. Malone-Lee and W. Mao. Two birds one stone: Signcryption using RSA. In M. Joye, editor, *Topics in Cryptology – CT-RSA 2003*, volume 2612 of *Lecture Notes in Computer Science*, pages 211–225. Springer, 2003.

132. Mastercard and Visa. *Secure Electronic Transaction Specification – Book 1: Business Description*, 1997.

133. Mastercard and Visa. *Secure Electronic Transaction Specification – Book 2: Programmer's Guide*, 1997.

134. K. Matsuura, Y. Zheng, and H. Imai. Compact and flexible resolution of CBT multicast key-distribution. In Y. Masunaga, T. Katayama, and M. Tsukamoto, editors, *Worldwide Computing and Its Applications – WWCA '98*, volume 1368 of *Lecture Notes in Computer Science*, pages 190–205. Springer, 1998.

135. A. May. Computing the RSA secret key is deterministic polynomial time equivalent to factoring. In M. Franklin, editor, *Advances in Cryptology – Crypto 2004*, volume 3152 of *Lecture Notes in Computer Science*, pages 213–219. Springer, 2004.

136. N. McCullagh and P. S. L. M. Barreto. Efficient and forward-secure identity-based signcryption. Available from http://eprint.iacr.org/2004/117, 2004.

137. N. McCullagh and P. S. L. M. Barreto. A new two-party identity-based authenticated key agreement. In A. Menezes, editor, *Topics in Cryptology – CT-RSA 2005*, volume 3376 of *Lecture Notes in Computer Science*, pages 262–274. Springer, 2005.

138. A. J. Menezes, T. Okamoto, and S. A. Vanstone. Reducing elliptic curve logarithms to logarithms in a finite field. *IEEE Transactions on Information Theory*, 39(5):1639–1646, 1993.

139. A. J. Menezes, P. C. van Oorschot, and S. A. Vanstone. *Handbook of Applied Cryptography*. CRC Press, 1997.

140. V. S. Miller. Short programs for functions on curves. Unpublished manuscript, 1986.

141. V. S. Miller. The Weil pairing, and its efficient calculation. *Journal of Cryptology*, 17(4):235–262, 2004.

142. C. J. Mitchell, M. Ward, and P. Wilson. Key control in key agreement protocols. *Electronics Letters*, 34:980–981, 1998.

143. S. Mitsunari, R. Sakai, and M. Kasahara. A new traitor tracing. *IEICE Transactions on Fundamentals of Electronics, Communications and Computer Sciences*, E85–A(2):481–484, 2002.

144. A. Miyaji, M. Nakabayashi, and S. Takano. New explicit conditions of elliptic curve traces for FR-reduction. *IEICE Transactions on Fundamentals of Electronics, Communications and Computer Sciences*, E84–A(4):1234–1243, 2001.

145. D. Nalla and K. C. Reddy. Signcryption scheme for identity-based cryptosystems. Available from http://eprint.iacr.org/2003/066, 2003.

146. M. Naor. Bit commitment using pseudorandomness. *Journal of Cryptology*, 4(2):151–158, 1991.

147. M. Naor and M. Yung. Universal one-way hash functions and their cryptographic applications. In *Proceedings of the 21st Symposium on the Theory of Computing – STOC 1989*, pages 33–43. ACM Press, 1989.

148. M. Naor and M. Yung. Public-key cryptosystems provably secure against chosen ciphertext attacks. In *Proceedings of the 22nd Symposium on the Theory of Computing – STOC 1990*, pages 427–437. ACM Press, 1990.

149. National Institute of Standards and Technology (NIST). NIST FIPS PUB 186-3 – Digital Signature Standard (DSS), 2009. Available from http://csrc.nist.gov/publications/PubsFIPS.html.

150. National Institute of Standards and Technology (NIST). NIST SP800-58: Security Considerations for Voice over IP Systems, 2005. Available from http://csrc.nist.gov/publications/PubsSPs.html.

151. T. Nishioka, K. Matsuura, Y. Zheng, and H. Imai. A proposal for authenticated key recovery system. In *Proceedings of the 1997 Joint Workshop on Information Security and Cryptology – JW-ISC '97*, pages 189–196. 1997.

152. T. Okamoto and D. Pointcheval. The gap problems: A new class of problems for the security of cryptographic schemes. In K. Kim, editor, *Public Key Cryptography – PKC 2001*, volume 1992 of *Lecture Notes in Computer Science*, pages 104–118. Springer, 2001.

153. P. Papadimitratos and Z. J. Haas. Secure routing for mobile ad hoc networks. In *Proceedings of the SCS Communication Networks and Distributed Systems Modeling and Simulation Conference – CNDS 2002*, 2002.

154. B.-N. Park and W. Lee. ISMANET: A secure routing protocol using identity-based signcryption scheme for mobile ad-hoc networks. *IEICE Transactions on Communications*, E88-B(6):2548–2556, 2005.

155. N. Park, K. Moon, K. Chung, D. Won, and Y. Zheng. A security acceleration using XML signcryption scheme in mobile grid web services. In D. Lowe and M. Gaedke, editors, *Proceedings of the 5th International Conference on Web Engineering – ICWE 2005*, volume 3579 of *Lecture Notes in Computer Science*, pages 191–196. Springer, 2005.

156. K. G. Paterson. ID-based signatures from pairings on elliptic curves. *Electronics Letters*, 38(18):1025–1026, 2002.

157. K. G. Paterson and G. Price. A comparison between traditional public key infrastructures and identity-based cryptography. *Information Security Technical Review*, 8(3):57–72, 2003.

158. C. E. Perkins and E. M. Royer. Ad-hoc on-demand distance vector routing. In *Proceedings of the 2nd IEEE Workshop on Mobile Computing Systems and Applications – WMCSA '99*, pages 90–100. IEEE Computer Society, 1999.

159. H. Petersen and M. Michels. Cryptanalysis and improvement of signcryption schemes. *IEE Proceedings: Computers and Digital Techniques*, 145:149–151, 1998.

160. J. Pieprzyk and D. Pointcheval. Parallel authentication and public-key encryption. In R. Safavi-Naini and J. Seberry, editors, *Proceedings of the 8th Australasian Conference on Information Security and Privacy – ACISP 2003*, volume 2727 of *Lecture Notes in Computer Science*, pages 387–401. Springer, 2003.

161. D. Pointcheval. Chosen-ciphertext security for any one-way cryptosystem. In H. Imai and Y. Zheng, editors, *Public Key Cryptography – PKC 2000*, volume 1751 of *Lecture Notes in Computer Science*, pages 129–146. Springer, 2000.

162. D. Pointcheval. The composite discrete logarithm and secure authentication. In H. Imai and Y. Zheng, editors, *Public Key Cryptography – PKC 2000*, volume 1751 of *Lecture Notes in Computer Science*, pages 113–128. Springer, 2000.

163. D. Pointcheval and J. Stern. Security arguments for digital signatures and blind signatures. *Journal of Cryptology*, 13(3):361–396, 2000.

164. C. Rackoff and D. R. Simon. Non-interactive proof of knowledge and chosen ciphertext attack. In J. Feigenbaum, editor, *Advances in Cryptology – Crypto '91*, volume 576 of *Lecture Notes in Computer Science*, pages 433–444. Springer, 1991.

165. R. L. Rivest, A. Shamir, and L. Adleman. A method for obtaining digital signatures and public-key cryptosystems. *Communications of the ACM*, 21(2):120–126, 1978.

166. R. L. Rivest and R. B. Silverman. Are 'strong' primes needed for RSA? Available from
     http://eprint.iacr.org/2001/007, 1999.
167. P. Rogaway. Authenticated-encryption with associated-data. In *Proceedings of the 9th ACM
     Conference on Computer and Communications Security – ACM CCS 2002*, pages 98–107.
     ACM Press, 2002.
168. P. Rogaway, M. Bellare, J. Black, and T. Krovetz. OCB: A block-cipher mode of operation for
     efficient authenticated encryption. In *Proceedings of the 8th ACM Conference on Computer
     and Communications Security – ACM CCS 2001*, pages 196–205. ACM Press, 2001.
169. J. Rompel. One-way functions are necessary and sufficient for secure signatures. In *Proceed-
     ings of the 22nd Symposium on the Theory of Computing – STOC 1990*, pages 387 – 394.
     ACM Press, 1990.
170. R. Sakai and M. Kasahara. ID-based cryptosystems with pairing on elliptic curve. Available
     from http://eprint.iacr.org/2003/054, 2003.
171. R. Sakai, K. Ohgishi, and M. Kasahara. Cryptosystems based on pairings. In *Proceedings of
     the Symposium on Cryptography and Information Security – SCIS 2000*. 2000.
172. K. Sanzgiri, B. Dahill, B. N. Levine, C. Shields, and E. M. Belding-Royer. A secure routing
     protocol for ad hoc networks. In *Proceedings of the 10th IEEE International Conference on
     Network Protocols – ICNP 2002*, pages 78–87. IEEE Computer Society, 2002.
173. C. P. Schnorr. Efficient signature generation for smart cards. In G. Brassard, editor, *Advances
     in Cryptology – Crypto '89*, volume 435 of *Lecture Notes in Computer Science*, pages 239–
     252. Springer, 1989.
174. M. Scott. Computing the Tate pairing. In A. Menezes, editor, *Topics in Cryptology – CT-RSA
     2005*, volume 3376 of *Lecture Notes in Computer Science*, pages 293–304. Springer, 2005.
175. M. Seo and K. Kim. Electronic Funds Transfer protocol using domain-verifiable signcryption
     scheme. In J.-S. Song, editor, *Information Security and Cryptography – ICISC '99*, volume
     1787 of *Lecture Notes in Computer Science*, pages 269–277. Springer, 1999.
176. A. Shamir. How to share a secret. *Communications of the ACM*, 22(11):612–613, 1979.
177. A. Shamir. Identity-based cryptosystems and signature schemes. In G. R. Blakley and
     D. Chaum, editors, *Advances in Cryptology – Crypto '84*, volume 196 of *Lecture Notes in
     Computer Science*, pages 47–53. Springer, 1984.
178. J.-B. Shin, K. Lee, and K. Shim. New DSA-verifiable signcryption schemes. In P. J. Lee
     and C. H. Lim, editors, *Information Security and Cryptology – ICISC 2002*, volume 2587 of
     Lecture Notes in Computer Science, pages 35–47. Springer, 2002.
179. V. Shoup. A composition theorem for universal one-way hash functions. In B. Preneel,
     editor, *Advances in Cryptology – Eurocrypt 2000*, volume 1807 of *Lecture Notes in Computer
     Science*, pages 445–452. Springer, 2000.
180. V. Shoup. Sequences of games: A tool for taming complexity in security proofs. Available
     from http://eprint.iacr.org/2004/332/, 2004.
181. V. Shoup and R. Gennaro. Securing threshold cryptosystems against chosen ciphertext attack.
     In K. Nyberg, editor, *Advances in Cryptology – Eurocrypt 98*, volume 1403 of *Lecture Notes
     in Computer Science*, pages 1–16. Springer, 1998.
182. D. R. Simon. Finding collisions on a one-way street: Can secure hash functions be based on
     general assumptions? In K. Nyberg, editor, *Advances in Cryptology – Eurocrypt '98*, volume
     1403 of *Lecture Notes in Computer Science*, pages 334–345. Springer, 1998.
183. N. P. Smart and F. Vercauteren. On computable isomorphisms in efficient asymmetric
     pairing-based systems. *Discrete Applied Mathematics*, 155(4):538–547, 2007.
184. R. Steinfeld and Y. Zheng. A signcryption scheme based on integer factorization. In
     J. Pieprzyk, E. Okamoto, and J. Seberry, editors, *Information Security Workshop (ISW 2000)*,
     volume 1975 of *Lecture Notes in Computer Science*, pages 308–322. Springer, 2000.
185. D. R. Stinson. Universal hashing and authentication codes. *Designs, Codes and Cryptogra-
     phy*, 4(4):369–380, 1994.
186. C.-H. Tan. On the security of signcryption scheme with key privacy. *IEICE Transactions
     on Fundamentals of Electronics, Communications and Computer Sciences*, E88–A(4):1093–
     1095, 2005.

187. C.-H. Tan. Analysis of improved signcryption scheme with key privacy. *Information Processing Letters*, 99(4):135–138, 2006.
188. C.-H. Tan. Security analysis of signcryption scheme from q-Diffie-Hellman problems. *IEICE Transactions on Fundamentals of Electronics, Communications and Computer Sciences*, E89–A(1):206–208, 2006.
189. C.-H. Tan. Forgery of provable secure short signcryption scheme. *IEICE Transactions on Fundamentals of Electronics, Communications and Computer Sciences*, E90–A(9):1879–1880, 2007.
190. G. Ungerboeck. Channel coding with multilevel/phase signals. *IEEE Transactions on Information Theory*, 28(1):55–66, 1982.
191. G. Ungerboeck. Trellis-coded modulation with redundant signal sets – Part I: Introduction. *IEEE Communications Magazine*, 25(2):5–11, 1987.
192. G. Ungerboeck. Trellis-coded modulation with redundant signal sets – Part II: State of the art. *IEEE Communications Magazine*, 25(2):12–21, 1987.
193. G. Ungerboeck and I. Csajka. On improving data-link performance by increasing the channel alphabet and introducing sequence coding. In *Proceedings of the 1976 International Symposium on Information Theory*. 1976.
194. E. R. Verheul. Evidence that XTR is more secure than supersingular elliptic curve cryptosystems. In B. Pfitzmann, editor, *Advances in Cryptology – Eurocrypt 2001*, volume 2045 of *Lecture Notes in Computer Science*, pages 195–210. Springer, 2001.
195. S. T. Walker, S. B. Lipner, C. M. Ellison, and D. M. Balenson. Commercial key recovery. *Communications of the ACM*, 399(3):41–47, 1996.
196. G. Wang, F. Bao, C. Ma, and K. Chen. Efficient authenticated encryption schemes with public verifiability. In *Proceedings of the 60th IEEE Vehicular Technology Conference – VTC 2004*, volume 5, pages 3258–3261. IEEE Vehicular Technology Society, 2004.
197. K. Yamaguchi and H. Imai. A study on Imai-Hirakawa trellis-coded modulation schemes. In T. Mora, editor, *Proceedings of Applied Algebra, Algebraic Algorithms and Error-Correcting Codes – AAECC-6*, volume 357 of *Lecture Notes in Computer Science*, pages 443–453. Springer, 1988.
198. G. Yang, D. S. Wong, and X. Deng. Analysis and improvement of a signcryption scheme with key privacy. In J. Zhou and J. Lopez, editors, *Proceedings of the 8th International Conference on Information Security (ISC 2005)*, volume 3650 of *Lecture Notes in Computer Science*, pages 218–232. Springer, 2005.
199. T. H. Yeun and V. K. Wei. Fast and proven secure blind identity-based signcryption from pairings. In A. Menezes, editor, *Topics in Cryptology – CT-RSA 2005*, volume 3376 of *Lecture Notes in Computer Science*, pages 305–322. Springer, 2005.
200. M. Yoshida and T. Fujiwara. On the security of tag-KEM for signcryption. *Electronic Notes in Theoretical Computer Science*, 171(1):83–91, 2007.
201. D. H. Yum and P. J. Lee. New signcryption schemes based on KCDSA. In K. Kim, editor, *Information Security and Cryptology – ICISC 2001*, volume 2288 of *Lecture Notes in Computer Science*, pages 305–317. Springer, 2001.
202. F. Zhang, R. Safavi-Naini, and W. Susilo. An efficient signature scheme from bilinear pairings and its applications. In F. Bao, R. Deng, and J. Zhou, editors, *Public Key Cryptography – PKC 2004*, volume 2947 of *Lecture Notes in Computer Science*, pages 277–290. Springer, 2004.
203. Y. Zheng. Digital signcryption or how to achieve cost(signature & encryption) $\ll$ cost (signature) + cost(encryption). In B. S. Kaliski Jr., editor, *Advances in Cryptology – Crypto '97*, volume 1294 of *Lecture Notes in Computer Science*, pages 165–179. Springer, 1997.
204. Y. Zheng. Digital signcryption or how to achieve cost(signature & encryption) $\ll$ cost (signature) + cost(encryption). Full version. Available from http://www.sis.uncc.edu/~yzheng/papers/, 1997.
205. Y. Zheng. Shortened digital signature, signcryption, and compact and unforgeable key agreement schemes. Submission to the IEEE P1363a Standardisation Body, 1998.

206. Y. Zheng. Identification, signature and signcryption using high order residues modulo an RSA composite. In K. Kim, editor, *Public Key Cryptography – PKC 2001*, volume 1992 of *Lecture Notes in Computer Science*, pages 48–63. Springer, 2001.

207. Y. Zheng. Message encryption and authentication methods (signcryption). Australia Patent Serial Number 721497, lodged on October 25, 1996, granted on May 10, 2000; US Patent 6,396,928, granted on May 28, 2002.

208. Y. Zheng and H. Imai. Compact and unforgeable key establishment over an ATM network. In *Proceedings of the 17th Joint Conference of the IEEE Computer and Communications Societies – INFOCOM '98*, volume 2, pages 411–418. IEEE Communications Society, 1998.

209. Y. Zheng and H. Imai. How to construct efficient signcryption schemes on elliptic curves. *Information Processing Letters*, 68(5):227–233, 1998.

210. Y. Zheng and J. Seberry. Practical approaches to attaining security against adaptively chosen ciphertext attacks (extended abstract). In E. F. Brickell, editor, *Advances in Cryptology – Crypto '92*, volume 740 of *Lecture Notes in Computer Science*, pages 292–304. Springer, 1992.

211. Y. Zheng and J. Seberry. Immunizing public key cryptosystems against chosen ciphertext attacks. *IEEE Journal on Selected Areas in Communications*, 11(5):715–724, 1993.

212. H. Zimmermann. OSI reference model – The ISO model of architecture for open systems interconnection. *IEEE Transactions on Communications*, 28(4):425–432, 1980.

Index